5

POWER AND
PERFORMANCE

POWER AND PERFORMANCE

Ethnographic Explorations through Proverbial Wisdom and Theater in Shaba, Zaire

JOHANNES FABIAN

THE UNIVERSITY OF WISCONSIN PRESS

The University of Wisconsin Press
114 North Murray Street
Madison, Wisconsin 53715

3 Henrietta Street
London WC2E 8LU, England

Library of Congress Cataloging-in-Publication Data
Fabian, Johannes.
    Power and performance: ethnographic explorations through
proverbial wisdom and theater in Shaba, Zaire / Johannes Fabian.
    332 pp.   cm. — (New directions in anthropological writing)
    Includes bibliographical references.
    1. Luba (African people) 2. Theater—Zaire—Shaba.
3. Philosophy, Luba (African people) 4. Power (Social sciences)
5. Groupe Mufwankolo. I. Title. II. Series.
DT650.L8F32   1990
305.8′96393067518—dc20   90-50085
ISBN 0-299-12510-6   CIP
ISBN 0-299-12514-9 (pbk.)

On Ethnography

Some social science research seems incredibly to assume that what there is to find out can be found out by asking.

Dell Hymes

On Performance

To learn to speak a foreign language really well and to be at ease talking in society, with the real accent of the people, one does not only need memory and an ear, but he must, to a certain extent, be a bit of a pretender/fake/performer [*Geck*].

Georg Christoph Lichtenberg

Poesis, rather than mimesis: making not faking.

Victor Turner

On Power

Le pouvoir se mange entier. Power is eaten whole.

A saying from Shaba

Contents

Maps and Figures

Maps

Figures

Preface

There seems to be a consensus in recent debates about the nature of ethnographic writing that our texts should be stories which are a pleasure to read and that this effect can be attained only if we abandon the form of the "monograph"—that systematic, and therefore basically spatial, presentation of knowledge pretending to "cover" a territory within our "field." However, everyone who has given the matter some serious thought realizes that liberation from the monograph has its problems. Like former convicts we must now face "life on the outside." We may be free but, as yet, little consideration has been given to our readers. What happens to their freedom (our freedom, really, because we are also readers) to walk in and out of a text (something which the classical monograph permitted and even encouraged)? The critique of misplaced scientism in anthropology has been a good thing, a hard-fought victory over a collusion of theories of knowledge, conventions of representation, and the practice of Western imperialism. It would be sad if the new problems which critique creates made us return to the comfort of our old prisons or veer off into the hidden conservatism of post-modern playfulness.

Now that interpretive and hermeneutic approaches have demonstrated their capacity to persuade producers and consumers of anthropology of viable alternatives to positivism, we face the task of a "critical anthropology" on a new level. History should have taught us that no power is more pervasive and insidious than that of the hermeneut, the authoritative interpreter of texts. And that there is no exercise of that power more dangerous than that which colonizes the texts of other cultures, especially in a world in which control over information is said to become more important than control over resources, manpower, and technology.

As I am about to present a study to which texts are central I see no other way of avoiding the dangers of interpretation except to make what

I am doing with texts as transparent as possible. I am counting on readers who are equally critical and have an interest not only in what I have to say (or what I demonstrate) but in how I got there. I shall assume that they share my conviction that ethnographies are questionable representations unless they show their own genesis. Those readers who need no further convincing may want to skip the first three chapters (except perhaps for the beginning of chapter 1 and the first part of chapter 3). They should begin with "The Experiment" related in chapter 4, most of which is a story in the literal sense of the word. If that story has the intended effect, readers will then turn with interest to the texts that make up chapters 6 to 13. Should they then decide that this is all they want to get out of this book I would be more than satisfied (and so would be the authors of the texts, the Zairean theater company who joined me in my ethnographic project). Of course, I also hope that by then my story will have become intriguing enough for the reader to want to know more about the world from which it came, postcolonial urban Africa—and the world into which it was made to fit, anthropology in search of understanding. Chapters 2 and 5 would be the next to turn to; chapters 1 and 14, finally, may look like attempts to place all that into a theoretical frame of reference.

If there are good reasons to disregard the outline provided by the table of contents (that shadow of the monograph which we seem to be unable to shake off) and begin the book with the "Experiment" and go on to the "Texts," why not change the sequence of presentation? That I nevertheless followed the numbered sequence of chapters has to do more with epistemology than with literary composition: I want to avoid, as far as this is possible, giving the impression that straightforward accounts of events and presentation of transcribed/translated texts are just preparatory to, or, conversely but worse, more fundamental than analysis and interpretation. This study has no other empirical ground to stand on than the history, experience, praxis (any of the above will do) of its author and the people who cared to converse with him. Nor is any "theory" that I am able to invoke or formulate outside that history.

If it is not to lead us up the blind alley of solipsism, such a position must pass the test of communicability (something quite different from passing the tests of logical consistency and theoretical significance, unless these are [re]interpreted as assessments of communicability). Communication is the proof of communicability. In that sense ethnography is, as the fashionable saying goes, "rhetoric." My interest in theories of performance is also rhetorical. Chapter 1, which reviews some of these, is not to be taken as a systematic disquisition preparatory to formulating my own variant to be applied in the remainder of the book. I am not interested in testing performance theory against ethnographic "data." I want to argue that what, perhaps for lack of a better term, we call "performance" is involved in creatively giving expression and meaning to experience; it is also required in studying such expressions. I shall call this a "discovery" because this is how is struck me at a certain moment during ethnographic research. As I think about it, it becomes clear to me that this experience of a sudden event was but an intensification of a process that lasted many years. It began with an attempt to overcome the prevailing positivist conception of anthropological knowledge production in the late sixties and has since resulted in the conviction that the asymmetrical view we used to take of our work (subject here, object there; theory/method on our side, reality and facts on theirs) is more ideological than epistemological in nature. Performance, this study will argue, is not what they do and we observe; we are both engaged in it. Our scientific, academic culture may take us along different roads, into other directions, but our attempts at making sense are not in essence different and certainly not of a higher order than those made by the people whom we study. Selecting a cultural axiom, such as "le pouvoir se mange entier," and working out interpretations with the tools of our discipline (and of a few others) I consider to be efforts guided by interests that may be common to, in opposition to, or in competition with popular wisdom and artistic presentation; they are never in a neutral relationship to the society of which they purport to convey a measure of understanding. This is why the book is "political," irrespective of the fact that its subject matter—thought about power—happens to be political. It does not follow, though, that this study is a place for me to take a stand regarding the current politics of Zaire, even less to impute such a stand to the authors and audiences of statements that will be documented. I give an account of publicly expressed ideas about power gleaned almost entirely from public events (what could be more public than a play broadcast on national television?). That books like this one may become pretexts for repression I have experienced earlier in my work on religious movements in the same region. But, then, anything may become a pretext. Oppressive powers have ways to make any shoe fit to wear. The alternative, to cover critical popular thought with silence, is not one I am ready to adopt.

There has been much talk about "multiple authorship" in recent debates about ethnographic writing. In this study, authors of statements or texts are identified and, whenever possible, named. But I shall not burden them with authorship in the sense of being the ones who present this story to a public and therefore have to take responsibility for its anthropological findings and political implications.

Amsterdam
June 1989

Acknowledgments

Many have contributed their knowledge, imagination, and time to this study, above all the Troupe Théâtrale Mufwankolo of Lubumbashi. My friend and mentor in the popular language of Shaba, Kalundi Mango, worked with me during the summer of 1987 on the final version of the texts and their translation. J. Dassas and his family and many other friends made my work in Lubumbashi possible and enjoyable. What would we anthropologists be without the hospitality extended to us by people who see meaning in what we do? The Faculty of Social Science at the University of Amsterdam provided the means to travel to Shaba in 1986 and to prepare the manuscript; thanks especially to T. Nieuwenhuis. Barbara Hanrahan of the University of Wisconsin Press saw the project through adversities it seemed to encounter initially. I also want to thank the critical readers who were called upon, especially Wyatt MacGaffey, and Jim Clifford and George Marcus for their decision to make this book part of the series of which they are the general editors.

I dedicate this book to my wife Gabi and to our daughter Anna, who was born when the work was completed.

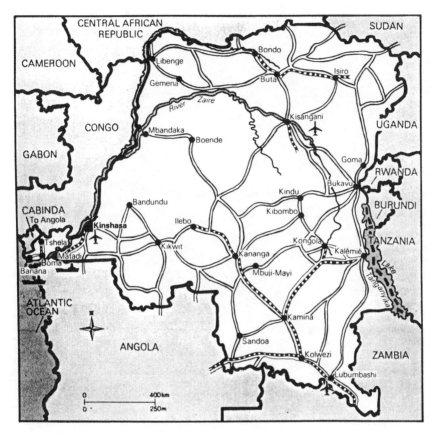

Map 1. Zaire

POWER AND PERFORMANCE

1

Reflections on Ethnography

Discovery: From Informative to Performative Ethnography

On the evening of June 17, 1986, in the midst of a relatively short stint of field work in Lubumbashi, the capital of the mining region of Shaba in Zaire, I was writing up the day's events when I made a discovery. At least that is how it appeared to me then. In the year before, while pursuing investigations not directly related to the topic of this study, I had come upon a statement that was clearly not formulated ad hoc and was pronounced with the authority of an axiom: *Le pouvoir se mange entier*, Power is eaten whole. The circumstances in which it was quoted to me (about which more in chapter 2) were such that I was unable to class it away as an interesting proverb. The more I thought about it, and discussed it with others, the more intriguing it became.

In the afternoon of that day in 1986 I had brought it up when I met with a group of popular actors whom I had known since the seventies. I did this with no particular purpose in mind and I was overwhelmed by their eagerness to explain "le pouvoir se mange entier" to me and to themselves. Spontaneously they decided that it would be just the right topic for their next play. On the spot they began planning—first suggestions for a plot were made, problems of translating the French term *pouvoir* were debated, several actors cited sayings and customs from their home country—in short, I had triggered an ethnographic brainstorm (all this will be reported on in more detail in chapter 3).

In the evening when I assembled my scribbled notes and reminders into a coherent account, I realized how much I had learned from this session. As I said, I was overwhelmed by the reaction to my casual inquiry; I was also extremely tired after many similar fourteen-hour days. It was difficult enough to keep up with my other projects; and here I was, faced with a wealth of information I had not really asked for. This is how the day's entry in the journal ended:

. . . but I simply cannot take in anymore information. Whatever else happened [on that afternoon], here is a "new ethnography"—the ethnographer's interpretive idea [to use the dictum as a key to cultural conceptions of power] is taken up, collectively discussed, cast into a play, tested on a public, etc., all this [starting] from a chicken gizzard in Kolwezi.[1]

In the days that followed I kept thinking about the implications of my discovery. As is often the case, ideas that strike us as new when we first formulate them begin to look less new as soon as we have had time to reflect and remember. Sometimes we must reluctantly admit that our excitement was hardly justified. In this case, I knew it was different. New or not new, I decided to spell out what I had called a "new ethnography."

To put the thoughts that follow in context I need to back up briefly. I learned some time ago that in the kind of projects I was involved with—studying a religious movement among mine workers, later expanding my investigations to language and work and to artistic expression—received methods and prescriptions for empirical research simply do not work. The phenomena I was interested in offered very little in the way of outwardly observable behavior, of traits that could be mapped or counted, in short, of the kind of "hard data" that, properly collected, classified, and analyzed, are said to produce ethnographic knowledge. Probably, working with an elusive religious movement that refused to be approached in any other way but talk, in and on their own terms, was decisive in shaping my convictions. Negatively, I first formulated my position as a critique of positivism and scientism in anthropology. Positively, I found many useful insights in the "ethnography of speaking" propagated by Dell Hymes and others, although I began to see that it too had its limitations.[2] Be that as it may, I came away from my reflections convinced that ethnography is essentially, not incidentally, communicative or dialogical; conversation, not observation, should be the key to conceptualizing ethnographic knowledge production. Later I tried to deepen this idea by exploring what seemed to me a paradox, or even a contradiction, in the practice of anthropology: Although we do our field research on the premise of coevalness, of sharing time with our interlocutors on equal terms, we then go on to produce an allochronic dis-

---

1. The "chicken gizzard in Kolwezi" is a reminder of the occasion on which the saying about power was quoted to me for the first time. That story is in and of itself important and will be told in chapter 2.
2. See Fabian 1971b, 1979a.

course based on temporal distancing; we construct an Other whom we relegate to times other than our own.[3]

When I returned to Shaba in 1985 and 1986, for the first time in more than ten years, I started out with the communicative and critical approach to ethnography which I had cultivated in the meantime. That I did not become complacent about it is due to the "discovery" I am reporting here. But first back to the journal. On June 19 (that is, three days after the first entry and after another meeting with the theater group and some intensive work with a religious community) I wrote:

> Throughout all this I continue to invent a new "method" (about which nothing is new but the formulation, pulling together established insights). It will be a step beyond "communicative" and "dialogical" ethnography. I am thinking of a theoretical article with the Mufwankolo [theater group] sequence as its ethnographic core. [Title:] "From informative to performative ethnology."

In what sense could and should one go beyond communicative and dialogical ethnography? That communication is no panacea for our research problems I had realized some time ago; it can in fact become a dangerous concept if merely to assert it is believed to guarantee "power-free" interaction on equal terms. When they are used to describe the nature of ethnographic research, communication and dialogue are above all epistemological concepts (they point to intersubjectivity and the constitutive role of language in formulating and sharing knowledge). But very often communication and dialogue are invoked in ethical arguments calling for freedom from constraints and domination and for encounter on equal terms. As I see it, these criteria are epistemological first (naming conditions that enable us to know) and only secondarily ethical (prescribing attitudes to be adopted by ethnographers toward their interlocutors). Moreover, if "epistemological" is to cover not only (and even not so much) rules of verification but ways of accounting for the production of knowledge, we must get beyond using communication and dialogue as cover-all protestations of good will and spell out in as much detail as we are capable of what actually happens when we communicate and engage in dialogue.

As far as I can oversee the current state of efforts in that direction there are two ways in which this is being done with some success. There is, first, the "ethnography of speaking" (and its theoretical cousin, ethnomethodology), which strives for more sophisticated and specific accounts of what is involved in (mostly verbal) communication. More

3. See Fabian 1983.

recently, there is a tendency to explore the fact that ethnography not only entails communication *with* members of other cultures but also communication *of* our findings, mostly through writing. The former grew out of a critical confrontation with linguistics, the latter profited from a reception of theories in the field of literary criticism; both draw to varying degrees on semiotics, i.e., the science that specializes in decoding the symbols that serve to represent cultural knowledge.[4]

But there is a third direction in which to probe and this brings us back, finally, to what I called a "discovery." Put in very simple terms, it is this: No matter how far away I got from a positivistic conception of research, no matter how communicative my approach had become, I still acted as an investigator. As long as one participant asks questions and the other is expected to respond with information (irrespective of how much grammatical or rhetorical questioning occurs in their dialogue) the situation will remain asymmetrical, to say the least. Now, a solution, or just a step further, may be to examine the one concept that often remains outside the debates on anthropological knowledge: information.

It seems to be a truism bordering on the trivial that an ethnographer is out to collect information and that he can get it from those who have it. But who "has" information? Members of all societies have, of course, certain kinds of knowledge and skills which they can convey directly or indirectly. An informant may be able to tell me his birth date, the names of his paternal aunts, describe how to get to the next village, and so forth. But what if he or she is asked how magic works, what sacrifices are good for, or—why not?—what the saying "le pouvoir se mange entier" means?

It is only fair to say that anthropologists have been aware of these differences; they have thought about reference versus connotation, instrumental versus expressive behavior, material versus symbolic aspects of society and culture. They have been ingenious in extracting "hard" information on social structure or ecological adaptations from myths, rituals, music, masks, and other "representations" of culture. What has not been given sufficient consideration is that about large areas and important aspects of culture no one, not even the native, has information that can simply be called up and expressed in discursive statements. This sort of knowledge can be represented—made present— only through action, enactment, or performance. In fact, once one sees matters in this light, the answers we get to our ethnographic questions

---

4. For the "ethnography of speaking" see the collected essays by its pioneer, Dell Hymes 1974; on "poetics and politics of ethnography," see Clifford and Marcus 1986.

can be interpreted as so many cultural performances. Cultural knowledge is always mediated by "acting."

Performances, on the other hand, although they can be asked for, are not really responses to questions. The ethnographer's role, then, is no longer that of a questioner; he or she is but a provider of occasions, a catalyst in the weakest sense, and a producer (in analogy to a theatrical producer) in the strongest. Victor Turner, pursuing a similar line of thought, has called the ethnographer an "ethnodramaturg."[5]

What is the significance of such a discovery? Does it bring some *thing* to light, or some *way*? Does it qualify as a new level of knowledge, or should it just be added as a new method to the arsenal that already exists? Answers to these questions require that we briefly look at uses (and abuses) of performance in social-scientific theorizing.

Performance: Some Uses in and around Anthropology

From a point of view above the many involved debates about performance—a vantage point which is hard to obtain and harder to maintain—it seems to me that the concept has served its users contrary purposes.

For those theorists who seek structural, logical, or quasi-mathematical, and ultimately neural, foundations for a science of man (or, at any rate, for a science of one aspect of human activity which is then hoped to become a key to others), "performance" refers to actual, physically palpable, doing, talking, moving, in short, to that which (often in a pejorative tone) is declared "empirical" behavior. "Competence" usually figures as the obligatory counterconcept to this notion of performance. The most influential contemporary proponent of this disdainful view of performance is Noam Chomsky. To be fair to him, it should be said that he would be the first to disclaim applicability of his views beyond that domain of the human mind he defines as language. Still, he has been able to create a climate in which other, less rigorous theorists seem to thrive because he can be seen as the current prophet of an age-old dream: to cut through appearances and reveal essences; to demonstrate timeless order beneath contingent confusion; above all, to attain "deeper," irrefutable, hence more powerful knowledge.

At about the same time when performance entered the vocabulary of the grammarians (in the 1950s) it came to prominence in the writings of folklorists (see Ben-Amos and Goldstein 1975 for relevant literature). Here it was opposed to "text" and its significance was positive: to stress

5. In his essay in Ruby 1982: 96.

the integrity of actual events of reciting myths, epics, and stories. Attention to performance made it necessary to study such events through participation, and through a full appreciation of their contexts (including the distribution of roles among participants, the uses of time and space in music and dance linked to oral performances). This was proposed against a praxis of "text-collection" followed by postmortem classification and analysis. To the extent that more attention was paid to pragmatic and rhetorical aspects of language this was certainly a turn toward a more empirical approach, although it is hard to discover in it any resemblance with the caricature of linguistic empiricism that seems to provide comfort to generativist linguists.

From the point of view of anthropology, one line of thinking about performance found its most fruitful formulation, up to now, when critique of generativist formalism, the new orientation toward oral "texts" (and a few other concerns that need not be specifically mentioned at this point), converged in the "ethnography of speaking." Who speaks to whom, when, where, how, and why—these questions were (once again) proclaimed crucial in understanding language as a "system in action."[6]

As might be expected, this established on the whole a positive notion of performance as a source of ethnographic knowledge. It was paralleled, or followed, by similar theoretical developments in ethnomusicology and visual anthropology. Now it orients inquiry even where Dell Hymes's work has not been directly influential. A recent example demonstrating the influence of this idea is Jan Vansina's thorough revision of his earlier classic on oral tradition. Attention to performance becomes the criterion that distinguishes the oral historian from his colleague who works with written documents:

> [The oral historian] did not find the piece of writing, but rather
> created it. He or she recorded a living tradition. The questions now
> are: what is the relationship of the text to a particular performance
> of the tradition involved and what is the relationship of that per-
> formance to the tradition as a whole? Only when it is clear how the
> text stands to the performance and the latter to the tradition can an
> analysis of the contents of the message begin. This means that the
> questions of authenticity, originality, authorship, and place and
> time of composition must be asked at each of these stages. *The*
> *crucial link is the performance. Only the performance makes the tradi-*

6. See for instance Hymes's essay and other contributions in Ben-Amos and Goldstein 1975 and the programmatic article, with supplementary essays, by R. Bauman (1977; reissued in 1984).

tion perceptible and at the same time only a performance is the source of the ensuing text (1985: 33f., my emphasis).[7]

Perhaps the most important insight to be derived from an "ethnography of speaking" approach is this: Text and performance are aspects of a process; they may relate to each other as phases (when production is considered) or as layers that can be discerned (when communicative events are analyzed), but they do not relate as tokens or representations to events. A text is not a representation, much less a symbol or icon, of a communicative event, it *is* that event in its textual realization. A performance does not "express" something in need of being brought to the surface, or to the outside; nor does it simply enact a preexisting text. Performance *is* the text in the moment of its actualization (in a story told, in a conversation carried on, but also in a book read). That performances can be staged, that they can be good or bad, that they can be genuine or faked, or simply go wrong, that some people are better performers than others—all this points to dialectical, processual relationships between texts and performances.[8] It reveals as misguided any sort of textual fundamentalism, which is a temptation especially for those anthropologists whom the idea to study culture as text(s) has liberated from positivism and naïve realism.

It would be comforting to be able to say that what we have sketched so far more or less covers the uses of performance in anthropology; as it is, the story is complicated enough. But we must take another step and this is perhaps again best done by contrasting two tendencies.

First there are the views of performance in anthropology character-

---

7. See also Jewsiewicki and Newbury 1986 for other examples for the turn to performance in recent African historiography.

8. The notion of performance I try to develop here differs from the one proposed by Bauman (1984: 2–58) even though I believe that convergences between our approaches are in the end more important. Bauman begins with a problem that is not mine in this study: to distinguish what he calls "verbal art" from other kinds of verbalization. Hence he sees performance (a) as systematically distinct from other ways of speaking and (b) as distinguished in the sense of having an exalted, extraordinary quality (8). Furthermore, developing the idea of cognitive/interpretive "frames" as first used by G. Bateson and E. Goffman, he comes close to equating frame with "genre" (25). This would mean that genre is given the higher logical status (in that performance is one genre among others). I would like to place performance at a higher level of classification (such that performance encompasses many genres). Bauman more recently (1986) proposed to distinguish between performance as practice, cultural performance, and the poetics of oral performance. Within this much wider frame I would situate my concerns somewhere between the first and the second approaches. On the "logical status" of performance in this study, see pp. 13f.

ized up to this point. They have in common an empirical orientation to verbal expressions, oral texts, and communicative events. Theoretically, these approaches emerged from critiques of various kinds of linguistics or linguistically inspired theories of cultural knowledge (text philology, structuralism, formal semantics, generativism). Orientation to language and linguistics, however, meant that certain aims and purposes have been shared among the critics and the criticized. "Performance," while signalling recognition of pragmatic, social, and esthetic uses of language, also stands for a program that seeks to extend the search for "rules and regularities" from language to speaking (see, e.g., Hymes in Ben-Amos and Goldstein 1975). In other words, sociolinguistically inspired uses of performance in anthropology, folklore studies, and related fields, often advocate a certain methodologization, a greater descriptive rigor, even if most of the proponents now reject excessive formalism.

Different from this is a trend that, although it shares some of the research interests and many intellectual preferences of the former, uses "performance" in a sense that is at once more literal and methodologically more diffuse. It is inspired above all by the work of Victor Turner and takes spectacular ritual, social drama, and theatricality in general as its points of departure. "Experience" (rather than communication or speaking), "symbols," and "interpretation" or "hermeneutics" (rather than text, speech events, and rules) are the keywords of its discourse.[9] Turner himself intended this focus on performance as a humanization of anthropology, as saving it from theoretical and descriptive pedantry and as a way of reintroducing an element of fun into its teaching. His recommendations also include many points of epistemological significance (for instance, the notion of reflexivity, which he ties to performative acts). His enthusiasm has influenced others and the revision of anthropology he promoted has brought about one of the most salutary changes to affect our discipline in recent decades even though certain elements in his thought remain open for criticism (some of which we will discuss later on).

Simply as a matter of completeness it should be noted that notions of performance also play a role in sociological analyses inspired by the brilliant, if somewhat ethnocentric, descriptions of public interpersonal behavior given by E. Goffman and in investigations where anthropological and psychological-cognitive interests converge.[10]

9. See a collection of essays by Turner published posthumously, 1986; his contributions to Ruby 1982 and Turner and Bruner 1986, but also Singer 1972, Geertz 1980, and Fernandez 1986.

10. Goffman's work, with references to his most important publications, is discussed in Schechner 1986. The cognitive use of notions such as "frame" was already mentioned, see Bauman 1984: 11ff., and a survey by Casson 1983, especially on the

Some Ideas Guiding this Study

Concepts and methods directly derived from the ethnography of speaking (or sociolinguistics) have served me well in the past[11] and the "discovery" which became a starting point for this study has led me to pay more attention to Turnerian "anthropology of performance" than I have previously. At the same time, I now find some problems in the sociolinguistic as well as in the theatrical approaches which, I believe, cannot be solved by enlightened eclecticism alone. Therefore I now include in these introductory reflections a summary of issues that arise when "performance" is applied in the context of a specific project such as this study.

(1) The first question regards *the nature of cultural knowledge and the nature of knowledge of cultural knowledge.* How introducing "performance" into thought about these matters might affect conceptions of ethnography has already been spelled out in some detail. But perhaps it is useful to add the following qualifications: First, performing is here understood in contrast to informing. This is a matter of epistemological preference, not of ontology. Performances may inform; information may require performances to be realized. But usually theories of ethnographic knowledge are built on models of information transfer, of transmission of (somehow preexisting) messages via signs, symbols, or codes. Perhaps they are descriptively useful; epistemologically they are deficient because they fail to account for historically contingent creation of information *in and through the events* in which messages are said to be transmitted. Second, the ethnography of speaking (and some kinds of ethnomethodology, or the analyses of E. Goffman, E. T. Hall, and others) continue, by and large, to view ethnographic research in terms of clear role differences between researcher and researched. This has probably been one reason why questions of intersubjectivity and shared praxis are often bracketed when it comes to observing and describing communicative events. The notion of performance I am exploring here proposes to abandon hierarchical (or, in D. Tedlock's word, "analogical")[12] definitions of relationship between observer and observed, questioner and questioned. Performing is in essence "giving form to." Giving form to only occurs whenever communicative exchanges are

closely related concepts of "scripts" for performance. Finally, in my search through the literature I also came across performance studies which turned out to be concerned with classifying and measuring how humans perform tasks (see Fleishman 1984). This approach would seem to have no relevance whatsoever to our project; but perhaps it would be interesting to ask whether we have here just an accident of polysemy.

11. See Fabian 1974, 1979a, 1985, 1986.
12. See Tedlock 1983, chap. 16.

initiated that involve all participants, including, of course, the ethnographer.

(2) Implied in the position just described is that emphasis on performance serves to stress *the role of time* in the production of ethnographic knowledge—of duration, timing, and, above all, of shared time. That the relation between the anthropologist and his interlocutors must be coeval in order to produce "results"[13] is evident when both are seen as participants in performances. Temporality asserts itself also through the fact that performances are tied to *répétition*, repetition and rehearsal. There would be no reason to qualify performance as a process ("a sequence of acts" would do) unless it is admitted that repetition *in real time* is as essential to what we called "giving form to" as it is to dancing or to playing a piece of music. The qualification "in real time" is necessary to distinguish this notion of repetition from concepts of linguistic recursiveness or sociological predictability (both of which have certain uses in understanding performance; but this is not the point here). An image that keeps coming up as I think about the texts and performances around the theme "le pouvoir se mange entier" to which this study is devoted is that of an iceberg. Performance is the visible tip; rehearsal/repetition the submerged body. Such a spatial or corporeal image may at first seem an inappropriate evocation of process yet it helps to clarify an important insight. As the tip of the iceberg does not represent its submerged part, cultural performances do not symbolize the work of repetition and rehearsal. They are *carried* by that work; there is an unbroken, material connection which is metonymic, not metaphoric. As far as I can see, process can—productively—only be conceived of metonymically. To relate this to our earlier discussion of uses of performance in anthropology: I share with the ethnography of speaking a processual view and I agree with Turner's more literal, theatrical idea in that speech events ought not to be isolated by synchronic analysis from their embeddedness in repetition and rehearsal in real time.[14]

This may have wider significance. If the material for anthropology is events rather than things, and if ethnography is unlike a collection of artifacts but like a repetition of performances, then it is in principle impossible for a culture to appear or be witnessed at a given time as anything but the tip of an iceberg. That tip is not (certainly not only) a token of the submerged body. It is a part, a moment of a process. At least, this should be our epistemological point of departure; that all cultures we know of also construct tokens, symbols, and representations

13. The idea of coevalness is developed in Fabian 1983.

14. Turner himself acknowledges "temporalization" as crucial in the turn toward postmodern anthropology which is signalled by concern with performance, see 1986: 76, 79f.

is a second-order theoretical proposition. In this way, thought about performance may lead to a materialist rather than symbolic position.

Time is of course but one of the dimensions that constitute communicative events as performances (albeit the most crucial one as long as we consider talking essential to intercultural communication). Perceptions of space, of movement, of objects and landscapes also deserve attention, as do tactile experiences, smells, tastes.

(3) Another *line of demarcation needs to be drawn against "sociologizing" the concept of performance.* After all, performing can easily be equated with enacting and one might justifiably ask what performance theory has to offer that has not already been adequately formulated in one or another sociological theory of action. The difference that justifies giving precision to action by calling it performance is this: In the standard sociological view (let us assume for the sake of the argument that there is such a thing and take Parsonian action theory as its classical incarnation) social action is social because individual actors act and interact, guided by values and beliefs which they have internalized as part of a shared culture. There is a platonic element in this inasmuch as sociality is exalted (as by Durkheim), but also in the sense that it is posited to predate any concrete enactment. From the point of view of contingent social acts, society and culture share the attributes of the deity—they are transcendent, immutable, unassailable (or they must at least be imagined as such in order to assure order and equilibrium in the social system). Performance, as I like to think of it here, certainly is action, but not merely enactment of a preexisting script; it is making, fashioning, creating. What I called sociality (better, perhaps: social praxis) is, in this view, the result of a multitude of actors working together to give form to experiences, ideas, feelings, projects. Performance can therefore have a guiding function in investigations where we encounter neither social order nor equilibrium, nor a homogenous shared culture embodying undisputed values and norms.

(4) Some remarks are now in order regarding the logical *status of the concept "performance" in this study.* Given its multiple filiation and complicated history, I do not pretend that all ambiguity can be removed, nor do I think that unambiguous concepts are very useful (unless they are parts of axiomatic constructs). Nevertheless, some of the possible sources of confusion ought to be pointed out now.

First, the proposition that performance might be crucial to our understanding of the nature of culture as well as of knowledge about culture is not meant to be reversible. Not everything that is crucial to culture and to knowledge about culture is performance.

Second, and perhaps more serious are the dangers of misplaced concreteness that always loom when scientific discourse makes use of concepts that come along carrying a heavy load of cultural connotations. Depending on whether the sources of inspiration are religious rites, theater, dance and music, or some other activity which *our* culture designates as performance, there is always the problem of avoiding extensions of the concept that displace our understanding laterally into the realm of similes and metaphors. In this manner, our understanding may be enriched, but its critical edge may also be dulled. Anthropologists should by now have had enough bad experience with topoi such as kinship, tribe, ritual, myth, magic, and so forth, to know that such seemingly innocent classifications amount to intellectual verdicts that serve to establish cultural distance and hegemony. Performance, in other words, should not be projected onto the societies whose images of theatricality we study in order to contrast them with our own, which we see as engaged in serous business.

Third, even if such a critical awareness is acquired in general, there is still the problem of avoiding equivocation in specific applications. On the one hand, I introduced "performance" as a concept marking an epistemological position; on the other, most of this study (apart from the reflections on proverbs) is based on material documenting actual theatrical performance. Am I therefore tailoring my ethnography to fit epistemological requirements, or is it the other way round? I don't think that it is desirable to formulate rules or safeguards that would eliminate ambiguity on this point. Nor do I want to dignify what might be in fact a weakness by declaring it a hermeneutic circle. The only safeguard I know of is to keep the account at all times open—open, that is, to the contingencies of the actual, social, and political context in which this ethnography has been produced. What I mean by openness will be spelled out in more detail in the last section of this chapter.

(5) Finally, attention to performance also determines *the aims of description*. When we give ethnographic accounts as accounts of performances we may employ various formal devices in order to highlight or summarize findings about the structure of events. But the aim cannot be, in any but the most loose sense of the terms, to define "rules" or construct "grammars." The ethnographer participates in, and gives accounts of, performances because he or she wants to report *what* is given form to.[15] That cultural content, always the result of contingent historical processes, could be generated from sets of abstract, transhistorical principles (be they structures of the mind, basic needs, or what not) is in my view extraneous to the tasks of cultural anthropology.

On the other hand, a focus on performance, will make it impossible to affect false descriptive modesty, as if the ethnographer's task were

15. See Fabian 1979a for a more detailed exposition of this argument.

just to present "scripts," cultural texts that speak for themselves. Those lasting objectifications of events that we produce through recordings, transcripts, and translations are without any doubt material for the "work of interpretation," as Tedlock calls it. But the book which carries that phrase as part of its title (1983) also demonstrates that records of the spoken word cannot be conceived of as data leading an existence independent of the projects in the course of which they were obtained. The passage from Vansina quoted above underlines this point.

Conversely, when actual records, texts, are included in the presentation this is not only, as it were, a matter of ethics or politeness ("giving a voice to our informants") nor a matter of literary theory (recognizing multiple authorship). It is required by the claim that such writing give accounts and interpretation of processes. Like verbal communication itself, ethnographic presentation may appear full of redundancy if measured by standards that presuppose an ideal reader, a perfect match of content and form between text and translation, and complete sets of findings covering the, and only the, announced subject of research. Parsimony is a supreme value for those who already know; ethnographers, although some of them can say what they have to say more clearly and succinctly than others, are destined to tell baroque and tortuous tales.

Moving Ahead: Performance and Survival

J'ai connu des sociétés composées uniquement de sociologues. Ils avaient un talent fou, dans la veille et le récit. Nous sortons à peine de cette Antiquité, nous ne sommes pas tous sortis de cette pauvreté qui a duré d[é]s âges mythiques jusqu'à naguère. Je me souviens de sociétés mythiques tout entières saisies dans la représentation, endormies dans le langage. La pauvreté ne se mesure pas seulement au pain mais à la parole, pas seulement au manque de pain mais à l'exces, à l'exclusivité, à la prison des paroles. La langue croît quand manque le pain. Quand le pain vient, la bouche, longtemps affamée, a trop de travail pour, en plus, s'occuper de parler. Nous avons appris à aimer les objets.

Michel Serres[16]

16. See *Les cinq sens* (1985: 38f.). Here is my translation:

I have known societies consisting only of sociologists. They had an incredible talent for staying up late and telling stories. We have just emerged from such ancient times, and not all of us have left this impoverished state which lasted from the mythical ages until not long ago. I remember mythical societies which were completely caught up in representation, asleep in language. Poverty is not only

Until now, this brief account suggests that the uses which social scientists have made of performance may be found somewhere between two possibilities: Either they methodologize performance such that the concept can cover almost any sort of action or they celebrate performance as an artistic achievement in which case the concept should be reserved to acts of extraordinary intensity and heightened significance. However, these differences appear less important as soon as one considers what most of their proponents share. No matter, whether preferences go to smooth routine or to rousing drama, performance theory tends to share two shortcomings with its predecessors: positivity and political naïveté.

By positivity (which may also appear as "authenticity") I mean the tendency to privilege theoretically and empirically, as "the rule," behavior which affirms or enacts presumed societal values. Conversely, action that denies, contests, lacks commitment, or simply dissimulates will be qualified as anything between curious and deviant. That this is a matter of theoretical inclination, not a logical concomitant of a focus on performance can be seen as soon as we recall the subtle analyses of clowning, insinuation, and subterfuge we have from folklorists and sociolinguists,[17] or Victor Turner's struggles with negativity in the form of antistructure.[18] I hope that this study will contribute to arguments that negativity needs to be incorporated into our basic conceptualizations of social praxis instead of being relegated to deviance or domesticated as drama, that is, "normal conflict" or, worse, "dynamics." This is especially important when we subsume the phenomena we investigate under the concept of popular culture. It is a notion that has been instrumental in

---

measured by bread but also by speech, not only by a lack of bread but also by an excess of words, by their exclusive claim, and by being imprisoned by words. Language grows when bread is lacking. When the bread comes, the mouth, which has gone hungry for so long, is too much occupied to go on talking. We have learned to love objects.

I believe—though I do not agree with most of Serres's larger argument concerning the superiority of the natural sciences—that this outrageous reflection is useful when we think about verbal performance under conditions of material deprivation.

17. See Bauman's insightful remarks on the disreputability of performance (1984: 29, 44f.) and the many concrete examples of playful but serious dissimulation in the work of Roger Abrahams (1972, 1975); see also Abrahams and Bauman 1971. That "participatory discrepancies"—deviating from the perfect score—may belong to the essence of successful musical performance has recently been argued by Charles Keil (1987) in an essay that contains much food for thought on performance in general.

18. See, for example, his essay "Metaphors of Anti-structure in Religious Culture" (1974). My own attempt to "recapture the negative" I formulated in Fabian 1979b. See also Washabaugh 1979 applying the notion of antistructure to languages such as the one on which this ethnography is based.

removing the stigma of inauthenticity from vigorous, creative expressions which do not conform to standards of "high" or "traditional" culture, but it also carries the constant danger of condescending folklorization.

Political naïveté is perhaps the more serious of the two shortcomings I see in some performance theory. Fascination with the communicative, esthetically creative, inspiring, and entertaining qualities of cultural performances all too easily make us overlook that the people who perform relate to each other and to their society at large in terms of power. Again, this does not only apply to the "normal" differential distribution of might and influence wherever a multitude of people are engaged in common projects (this is why the matter is not taken care of by introducing the notion of differential roles into the analysis of performance). Recognition of power relations acquires a heightened significance when we investigate societies under colonial domination or postcolonial, quasi-totalitarian regimes, where expression of opinion, social criticism, and the free play of imagination are severely restricted. Colonial rulers and their successors have been aware of these threats and challenges and often have, with true machiavellian determination, encouraged performance as entertainment and as a way of channeling or co-opting social protest (later on, we will provide some detail on how this works). There is, therefore, always the possibility that an interest in the creations of popular culture which professes to be strictly academic and theoretical works into the hands of oppressors. I should hope this study will avoid such naïveté, partly because, on reflection, I have become aware of it, but much more so because the Zaireans who allowed me to be part of this ethnography of power saw to it that their own political predicaments were expressed, albeit in ways that often are not immediately clear to the outsider.

The points I am trying to make here can be clarified by some observations on the direction Victor Turner's thought took in his last essays before his untimely death in 1983. For some years he had been moving away from ritual interpreted as social drama to a more literal concern with theatrical performance. Together with this apparent narrowing of focus, however, went a theoretical reorientation. It is as if he had become disenchanted with the rather flat moralism or sociologism that besets metaphorizing social conflict as "drama" (what I qualified as "positivity"), on the one hand, and with the temptations of noncommittal estheticism (one form of what I called political naïveté), on the other. Turner began to feel the need to ground performance, to seek its foundations in those depths of human acting that are about survival. To the consternation, I imagine, of many who had followed him as one of the prophets of symbolic anthropology, he proposed to look for these foundations in the evolutionary history of the human species and its neuro-physiological equipment.[19] With that he chose an option that is not new in anthropology; Lévi-Strauss comes to mind, perhaps also the more original and interesting thought of Gregory Bateson,[20] not to mention the renaissance of evolutionism associated with the rise of sociobiology. In one sense, these visions express a yearning for a scientific grounding of anthropology. But, until we have better solutions to the problem of translating the results of scientific experiments (which are formulated and reported on in terms of quantitative measures and mathematical probability) into historical accounts, such scientific grounding quickly degenerates into metaphysics, at best, and ideology, at worst.[21] I share Turner's conviction that our inquiries into cultural performances need to be grounded in something that is real, something more serious than the contemplation of drama. Yet, as long as our contributions to knowledge are based on participation in uncontrolled, contingent events, I doubt that we can find anything "harder" than political praxis. I, at least, am unable to see how reductions to brain structure and ethology could justify explanations or interpretations of performance that would lead us to ignore historically established conditions of power and oppression.

Let me now come to a conclusion of sorts. These reflections began with the report on a discovery: "Performance" seemed to be a more adequate description both of the ways people realize their culture and of the method by which an ethnographer produces knowledge about that culture. In search for a catching phrase to designate the reorientation which that discovery would entail I proposed to move "from informative to performative ethnography." This has epistemological significance inasmuch as I recommend an approach that is appropriate to both the nature of cultural knowledge and the nature of knowledge of cultural knowledge. But the recommended reorientation also has a historical, political background.

It does not take much reflection to suspect that what appears as a merely theoretical advance is in fact related to changes in research

19. See his essay "Body, Brain, and Culture" in 1986, and Schechner 1986. Schechner worked with Turner during his last years.

20. Summarized perhaps most poignantly in Bateson 1979.

21. I cannot resist citing a similar expression of skepticism made forty years ago by none other than Norbert Wiener. He acknowledges the interesting contacts he had with Gregory Bateson and Margaret Mead concerning the applicability of cybernetics to social systems. Yet he puts a damper on their and other social scientists' hopes precisely because he is aware of what I called translation problems from statistics to human concerns (see Wiener 1948: 33f.).

practice dictated by other than academic considerations. Informative ethnography—collecting data and information about another culture—corresponds to a political situation of more or less direct control, one in which the ethnographer as the emissary of the dominant power (wittingly or not) has the upper hand; where he or she can ask the questions, determine what counts as information, control the situations in which it is to be gathered, and so forth. Performative ethnography—the kind where the ethnographer does not call the tune but plays along—would be the approach that fits situations where our societies no longer exercise direct control. There is some truth in this and future critics of anthropology will probably point to the hard realities of changed political relations when it comes to account for the emergence, in the sixties and seventies, of humanistic, communicative, and dialogical anthropology (as a program, not just a matter of human decency).

However, although exploring the idea of performance is for me a way to continue with communicative approaches, it also makes me realize that more is involved than adjusting to changed political situations, or rather, that more thought needs to be given to exactly what the changes from colonial to postcolonial relations amounts to. If anything, domination has intensified. Western imperialism is all the more pervasive and powerful for having become an absentee regime of organizations that remain anonymous to the ruled. "Improved" communications technology and intensified circulation of consumer goods see to it that more and more of the things Africans know and like are shaped and selected outside. Locally, governments and regimes who are powerless in global terms must compensate for lack of legitimacy with measures that are either oppressive or corrupt, and often both. If we further consider that increasing integration into a world system goes together, for most Zaireans, with pauperization that does not seem able to hit bottom, then we realize that there is nothing in the postcolonial situation that would make ethnography by and of itself more humane, playful, or fun, or that would make "performance" a more germane concept to describe its nature. No, the kind of performances we find in popular culture have become for the people involved more than ever ways to preserve some self-respect in the face of constant humiliation, and to set the wealth of artistic creativity against an environment of utter poverty. All this is not to be dismissed off-hand as escape from reality; it is realistic praxis under the concrete political and economic conditions that reign.

This brings me once more to some thoughts about "performance" that are likely to cause consternation among no-nonsense practitioners of the social sciences who have kept their faith in straightforward scientific inquiry. One of the connotations from which performance should *not* be purified is that of being just performance, of putting up an act, of tricking and dissimulating. Colonial history, and social history in general, have taught us that the "shuffle and dance" to which the oppressed had to resort in everything, from how they speak their languages to the ways they move, and the manner in which they relate to those in power, have been so many ways of surviving. An ethnography/ anthropology that does not contemplate performance from a safe distance but realizes that it must itself become performative will—correctly—be qualified as "shuffle and dance" by those who have never experienced difficulties with the methods and approaches we inherited from times when our discipline fought for, and achieved, academic respectability as a positive science.

Superficially, what I am more insinuating than expounding here may look similar to arguments that are advanced in favor of a postmodern anthropology. But I cannot overcome a profound sense of distrust in postmodernism. Although some of it is motivated by reflections on research experience such as mine, much is inspired by problems we have with our own literary practice in which those whom we investigate do not directly participate. If the proponents of postmodernism tell us that nothing is to be taken seriously about anthropology (because nothing about it is real) and that free experimentation in the sphere of representations is all that remains, then this reminds me of a saying attributed to Woody Allen: "Symbols are extra." Indeed, literary *dégustation* of anthropology is a luxury which we owe to the wealth our societies extract from the ones we purport to study.[22]

22. The most encompassing collection of essays on anthropology in the postmodern spirit is the one edited by Clifford and Marcus (1986). A companion piece—at once partial refutation, or at least gently chiding, and a demonstration of how literary appreciation of anthropology is done—is Geertz's latest essay (1988). Lest my remarks be misunderstood as a defense of modernism, I want to say that books such as *Writing Culture* and an earlier study by Boon (1982) represent a significant step forward in the critique of anthropology. It is just that I am wary of a critique that is not constantly made to confront ethnography "on the ground."

2

The "Problem": Power and
Cultural Axiom

In the project I am undertaking with this study, preoccupation with performance, apart from being forced on me by circumstances, grew out of epistemological concerns. Not the idea that social life consists of performances, but an insight that knowledge about social life is, in important respects, performative rather than informative, has been my starting point. That a theatrical play, a performance or series of performances in the most literal sense of the term, will eventually be the empirical core of this book, does not, in my view, weaken the epistemological argument; it only makes it more urgent and interesting.

In this chapter, I want to show that sociocultural performances (social drama, ritual, story-telling, interpersonal games)—so many ways of conceptualizing the "how" of interaction—are not the problem I started out addressing; what made me undertake this uncertain journey has been a "what." Even though I shall eventually offer some generalizations, as does every author of social scientific discourse, I did not start out by applying generalized concepts or interpretive schemes to interesting data. Nor did I have in mind a contribution to a specialized subdiscipline such as linguistic or political anthropology. I simply began by being intrigued with a specific pronouncement, ostensibly about the nature of power, made by specific persons on a specific occasion. Did what was said express actual experience with power? Did it posit some conventional or ultimate principles? Or both? Was it an echo of a traditional way of life, or did it speak to the present situation? Or both? Could a saying that so obviously made sense to those who quoted it help me understand what at that time was my own principal quest ("revisiting" a religious movement that I had first studied almost twenty years earlier and finding it alive yet transformed and engaged in a new struggle)?

I shall now report on the event that triggered my questioning. I will then look at a few ethnographic sources in order to provide some wider context and historical depth. I shall conclude with some reflections that will bring us back to theme of performance and take us to the ethnographic experiment to be reported on in the following chapter.

Of Power and Chicken Gizzards

About halfway through my visit to Shaba in 1985 I found myself one evening in the company of three Zaireans: an electronics engineer, an architect, and an agronomist by profession. The liveliest contributor to the conversation was the agronomist, a colorful character who had turned from government official into big-time cattle and grain farmer. In the course of that transformation, he had also become the founder and leader of a small independent church called *Sifa Lwa Bwana*. In a religious register this means "Praise to the Lord." But a more worldly translation is also possible and then it says "Hail to the Boss"— not such a farfetched idea because, as I learned later, most or all of this church leader's followers are small peasants and agricultural workers who are employed by, or otherwise dependent on, his farms.

We all had met a few days earlier in Kolwezi, the most important of the mining sites in Shaba, where I had gone to revisit with some Jamaa groups I had worked with during my first field research in 1966–67. Because I had only a week or so, I stayed in a hotel to which I returned at night when I was through seeing Jamaa people in workers' camps and townships. Almost every evening I was invited by this group of friends to join them in their rounds, eating, drinking, and talking in their houses and those of their women friends. That particular evening, having already taken a copious meal in one home, we went to one of the houses belonging to Lukasu ("the hoe," in Luba), as the farmer and prophet was called by his friends. In a large, barren, and ill-lit room whose walls and ceiling still showed the damage done by bullets and shrapnel during the last Shaba war, we settled down at a low table. On it were placed a bowl of chicken, a huge *bukari* (a maize and manioc mush, which is the staple of the area), and crushed peppers in a small wooden mortar. An enameled basin filled with water was placed on the floor next to the table. A young man and several women were ready to wait on us but kept themselves in the dark at the far end of the room. Earlier we had gotten into an animated discussion about religion, Bantu philosophy, and Placide Tempels and his Jamaa movement. We went on talking as we approached the table. I suddenly had a feeling that, unlike the earlier meal, which had been served in a bourgeois fashion with plates to eat from and forks and knives to use, this one was offered to me as a challenge or test. This was not just food, it was material for some kind of communion. My feeling was confirmed presently when our host announced that this was a very special occasion. After we were seated there was a moment of tension. My companions watched me. I wetted my hands in the water and asked for a towel. Then I took a handful of *bukari*, kneaded it into shape, dipped it into the sauce accompanying the chicken and took the first bite. The tension broke; I had performed the appropriate acts in proper sequence and passed the test—at least part of it.

One of the men then reached out to the bowl of chicken and offered me the gizzards. This is the piece reserved to the person of the highest rank, he told me. Somewhat confused and embarrassed I offered to share the choice piece. All three protested. The one who had offered it said, rather curtly, either you eat it or give it to me. It must have been obvious to them that I did not understand their reaction, certainly not its strength and unanimity. The explanation was quick and concise: "Le pouvoir se mange entier." Power is eaten whole. That this phrase was pronounced in French took nothing away from its significance and authority. That it was a saying of Luba origin I knew because I had heard similar expressions earlier. This invocation of ancestral wisdom made us return to our discussion of African philosophy. The meal continued pleasantly. (Incidentally, I gave the gizzard to the one who had offered it to me and he ate it, alone.)

The episode was duly noted in my diary, without comment or reflection. I really began to think about it months later, when I tried to formulate a first report on recent developments in the Jamaa movement.[1] What intrigued me most was a contradiction between the saying's axiomatic insistence on the wholeness and integrity of power and the actual situation in and round the Jamaa. Where there was once a concentration of power there now seemed to be disintegration and dissipation. At one time, the Jamaa had almost had a monopoly on religious enthusiasm in the Catholic context. Protestant-inspired movements were more numerous but charismatic power seemed concentrated in a few major ones. In 1985–86 hundreds of churches and cults competed among each other, and even the Jamaa had to face more internal divisions than in earlier years, as well as competition from other movements among Catholics. How could such disintegration or dissipation be viewed in the light of what obviously was still a powerful cultural principle, "le pouvoir se mange entier"?

The report I mentioned was drafted at the end of 1985. In it I formulated a number of ideas which I thought were helpful for the task at hand. The method I followed was to combine an analysis of the logical implications of the saying with some lexical and ethnographic

1. See "Jamaa: A charismatic movement revisited," to appear in T. D. Blakely et al., in press.

information about Luba language and culture. I should like now to report the results as they were formulated then.

Two things are remarkable about the saying. First, it makes a connection between acquiring power and eating. That in this case a meal was the occasion to invoke this cultural axiom only adds force to an image long established.[2] In the Luba languages of Zaire "to eat" is frequently used to denote access to power (kudia bulopwe, literally: to eat the office of chief). It can also signify the conclusion of a special relationship or pact of friendship (kudia bulunda, literally: to eat friendship).[3] I myself had heard the expression for the first time in one of the linguistic jokes which workers made to ridicule pretentious but not quite competent use of French, especially by some politicians of the first generation. It was, I believe, Jason Sendwe, the Luba leader around Independence, who was reported to have begun one of his speeches with the phrase "Depuis que j'ai mangé mon pouvoir," meaning: Since I took my office. Those who told the joke played on the quaintness of what linguists would call a French calque of an idiomatic expression. In Sendwe's Luba-French they saw symbolized a less than complete transition from traditional chieftaincy to modern political office.

Indirectly, the image of ingestion is operative in honorific titles or, for example, when the elephant is said to symbolize chiefly power. It does this not only because of its strength, size, and so forth, but because it eats more than other animals.

In sum, these are images which depict access to power as ingestion/incorporation rather than occupying a position or territory, or imposing order. Once ingested, as it were, power is internalized; it becomes like a person's weight, a property rather than a function. Of course, there have been Luba potentates in the past (and there are Luba politicians in the present) who were also strategists of power and knew the uses of diversification and delegation. Still, it can be said that the dominant connotation in the cultural image we encounter in our saying comes

2. Notice also that the expression occurred in a complex, layered symbolic setting. As it was put in one of the many discussions about the episode, the gizzard first of all "stands for" the chicken. The whole gizzard represents the whole chicken. The thought behind the custom is that the guest receives the whole chicken and that it is the guest, not the host, who invites the others to share the meal. Eating the whole gizzard signifies acceptance of hospitality, that is, of a specific relationship which is expected to be whole, without reservation. That the gizzard may also be a choice piece reserved to the person of the highest rank is another matter.

3. For the rich semantics of kudia, illustrated by a series of proverbs, see Van Avermaet and Mbuya 1954: 106ff. Among terms denoting political office is mudyavita, literally "he who eats war/battle," translated by Reefe as "general of the army" (1981: 43; see also Van Avermaet and Mbuya 1954: 790, where the term is said to designate nowadays one kind of notable).

close to Weber's notion of charisma as a personal property. What we catch in these societies with our sociological category of charismatic authority should therefore perhaps be regarded as the routine and not as an exception. For societies where "le pouvoir se mange entier," it would then follow that to postulate logical or actual opposition between charismatic authority and the forms designated as traditional or rational-bureaucratic may be an ethnocentric projection on our side.

But our axiom has another implication that requires interpretation. This is the stress laid upon the *wholeness* of power. A paradoxical thought—because eating entails destruction (or digestion), and incorporation in one body means separation from others. In one respect (but not in all, as we shall see) the paradox can be removed if we assume that in Luba political thought power is tied to concrete embodiments, persons, and material symbols, rather than to abstract structures such as offices, organizations, and territories. The point about wholeness is not that power cannot be shared. Rather, one refuses to acknowledge disembodied divisions of power of the kind that characterize Western political thought.

How—this was, for the time being, the last step in my reflections—can "le pouvoir se mange entier" be made to shed some light on the incredible proliferation of religious groups and other forms of the dissipation of power which I witnessed all around me? Stress on incorporation and on the notion of wholeness, ontological ideas in the last analysis, create a cultural logic in terms of which "concentration of power" is tied to personal carriers. Their behavior will not meet Western expectations. Our notions of political power express belief, to cite Weber one more time, in the historical quasi-law of rationalization. Accumulation of power is in that case envisaged to occur like the accumulation of wealth with its attendant problems of impersonal planning and organization. Therefore, what looks to us at first like dissipation of power in the stronger, or diversification in a weaker meaning, may not be indicative of forced adaptation to the external circumstances of postcolonial political economy, much less of internal disintegration and self-inflicted decline. It may be the very form in which a particular cultural notion of power realizes itself. What looks paradoxical or simply confusing from the outside—the ardent pursuit of power in its entirety and the proliferation of its embodiments—may express a cultural preference for a state of anarchy, be it in religion, economics, or politics.

Such a conclusion needs to be expressed hypothetically. After all, up to now our argument has been more or less deductive, a teasing-out of the possible meanings of one saying. But there are good reasons to believe that it is not entirely off the mark. In an ethnography of power from a Zairean society which is not that different from Luba culture (and has had as much of an influence on modern politics as the latter), W. MacGaffey speaks of the "Kongo ideal of complete anarchy" (1970: 254). His assessment is backed up by a long and detailed analysis of traditional as well as colonial and contemporary notions, structures, and processes, and although this study will follow a different road, the aim—to understand the cultural specificity of conceptualizations of power—is similar. We must now seek to broaden the empirical basis and clarify the methodology.

The Missing Proverb

This is how far I had proceeded when I first tried to confront "le pouvoir se mange entier" with what I knew about current uses and abuses of power in Shaba. Even from the brief discussion above, it is clear that this is not a simple matter at all. It is not as if the meaning of the dictum were fixed and distinct. For that reason alone its function cannot be just culturally to classify and thereby determine behavior. As we have seen, even though it is apodictic in its linguistic form (the saying simply asserts; it does not imply, allude, question, etc.) and even though it may be reinforced by a distinct symbolic referent (the whole gizzard in our anecdote), the meaning it attributes to power remains paradoxical (logically). Nor did it become clear just how much authority, how much cultural weight the saying carries, something one would have to know more about in order to assess its explanatory meaning.

The question of authority would seem to be resolved if we can identify a statement as a proverb, expressing traditional and probably ancient wisdom. But folklore and linguistic research have taught us that to understand what proverbs mean and how they convey meaning requires attention to much more than the semantics of a statement.[4]

4. Folkloric, literary, linguistic, and anthropological studies of proverbs in Africa alone have produced a voluminous literature. In some recent studies which discuss questions of theory and method I found much divergence in terminology together with much agreement on substantial questions such as communicative context, generic status, rhetorical function, and linguistic form. See Arewa and Dundes 1964; Burton 1981; Cauvin 1980, 1981 (among the best I found); Dundes 1981; Eastman 1972; Faik-Njuzi 1976; Finnegan 1970; Girard 1981 (comparison between Bemba proverbs and Zambian state ideology); Kaphagawani and Chidam'modzi 1983; Penfield 1983; Rodegem 1985; Seitel 1976, 1977; and Yanga 1977. In her study of Igbo "quoting behavior," Penfield, following Mukařowský, lists the following "functional properties" of proverb use: *depersonalization*, which "allows the speaker to bring out a very sensitive matter in a nondefinite or abstract manner; as a result, speakers are not held personally responsible for their statements"; *foregrounding*, which refers to contrast (linguistic, cognitive) between proverbial expressions and the surrounding context; *authoritativeness*, based on community acceptance and "expert" authors such as famous chiefs or

Without going too much into technicalities, I believe that at least three considerations are of importance: There must exist a communicative-rhetorical practice which encourages or even requires the use of proverbs; there must be a tradition, or more exactly, a repertoire of statements that can be quoted as proverbs when the occasion arises; and there must be properties which make a statement recognizable as a proverb. Not one of these three criteria is independent of the others. A practice cannot be practiced without a repertoire, a repertoire cannot grow without a continued practice, and a saying is not a proverb unless it has properties that will admit it to a repertoire.

Where does this get us with "le pouvoir se mange entier"? Because it seemed to be such an important and intriguing statement about the nature or power, I was naturally inclined to take it as the French version of a Luba proverb. Its rhetorical intent (as an appeal to received wisdom), linguistic form (as a metaphorical expression), and communicative setting certainly met my nonexpert expectations regarding the use of proverbs. But was the saying indeed part of a repertoire, and was it therefore worth exploring beyond the occasion on which I reported? I must admit that, at first, I was absolutely convinced that such was the case. None of that certainty remains now that I have had the time to make further investigations.[5] These were of two kinds. Although neither of them can claim to have been exhaustive, they brought results which made "le pouvoir se mange entier" a more interesting subject than if I had been able to class it away as must another traditional proverb.

First, as I have already mentioned, during the remainder of my 1985 stay, and then again in 1986, on every occasion that seemed suitable I made it a habit to ask my African friends and acquaintances whether they knew the saying. My question was usually formulated in Swahili, occasionally in French; the saying was always quoted as I had heard it, in French. Almost everyone responded in the affirmative. Often they

---

ancestors; *reference to societal norms and values;* and *prestige,* based above all on the fact that using proverbs gives evidence of "skillfulness in the language and ways of the culture" (1983: 5, 6f., 8f., 10). For a useful treatment of proverbs as expressive of "cultural models" (a notion related to what I have been calling cultural axioms) see White (1987). The most comprehensive recent bibliography was compiled by Mieder (1982).

5. There would not be much of a problem if one were to accept Penfield's maximal definition of proverb use as "quoting behavior," which, in a multilingual, multicultural situation, can include quotations from the Bible or from classical authors (1983: index under "quotes"). "Le pouvoir se mange entier" was quoted by a multilingual speaker with a Western education. It could be shown to have the required "functional properties" (see note 4 above). Therefore, the saying would qualify as "proverb." But such a maximal definition would have cut short the kind of questioning we are now about to undertake.

qualified their answer: Yes, this is said. Yes, I heard it before. Several respondents declined, as it were, to adopt my ethnographic meta-perspective (inquiring after the occurrence of such a statement about power) and answered as if I had intended to confront them directly with the saying. In that case, most of them again said that it was "true," although a few persons found it necessary upon reflection to add that in the tradition to which the saying belongs there would be other sayings that insist on the sharing of power and on the responsibilities that power carries (some examples of such reflexive reaction will be discussed in chapter 3). Incidentally, I do not recall a single case in which the respondent remarked on the use of "eating" in connection with power as being in any way odd.

My first question was always followed up by a second one: Could they cite a corresponding proverb in Swahili or, preferably, in one or the other autochthonous language they spoke?[6] At that point my inquiry took an unexpected turn. *Not a single person was able to quote a "traditional" proverb corresponding to "le pouvoir se mange entier."* Most of the respondents were adults of a certain age who otherwise habitually used proverbs. Two among them were colleagues, one an anthropologist, the other one of the foremost Zairean experts on Luba folklore and oral literature.[7] One old friend, a priest of Lunda background, became all excited about the interpretation I proposed (along the lines indicated above). He wanted us to discuss this immediately with one of the leading Lunda politicians who happened to be in town. But he—the priest— also categorically stated that there was no such proverb in his language.

There remained another line of inquiry: to search the ethnographic literature. To do this exhaustively would have required an effort far beyond what can reasonably be expected for the purpose at hand. In the end, I decided to concentrate on sources from the core of Luba country as these would most likely contain hints or actual examples if our saying was indeed such a well-known formulation of traditional wisdom as it appeared at first. The literature I have been consulting includes Luba ethnographies that have become classical, articles on the use of proverbs and on traditional oral literature in general, and actual collections of proverbs, among them the unique list of almost 1800 proverbs "gathered from all over Lubaland, from Kongolo and Katompe, in the North, to

6. These languages would have included at least the following members of the Luba family: Kiluba (and varieties), Tshiluba, Lunda, Chokwe, Kaonde, Sanga, Lamba/ Bemba, and Tabwa.

7. They were Dr. Mufuta P., professor of African literature and folklore, and Abbé Musenge, lecturer in anthropology, both at the University of Lubumbashi. Mufuta's background is Luba-Kasai; Musenge's native language is Rega.

Bukama and Kamina, in the South," by the missionary-ethnographer W. F. P. Burton (1955: 69).[8] So far, the literature search has proved as negative as my other inquiries.[9] By itself, this would be of doubtful significance because, as I said, the sources consulted do not cover the entire Luba area and, at any rate, failure to report the proverb I am looking for does not constitute proof of its nonexistence. Nor is such a proof, positive or negative, really required for the argument I should like to advance.

A proverb is presumably a token of well-established ideology, realized in a certain form and according to the rules of a communicative-rhetorical praxis. Just because anthropologists, like other "experts" on traditional culture, have a tendency to folklorize tradition and therefore expect to find it articulated in texts that can be classed among recognized genres, this does not mean that cultural beliefs can exist only as lore. In other words, failure to find an expected proverb, either in the literature or from persons questioned may be due to gaps on the side of the sources; more likely it points to mistaken conceptions or wrong expectations on the side of the student of tradition. At any rate, our "case of the missing proverb" leads us to ask questions about cultural knowledge and its formulations that might not have been asked had "le pouvoir se mange entier" indeed proved to be nothing but the translation of an existing proverb.

---

8. A partial list of these sources includes, apart from Burton, the following ethnographies and collections of proverbs from the Luba and a few neighboring regions: Colle 1913 (Luba); De Clercq 1911–12 (Luba); Kalunga 1980 (Tabwa); Girard 1981 (Bemba); Hulstaert 1958 and Korse 1983 (Mongo); Mpandajila et al. 1986 (Luba); Dimandja 1979 and Shala Lundula 1985 (Tetela); Rodegem 1983 (Rundi); Theuws 1954, 1962, 1983 (Luba); Van Caeneghem 1935, 1937, 1939 (Luba); Van der Beeken 1978, 1982 (Yaka); Verhulpen 1936 (Luba); De Sousberghe 1983, Van Bulck 1936 and Wannyn 1983 (Kongo); Evans-Pritchard 1963, 1964 (Zande). Finally, I also searched a recent compilation of more than 2000 proverbs in East Coast Swahili by Scheven (1981), as well as a collection in Swahili as spoken in Zaire (Taabu Sabiti n.d.). Finally I consulted a multilingual collection compiled in Lubumbashi (Cornet et al. 1975, for use in secondary schools). Most of the entries are in Tshiluba or Kiluba, some in Bemba, Hemba, Lulua, Lunda, Kanioka, and Sanga; only three are identified as being in Swahili, one of which is really Luba.

9. Only in Shala Lundula's collection did I find two examples (in translation only) which might be read as coming close to "le pouvoir se mange entier":

(P. 34) Le chef ne laisse pas de reste (lorsqu'il mange) excepté quand il y a des légumes. (1985: 155)
(P. 42) Le léopard ne mange pas le cordon umbilical.
[Compiler's comment added:] Le chef se doit de par ses fonctions de se garder de tomber dans la médiocrité non seulement sur le plan de comportement, mais aussi sur le plan alimentaire. (158)

Power and Lore: Some Elements in Luba Culture

Search for the proverb may have been without success; it was not entirely in vain as regards our efforts to understand "le pouvoir se mange entier." Much valuable information and food for further thought came up in conversations and in the ethnographic literature. I shall now summarize and illustrate these findings.

Among the three semantic elements that can be distinguished in "le pouvoir se mange entier" one is an abstract concept ("pouvoir"), one an adjective ("entier") and the third a metaphorical expression ("se manger"). The notion of eating power is the one that is most striking about the saying. It appears odd to the outsider whereas even to someone who can only claim superficial familiarity with Luba tradition[10] it gives to the saying a special significance, an authentic flavor. We have already noted the rich semantics of the verb *kudia*, "to eat," in Kiluba. A glance at a collection of Luba proverbs such as Burton's gives us an idea of how such an accumulation of meaning may have come about. Although I did not bother to count them, a very substantial number of the sayings on Burton's list makes use of the semantics of food and eating. Cooking, meals, ingestion, sharing (or not sharing) of food are all-pervasive manners to designate social positions and relations, virtues and vices, positive and negative consequences of conduct, and so forth. Here are a few examples illustrating some of the more general applications:

764. *Kitole wa mpopo, kape mukaji koshya, amba leta ne kuno kudi kyaba.* The selfish man. He does not call his wife to cook food lest she should want some, but says "Bring it here where there is room." (Burton 1957/4: 117)

1448. *Nzevu mubangi i kalulu.* A (dead) elephant, shared ub [sic] among many, is no more than a rabbit since each gets so small a piece of meat. (Burton 1958/12: 376)

---

10. I am aware of the problematic nature of the designation "Luba." I realize that a simple disclaimer may not be enough given our present state of knowledge regarding ethnic labels. Nevertheless, this much can be said: The term began its career as an ethnic label perhaps a hundred years ago and has served various colonial interests in ethnic categorization. It is also true that it has been used for cultural and political self-identification (with a major internal opposition between Luba-Kasai and Luba-Shaba). Still, colonial and postcolonial interests that made ideological use of the term did exploit a linguistic, cultural, and historical substance. It is to that substance that the designation "Luba culture" refers (see also Reefe 1981: 8f.). For a most impressive and convincing account of the "making" of an ethnic category see Wilmsen (1989). A full understanding of "Luba" would require a similar study.

S 20. *Kudya wailo madimbo. Upwa kadi lukambo.* He who wants to eat more than his fair share will reap bad feeling. (Burton 1959/2: 43)[11]

I did not find the expression "to eat power" documented in Burton's work. I came upon several examples in an earlier collection of proverbs in Tshiluba (or Luba-Kasai):

119. *Kudia bukalenge nkudikebela malu:* de overheid hebben is zich moeilijkheden aantrekken [To assume power—"to eat *bukalenge*"— is to call for trouble]. (De Clercq 1911–12: 999)

120. *Wadia bukalenge, wabatamija malu,* wie de overheid voert moet de ruzies stil leggen [Those who govern—"those who eat *buka-lenge*"—must stop quarrels]. (Ibid.; other examples for *wadia buka-lenge* in proverbs 123, 124)

Because the food/eating metaphor is so important in making statements about human relations in general, it is not surprising to find it used in sayings that refer to holders of office and power. Confirming the kind of response that "le pouvoir se mange entier" elicited from many persons, proverbs that express power relations in terms of food and eating stress above all the aspect of sharing.[12] In other words, they seem to assert just the opposite of our saying.

1578. *Udya nombe na bobe. Utala nombe yakapwile.* If you are eating ox, share it with those about you, O chief. (Burton 1959/1: 7)

707. *Kilemena mulopwe. Mulopwe kadile kilemena kadi.* He is given dignity by the chief, but if the chief has no food his protégé will also suffer. (Burton 1957/3: 89)

860. *Kupwana na mulopwe i kudya kwaya.* If you are intimate with the chief, you must eat what he eats. (Burton 1957/6: 164)

---

11. Burton does not distinguish clearly between literal translation and paraphrase or explanation. This is a problem that all collectors of African proverbs face. Penfield (1983) meets it by always giving two translations, one "literal," the other "philosophical."

12. See also the one relevant item I found in Scheven's collection of more than two thousand proverbs in East Coast Swahili:

240 A. KWA SULTANI CHAKULA HAKIKOSEKANI. At a king's place food is not missed (or, does not lack).
If you are interested in acquiring anything, you should associate with those that can provide it. (1981: 61)

S 48. *Wabuntu ni mulopwe. Wamwino i mununwa.* The generous one is the chief. The selfish one a slave. The open-handed man is surrounded by friends, but the miser eats alone. (Ibid.: 48)

Of course, it may be argued that, strictly speaking, these sayings do not apply to power itself but to the virtues expected from those who hold power. Sharing of power is one thing, sharing of food another. The metaphorical referents of (shared) food would then be such values as generosity, solidarity, loyalty. However the last proverb in the series quoted (unless it is only Burton who uses the eating metaphor in his paraphrase) contains at least a hint that the intended connection may be more direct (that eating a lot signifies acquiring great power). Such is in my view the case in the following example:

1400. *Nsaba bukata kaso nkose.* He who would grow big must not be fussy about his food. (Burton 1958/12: 369)

Although I have only very general notions of Luba, I suspect that Burton's gloss is not a literal translation. Nevertheless, for what it is worth, it gives us an instance in which increase in power is metaphorically linked to voracious eating habits. The same general idea is expressed in the following dictum from a collection of Luba texts by Theuws. In this case it is predicated on *vidye*, the Supreme Being. But the term *vidye* is not exclusive; it can also designate a chief and inasmuch as this proverb says something about the nature of power it applies to chiefly power at least by connotation.

10. Vìdye ludyà bibìsi: *L'Esprit mange les choses crues. —ludyà:* qui mange parfaitement, même des choses qui ne sont pas préparées, des choses vertes. Il fait ce qu'il veut. On cite le dicton souvent en cas de malheur. . . . (Theuws 1954: 74)

Theuws, a more sophisticated ethnographer than Burton, also provides us in this context with some precious information about the nature of proverbial speech. Following the one just quoted, he lists a saying that makes precisely the opposite assertion:

11. Vìdye ke ùdyanga bibìsi nì? Kàdi po bibìsi: *L'Esprit mange-t-il des choses crues? Il ne mange pas des choses crues.* Le dicton sert parfois de réponse au précédent. Un père qui vient de perdre un enfant citera le premier, son ami, qui a un enfant en vie, répondra par le deuxième. Aussi: Dieu a le temps. Il n'est pas pressé comme celui qui n'a même pas le temps d'attendre que le repas soit tout à fait prêt. (74f.)

It is only to be expected that to coexist in one and the same repertory with its own contradiction be a characteristic of sayings we call proverbs. This is required by the rhetorical function of proverb quoting, which often includes arguments, disputes, and litigation. That, furthermore, contradictory proverbial assertions can be based on the same or a similar saying is made possible by the fact that the expressive element of proverbs—the metaphorical form—appeals to the imagination; it entertains and seduces more than it proves and prescribes. Proverbs are neither legal rules nor philosophical maxims.

Before I explore this line of thought further, I want to note a few more observations on the food/power connection in Luba thought. First, it seems that accession to power and chiefly office were marked by ritual ingestion. One or several people (slaves?) were killed and "food is next prepared with water from the sacred spring, and mixed with the blood of the slain" (Burton 1961: 24). A more gory version is reported by Theuws where the chief drinks the slain subject's blood from a human skull (1962: 216). He also records an expression that at first seems to offer yet another example for the use of oral/ingestive imagery in connection with power. The rites just mentioned are performed because a newly invested chief must be "bitten by *bulopwe*" (the expression is *kusimisya bulopwe*, to make *bulopwe* bite; ibid.). So now, if "pouvoir" is a possible translation for *bulopwe*, it is power that bites (into) the chief. However, a check on the verb *kusimika* (Van Avermaet and Mbuya 1954: 611) shows Theuws's translation to convey a minor, perhaps metaphorical variant of the verb's primary signification which is "to fix, to establish, or to take hold of something." In other words, accession to power is here conceptualized as a kind of possession by *bulopwe*.

This notion of being possessed by the chiefly office may provide the logical link to another set of symbolic uses of food and eating in connection with power. The statement quoted above from Burton continues:

> While the chief eats this, he is told by the chief "kilumbu" (necromancer) of the realm: "Henceforth you must never be seen eating or drinking, and you must always eat alone. If you break this rule, and eat in the company of any other person than your 'mulunda'—personal adviser—then your power will depart, and you will die."
> (Burton 1961: 24)

This eating taboo is confirmed by other ethnographers.[13] In fact it is one of the symbols most often associated with chiefly power in Africa (and

13. See, for instance, Colle 1913: 2:840; Reefe 1981: 25f., where it is shown to be part of the Luba genesis myth; and Theuws 1962: 143, 209, 214.

elsewhere), but that does not concern us here. What needs to be retained for our discussion is that it provides cultural confirmation of the inherently paradoxical character of the ingestive metaphor which we found, speculatively, when we first considered how eating and wholeness, destruction/disintegration and integrity could both be predicated on power in "le pouvoir se mange entier." Everything points to the eating taboo being not so much (or not only) a symbolic expression of the sacred, hence separate, secluded nature of the chiefly office but rather part of a complex of prescriptions that link power to wholeness. The chief's body itself then becomes a symbol. As we know from the Luba (see, e.g., Theuws 1962: 217) and many other examples, physical wholeness is a requirement for being *mulopwe;* any weakness or deformation due to illness or accident could cause a chief to be deposed and even killed. The factual seclusion/separation which the eating taboo entails is therefore not a literal expression of social rank and exclusiveness. It has nothing to do with notions of royal absolutism. To the contrary, it is a symbolic marker of the wholeness and integrity which legitimize power in and for the community.

That solidarity is the signified of ritual seclusion is confirmed by yet another tenet of Luba thought and custom: Traditionally, an accepted and apparently quite common way to contest or reject a chief's claims to power (one, incidentally, for which colonial "legalization" of chiefly office understandably made no provisions) was simply to abandon a chief, "leaving him without power and influence" (Colle 1913: 2: 843; see also Theuws 1962: 142).

Given our fragmentary knowledge of Luba culture it is difficult to speculate on reasons why food/eating imagery should be so important.[14] As we have seen, the sayings that use such images exploit above all social aspects such as sharing and generosity (and their opposites).[15]

14. Perhaps I should point out that the figurative productivity of eating in Luba lore has been noticed by others, see most recently Tshibabwa and Elia (1987). That there might be considerable variation even among closely related cultures is suggested by Hulstaert's collection of Mongo proverbs. Although this is only based on impressions when searching through the book, the lesser importance of eating and related metaphors (as compared to Burton's Luba collection) is striking. Then, again, see the importance of eating in Wannyn's collection of Kongo proverbs (1983). Incidentally, Wannyn exemplifies the interest taken by many colonial administrators in collecting proverbs.

15. Proverbs speaking of generosity (and its opposite) are amply documented in the collections by De Clercq and Van Caeneghem. The latter offers a generalization whose colonialist overtones should not detract from the interesting point it makes:

Uit al die spreekwoorden blijkt dat geven bij ons negers opgevat wordt als een plaatsen van hun goed waar het kan opbrengen. Ze zijn niet gierig of krenterig, maar geven niets als zij er geen profijt kunnen van verwachten. Daar is maar een

Some evoke the physical act of ingestion as an image of acquisition and then stress quantity—the appetite for power is stilled, and possession of great power is demonstrated by eating a lot and indiscriminately. But, although the imagery of food and eating is striking, one may still ask why this domain of experience has such a prominent role in metaphorical (and proverbial) speech. There may be something more than social significance and physiological analogies. Food goes with power because what we translate as power from our sources is a matter, not just of organization, not only of domination, but of life and death.

> 660. *Kibundji kyampikwa mukulu i kifwe.* The village without one in authority will die out. (Burton 1957/3: 83)

With that we touch on another set of ideas that may have a bearing on this discussion. Extraordinary means of protecting and increasing life are designated as *bwanga*, a term usually (mis)translated as "magic" or "magic charm." It is not surprising that we once more encounter the imagery of eating in a proverb worth quoting here because it shows that traditional wisdom was capable of relativizing its own central tenets:

> 46. The real medicine *[bwanga]* of happiness is to be at peace with everybody.
> Bwanga bwà dyesè i kudyà na bantu.
> Literally: to eat with, to share food with people. To share food with somebody is a token of trust, of brotherhood, of oneness. (Theuws 983: 60f)

A variant of the saying just quoted in which *buneme* ("importance" ?), here apparently used as synonym for *bukalenge*, is the subject I found in De Clercq's Tshiluba collection:

> 116. *Buneme nkusombelela ne bantu, nkudia nabo, nkuyikila nabo, nkuseka nabo bimpe, ke buneme buakane abu:* in't gezelschap leven der mensen, met hen eten, met hen spreken, zich met hen verzetten, dit geeft echt gezeg [To live in the company of people, to eat with them, to talk with them, to have fun with them, that gives real authority]. (1911–12: 98)

That holders of power possess powerful *bwanga* is doubted by no one. Of *bwanga*, as of *bulopwe*/chiefly power, it is said that it is indivisible (see

---

uitzondering: het eeten. Eeten mag men nooit weigeren en aan niemand. . . . (1937: 411)

(It is clear from all these proverbs that our Negroes conceive of giving as placing their goods where they can earn. They are neither mean nor stingy, but they give nothing unless they can expect some profit. *To this there is only one exception: Food. Food may never be refused, and to no one.* [My emphasis])

Theuws 1983: 6, 15), and here may be yet another logical link between the notion of power and wholeness.

The wholeness of *bwanga,* Theuws explains quoting a Luba explanation, is like that of the wind. "Can the wind be split up, cut in pieces? If I open a room to the wind and the wind streams in, does that decrease the wind outside?" (1983: 15). Similarly, to predicate wholeness on *bulopwe* may express the idea of each individual holder or embodiment of power participating in the one power that is indivisible. A Tshiluba proverb elaborates further on the idea of integrity:

> 111. *Bukalenge kabuena kuiba; bukalenge amu bakupabo biakane; kuiba bukalenge nkukeba lufu lunene:* het heerschap is niet te stelen: alleenlijk de overheid die men gegeven heeft is recht, de overheid stelen is en geweldige dood zoeken [Power/authority/office cannot be stolen. Only power that is given is legitimate. To steal power is to seek death indeed]. (De Clercq 1911–12: 97)

Moving for a moment outside the confines of Luba culture, a Mongo proverb can be quoted which makes a similar point:

> 2018. *Ntaa'taka botale la bonano.* On ne devient pas grand en s'étirant. . . . Surtout: On n'obtient pas l'autorité en la prenant de force ou par intrigues; on l'a de naissance. (Hulstaert 1958: 516)[16]

Yet another element in the notion of wholeness may be continuity. This is indicated in the following example from Hulstaert's collection:

> 1749. *Mpito ndé botsikali . . .* L'authorité est un survivant. A ta mort, elle restera sur terre et d'autres l'hériteront. (Ibid.: 452)

In sum, the connection of power, eating, and wholeness is amply documented in the sources I consulted. But that does not mean it is always, or even most of the time, intended and interpreted in a metaphysical or axiomatic manner. Being the metaphorical expression it is, it must remain ambiguous, playing on shades of meaning between wholeness as integrity and wholeness as all of it.

Cultural Axioms and Performance

Can we assume that the saying, or the principle it seems to state, expresses specific—Luba or "Zairean"—conceptions of power? If so, how is expression achieved? I have begun to formulate some answers and hunches after consulting dictionaries, questioning people, and mak-

---

16. In his transcriptions Hulstaert uses a complicated system of diacritic symbols. These are omitted in this and other quotations from his work.

ing forays into the ethnographic literature. By now, it is more than a suspicion when I say that some of the problems which made this inquiry so difficult and the answers somewhat tortuous were self-imposed.

To begin with, the episode that produced "le pouvoir se mange entier" was indeed but an episode. It left an impression powerful enough to get this project going. But, as an episode, it did not really provide sufficient context or substance from which to extract meaning capable of being attributed to such complex phenomena as the dissipation of power in religious movements and other areas of Zairean society. With the hindsight provided by this study it is not difficult to guess the reasons for my taking a short cut from experience to inference (one which, if we were to look in the ethnographic literature for similar "interpretations," would show that I am in the respectable company of many colleagues). Foremost among those reasons is a propensity, undoubtedly culturally engrained, to expect that crucial tenets of cultural knowledge come, somehow, as rules and that rules are "naturally" expressed in sententious sayings (or, conversely, that sententious sayings make statements that are considered axiomatic in the culture under study). It is even likely that such a narrow connection between sentence and rule belongs to the kinds of rationality which our scientific tradition has discarded as lore and therefore projects on the societies anthropologists study. That this is in turn not rationally justified but a matter of received conventions and topoi of ethnographic discourse is now widely acknowledged and made the subject of critical inquiry.

Be that as it may, the hunt for a traditional proverb behind "le pouvoir se mange entier" that seems to have led us up a blind alley can now be booked as a salutary experience. Not that it was entirely useless (see above) or misdirected. By looking for a proverb we began, first intuitively, later with a clearer purpose, to lead our inquiry in a direction in which it should go from now on. This is the direction opened up by realizing that proverbs and proverbial expression are not only characterized by certain formal linguistic and literary criteria; they are also always part of a communicative-rhetorical praxis which is wider than one type of instances. A way of speaking cannot achieve generic status in a community unless it is in contrast to other genres. And all genres of speech or discourse are first of all realized as cultural performances. That such performances are based on, imply, or operate classifications (hence logical, moral, esthetic, and other categories) is—ethnographically speaking—*post factum*. Typologizing is not unimportant, but taxonomic analyses do not deserve the quasi-monopoly granted to them by certain structuralists and ethnosemanticists.

Since we are talking about lines of inquiry inspired by ideas ultimately derived from linguistics, I should like to mention one that could

perhaps help us to delve more deeply into connections between proverbial expressions and cultural tenets that are axiomatic. Many
observers have found that proverbs contrast with their linguistic environment in that they show unusual, often archaic, or obsolete forms. It is
not unusual, for instance, to find words and expressions in proverbs that
are not currently used, or even understood. Proverbs may be syntac-
tically peculiar and often they are characterized by (obligatory) metric
patterns. Above all, they are to a high degree stereotypic, unchanged. A
way to generalize this tendency is to assume that proverbial expressions
have become removed from the free syntagmatic realization of speech
or, which comes to the same thing, that they have taken on a paradigmatic character. One may use proverbs to change the course of an
argument, but one does not argue to change a proverb. All this can be
interpreted as a kind of grammaticalization expressive, as I have argued
about certain features of religious doctrine, of dogmatization.[17] In this
sense, proverb-quoting behavior implies that by

> using a proverb sometimes the speaker can escape being under the
> control of realities which would be in conflict with the assertion he
> has made by using a proverb. (Mukařowský 1971: 294; English
> translation by P. Garvin, quoted from Penfield 1983: 99, see also
> p. 19)

Our reflections on ethnography and performance in the preceding
chapter have taught us *not* to expect relations between knowledge and
cultural expressions to be straightforward. Even to acknowledge that
they may be mediated and refracted by metaphors is not enough.
Among the things which taking the idea of performance seriously
requires is to stay attentive to the aleatory, artistic, and therefore unpre-
dictable, and, indeed, to the devious, dissimulating potential of cultural
expression.

It would be unwise, and certainly contradicting my own experience,
to discard the possibility of communicative key-events, such as the
chicken gizzard episode, all of a sudden creating a deeper understanding
or causing diffuse insights to "fall into place." Semantic investigations
have shown that our understanding of entire domains may be dependent on key-terms or concepts. This has been extended even to the
sphere of metaphors.[18] Why should something analogous not occur on a
level that does not lend itself easily to formalization? (Existing attempts
to formulate rules or even grammars governing speech events fail to
convince me, so far.) At any rate, it is now clear that isolating proverbs in

17. See my paper "Taxonomy and Ideology" (1975).
18. See, for instance, the approach used by Lakoff and Johnson (1980).

the hope of getting at the axiomatic core of a cultural tradition, at that part of it which is most practical because it is most theoretical, most directly expressive of a way of reasoning, is a misguided enterprise. A lesson from the work of M. Foucault, which I have put to use in another context,[19] has been that it is precisely their *dispersal* in many kinds of expression that make tenets of a discourse "central" in the sense of being ideologically and practically effective. Anthropologists, folklorists, and, of course, literary critics have known this for some time. Not for a moment do I pretend to have come up with a novelty. But to the nonspecialist it may have been of interest to witness how this kind of knowledge, which is generated systematically and routinely in "normal" investigations, can come about as a discovery, in a moment of surprise, and how it is then transformed into a project of which a story can be told. And this is just the beginning.

19. In a paper entitled "Popular Culture in Africa" (1978).

3 ——————————

The Experimenters

The Troupe Théâtrale Mufwankolo: First Encounter and Some History

Between October 1972 and December 1974 I lived and worked in Shaba, mainly in Lubumbashi, with occasional stays of a few months or weeks in Kolwezi. I had arrived with a grant to study problems of language and work. The idea was to gain, through ethno-semantic and sociolinguistic analyses, an understanding of ways in which Swahili-speaking workers express and communicate their skills, tasks, and experiences.

In the beginning, I concentrated on two projects; one was carried out in a modern zinc production plant near Kolwezi, the other in two small workshops in Lubumbashi which manufactured what might be called neo-African carved furniture, mainly for expatriate customers. Soon it became clear that my research would profit from widening (and deepening) the topic of "work" by looking also at various forms of artistic creativity. Together with I. Szombati I concentrated on a study of popular painting (and painters) in Lubumbashi and Kolwezi. It was then almost inevitable that, once I had entered the fascinating world of popular culture, I would have to extend my interests to the verbal arts.

I had served an apprenticeship in Swahili verbal artistry in the mid-sixties when I studied the Jamaa, a religious movement grown out of a Catholic context. In the early seventies, after many years of working on Jamaa texts, my competence in Shaba Swahili was good to excellent as far as religious discourse went; it was growing in matters of technical communication about metallurgy, industrial processes, and woodworking craftsmanship. But I became painfully aware of my limitations in everyday conversation, especially when, in 1973, my ethnographic work took second place to a professorship in anthropology at the university. Suddenly I no longer had the privilege (or excuse) of the visitor from outside who may limit his attention to topics selected for research. Like other anthropologists I had, of course, always made sure to place my projects in context; now, having been assigned a place in this society, I became part of that context. Formal and informal contacts which I could not control, and did not want to, increased and so did the linguistic demands and fortunately also the rewards. Watching the famous Kinshasa fight between Muhammad Ali and George Foreman on television in a little drinking place together with African friends and then being able to discuss it in Swahili over many bottles of Simba beer, seemed, and probably was, more of an achievement than being able to translate Jamaa religious doctrine or analyze lists of technical terms used in a factory.

Checking these recollections against my notes, I find that this nondirected, nonethnographic learning process began long before I fully realized its importance. On January 3, 1973, I was first introduced to the actor Mufwankolo[1] and his theatrical troupe. I had already watched some of their weekly television plays. Friends from the university who were monitoring my progress in local Swahili decided that I should meet these undisputed masters of the common language of Shaba. They took me to the makeshift studio where the group had just finished taping the weekly show. The first welcome was polite and somewhat reserved. But things changed quickly as most of us moved to the Tam Tam du Shaba, then one of the fashionable *dancings* in Kamalondo township. The evening ended at 3 A.M. in another township where we sealed our new friendship over a nightcap at the *buvette* which the late Balimuacha, then one of the principal actresses in Mufwankolo's group, kept in her house.

Similar evenings followed. Eventually, I became somewhat of a habitué at Balimuacha's and she liked to visit our house. Soon after the first meeting with the group I went to a few rehearsals. I began to take notes from which I shall now quote a brief passage. It anticipated a discovery made (again) thirteen years later which will play a crucial role in understanding the experiment I want to report on in this and the following chapter:

> 15. 1. [1973] Went to a rehearsal of the Mufwankolo group. I am struck by the facility with which, starting from a simple story, the actors develop a dialogue. In fact, during rehearsal, the situation is such that no clear line can be drawn between informal exchanges, *plaisanteries*, private discussion among two participants or within a subgroup, and the actual "theater." The two leaders [Mufwankolo

---

1. Throughout I shall be using the stage names under which the actors are known in Lubumbashi. For a list see p. 121f.

and Kachelewa] seem to exercise very little direction; they have trouble with discipline and often have to assert themselves to keep the actors to the *sujet.*

That I began to take down these notes shows that the Mufwankolo group could have become for me an object of ethnographic study. Luckily, in retrospect, this never happened. One reason was above all practical; I was already overwhelmed with the results of three other projects. As I began to anticipate the problems and labors of transforming my data into writings, I knew that I had to draw a line somewhere. But there was another reason of which I was only dimly conscious at the time. It occurred to me that the group's work—giving form to everyday experience in the urban-industrial world of Shaba and thereby making it possible to reflect and comment on it—was not in essence different from my own groping for an ethnography of work and language. My "method" had always been to rely on recordings and texts. Now I realized that their plays and sketches would make documents of the kind I tried to produce but would be superior in their linguistic quality. I discussed the idea with Mufwankolo and Kachelewa; they were enthusiastic about it and offered their help. Two weeks later (on January 30, 1973) we recorded an improvised sketch entitled *Kazi* ("Work"), in which the two were joined by Balimuacha and the other principal actress of that period, Bibi Kawa. I arranged for the recording to be done under optimal conditions at my house. When I attended rehearsals and watched some of the plays on television I noticed that their free, often anarchic way of delivery would make transcribable recordings all but impossible. On the other hand, performing a sketch around a dining table was not too artificial a situation since it resembled that of their weekly radio sketches. Anyway, the recording was made and filed among various "background information." Only a few years later, when I got around to working on the tape, did I realize how rich a source it was.[2]

2. In 1973, the recording of *Kazi* was to remain our only piece of ethnographic collaboration. In February of that year, Walter Schicho, an Austrian colleague, arrived in Lubumbashi to do linguistic and sociolinguistic research on Shaba Swahili. I was glad to put him in touch with Mufwankolo and his actors. Eventually they became the core of his project. In 1981 he and his Zairean assistant published an excellent collection of texts (interviews with individual actors and four radio sketches) in the original and a French translation, together with some notes on the way the group works. Also of interest is an earlier essay on the expressive use of language varieties in the Mufwankolo plays (Schicho 1975). When John Povey visited Lubumbashi in 1974 I took him to meet the Mufwankolo troupe (see Povey 1975). In my account of the group's history and composition I draw on Schicho's publications as well as on my own nonsystematic notes from the seventies and especially on recorded interviews made in 1985 and 1986.

Thus, to do ethnography *with*, not *of*,[3] the Groupe Mufwankolo has been a project ever since we first met. It never occurred to me to analyze this company of actors as a product of their environment (which, in a sense, they are) or as a case contributing to a comparative understanding of similar phenomena in urban Africa (for which they may be well suited). Because it never became a matter of formal investigation I cannot offer the sort of detailed biographical and socioeconomic information more sociologically minded readers might require at this point. On the other hand, defining our interaction as a common ethnographic enterprise, does not mean that we acted and interacted outside history and all those enabling and restrictive conditions which determine communicative events and competences. I had my history of trying to understand life in Shaba, they had theirs; our ability to communicate across experiences depended on our ability to share them. On more than one occasion, in the course of the years, we found reasons to look back to the past. Unavoidably, this took us back to colonial times. Improvised theater in the common language of Shaba belongs to artforms (such as popular painting and music) which go back to colonial imports and institutions but have long ago acquired a vigorous life of their own.

In 1985 I had conversations, some of them recorded, with Mufwankolo himself and with Citoyen Kisimba which make it possible to reconstruct at least the great lines of that history. There is, as we shall see, something remarkable about the reminiscences of these pioneers: their own progress from childhood to mature age coincides with the emergence of popular theater as a childrens' entertainment and its development to present levels of virtuosity and mass appeal. No wonder that they identify with their work as actors and performers and have little interest (and patience) for historical detail and accuracy. Talking to Kisimba and Mufwankolo is to meet history as it still occurs.

Their story takes us back to the mid-thirties, to a juncture in the colonial history of what was then Katanga, at which it became imperative for the largest employer, the mining company *(Union Minière du Haut Katanga)*, and the largest service organization, the Catholic missions (who had the quasi-monopoly on education and professional training), to do something about a growing "youth problem." In the mid-twenties policies had been introduced, aimed at stabilizing the labor force by switching from short-term recruitment to long-term settlement

3. First reactions to this formulation in a draft of this study lead me to expect that my choice of words may rub some colleagues the wrong way. When I plead for "with" rather than "of," I try to evoke an issue which to me is epistemological, not ethical, and certainly not guided by old anthropological pretentions of going native in a new garb. It will be the burden of my story to convince the reader that an "ethnography with" is possible.

of workers together with their (nuclear) families. These measures had proved successful. Population growth in the miners' settlements and the urban areas made a situation foreseeable where labor would be more or less self-reproductive.[4] Schools were the main route along which children were channeled on their way to becoming wage earners. But there was also the problem of controlling leisure time. An ingenious solution was found when lower-level expatriates and upper-level African employees (as much as they existed then) were encouraged to use their own free time to promote sports, useful artisanal activities, and, above all, youth organizations such as the Boy Scouts.[5] Donors for uniforms and badges were found, camps and outings organized. An elaborate system of ranks, rewards, and distinctions (similar to the largely symbolic system of *cotes* (promotions), which was designed to keep their fathers in the mines and factories under the illusion of professional progress) provided prospects and perspective for large numbers among the urban youth. Occasional meetings with groups in other regions and other colonial territories formed and expressed links to international *scoutisme*. As elsewhere in the world, scouting provided experience

4. On the labor history of Katanga/Shaba as it relates to education, language, and other cultural policies (and with special attention to the role of Swahili) see Fabian 1986 (also for references to other sources).

5. A chronicle of Elisabethville (*Elisabethville 1911–1961* [1961: 144]) states that scouting was introduced there by "MM. Durant and Clajot, assisted by Dom Grégoire Coussement" and that Pius Sapwe, now (1961) the police commissioner, was one of the first Cub Scouts. The date fits what has been said about the change in social policies. The earliest documentary evidence of *scoutisme* in Katanga being part of the close collaboration between the Union Minière and the Catholic mission I found in correspondence between the company's department of native labor (M.O.I., *main-d'œuvre indigène*) and Father Grégoire Coussement, representing the Benedictines. A note by Father Grégoire (dated March 24, 1937) formulates the project of a *foyer social* (social center) to be organized and directed by the mission in each of the workers' camps. A confidential memorandum from the M.O.I. department (dated March 26, 1937) discusses implementation of this proposal and mentions "le scoutisme" under the rubric "Service d'assistance récréative" (Archives UMHK-MOI-Lubumbashi, dossier 11, "Dossier M. Rolus"). That scouting was by then already organized for the children of mine workers is attested to by a few highly interesting documents that somehow found their way into the UMHK archives. These are three short essays in Swahili (typewritten) in which Boy Scouts from Kikole report on outings and other activities in mid-1937 (these are, incidentally, among the earliest examples of written Shaba Swahili known to me). Most likely these little essays were appended to a report (under the heading "Union Minière du Haut Katanga—Scouts de Kikole," unsigned but obviously submitted by the European Scout Master) on activities during the months of April and May 1938 (almost all of which consisted of professional training). The author mentions another Boy Scout group in Luisha under a "jeune chef indigène" and asks for permission to go to Elisabethville to meet Father Grégoire and work toward a "federation" of various Boy Scout groups in the area (Archives UMHK-MOI-Lubumbashi, dossier B 21).

with, and early selection for, leadership.[6] A certain degree of Africanization was encouraged through the use of traditional folklore and music.[7]

This is where Kisimba placed the origins of popular theater in Lubumbashi/Elisabethville.[8] Taking off from theatrical texts and performances that were part of the school curriculum[9] or of cultural programs organized for the expatriate population of Elisabethville, Boy Scouts began to invent sketches and to perform them on outings in their

6. On the historical role of scouting in meeting the "Imperatives of Empire," see the excellent study by Rosenthal 1986. Also relevant are recent works on the social history of games and sports as an instrument of imperialism by Mangan 1986 and Baker and Mangan 1987.

7. Apart from the documents cited already, I have found only scattered historical information on scouting in the former Belgian Congo. In the journal *La Voix du Congolais*—at the time the only major tribune for educated Congolese published under governmental guidance—I found two short articles. Antoine Ngwenza says that scouting began between 1926 and 1935 "under the direction of the late M. Paul Van Arenberg in Katanga and of M. Henri Durand in the Bas-Congo" (1946: 408). Later he adds that in Katanga several groups have existed for ten years (i.e., since ca. 1935), some of them for European children only (ibid., 409). The earlier date (1926) probably applies to the Lower Congo. This is confirmed by Mikeno who puts the beginning of scouting in Léopoldville with "the St. Norbert troop at Sainte-Anne [parish] around 1925" (probably for the children of expatriates). Scouting was established in the native townships at St. Pierre parish by the Reverend Father Van den Heuvel (Mikeno 1953: 802). The same journal reported a scout rally at Kimwenza (Lower Congo) in 1951 with photos showing racially mixed groups (Cigogne Patiente 1951) and also ran photos of a scout ceremony in 1948 (*La Voix du Congolais* 1948, no. 4: 484) and of Lady Baden-Powell visiting guides and scouts at Léopoldville in 1950 (1950, no. 6: 290). An article by a missionary, P. Lizin, published in 1968, gives statistics for that year but, except for mentioning that the author started his own first group in 1947, does not treat of the early history.

8. A study of popular theater in Bandundu (the former Banningville) by Mikanda et al. (1980) confirms the historical picture drawn by Kisimba. There, too, "children" playing sketches are said to have been the beginning; the Boy Scouts and other Catholic youth movements are mentioned, as is the *cercle d'évolués*. All this started in the forties but really got off the ground after independence in 1960. The major difference with Lubumbashi is in the language. Bandundu lacks a common language—although Lingala has some currency, a situation of stable multilingualism seems to obtain there, including Pende, Mbala, Yanzi, and a few other languages—and so most plays were performed in French. The study cited contains the texts of six pieces.

9. The use made by missionary schools of theater as a means of education is an interesting topic in itself. In some former colonies it goes back to the nineteenth century (see Abedji 1971, 1973, for Nigeria). An article by Yoka (1982) on "La conception missionnaire du théâtre naissant en Afrique et notamment au Zaïre" is somewhat disappointing. Yoka mentions that school theater in Kinshasa goes back to "around 1925" and a play called *Katikiro* about the Ugandan Martyrs. See also two articles by the same author (published under two different versions of his name), Mu-Daba (1975) and Mudara (1972).

camps under the leadership of a certain Michel Makassi.[10] These short plays were above all moralizing (a typical theme: *Mutoto muzuri anasaidiaka maskini*, The good child always helps the poor). But it was decisive for the later development of the genre that the emphasis was laid from beginning on humorous entertainment *(kucheka, kuchekesha)*. Sketches that proved successful were given more elaborate performances on holidays and feasts of patron saints. Girls, incidentally were at that time not involved (female roles would be performed by boys dressed as women). The *guides* (Girl Guides, the female branch of the scouts) specialized in singing. As Kisimba sees it, the Boy Scout actors achieved with their sketches a breakthrough from the mission-sponsored plays performed in French by their elders to improvised theater in Swahili. By 1940, he recalls, he and his peers had risen in the ranks of scouting to become *routiers* (Rovers). They began to take their work more seriously and to write down scenarios *(aides-memoires)* and to put on "real" plays.

Singing had always been part of the sketches. Accomplished musicians such as Martin Kibunka and Michel Lukonga[11] taught the younger ones instruments (guitar and accordion) and then, Kisimba says, we began to play a sort of jazz—taking off from traditional songs put to modern rhythm *(tunarythmer)* and from recorded Latin American dances such as the tango, rumba, cucaracha, and many others. Playing this sort of music seems to have been the point at which these young performers grew out their "scoutisme" and began to assemble their own groups.[12] With Kitenge Gabriel[13] as a leader they formed the VJKat *(Voix de la*

10. Michel Makassi was born the son of a soldier in Lubumbashi (he was, according to popular categories, "Mangala," i.e., "Lingala-speaking"). He worked as a driver and was the sexton at St. Jean parish in Kamalondo. He was known as guitar player in various groups formed by the "Mangala" ethnic association. (Information provided by Kalundi Mango, August 1987).

11. Martin Kibunka, a Yeke from Bunkeya, attended St. Boniface School in Lubumbashi where he graduated in 1937. He became an elementary school teacher in St. Jean parish. He played the guitar in a dance orchestra, the harmonium in church, and the trumpet in the parish brass band. After World War II he moved to Kasenga where he died young (he suffered from asthma). Michel Lukonga was born in Lubumbashi. His father, like Michel Makassi's, was a "Mangala" soldier. Lukonga also graduated from St. Boniface, and found work as a government clerk. He too played guitar and trumpet and sang in Father Anschaire Lamoral's church choir. (Information provided by Kalundi Mango, a classmate and friend of Kibunka and Makassi, August 1987).

12. This new music also constituted a break with the kind of social dancing ("European style") known as *malinga*, which was popular among the upward mobile of the times (see Gansemans and Schmidt-Wrenger 1986: 184f., Kazadi 1973, and Low 1982).

13. Kitenge Gabriel, also a former Boy Scout, was born in Lubumbashi of Songye ("Kabinda") parents. He graduated a few years later than Kibunka, Lukonga, and

Jeunesse Katangaise), some of whose members had left school and youth organizations and had started working. Kisimba himself did not play an instrument well but he "knew how to direct" and organized his own group, the famous *Je-Co-Ke (Jeunesse comique de Kenya,* named for one of the African townships of Elisabethville).[14] They began with imitations and impersonations of pieces and performers they had heard on the radio or seen in films, interspersed with comical sketches. Together with Mungobo Joseph, who was then a very popular actor, he continued to perform improvised plays. These, too, were always mixed, "multi-media" entertainments. Kisimba remembers how they got their inspirations and topics. They would go to drinking places *(cabarets)* and watch "people hanging around, how men would play up to women, and vice versa." They would go to the railway station or to bus stops and observe people. An especially rich source for *sujets* was the night court *(Tribunal de nuit)*, where petty offenders and all sorts of litigating parties provided types and situations. Eventually they also began to perform for a paying public in bars. By 1950 there was at least one other group called Naku-lika,[15] led by a certain Baba Mateo.

Kisimba then became a member of the Cercle St. Benoit, the mission-sponsored club for *évolués*.[16] There he began to concentrate on producing folkloric *ballets,* performances of traditional dance by accomplished musicians and dancers from different ethnic associations. Directly or indirectly, these diverse activities—improvised theater, vaudeville-like mixed entertainment, and traditional dancing—were in various degrees supported by the missions and other colonial agencies without being directly controlled. However, it was in line with the then dominating ideology of assimilation that the missionaries and other cultural promoters among the expatriates looked at this development as

---

Kalundi. He was hired by the B.C.K. railway company, now S.N.C.Z. (where he still works).

14. Kisimba must have acted as a kind of manager or impressario of this group. He allowed me to copy a kind of prospectus from his collection advertising records (singles) by *Je-Co-Ke* on "ECODIS Disques 'FIESTA'" with a photo of the group. He identified the five members shown as Kabeya (stage name Corbich), Masengo (Kateti; is this the famous Masengo Edouard? [see Low 1982: 92ff.]), Mwale, Mungobo (Le comique) and Nikulu (Rossignole). Ten records are listed on the sheet, six of them in Swahili, two in Lingala, and one each in Lunda and Zulu(!).

15. *Nakulika* is probably Bemba, literally meaning "I hang (something)."

16. On the historical role of the *Cercle St. Benoit,* see Fetter 1976: 164f. One of the founders was Attorney General Paul van Arenberg (whom we met earlier as one of the earliest promoters of scouting in Katanga; see Ngwenza 1946). Fetter also mentions that in 1932 Auguste Verbeken, a prominent sponsor of *évolué* activities, directed "a play which he had written especially for the club: quite unconventionally the cast included both European and African actors" (1976: 164).

but a phase in the introduction of Western culture.[17] Classical French plays continued to be performed and official sponsorship of music was directed to religious choral singing[18] and brass bands. As was the case in Kinshasa and Brazzaville, Greek merchants in Elisabethville representing the recording company Telefunken were the first to recognize the commercial potential of Congolese popular jazz.[19]

Like Kisimba, Mufwankolo first discovered his talents when he attended St. Boniface, the elementary and secondary school (now Institut Kitumaini) in Kamalondo township (the former commune Albert). He was in the fifth grade when he caught the teacher's attention with the way he told a story he had heard from his maternal grandmother.[20] He recalls the teacher's name, Mumba Cornelis (now an employee with the railway company SNCZ); apparently Mumba was the one who encouraged him to try acting. Not much later, in 1952, he assembled a group of actors who called themselves Jeunes acteurs du Katanga. Their first successful piece was Sikia shauri ya wazazi (Listen to your parents' advice). Performances were given in bars. The owner would add 50 centimes to the price of a bottle of beer (which cost 6 francs at the time) and also charge a 2 franc entry fee. This was mostly in commune Kenya, where Mufwankolo lived in the care of his *muyomba*, his maternal uncle. The uncle did not support Mufwankolo's artistic ambitions; he saw to it that his nephew first learned a decent trade. After finishing elementary education, Mufwankolo went on to Don Bosco trade school where he learned to be a cabinet maker.

Mufwankolo's and Kisimba's careers converged in the mid-fifties. Their involvement with theater had grown along with developments in

17. It is remarkable that Kisimba's and Mufwankolo's accounts do not mention the puppet shows *(théâtre de marionnettes)* which were then promoted by expatriates as a means to introduce natives "slowly" to European theater. On these puppet shows, which date back to the late forties, see Anonymous 1950; H. Drum [pseudonym for van Herreweghe) 1948, 1950; Jadot 1950; Theys 1952. A comprehensive study of puppet theater in sub-Saharan Africa by Darkowska-Nidzgorska 1980 comments on these efforts but also demonstrates that this art form predated colonization. Concern with a slow, "evolutionary" approach to Westernization has been characteristic of much of Belgian colonial policy. It is not surprising, therefore, to find it in some of the reports on promoting theater in the Congo almost up to Independence; see Bissot 1952: 626, Brasseur 1957, Scohy 1951, Weterings 1936–37.

18. For a contemporary report on these efforts, with a photograph of the composer Joseph Kiwele, see Falasisi [pseudonym] 1948.

19. On the first Greek-owned record companies in Léopoldville/Kinshasa, see Bemba 1984: 33. On the recording stars from Katanga (not mentioned by Kisimba and Mufwankolo) see Low 1982.

20. In 1985 I recorded that story with Mufwankolo.

the colonial situation. By 1956 colonial authorities acknowledged that something had to be done about future developments.[21] The Brussels World's Fair of 1958 made possible a meeting of Congolese political leaders. It can be seen as the beginning of events that led to independence in 1960. As a sort of last ditch effort (although it was hardly perceived that way), Belgians of various political persuasions and with different degrees of involvement in colonization became active in the promotion of indigenous artistic expressions. In Elisabethville several expatriates (Kisimba and Mufwankolo recall some of the names: a M. de Koninck, who went by his artist's name, M. Landier; a M. Schumacher, nicknamed *kamukonzo*[22] because he was tall but thin; a M. and Mme. Leloup; and a Mme. de Dekker[23] began to promote what they called *spectacles populaires*. Although, apart from acting out their private enthusiasm and, probably, idealism, they served Belgian propagandist interests, they also gave the likes of Kisimba and Mufwankolo the first chance at professional theater. They recognized the local talent, taught them some basic skills, such as lighting and sound, and produced, in 1957, the first major folkloric *spectacle*, "Shangwe Yetu" (Our Feast).

"Shangwe Yetu" was indeed a spectacle, a huge production made possible by grants from the government and the big companies. One of the initiators was Maurice Huisman, director of the Belgian national theater. Jean-Marc Landier produced the project. In a first phase, dance groups from Katanga and Kasai provinces and from Rwanda were recruited locally. The groups then came by train or airplane to Elisabethville/Lubumbashi and were housed in a special camp at Lukuni, an abandoned mine some fifteen kilometers from town. Here they spent some time rehearsing and probably coordinating their performances. Meanwhile a football stadium was prepared for the presentation. The decor (large, decorative panels) was by the then young painter Mwenze. Kiwele and his singers were also involved as were smaller groups of vaudeville-like entertainers. The performance itself was a true multimedia entertainment. Traditional dances, masks, folkloric adaptations, old and "modern" music, staged ritual, comic sketches, choral music, and

21. Colonial publications of that period report on stepped-up artistic activities in the Congo, such as tours of the National Theater, of many individual performers, and even of a circus. Although these were above all intended for the European public, interest among Africans was noted and encouraged; see Brasseur 1957, Gascht 1958.

22. *Kamukonzo* means "the skinny one" (probably from Shaba Swahili *kukonda*, lose weight).

23. The names are transcribed from conversations and recorded interviews. I have not been able to verify the spelling. At any rate the most important among the persons named was Jean-Marc Landier, the director of *Shangwe Yetu*.

imitations of black gospel song (by a group who called themselves Les jeunes soumarins) were watched by a huge audience on the evening of August 3, 1957.[24]

"Shangwe Yetu" brought Kisimba and Mufwankolo together. For a while, Kisimba seems to have put aside his interest in ballet in order to work on some major plays together with Mufwankolo. Their great success came in 1959, on the eve of Independence. With a group of seven they went on a European tour, performing in major houses such as the Théâtre de la Monnaie in Brussels. They had two plays in their repertoire: *Le chasseur et le blanc*, or *Kilolo kalambatila*, conceived by Mufwankolo and translated as "The Hunter and the White Man,"[25] and *Le docteur malgré lui* (The physician in spite of himself), a play Kisimba and Mufwankolo adopted from a story which, Kisimba says, had served Molière as a source for his *Le médicin malgré lui* (1666).[26] They played in Swahili with enough French clues mixed in to enable Belgian audiences

24. This is based on viewing a film titled *Changwe Yetu*, "*Notre plus grande fête à nous tous*" (both the spelling and the translation are not quite correct) in the historical archives of the Royal Museum at Tervuren (Filmotheque Index 142). The film, directed by Jean-Marc Landier, documents preparations and the production of the spectacle; it only contains a few takes of the performance itself. It is also an interesting document about "documentation." The film is cast as a sort of adventure story intended to strengthen its propagandistic appeal. Some of the scenes are obviously reenacted. Nor is it possible to tell the difference between "authentic" performances filmed in their own context and staged, folklorized versions prepared for the show. As far as I know *Shangwe Yetu* was a one-time event (although it may have had several performances in Lubumbashi). At about the same time several groups promoting theater were active in Léopoldville/Kinshasa, most prominent among them the *Ligue Folklorique Congolaise*, organized by Jean van den Bosche and the painter-musician-actor A. Mongita (see Collard 1958). On Mongita, see also Bissot 1952, Schohy 1951, Trussart 1972; for other names/groups see Cornevin 1970: 127–34, based largely on Jadot 1959. Cornevin also mentions, and reports on the outcome of, two competitions or "tournaments" for Congolese playwrights and actors, one organized in 1950 by *La Voix du Congolais* (6: 665f.; notice that the jury for submissions in Swahili, one of the "four dialects" admitted for the competition, was to be located in Costermansville/Bukavu), the other in 1957 in Lubumbashi (ibid., 129, 131f.). *La Voix du Congolais* had reported on a "native theater troupe" as early as 1948 (4: 202); later it published several texts (by Albert Mongita, 13 (1957): 779–82, 868–69, 967–70; 14 (1958): 47–50, 655–57, 712–17; Pascal Kapella, 14 (1958): 139–43; Christophe Tshimanga, 14 (1958): 363–65, 425–26, all in French). A Swahili-French edition of a piece by Joseph Kiwele was published in Elisabethville/ Lubumbashi in 1953 (Kiwele 1953).

25. This refers to the plot that was constructed around a European and an African hunter. *Kilolo kalambatila* needs explanation. *Kilolo*, the bugler, was at that time Mufwankolo's stage name; *kalambatila*, is of Bemba/Lamba derivation and means "he who goes hunting."

26. Interestingly, among the illustrations in Gascht 1958 I found a photo (no. 53) of a presentation of *Le médicin malgré lui* by a group of Africans identified as Théâtre de l'Union française de Léopoldville. The principal actors are in seventeenth- or

to follow. Apparently Mufwankolo also gave some solo performances as a mime.

This brief period of international success came to an abrupt end with Independence and the Katanga secession in 1960. Their efforts were redirected to local audiences and for a while they continued to produce sketches. An actor who called himself Kalwasha (whom we will meet later) was then the specialist for tribal accents. Ethnic humor was popular. However, it lived less on characterizing differences between groups in town than on comical exaggerations of the speech and demeanor of the up country visitor or recent arrival. In 1960, Kisimba took his folklore ballet to Kinshasa to perform in the festivities of Independence. Later he had much support from the separatist Katangese government, as long as it lasted, but does not seem to have suffered from that association. In 1966 the central government chose him and his group to represent the Congo at the Festival de l'art nègre in Dakar. Eventually he found employment in the social services of the mining company (which was nationalized at the end of 1966). There, until recently, one of his main duties was to organize theater and dance groups (and competitions) in each of the fifteen miner's settlements.[27]

Mufwankolo also found a new sponsor during the brief period of the Katangese secession. Mbuyu Darbo, known as Bwana Cheko (he too will be part of our story later on), was then director of Radio Katanga. He arranged for weekly radio sketches on topics of current interest. These were at first broadcast live, and later on taped. As a result, Mufwankolo and several actors of his group were employed at the radio station (where they still hold jobs), and it was in this new medium that their improvising skills were honed to perfection. These radio broadcasts put limits on the number of players (usually four); they were a constant challenge to come up with fresh topics reflecting life in the towns of Shaba and to make the sketches entertaining; they forced them to develop the high art of *double entendre* and *sousentendu* whenever their social criticism got too close to the powers that be. Above all, working for the radio favored a verbal, discursive, and often pedagogical style. A sketch was always followed by a *morale*, an epilogue in which Mufwankolo, switching to a "higher" linguistic register, would spell out message and applications. Performing on radio also meant that invisible audi-

---

eighteenth-century costume but they are surrounded by dancers in native dress. So, although the play was in French, Molière had been Africanized in one way or another. The same group played Molière's *Le malade imaginaire* in 1956 before an audience that included Governor General Pétillon and other high officials (see notice in *La Voix du Congolais* 12 (1956): 210f.).

27. In 1987 Kisimba suffered a stroke and has been disabled since.

ences had to be moved by the power of words and arguments alone; other theatrical means, such as facial expressions, body movement, a stage, costumes, and props could not be used. This (and a chronic lack of funds) explains the minimalist approach to theatrical productions which the group maintained even when, in 1971, it added television broadcasts of sketches to their regular radio program.

When I left Zaire in December 1974 the Mufwankolo group was at the peak of its popularity. Their (almost) weekly television program called "Zaire ya Kesho" (The Zaire of tomorrow),[28] was always eagerly awaited and watched by everyone who could get near a television set. The actors became local stars, they were recognized on the streets (as I often noticed when I walked with Mufwankolo or Balimuacha) and each play was discussed at length on the days following the broadcast. For a while (we were in a period of relative economic prosperity that came to an end with the oil crisis) the group could enjoy and occasionally celebrate its success.[29]

Then came the upheavals of the Shaba wars of 1976 and 1978. The radio broadcasts of sketches continued but things changed at the television station. Although limited by inferior technical equipment (the studio was set up in a classroom at the St. Francis College, now Institut Imara), programming in the seventies had been more or less under local control. When I returned to Lubumbashi in 1985, television was broadcast in color and by satellite, and it now emanated from Kinshasa; only a few local news programs and panel shows were produced in Shaba. "Zaire ya Kesho" was no longer a regular feature. When I probed into the reasons, most respondents hinted at political directives to play down everything that could foster Shaba regionalism (to which, intended or not, improvised plays in Swahili undoubtedly contributed).

Popular Theater in Shaba: Settings and Contexts

The key to understanding the world of urban-industrial Shaba is its labor history.[30] By the time the Berlin Conference had recognized the existence and boundaries of King Leopold II's private

---

28. Ironically, the title tune of this program was a popular song recorded in the early fifties—Mufwankolo claims to be the lead vocalist but that does not check with information on the record—which celebrates a city dweller's nostalgia for the "village back home" (for a text and translation see Fabian 1978: Appendix 1 and note 9, p. 331; see also Schicho and Ndala 1981: 124f.).

29. None of the plays of that golden era is preserved on videotape. The only sound recordings I know of are those made by W. Schicho and myself.

30. For the following see Fabian 1986 where I draw on the writings of Fetter (e.g., 1976) and Perrings 1979.

colony as the Congo Independent State (1885), its southeastern region, Katanga, was already known for its mineral wealth. Around the turn of the century, although the country had not yet been militarily "pacified," international organizations were set up in order to channel capital in search of profitable ventures toward this region. The Comité du Katanga (founded in 1900) was given sovereign powers over the soil and, for all practical matters, over the population. The Union Minière du Haut Katanga began mining and smelting copper in 1906 (with strong participation of organizations operating in the British colonies to the south and east, such as the Tanganyika Concessions Ltd.). The railway was brought to Katanga in 1910, and a year later Elisabethville, now Lubumbashi, was incorporated as an "urban district."

As might be expected, the mining company faced the problem of assuring an adequate supply of cheap labor. Stressing in their propaganda that the highly mineralized semi-arid environment of South Katanga supported only a sparse population (and downplaying the fact that the peoples of Katanga resisted colonization or found agricultural production more profitable than work in the mines) the Union Minière first opted for long-distance, short-term recruitment of able-bodied workers from British and Portuguese possessions to the south. That this sort of recruitment, which was done by subcontractors, differed little from slavery in the eyes of the people did not cause much concern among colonial administrators and company managers. It only became a problem when, due to losses during transportation, desertion, and the squalor in the labor camps, labor costs rose to a level where they threatened the profitability of the enterprise. Added to this was the political threat of dependency on South African and Rhodesian collaboration. By the end of World War I, a policy of Belgianization was adopted to counteract the danger of losing this region to British interests. This involved changes in the recruitment of expatriate personnel, measures to establish French as the official European language, and search for native labor in the populous regions of northern Katanga and Kasai. Mining sites spread from Lubumbashi to the west (in the area of what is now Likasi); railway links were established with the Congo River and eventually with the Atlantic port of Lobito. Around the mines and railway crossroads, administrative centers were established, and urban agglomerations began to grow. The services of the missions were secured by land grants and a monopoly for education.

Apart from the workers needed for the mines, these towns began to attract Africans who found work in subsidiary industries, in government and domestic services, in the military and the police. The need to provide services to the African population in turn provided opportunities for day laborers and petty traders and by the mid-twenties the authorities were faced with the unexpected problem of controlling an "over-flow" of Africans who settled in the towns. Company and administration introduced rigorous limitations on mobility to, and within, the mining region. Mostly with a certain pride, only occasionally with resentment, it was pointed out that everything in Katanga depended on the Union Minière. Wages and prices were dictated (and reflected fluctuation in the world market for copper and other minerals). Labor unrest among expatriates and Africans was quickly suppressed and counteracted with one of the most paternalist styles of colonization. Directly or indirectly, the company assured basic services such as housing, health, and education. It meddled with family life, leisure activities, and religion. But, all the self-congratulatory talk about successful, progressive colonization not withstanding, we know now with historical hindsight that, as the cities expanded and a new generation of Africans grew up having only tenuous links with their rural origins, large areas of African life were never successfully brought under control. More humane labor conditions created more leisure time, education opened up new cultural resources, aspirations to a petit-bourgeois life developed. Congolese began to take over skilled technical and clerical jobs that had at one time been reserved for whites or for such immigrants as the "Nyasaland boys," who formed the first literate elite in Lubumbashi.

With modernization awareness of the value of traditions grew, and where political channels were closed to them, Africans asserted their independence in new cultural and religious associations, in peer groups who spent much time together playing and watching sports or just being "about town." The economic crisis which hit the area in the early thirties acted to reinforce urban solidarity, even across ethnic boundaries. All in all, life was tough for those who had work and tougher for those who did not; police controls and punishment for minor offenses were severe; economic and commercial initiatives were tolerated only as long as they did not compete with expatriate residents; education was kept at a low level, which caused frustration among new intellectuals, who were made to pay twice when contempt was added to repression because the new *évolués* developed aspirations beyond their means to fulfill them. Still, Africans survived with dignity and even a measure of joy under mostly adverse circumstances and political oppression. They learned the arts of parody and subterfuge all the while they gave form to their life in the cities and they did this with the help of the popular arts.

Against this background, the story of the emergence of popular theater in Lubumbashi remains sketchy. Enough is known, however, to permit a few generalizations that will enhance our understanding of the account to come, always keeping in mind the aim of this study, which is to explore the meanings of "Le pouvoir se mange entier" and to do this following a "method" that works as an ethnography with, not of, the Groupe Mufwankolo.

To begin with, we can discern, through the reminiscences of Kisimba, Mufwankolo, and others, characteristics and determinants of popular theater. Having been made aware of history, we no longer have the choice (often taken by anthropologists for want of an alternative) to seek explanations mainly in synchronic, systematic terms. What popular theater in Shaba is, how it is practiced and received, is to a large extent the outcome of processes and events that were larger than the subject we happen to focus on now. Of course, everything that is, is in some sense the outcome of processes and events. The reason to stress this here and to insist on the attribute "historical" is to introduce an argument which will allow us to see the emergence of popular theater as one form of a larger struggle for the production and expression of communicable knowledge about life in urban-industrial Africa—factual, but also esthetic, emotive, reflexive, and so forth.[31] Those forms that did develop to the level of mass media (music, painting, theater) owe their existence, not to a more or less predictable evolution following some general laws or patterns, but to specific constellations, accidents in fact, and to an interplay of personal choices and sociopolitical conditions which have always been ridden with conflicts and contradictions. If it was developmental, this history has been characterized by breaks and breakthroughs more than by stages and transitions; accordingly, its present result—"present" being the time at which we study it—is far from being an institution that has settled down into functionally integrated structures, more or less peacefully serving well-defined societal needs.

Let us try to spell this out in some detail. On the one hand it is true that theater[32] was introduced to Shaba in its "classical" Western form (as filtered, of course, through uses and abuses in a school system, primarily as a vehicle of language teaching; but that would be no different from the first experiences most Westerners have with theater). As such it was eagerly adopted already by Kisimba's and Mufwankolo's elders, some time in the late twenties. When Africans began to develop their own initiatives they accepted "theatrical" as a definition of their activities.[33]

---

31. A unique document for this—a colonial history of Elisabethville/Lubumbashi written in Swahili by a local author and sponsored by an association of former domestic servants—is now available in print (see Fabian 1990).

32. It should be clear that the term is here taken in its narrow sense of Western-type staged performances. This is in no way meant to imply that theatrical forms of expression, often highly developed, were absent from precolonial African societies.

33. Here lies an important difference between popular theater and other, often earlier, forms of dramatic performance, such as Kalela and Bene Ngoma (see Mitchell [1956] 1968; Ranger 1975). I brought this up in the conversation with Kisimba. He

But this adoption was by no means an instance of straightforward, one-way acculturation. Acceptance only created a common ground, perhaps one could say a cover, for asserting creativity, independence, and critique in a political situation that had no use for any of this. Some colonialists may have marveled at the ease with which young Africans took up various kinds of artistic expression; less well intentioned observers took it as proof for their conviction that Africans liked to ape the culture of their European overlords. Neither understood that mimesis had opened a battleground, that it was an active mode of coping, not just passive imitation.[34]

Theater was not adopted as a sort of cultural present from Europe to be nursed and cared for. It was quickly dissociated from its place in the schools and in the workplace for which the schools prepared. First it was displaced laterally to leisure activities organized by the youth movements, then it descended into the uncontrolled areas of life in the African townships. In the course of such displacement, theater was stripped of its cultural "seriousness" and solemnity. Our account makes it clear that the new groups of actors chose to practice the "low" genre of comedy—the sketch, as they themselves called it—rather than enacting high and noble drama and tragedy. This gave them freedom from the Western classical repertoire. When they occasionally did use that repertoire they chose classical comedies.

What I described as displacement and descent (the latter not to be understood as decline but as reaching for deeper levels) was made possible by another break with the imported practice. Classical pieces in French were rehearsed and produced in schools for Africans because it was thought that their "natural" talent for acting could in this way be made to serve the implantation of the French language and francophone culture. By switching to Swahili the new theater groups made an imported cultural form serve their own purposes. In the mid-thirties (when our story begins) a variety of Swahili (different from both East Coast "Standard" Swahili and the so-called Kingwana spoken in the northeast of the then Belgian Congo) had just been fully established as the common language of urban Shaba. This is not the place to go into detail about questions of linguistic policy[35] except to say that the Belgians had promoted Swahili for their own political aims: to counteract

---

remembered the *beni ya Nyanzaland* [Nyassaland, now Malawi] and another "dance" of Bemba origin, *Ngwaya*. But he insisted that the emphasis was on music, dance, and mime rather than on spoken dialogue.

34. The most comprehensive and illuminating study of cultural mimesis (including forms of possession) in colonial Africa is a recent book by Kramer (1987).

35. See on this Fabian 1986.

the influence of English and other African work languages that dominated Lubumbashi well into the twenties. Ironically, Belgians went about appropriating Swahili in such a way that they unwittingly created spheres of freedom where they wanted to establish controls. Missionaries, government agencies, and private companies described, codified, and thereby, they thought, promoted Swahili in two forms. The missions, above all the White Fathers, chose a "high" variety modeled on the classical (Zanzibari) dialect spoken by the Swahili traders of the nineteenth century; private European employers pushed a pidginized form reduced to the bare essentials of work and command situations; the government oscillated between the two. None of the descriptions published and circulated during colonial times corresponded to the Swahili actually spoken by the population for whom it soon became the first and often only African language. Although this constituted a barrier against official literacy, it did not prevent uncontrolled, grass-roots literacy and, above all, it guaranteed liberty of language use. Swahili became an important vehicle for all sorts of private communication but also for contestatory religious movements—a case of a medium becoming the message—and, which is what interests us here, for creative artistic expression in the lyrics of songs and the dialogues of improvised theater.[36]

Thus, by its linguistic vehicle alone, theater became firmly anchored in an emerging, vital popular culture. This had other consequences to which we must now turn our attention. Popular theater broke with the conventional distinctions that characterized the imported classical form and, in the eyes of Western propagators of high culture, guaranteed its seriousness. Above all, it abolished divisions between creators and performers, writers and actors. Because it was essentially oral, popular theater had no place for definitive texts. Topics and plots were developed and given repeated performance but always in such a way that improvisation and constant adaptation and responsiveness to changed settings, social circumstances, and political exigencies remained central. Nor was the separation of other media such as music and dance from theatrical performance ever accepted. Where it seemed to obtain to a

36. To my knowledge the only text of a theater piece in "popular" Swahili was published by Van Spaandonck (1959). It was performed in 1958 in Kolwezi. The piece was not transcribed from a recording but written down by the author, Christophe Makongo. Linguistically, it differs significantly from texts recorded with the Mufwankolo group. It is much closer to the kind of pidgin varieties that were used in communication with expatriates in exaggerating phonological and morpho-syntactic traits of what the editor calls the "Potopot [i.e., mixed-up] Kingwana of Katanga." This may reflect how the author perceived Van Spaandonck's linguistic competences, or the editing by the latter, or both.

certain degree, this was due to technical necessity, for instance, when in the sixties and seventies radio and television broadcasts became the most important outlets. Up to this day, groups such as Mufwankolo's are able to use all available resources whenever the occasion allows this. Almost all the principal actors are also accomplished musicians and dancers.

True, similar conceptions of a "total theater" or, in Wagner's term, of a *Gesamtkunstwerk,* characterized Western theater in its beginnings and have been revived since the nineteenth century. This is why expatriate promoters of *spectacles populaires* in the fifties were so impressed by what they found in Africa. But the upheavals of independence were not the only reason why their attempts to channel these activities into an international, fashionable scene eventually failed. Popular theater in Shaba resists transformation into a commodity that can be marketed elsewhere; it refuses to be rendered harmless by folklorization. With all its improvised comedy and slapstick it continues to address matters that matter in ways that have a chance of carrying messages under the most severe forms of cultural and political repression. Because it rises from the masses, talks their language, and expresses their feelings, popular theater is much more serious than imported classical drama could ever have been.

Before I conclude this chapter I should like to present in full (translated from French) a most striking document. It is an advertisement by Mufwankolo's sponsor in the early sixties, Bwana Cheko, now one of the members of the troupe.

THEATER
The Group Bwana Cheko
or
The King of Laughter Announces

Whew . . . . . it's enough . . . . now we need . . . . .
THEATER . . . . .
He who says Theater thinks of Peace
Nothing is more cheerful than the Theater
Nothing is more beautiful than Peace
Rich and Poor, Young and Old want to live in Peace
In the Theater all peaceful people find wholesome distraction
Quiet!! . . . . Even for politicians there is a measure of appeasement
Attention:
Time passed in the "THEATER" is not time lost, as is often believed
Time passed in the "THEATER" will do you a lot of good and thus spare
    you other useless expenses
THEATER forgotten and the ARTS neglected . . . . . Why is this??

Yes . . . . . I see . . . . LACK OF SUPPORT . . . . . But how to remedy that
situation

STOP . . . . . Here is a remedy . . . . . .

**THE THEATER-GROUP "BWANA CHEKO" or "THE KING OF
LAUGHTER"** brings you a very precious message . . .

- a message that does not touch politics
- a message that interests above all the masses
- a message that will help our Congolese artists

**THE THEATER-GROUP "BWANA CHEKO" or "THE KING OF
LAUGHTER"** is going to present in the very near future, for the first
time after independence, at the theater of the *Cinquantenaire* of the
Town of Elisabethville lively variety shows which will make you
CRAZY WITH LAUGHTER!

Come and pass your time with "BWANA CHEKO" OR "THE KING OF
LAUGHTER" The date will be announced later.

M'BUYU-DARBO Emile
President-Founder of the group "BWANA CHEKO"
Elisabethville, June 8, 1963[37]

In this theatrical presentation of theater (printed, incidentally, in the
kind of notation D. Tedlock has recently proposed as a means for
making oral text come alive!) we have a manifesto reflecting the spirit of
emerging African theater in Katanga/Shaba: It appeals to the impecun-
ious masses; it makes a political statement by pleading for peace and
disclaiming political intentions (and, characteristically, throws a barb at
politicians); it stresses the seriousness of comic entertainment and expresses consciousness of an artistic vocation. We will reencounter all
these themes in the chapters that follow.

This very condensed overview leaves, I am sure, many questions
unanswered.[38] Some of them will be addressed when the occasion

37. This advertisement appeared in the short-lived (1963–64) Katangese journal
Notre Afrique-Afrika Yetu, Friday, June 14, 1963, p. 7.

38. Among them the question how the history and present development of
popular theater in Shaba fit into the wider picture of theater in Africa. As much as it
was possible and necessary I have consulted some of the growing literature on the
subject: *Actes du Colloque sur le théâtre nègro-Africain* 1971, Banham and Wake 1976,
Coplan 1986, Cornevin 1970, East 1970, Epskamp 1987, Etherton 1982, Fiebach 1986
(perhaps the best documented and argued survey to date), Graham-White 1975,
Harrison 1974, Hourantier 1984, Kennedy 1977, Nidzgorski 1980, Okpaku 1970, Oyin
Ogunba and Irele 1978, Schipper-de Leeuw 1977, Traore 1972, Vaz 1978, Warren 1975,
to name but some of the more comprehensive studies that also contain further
bibliographic references. But I must repeat that I do not think of this study as an
ethnography of theater; hence I feel neither inclined nor obliged to situate my account
in an existing field of knowledge. Specialists of African theater may find the approach I
chose interesting because it does not follow the main road.

arises. But now, I hope, the excitement I felt can be appreciated when, in the summer of 1986, I got a chance to work with Mufwankolo and his group on an ethnographic experiment, which, although not planned as such, turned out to be one, and a very fruitful one at that.

4

The Experiment

The Setting: Glimpses of Power and Play

The colonial planners of Elisabethville created a city which was an icon of power (see map 2). At first they must have envisaged a perfect square. Concessions were made to physical contours on its western side where the valley of the Lubumbashi River cuts into the plateau, and to economics and communications on the eastern side where the railroad, running diagonally from north to south, cuts off the eastern corner. The circular Place Royale, in the dead center of the original ideal quadrangle, marked the seat of power.[1] Here the Avenues Tabora and Lomami crossed, and from here the Avenue Royale, a diagonal "flaw" in the otherwise perfectly rectangular grid of streets led to the commercial center, the post office and the railway station. Around the Place Royale were grouped the first (provincial) governor's residence (later moved to the western periphery), the district commissioners' offices (now city hall), and the Palais de Justice. The commercial center asserted its symbolic importance by intruding on the southeastern corner. The northwestern corner was reserved for the Cercle Albert-Elisabeth, a seat of power which is of special interest to us because it will be a principal site of the story to be told here. This is how a historian of Elisabethville describes its foundation:

1. At least, of the usual institutions endowed with power, such as the court, provincial government, and so forth. But, to be accurate, in Katanga ultimate power rested with an organization called Comité Spécial du Katanga (CSK)—a mixed private and public institution, which, among other things, held title to the land and mining rights. Their imposing headquarters were off center, to the northwest of Place Royale. Maybe the reasons for that were accidental; still, its physical location in the city reflected the *modus operandi* of the CSK—off center, as an agency that liked to work behind the scenes. For a richly illustrated colonial history of Elisabethville, see *Elisabethville 1911–1961* (1961).

[In 1911] foreigners controlled the city's industry, commerce, and even the treatment of its African workers. Belgians felt themselves to be a minority in their own colony, so they banded together to form a club expressly designed to protect Belgian interests. . . . This institution was particularly well adapted to the leaders of Elisabethville's Belgian community, ambitious men who had gone to the colony to make their fortune and who were unable, in the primitive conditions, to show the world how far they had progressed on the social ladder. Almost immediately the Cercle Albert became a semiofficial body for protecting Belgian interests.

[It] . . . became the focal point of social life in the European community—for those fortunate government officials and mining engineers permitted to join. Although primarily a men's club where tired members met for a gin and tonic at the end of a hard day's work, the Cercle Albert also sponsored formal dinner parties where the few wives who had accompanied their husbands to the copperbelt held court and could forget, if only for a few hours, their primitive housing and cultural isolation. (Fetter 1976: 42f., 31).

Seventy-five years later, in 1986, the club had changed its name—it was now called Makutano (Encounter)—but the ghosts of the powermongers of yore, had they returned to their somewhat dilapidated former haunts, would have experienced a certain *déjà vu*. At dusk, men of the new bourgeoisie, not the really rich, nor the really powerful (because Zaire will not tolerate concentrations of real power outside the capital), meet at the bar. They are engineers and management personnel of the mining and other large companies, government bureaucrats, an occasional officer of the army, university professors: the sons and grandsons of the Africans who had swept the clubrooms and groomed the grounds in colonial times. As did their European predecessors, they use their club for an occasional social event, a private reception to celebrate whatever the bourgeoisie celebrates, a *diner dansant* for club members, their ladies, and guests.

Such a dinner took place on June 28, on the Saturday preceding Independence Day. I was the guest of two members; one was a colleague from the university, the other was Kachelewa, manager of a company that manufactures cardboard products and president of the Troupe Théâtrale Mufwankolo. A guitar band warmed up with some European popular tunes before it switched to Zairean music. In a room adjacent to the banquet hall a copious buffet of African delicacies was laid out. There was a delay, because in the dining room someone had set up the television for one of the most important matches of the Soccer World Cup being played in Mexico. Eventually the sound was turned off, and the company was seated. The president of the club called for order.

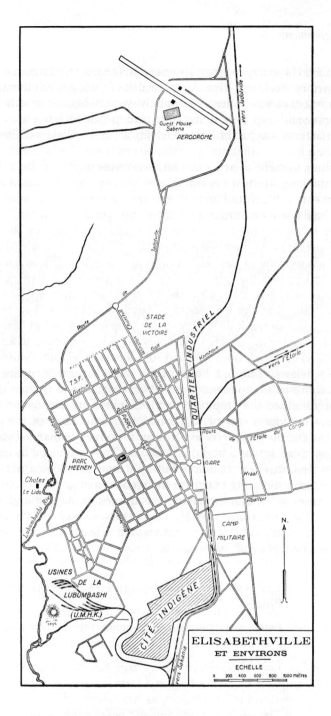

Map 2. Elisabethville/Lubumbashi, an icon of colonial power. (From *Guide du Vogageur au Congo Belge et au Ruanda Urundi*. Brussels: Office du Tourisme, 1951.)

Introductions and speeches were made. References to the occasion were perfunctory; decidedly, this was a social event, not a revolutionary rally. The thirtieth of June, once a day of boisterous political celebration, even of occasional riots and some army and police violence that caused expatriates to stay at home locked up in their villas, had become a holiday.

When the official part was over, everyone lined up at the buffet and some dancing was just beginning after the meal when it all came to an abrupt end. A blackout had left Lubumbashi in the dark.

I had not given much thought to the *genius loci* when, ten days earlier, I dropped in at the bar of Makutano, knowing that the Troupe Mufwankolo had scheduled a rehearsal for 5 P.M. The Cercle Makutano lets them use one of the club's rooms as a sort of public service. I was early and passed the time chatting with a personnel manager of the railroads, who had been an assistant in the anthropology department when I taught at the University of Lubumbashi more than ten years earlier (come to think of it, almost every time I stopped at Makutano I met a fellow anthropologist). Members of the troupe began to arrive and assembled in a backroom reserved for rehearsals. Finally, Mufwankolo and Kachelewa appeared. Some of the actors were still missing, so we had a drink and exchanged news. It was a year since we had last met. The occasion seemed propitious and I submitted my friends to what had by now become a sort of test. I told them the story of the chicken gizzards. Did they know the expression "le pouvoir se mange entier" and did they think it was a traditional saying? They answered as expected: Yes, indeed, this was tradition, but right now they could not recall a proverb corresponding exactly to the French saying. I then reported on the occasion on which the saying was quoted to me first and added a few hunches regarding possible application to uses of power in the current sociopolitical situation. But we had to leave it at that because it was time to begin with the meeting.

The Work: A Chronological Account of the Rehearsal Process

From bar-talk to topic: First group meetings, discussions in committee

Tuesday, June 17. Contrary to my expectations, the event that was now to take place turned out to be a formal meeting. It was declared open by Kachelewa in his capacity as "president." He had noted down an agenda and began by introducing and welcoming me in the name of the troupe. Then, to my great surprise, he announced that the principal point for today's discussion was to be "Le pouvoir se mange entier."

Response was immediate and enthusiastic. Even though I finally took some notes, I can only give the barest outlines of the collective search for the meaning of this saying that followed.

Exegesis begins with proposals for a translation of the French formula into Swahili. A satisfactory equivalent is not found at once. Kachelewa suggests that the saying is appropriate to situations where power is in transition. Members of the group agree and several point out that this is the sort of thing one pronounces at the installation of a new chief, hence the term *kudia/kulya* (to eat [power]). It is a situation of crisis and trial: Before the new candidate became chief, *balimuteswa*, they made him suffer. Then, *yee anabateswa*, he makes them suffer. *Mateso ni fini, anakulya usultani lote*, when the suffering is over he eats the chieftaincy whole. From then on, *yote inamuangaria*, everything becomes his concern, he can exclude nothing from his attention and responsibility.[2]

Kachelewa continues to lead the discussion and tells the anecdote of the chicken gizzards. In his version it is not the post powerful person present, but the invited guest who is offered the choice piece. At first this seems to distract from the power theme but then he adds another touch by going back to the preparation of the chicken: How do you cook it? Whole. (So the symbolism of wholeness extends beyond consumption.) But before serving it, the chicken is cut into pieces. Do you also cut up the gizzards? Unanimous response: Never. In fact, it is pointed out, if the chief does not see the gizzards he refuses to eat from the chicken. By now it is confirmed, if confirmation is needed, that the gizzard is a choice piece because it symbolizes wholeness. Which need not prevent it from being a delicacy.

There has now been some time to search memory and one of the actors comes up with a version of the saying in Tshiluba (where "power" is rendered as *ukalenge*, corresponding to *bulopwe* in Kiluba). This causes a discussion on how best to translate the French term *pouvoir*, a difficult matter, as everyone agrees. One actor suggests that it could be rendered as *uwezo* ("strength, might, power, capacity, authority, ability, faculty," according to the Standard Dictionary).[3] But, it is agreed, *uwezo* is

---

2. In quoting these and other expressions in Shaba Swahili my purpose is above all to add precision to my account and to point out semantic subtleties that would not be conveyed by paraphrases alone. Swahili specialists may require additional information regarding the peculiarities of this variety of Swahili. I will provide these whenever it serves the task at hand; for the rest I must refer to other sources, most of which are listed and utilized in Fabian 1986.

3. Here and in the following this refers to the Oxford *Standard Swahili Dictionary* (1939). I also often consulted the Swahili-French Dictionary by Lenselaer (1983), which is based on the Standard Dictionary but is updated and contains many items of Swahili as spoken in Zaire.

something shared by all who are here. *Busultani,* chieftaincy, is power above shared power. Another person comes up with *utukufu* ("exalted state or station, majesty, glory, aggrandizement"). This is rejected on the grounds that it only applies to God.[4] Things get even more complicated when yet another actor remembers that *uwezo* can also be a translation for *responsabilité,* indicating an interesting semantic shift which goes back to the use in French of *responsable* for the head of a company, whereby the element of power is foregrounded against the denotation of "responsibility."

Next, Kachelewa puts up for discussion my hypothesis that the saying may also apply to the ways in which Zairean businessmen behave (earlier, at the bar, I had remarked on their inclination to operate alone rather than in associations). Again, he distracts from the theme of wholeness when he moralizes on the issue of exclusiveness. He cites as a counterexample the case of someone whose car has broken down. Is he going to deal with this all by himself, or will he not rather seek help from others? When this is taken up in general discussion one participant puts us back on the track by insisting that a chief never appeals to others, nor does he speak about his problems to others. Indeed, says Kachelewa, but when he becomes weak he is no longer *muzima* ("healthy," in current language, but literally "whole"), he loses his chieftaincy. It is not as simple as that, someone objects, there are situations where the chief first shows weakness, then takes things into his hands. This evokes the transition theme: Power is never a static attribute, it is something constantly to be acquired because it is always in danger of being lost.

Then another aspect of *busultani* is brought up: *sultani hana na rafiki, hana na nduku,* the chief has no friend, no relative. Kachelewa feels that this is getting us off on a tangent and tries to get us back to power in the business world. Someone says: *kwa kupata makuta anapashwa kuwa mauvais,* to make money (a businessman) must be evil. Another actor rubs this in by reminding Kachelewa of his position as a company manager. At work he would not treat his fellow actors as friends but like any other employee (at least two members of the troupe work in Kachelewa's company).

Kachelewa tries to move the discussion away from this potentially embarrassing turn and reminds the group that they are here to discuss a possible theme for a play to celebrate June 30, the anniversary of Zairean independence. The line he proposes to follow is that power must be

4. In fact, the term is not used in Shaba except in the register of religious/ liturgical speech, with a typical occasional spill-over into official political language such as in *chama chetu chitukufu,* our exalted party (the Mouvement Populaire de la Révolution, MPR).

concentrated, not *dispersé*, if it is to be effective. This is met with general agreement and more examples from tradition are cited. One actor, a Luba Hemba, who has some experience with the matter, being himself a dignitary, returns to the installation of a chief. An important point is that upon accession to power the future chief is "told everything" by the elders of the court. His actions—judging cases, meting out punishment—will have to be based on information that is "whole." Then, in contradiction to earlier pronouncements, he muses about the fact that a chief's relations to his subjects are never from individual to individual, they are always mediated by *kizazi*, the kinship group. The chief's power, therefore, accounts for the fact that *kukata bidomo ilianza ku bankambo*, corruption began with the ancestors (meaning: it is not only characteristic of modern times).

For Kachelewa, this is going too much into detail and he tries to end the discussion, asking everybody to keep thinking about June 30, a day on which power is celebrated. This is ignored by the group who go on to give examples, trying to bring further precision to the issue by distinguishing between major and minor chiefs. Kachelewa then uses his privilege as president and declares discussion on this point closed for the day. Another agenda point is taken up, a play to commemorate the seventy-fifth anniversary of the Catholic mission in Lubumbashi. The archdiocese commanded a performance for the day of the anniversary (August 12); others may follow. The project means hope for paying audiences and some modest remuneration and this is greeted with approval. The subject causes less enthusiasm. Mufwankolo suggests that the piece should cover the history of Christianity in Shaba "from Monseigneur de Hemptinne" (remembered by most Africans as an authoritarian racist). Then he hesitates a moment, searching for a point of arrival; someone calls out "to Pius Kasongo" (Abbé Kasongo is a dissident charismatic priest who lives in open conflict with the archbishop). The group approves with laughter—not because the suggestion is thought to be joke; on the contrary, it is perceived as being serious and to the point. There is now an atmosphere of conflict and contestation in the meeting. Kachelewa, joined by Mufwankolo, who until then had remained largely silent, has difficulties controlling the group. With an admonition that the actors are here to make positive contributions, not to indulge in criticism, he officially closes the meeting. However, some of the players are unwilling to break the momentum. They begin to distribute the parts of the pioneer missionaries and current holders of office. The suggestions and remarks that come from all corners are quick and witty. The actors may have reservations about a command performance glorifying the colonial past but the topic fires their imagination.

Thursday, June 19. I get to Cercle Makutano around 5 P.M. Only a few members of the group are there. Kachelewa has to see after one of his trucks, which broke down, and is not expected at all. Chairs have been brought out to the terrace at the main entrance to the club and we pass the time with some small talk, with questions about my work, anecdotes, and stories. When the group is more or less complete we go to the backroom and the meeting is presided by the "secretary" of the troupe, Bwana Cheko. He had missed the Tuesday meeting and the others first inform him of the chosen theme and the occasion when "le pouvoir se mange entier" was first quoted to me. Without hesitation he takes up the theme and explains once more the significance of the gizzards. First of all, the innards are an animal's vital parts. A chicken served without them cannot be considered complete. Second, elementary politeness demands that a guest be offered the whole chicken. It is up to him to share the meal with his hosts. But even if he chooses to do so he is not expected to share that which symbolizes the wholeness of the chicken.

Kalwasha (I begin to retain the names at least of the principal actors) thinks that all this takes on significance when placed into a concrete context, such as the family *(jamaa)*. A family, he argues, is strictly hierarchical: *baba ni sultani*, the father is the chief; *mama ni sawa prémier ministre*, the mother is like the prime minister; *watoto sawa ministres*, the children are like the ministers. This is how it ought to be in the family (specifying the meaning of *jamaa* so as to exclude uncles and nephews—the extended family or kinship group). Coming up with yet another synonym for power, he insists that there must be *autorité* in the family. Bwana Cheko now applies this to *l'état* (the state) and to *l'entreprise* (a company). The state exists because there are *lois*, laws, the company follows the *code de travail*, labor regulations. As the French terms pile up he actually switches codes: "famille bila règlement intérieur c'est une famille morte," a family without bylaws is a dead family. Then, as an afterthought and apparently without much connection to the foregoing, he adds: A chief, like a pregnant woman, is *kivuko*, literally "a place where one crosses a river," a ford, but also the means for crossing, a ferry. Whatever else is intended by this image, it does evoke the theme of transition that seems to come up whenever power is discussed.

The group then considers the possibility that "le pouvoir se mange entier" may apply to the behavior of businessmen. Why are they so reluctant to form associations and to share risks and profits? Bwana Cheko interprets this morally (and perhaps politically): Zaireans are still on a low level of development, there is no spirit of cooperation, jealousy and pride determine conduct. Even if competent people get together they soon begin to steal and embezzle, to give in to demands from their relatives. He recalls the disastrous Zaireanization in the early seventies.[5] No one cares to contest his views.

At this point, I get uneasy. Perhaps Bwana Cheko, whom I had never met before and who does not know me, is putting on a performance for my benefit. I abandon the role of the passive observer and listener and intervene in the discussion: What you have told us sounds like an outsider's opinion. This is how Europeans talk about Zaireans. The fact is that there are lazy, dishonest, and incompetent people everywhere. Still, in Europe business associations, one form of sharing power, function; they don't seem to do so in Zaire. Must we not look elsewhere for an explanation, perhaps in the *kanuni ya tabia*, the rules of custom? Not a very helpful choice of words, as it turns out in the exchange on the meaning of *tabia* that followed. Several insist, correctly, that it means "nature," or "character." On the contrary, speaking from anthropological conviction, I tell them, it is not nature but custom, the teaching of the ancestors.[6] All right, Bwana Cheko replies, but *inafaa kubadilisha*, (customs) must be changed. Even in the old times custom was not absolute but continually changed and "improved."

Now a kind of subplot causes the debate to take a different direction. Tala Ngai, one of the younger, educated actors, takes this to be a statement on the *évolution* of custom. To give weight to the disquisition he is about to make he switches to French. This meets with loud protest, for some reason especially from two or three young women (who are bilingual; for them French as such would not have been a problem). Tala Ngai plays offended (rather well, he is an actor) before he lets himself be persuaded to continue in Swahili.

So we have another problem: How do we translate evolution? We suggest *maendeleo*. This, quite appropriately in retrospect, makes other members take up once more the question whether or not *tabia* should be translated as "nature." The discussion gets more and more heated until Mufwankolo intervenes, reminding the group of the task at hand, which is to arrive, by an exchange of thoughts and examples, at a play that can

5. Late in 1973 measures were announced and implemented to varying degrees to bring sectors of the economy that were foreign-owned and -run under Zairean control. See Young and Turner 1985: chap. 11; see also Callaghy 1984 and Nzongola-Ntalaja 1986: index under "Zaireanization."

6. I had heard the word *tabia* in expressions such as *tabia ya bankambo*, which in my mind I had always translated as "the customs of the ancestors." As this exchange shows (and it may be exemplary in this respect), my translation had really been a matching of topoi: *tabia* = "customary law." My attempt to project an anthropological concern such as the nature-culture distinction on my interlocutors was simply besides the point. That we could go on talking may be explained by the assumption that in Shaba Swahili *tabia* denotes above all "habit(s)," a concept capable of bridging "nature" and "culture."

be performed. We cannot go on arguing endlessly. But the others are not willing to drop the subject. Then Mufwankolo and Bwana Cheko propose a complicated compromise: *Tabia* does not exist in the (abstract) singular; if everyone here insisted on contributing examples from the *tabia* of his home country there would only be confusion. So, if we use illustrations we must take the risk and choose *one* such *tabia*. The public can then recognize similarities and differences and draw their own conclusions. But this does not settle the matter and the debate about *tabia* continues. Mufwankolo puts an end to it by announcing the following steps and another point on the agenda. A plot needs to be outlined for *Le pouvoir se mange entier* and the parts distributed.

Then there is the matter of the play for August 12. Mufwankolo was late for today's session because he had been in another meeting at the archbishop's residence, where clergy and church leaders discussed projects for the anniversary celebrations. He was also given "texts" on the history of the missions in Shaba to be followed in constructing the play. Immediately, this causes a new discussion. Fear is expressed that the troupe will be used for propaganda glorifying mission history. One would like to know whether the play can also show the dark sides of that history, for instance, the pressure put on people to convert to Christianity if they wanted to find schooling for their children. And what about the many denominations and churches competing with Catholicism, indeed, what about traditional religion? After all, God was revered by the ancestors before the whites came. The leaders of the troupe and some older members reject the idea of taking up such controversial issues. The play should stick to the history "from De Hemptinne to Kabanga" (the current archbishop). The purpose of such a play is to be *éducatif*. Kalwasha, who emerges more and more as the spokesman for the dissenters, asks in his dry, abrupt manner: "Educate whom? The clergy?"

In the end, Mufwankolo resumes control, not with arguments but with one of his brilliant performances. He acts out a synopsis of the play as he sees it. It will be a sequence of *tableaux* (each scene should be introduced by a poster showing a date and marking a period, a method, he reminds them, they used with success for a similar historical play commanded by the mining company). His account includes most of the "negative" elements and controversial issues, but obliquely, evoked through events and scenes, not argued as political rhetoric. We all are impressed by this demonstration of the difference between art and propaganda. A measure of harmony is reestablished and the meeting ends with arrangements for further work. During the weekend, the *comité artistique* will meet to determine the plot and the distribution of parts for *Le pouvoir se mange entier*. The first rehearsal will be on the following Wednesday.

Friday, June 20. I arrive at Cercle Makutano at the usual time. Inside, a reception is going on. The people are dressed formally; a prelate in a white cassock and red cincture seems to be the center of attention. I don't feel like walking through the reception crowd alone (I begin to recognize several acquaintances) and decide to wait on the steps of the front entrance until members of the artistic committee show up. A well-dressed gentleman, who looks to me like someone who strayed from the party, approaches. He greets me like an old acquaintance: "Aren't you the friend of Monsieur X [giving a friend's name]. I work with him, my name is Ingenieur Kalenda, of the planning department at Gécamines. Trouble is, my car broke down, just around the corner. I wonder if I could borrow 400 Zaire until tomorrow. I see your friend everyday." By now our little exchange is being watched by several spectators. Also by now, I am almost, but not quite, certain that Ingenieur Kalenda is a con man; there are some odd linguistic clues, something in the information he imparts, and above all the genre of the event, which make me suspicious. Because there is still the slightest chance that I might offend either him (if he is genuine) or the onlookers (who could take my refusal to help for some kind of racism), he has me at a disadvantage and I don't dare to call his bluff. So we settle for 200 Zaire, a high, but adequate price, given the extraordinary quality of his performance; and a contribution to the local economy. Incidentally, there was no Ingenieur Kalenda at my friend's service.

Meanwhile the committee, consisting of Kachelewa, Mufwankolo, Bwana Cheko, and Tala Ngai, is complete and we go to a backroom to begin the deliberation. There we are joined by a linguist and literary scholar from the University of Lubumbashi (as I learned later, because we were not introduced to each other).

So there are now two academic observers, a situation that must cause my colleague some uneasiness; throughout the evening, he refuses to acknowledge my presence. I never saw him again after that evening. Later I am told that he had taken an interest in the group's work and had been acting as critic/advisor for some time. Perhaps he saw in me an outside intruder or competitor. At any rate, he takes direction of the discussion that follows.

First, the professor is informed of the theme chosen for the June 30 play. He is also told the story of the chicken gizzards. We had been using the term current in Shaba Swahili, *kifu*. This, we are told by the expert, is incorrect, because it only designates the innards of cattle. The correct term is *finyango*. Then he explains to us the function of gizzards among birds. They have no teeth and need this organ to grind down their food. The committee is impressed and the professor's authority established (even though the linguistic information he imparts is not quite as correct as it sounds).[7]

Then follows another search for a translation of *pouvoir*. *Uwezo, être capable*, comes up again. Another proposal is *alama ya ukubwa*, literally, the mark of being big, great, important, senior. Neither meets with much enthusiasm. In the course of this conversation, incidentally, the professor has switched to Shaba Swahili (from French and a more literate Swahili variety). He speaks it quite well.

Bwana Cheko submits to the committee what he calls a *conducteur*, an outline of the guiding ideas for *Le pouvoir se mange entier*. This one-page document in French (see Appendix)[8] is typed in a formal manner, with the group's letterhead, dated and signed by Bwana Cheko in his capacity as *secrétaire administratif*. It has two parts. The first one lists three items: (a) characters; (b) decor: a traditional village, a modern town, one poster on which is written: to reign in disorder, one poster with the inscription: peace, justice, work (this is the motto of the Republic of Zaire); (c) dress as usual (every actor and actress are going to do the necessary [to find a costume]). Part two is titled DETAILS and has two entries:

1. - a tamtam, accompanied by a song, announces the beginning of the theater piece;
   - the chief and the queen in official attire;
   - the *notables* and the villagers are assembling in the chief's courtyard;
   - a folkloric dance to the rhythm of the tamtam before the chief;
   - the villagers do something else because there is no organization[9]—there is total disorder in the village and the chief no longer has authority.

7. *Kifu* is a local loan from Luba, see Van Avermaet and Mbuya 1954: 151: "estomac (d'homme ou d'animal), ka-fu: petit estomac; pour estomac d'oiseau on dit: kuzingila." *Finyango*, derived from the verb *kufinyanga*, to knead clay (as potters do), does not occur in the Standard Dictionary (which has *firigisi*); it is listed with the meaning "gizzard" as a form typical of "Kingwana" by Lenselaer 1983: 108, and, as *finyanga*, a ki-Mrima form, by Sacleux 1939: 223. Incidentally, the chicken, being an important food item, became in some Luba cultures a central symbol; see the comprehensive analysis by Kantshama and Luboya 1986 (which, however, does not contain any specific references to the gizzard).

8. In the summary and translation that follow I keep as closely as possible to the original, also regarding the form of presentation.

9. In the text, the term is *encadrement* (literally: framing). In the (party) political jargon of the day it is used for coordinating, or integrating groups and activities. The

2. - a "mixed meeting"[10] of chief and *notables*[11] is called;
   - measures are taken to reestablish order in the village; (counsel and remarks)
   - the chief acts and takes the situation in his hands;
   - order reestablished, respect, justice, protection of goods and persons, work for progress;
   - MORAL: LE POUVOIR SE MANGE ENTIER, i.e., the chief is there for everyone and cannot take sides, he must serve his people as an equal[12] but with authority.

To me, this sounds quite conventional, rather weak stuff for drama. The others seem to have similar feelings. Kachelewa suggests that, as it is, the play lacks a necessary element: change, transition. He points out that every piece of theater needs to move from *début mauvais*, a bad beginning, to *fin corrigée*, to an ending where things are set right—or the other way around. But dramaturgical considerations are not the only thing that preoccupies the committee. One of the discussants, in his usual blunt manner, puts the issue on the table. This is a political *sujet*, and it will be applied to *the* chief. Perhaps the desired element of change and transition could be brought in by taking up matters such as the (frequent) reshuffling at the political top, or the famous Zaireanization and *rétrocession*.[13]

All this gets rather touchy and the members of the *comité artistique* take refuge, as did Mufwankolo on an earlier occasion, in the safe notion that the purpose of these plays is to be "educating" (meaning: not politically instigating). Someone says: "Change? *Tout peut changer dans ce*

---

common people of Zaire, perspicacious as ever, know that, more often than not, *encadrement* is a euphemism for taking control or exercising outright oppression. So the term is used mockingly to refer to all sorts of efforts at organizing considered unwanted and futile.

10. With *réunion mixte*, Bwana Cheko uses another term of political jargon. As in the case of *encadrement* and some of the expressions in the following, it is quite possible that he intends this to be ironical.

11. A decision had to be taken at this point regarding the translation of *notable*, which is used throughout these texts as a French loan (following colonial usage). The term may be a bit awkward but the alternatives, such as counselor, dignitary, elder, sage, person of repute, and so forth, are too vague (although I shall occasionally use some of them as synonyms for *notable*).

12. The French expression here is ambiguous; it could also be translated as "serve all of them equally."

13. The latter term was used to give a legal flavor to what was in fact an admission of political and economic failure of measures to "Zaireanize" small and middle-sized business and agriculture. Whether the policy could have been successful, given the national and international economic constraints and dependencies, is of course another matter.

petit monde, everything can change in this little world."[14] One principle, however, is agreed upon: *pouvoir, unapashwa kuwa na peuple ku muko-ngo*, (if you want to wield) power, you must be backed by the people.

The professor, who has been silent until now, taking notes, redirects the debate to drama theory: *l'échec doit frapper plus que la réussite*, failure should be more impressive than success. Otherwise, *hakuna réflexion*, there is no reflection. The aim is to make people think. This play should not be "like a Hollywood movie with a happy end." In this piece, the chief should be a failure from beginning to end. The others find this convincing. Then they ask me what I think. My response is that I agree; after all it was a failure, my failure to comprehend, which produced in the first place the saying whose meaning we now explore.

In order to achieve the desired effect, one member suggests that the order in Bwana Cheko's outline should simply be reversed: first order, then disorder. The committee is about to adopt this as a basis for further work when Kachelewa takes us back to politics. Is such a construction not going to be interpreted "in a bad way"—as antiregime and politically subversive? One member insists: "The truth is the truth." Again, a safe way out is chosen by deciding that the play will be submitted to the *commissaire sous-régional* (roughly, the mayor of the city) for approval. But there is still one who does not want to give in: *il reste à nous acteurs kudévier*, it is up to us, the actors, to deviate. It turns out that no one feels much for official approval. Then another compromise is put on the table: They will stick to the negative scenario but possible "negative" interpretations will be "annulled" by Mufwankolo's customary moral at the end of the play. There is resignation in this way out, but it is also more than hinted at that it will work because of the integrity of artistic perfor-mance. As the professor tells them repeatedly, beyond all politics and moralizing, what really counts is *les paroles et les gestes*, the words and gestures. Here the meeting ends officially. Over a bottle of beer we continue to chat and I tell them of my work on another project.

Monday, June 23. At Cercle Makutano, the last session of the com-mittee before the rehearsals. At first, only Kachelewa, Mufwankolo, and Tala Ngai are present. Bwana Cheko and Malisawa join us later. Today's first task is to settle on a scenario. Kachelewa asks for suggestions for a *prémier tableau*, the first scene. Mufwankolo: There are villagers, they

14. This somewhat enigmatic remark, made in the manner of sententious expressions, "philosophically" asserts the deep pessimism shared by most Zaireans I met about the prospects for "change." By pronouncing it in French in a Swahili conversation the speaker gives to it a function not unlike that of proverbs (see chapter 2); he "quotes" anonymous wisdom and thereby protects himself (in this case politically) against having to take personal responsibility for his lack of confidence in change for the better.

make trouble.[15] They ought to be working as the chief had ordered them to do, but when he sends out his men to see what happens they find the villagers drinking and dancing. He then sends a policeman but he, too, is drawn into the general merriment. Finally, the chief arrives on the scene and is informed by his advisers, especially one woman, that the villagers disobey his orders. Unless I failed to catch it, at this point, the woman is not yet identified as the chief's wife.

That, as it turns out, was more or less the plot of a play they did for television some years ago. Kachelewa thinks that this is not sufficient for the current project. In this manner the play would end before anything much happens. Also we must not lead up to an end that only demonstrates the chief's failure without first having shown his power.

Mufwankolo starts again. He now sets the scene in the chief's court, including his wife and his dignitaries. A culprit is brought to him. He is accused of having stolen bananas from the chief's plantation. The chief pronounces *kanuni ya mugini*, the law of the village: The thief should be executed. But then he does not see to it that the sentence is carried out; the culprit is freed and leaves.

Kachelewa objects. This is no good as a beginning. The crime is "too banal." Instead, he proposes to locate the prime source of conflict among the chief's councilors. The culprit must have done something serious and the chief is about to punish him, but then the *notables* each drag the case into a different direction. Their principal fault is that they do not properly inform the chief. Each of them uses the affair for his own advantages. Thus *kishilani inatoka kwa notables*, mutual hate, contempt, arises among the *notables*.[16]

Bwana Cheko now takes over and develops Mufwankolo's ideas in more detail. He paints the scenes of drinking, drumming, and dancing. The *notables*, instead of enforcing the chief's orders, criticize him. The chief begins to react, but the councilors neutralize his actions by splitting into groups.

We sense that the discussion of the plot has now taken off and Kachelewa asks me to record it from now on. The result is much too complex even to attempt a summary. As a general impression I note that the construction of the scenario follows more or less the lines agreed on in the previous meeting. At the beginning are the chief's orders to the

---

15. The term he uses is *banasimanga* (literally: they rejoice in someone else's weakness). In Shaba Swahili, *kusimanga* also means to criticize or contradict (synonym: *kuteta*).

16. *Kishilani* is current in Shaba Swahili, heard only as a noun, possibly derived from the Shaba Swahili *kuzia, kuzira*. In Shaba the verb corresponding to *kishilani* is *kusirika*. *Kuzira* (or *kuzila*) seems to be used only for "to swear off" (drinking, for example). *Kizila* signifies "prohibition, taboo."

villagers; the *notables* mobilize the people, but then they quarrel among each other and give bad information to the chief, the end is *potopot*, chaos.

Then I ask what happened to the saying "le pouvoir se mange entier"? It has not played much of a role in our discussion of the plot. No one sees this as a problem, except Malisawa who wants to know: What *is* the message? Does the saying support the chief or does it contest his power? The others think that this must remain open. Right now it is important to have the *charpente*, scaffold or framework, then the saying/proverb can "infiltrate" (their expression) the piece through *masemo*, sayings, the things that are said. Incidentally, Kachelewa translates the saying, for the first time, as far as I can tell from my notes, as *busultani banakulyaka bote buzima*, they eat [one eats] the chieftaincy entirely whole.

The ending of the play, it is agreed, will be open and the public must be moved to react by telling themselves: but this or that should have been done. Matters are not left at that, however, and various aspects especially of the conflict among the *notables* are rehearsed again and again. Suggestions for improvement are adopted, others are rejected, some on purely technical grounds (such as questions of setting and decor), others for dramatic reasons. Kachelewa takes the recording home and will write a more extensive *conducteur* between now and Wednesday.

Rehearsals

Wednesday, June 25. The first rehearsal for *Le pouvoir se mange entier* is scheduled for 5:30 P.M. at the Cercle Makutano. As usual, the actors take time to arrive. Most come from their work or their homes in the townships. Public transportation, as much as it exists, is erratic; by walking an hour or two one can save the fare. Kachelewa has brought along his cassette player and while we wait for the group to be complete we listen to the recording of discussions in the committee. Citoyen Shango, program director at the Lubumbashi station of TéléZaire, joins the meeting. Kachelewa was not able to write a *conducteur*; instead this is now done on the spot by Bwana Cheko while he listens to the tape. Kachelewa then gives a summary of the scenario. For the benefit of the program director he tries to justify at length the planned open ending: This play should not finish with a prefabricated solution. As after a football match, when the supporters of the losing club go on for days discussing what should have been done to avoid defeat, their audience should go home and think about alternatives.

Then follows a first exchange on the technicalities of filming the piece. The program director is very firm about a time limit. He cannot give them more than one hour of air time. This causes concern, because it seems impossible to fit the current scenario into one hour, especially given the recording technique they are used to. Plays are filmed without multiple takes, changes of scene and decor are made on the fly, very much like in a live broadcast. The program director is adamant but generously offers the station's mobile unit and crew so that the play can be shot in a "pittoresque" village near Lubumbashi.

The next step is to assign the parts. This goes surprisingly fast, without much discussion. Only minor adjustments are made here and there, mostly in view of matching the importance of roles with the players' rank in the group. Costumes are planned in general, but details are left to every actor and actress who must somehow find the necessary material. A small make-up kit I brought along from the Netherlands will do the rest. Then, a magnificent performance in itself, Bwana Cheko assembles a definitive *conducteur* in Swahili from the notes he took earlier. This part is recorded.

Kachelewa is about to close the meeting with a perfunctory request for further suggestions when drama happens within the drama. First Shebele proposes some minor additions, which are approved. Then the program director says that he has a small point to make. He sees a problem with the saying as the title for the play. Also, we are in Zaire and play for black people, and they always cling to the ending. A play in which things end badly is no good. The sequence in the scenario should be reversed: disorder first, then order reestablished. His remark appears off-hand but is in fact a frontal attack on the artistic integrity of the play. Kachelewa tries to save the scenario with a device discussed earlier: The play will be followed by a moral in which things will be set right. But the program director is not convinced and the real issue is brought out into the open: This is a political play to be broadcast on a highly political occasion. Only yesterday, the president announced in a speech that he has had enough patience with his critics.[17] "J'en ai marre," he said (in a discourse otherwise given in Lingala). With an open ending in disorder the play cannot but be taken as a negative statement.

One actor still resists: In that case *tunafausser sujet yetu*, we falsify our topic. It would be better to do a play glorifying the achievements of the regime (implying: and who wants to do that?). But Kachelewa gives in to the director's demands. Bwana Cheko then pulls out his first typed

17. The occasion was the *fête du poisson*, literally the "feast of fish." This is an annual occasion celebrated at the fishing village of Konkole near Kinshasa to celebrate the economic efforts and success of the country (on June 24). The speech was broadcast nationally on radio and television.

conducteur, the conservative version, and hands it to the program director. He reads it, approves, and the matter is settled. Arrangements are
made for further rehearsals and the meeting ends. Throughout I was
tempted to intervene but decided against it. Obviously we had left the
space of free exchange.

Thursday, June 26. At 5:30 P.M. we are back at the Cercle Makutano.
This time the group assembles on an open terrace in the back of the club.
Mufwankolo once more assigns the parts as the actors arrive. At 6.00 P.M.
the group is complete, I get my cassette recorder ready. It is getting dark
by now and later the only light will come from the door and some
windows looking out on the terrace. Bwana Cheko, assisted by others
who improvise drumming on the seats of some chairs, intones what will
become the introductory song. Everyone joins in the refrain, some try a
few dance steps. After that the actors talk among themselves until Tala
Ngai, now taking on the role of the coach, intervenes: "Let's go." I
witness a terrific moment. With nothing to go on but imagination and
the memory of previous discussions the group bursts into action.
Moving along with the microphone and staying as close as possible to
the speakers, I try to catch the emergence of the play. While I take in
what is happening around me, my anthropologist's mind is ahead of me.
How will I get my TEXT? Will it be possible to transcribe the recording?
The actors speak fast, often several at the same time, there is much
switching to Luba, required by topic or parts. Many brief debates
momentarily interrupt the performance and it becomes increasingly
difficult to distinguish between the play and talk about the play. There is
now total attention to performance, no more meta-discussion of politics
and morals. Part of the group constantly acts as a critical public; they call
for improvements and refinements and applaud virtuoso performances
by Mufwankolo and Bwana Cheko. Tala Ngai keeps things together;
Kachelewa does not show up until just before the end.

I cannot really describe just *how* the whole thing happens except to
say that it is pure improvisation—preceded and accompanied by a lot of
hard work. What I witness seems so anarchical that I don't see how they
will get their act together for Sunday's shooting. We did not get much
beyond the first scene by the time the rehearsal ends at about 19:45 P.M.

Friday, June 27. Rehearsal at the usual time and place. As we wait
near the front entrance for everyone to arrive, one of the actors tells of
the dreams he has had recently. They were all about snakes he had to
fight. To those who listen it is obvious that this has something to do with
fertility (no one hints at sex). When he tells of one dream in which a
snake falls to the ground, bursts open, and spills small children, they
want to know whether his wife is pregnant. It turns out that one of his
women is. Kato is certain that the dream signifies he will have twins. The

rehearsal again takes place outside, on the terrace behind the club. Tonight it lacks the excitement of the first tryout. More and more it becomes, as the French term for rehearsal suggests, *répétition*. I have the impression that it will be possible after all to extract some text from the recording. Not that there is any rote; every scene is fresh and hard work on details continues. The television program director briefly visits. This is enough to slow down the action. Drumming and singing, which are part of several scenes, help to regain momentum. For one final time the political implications are briefly touched upon when Mufwankolo rehearses his moral. Everyone appears relieved that the play will not be interpreted "badly." The meeting ends quietly; how matters will go on from here is left open. So much needs to be done before the filming but this does not seem to cause concern.

Saturday, June 28. In the afternoon we should have gone to select a village nearby for the shooting of *Le pouvoir se mange entier*. But the program director excuses himself. He and his crew are busy filming the festivities commemorating the seventy-fifth anniversary of Lubumbashi. Our exploratory trip will be for tomorrow and the filming will have to wait until Monday, June 30. Which means that the play cannot be broadcast on that day. Is this intentional, another way to defuse its political explosiveness? Then, around 4 P.M., Kachelewa calls; we'll go after all. The first candidate is Kabula Mweshi, a large squatters' settlement in the northern part of town, bordering the chic *quartier du golf*. The place has preserved some village scenery, especially as one leaves the main road. As soon as Kachelewa parks his car and we enter the settlement there is excitement. Mufwankolo was recognized. Within minutes the news spreads through the neighborhood and hordes of children hurry to see the star. Some teenage boys appoint themselves as our guards and feel important. We come to one of the rare houses that has a thatched roof and is built with sun-dried bricks. It has a large front yard and a little garden with a few banana trees in the back that could serve for the scenes playing in the fields. But a power line serving the nearby Lubumbashi smelter and other signs of civilization intrude as we consider possible angles and takes. Although Kachelewa has a preliminary talk with the owners regarding permission to use the place, in the end we decide against Kabula Mweshi. It is too crowded and too urban. To make our outing worthwhile after all, we drop in for a drink at a well-known bar—*Les deux verités*, an intriguing name. The place is crowded and, although this huge settlement has no electricity, Zairean music is played full blast on a battery-fed hifi. Conversation is almost impossible and we leave after a glass or two. On the way out we pay our respects to the owner who is taking the evening air on a chair outside. He is a well-known figure in town, an executive in the mining company. He greets the foreign *professeur* with exquisite politeness and shows interest in our project. He promises to watch the play and we leave. Another expedition is planned for tomorrow but I will not be able to participate because of other obligations.

Later I learn that the actors could not be notified in time of the change of date for the filming. On Sunday, June 29, they all showed up at the Cercle Makutano and waited for hours. Finally they decided to do another rehearsal, of which I have no record.

The Play: Dress Rehearsal and Shooting *Le pouvoir se mange entier*

Monday, June 30, Independence Day. At this time of the dry season the days begin crisp and cold. Not a cloud in the sky. Since 8 A.M. I have been waiting to be picked up; Kachelewa finally arrives at 9:45. As we drive through town I notice a difference from other holidays and Sundays. Usually men and women, young people and children go their separate ways. Today there are families and groups of families on the streets, carrying bags and walking toward the outskirts of town. Kachelewa explains to me that June 30 has become a "normal" holiday. This year, it seems, even the obligatory parade and rally were held on the day before. Now is the time for family visits and a picnic in the green.

A picnic is what Kachelewa calls our expedition. After we had made several unplanned stops (getting the video cassette that was forgotten, dropping off his daughter somewhere in town, picking up some more equipment, filling up with gasoline), we set out from the television station. We don't travel very far. Just around the corner we stop to load a few cases of beer and soft drinks. Finally the convoy leaves town taking the road to Likasi. Kachelewa's car leads, then come the two vehicles of the television unit, the generator truck and the mobile studio. One of Kachelewa's trucks is at the end, carrying actors, props, and supplies. After a short ride of about fifteen kilometers we take a left turn onto a gravel road. It is in good shape and takes our heavy trucks right into Kawama village, chosen yesterday by Kachelewa as the location for filming *Le pouvoir se mange entier*. As we pass the first houses a group of four or five women and a man come toward us. They are dancing, singing, and gesticulating. Their heads are covered with white clay and their faces are painted white. As we get closer they call out to us: *balizala nampundu*, twins are born; this very day, in that hut over there. There is more to a village than a "pittoresque" scenery of wattle-and-daub huts with thatched roofs; the dancers celebrating the arrival of twins

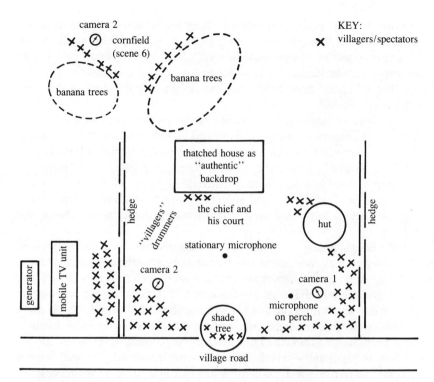

Map 3. The setting in which the play, *Le pouvoir se mange entier*, was filmed in the village of Kawama.

establish a presence that is going to assert itself in more than one way before the day is over.

The convoy continues for another two hundred meters before it stops at a place where we find space for parking our vehicles. Villagers have been expecting us and we are greeted by men and women as we pass their houses. There is the inevitable crowd of children surrounding the visitors, but everything is more quiet, and perhaps more guarded, compared to the minor riot we caused with our visit to Kabula Mweshi. A village has dignity.

Kachelewa and the TV program director make their decisions regarding the actual site. A "typical" house with a large front yard and a garden in the rear is found nearby and the crew begins to unpack and set up their equipment. Then Kachelewa and I walk a short distance to pay our respects to the chief. He awaits us in a reclining chair, outside his house. He is an older man, dressed very simply; he displays no insignia of his office. A younger man stands nearby and acts as his spokesman.

We are received with a friendly greeting, introductions are made, and, mainly for my benefit, the young man explains the village's status. Kawama is part of a larger community, which in turn is part of the *zone annexe* of Lubumbashi. Our host, it turns out, is a minor subchief but his and the villagers' demeanor leave no doubt that the respect he commands is "whole."

Kachelewa has a delicate problem. The chief had hoped that his *lupango* (enclosure or compound) would be the site for filming. But it is obviously not suitable. His houses, including a grain mill and workshop, are built of bricks and covered with corrugated iron; the village well occupies the middle of the yard. Kachelewa finds an acceptable compromise. The chief's place will be the troupe's headquarters. Their truck will be parked here and they will dress and make up in one of the houses.

While Kachelewa makes these arrangements, I return to the site. The television crew—about ten technicians, chauffeurs, camera men, cable carriers, and a few hangers-on—seem to know what they are doing. But there is chaos among the actors. Tala Ngai forgot to bring the *conducteur*, so another outline has to be written on the spot. This is done in the studio truck, where one of the television crew members is also busy preparing *cartons*, the graphics for title, credits, and scenes. Meanwhile it is 12:30 and everything is ready for the dress rehearsal, except that Mufwankolo, Bwana Cheko, Manyeke, and some others have gone off to a nearby market to buy a supply of *mukoyo*, maize beer, one of the props needed for the play, which is all the more important because it will be consumed during the performance. The program director decides to make a quick trip back to Lubumbashi, where he wants to finish another job. This gives me time to take a closer look at the site. It is indeed ideally suited (see map 3). Two cameras are set up such that they command the village street, the yard where most of the action will take place, and the house and a smaller hut which make up the background. Stands of bananas and a cornfield are just behind the house so that only one of the cameras needs to be moved when the scene changes to the fields. Only two microphones are available: one is placed, hidden by some shrubbery, in the middle of the courtyard; another one will be carried on an improvised perch.

1:10 P.M. The beer-buying expedition has returned with a huge calabash and a supply of cups. Everything is ready for the final rehearsal. But the start is slow. There are still last-minute debates and suggestions. Finally Mufwankolo, as the chief, accompanied by his wife, his *notables*, and guards, settle down in front of the house. The drummers are ready. Two old men and a woman had been sitting on the veranda in front of the house when our party arrived. They stay there throughout the rehearsal and the play, watching and commenting. An audience of villagers, perhaps a hundred at the beginning, later growing to some hundred and fifty, surrounds the courtyard. Together with some technicians I find a place under a shade tree just outside the angle of the cameras.

Then Mufwankolo rehearses the chief's introductory speech, where he lays down the law of the land. When he comes to the point when he says *sitaki busharati, sitaki buivi* (I don't want to have fornication, I don't want to have thievery), someone from the public calls out: *sasa namna gani batazala mwivi?* How, then, are thieves going to be born? General laughter expresses appreciation for such finesse. As Mufwankolo goes on to praise hard work and loyalty and as he slips into the style of party orators who shout slogans and move the audience to respond I overhear another person saying: *anafanya meeting?* What is this, a political rally? The village audience is ahead of the play's plot; they have already begun to contest the imaginary chief's authority.

The rehearsal moves on, the scene changes from the court to the fields and back, the actors work with consummate energy. Some final directions are given, a few changes made. The TV crew run audio and video tests. The villagers mill around; some of them are now recruited as extras. A large mortar and pestle is found, the kind that serves to pound manioc and maize, and the woman who owns it now gets a walk-on part in the play. Some baskets, reed mats, and reclining chairs complete the "authentic" scenery. Finally, the troupe leaves for the chief's compound to dress and make up.

By 3:30 everything is ready; the light is ideal, and the shooting starts. It is amazing to watch what happens now. The action is continuous without retakes or breaks, except for carrying camera 2 to the fields and back.[18] In take 1, camera 1 turns to the left. On the village road the party celebrating the birth of twins approaches the scene dancing. Then, switching from the documentary to the imaginary, the camera swings to the opposite direction to show the arrival of the chief and his entourage, accompanied by a throng of villagers. The actors wear improvised costumes. The chief and dignitaries have headdresses made from cardboard, and the guards somehow assembled pieces of clothing that give the effect of a uniform.

The first scene is set in the chief's court, with cameras 1 and 2 alternating between close-ups and sweeps. The chief makes his speech,

---

18. In this account I must make references to specific scenes, that is, to the content of the play. Some of these may be too elliptical for the reader who has not yet been informed about details. The chapters that follow will answer questions that may arise now.

then follow the court cases, the visit of the hunter, and the quarrel among the *notables*. Then the scene changes to the fields. It shows the villagers' insubordination (the arrival and corruption of the guards and *notables*, who are supposed to check on the progress of work, drinking and dancing, and finally the chief's wife spying the scene through the banana stands). In the final scene we are back in the courtyard: the chief takes control, deposes his *notables*, and delivers his concluding speech. Throughout, the people of Kawama who are not participating as extras have to be kept out of the picture. They respond noisily to the play, without respect for technicalities such as a nearby microphone. Again and again the technicians signal them to keep quiet. Once a young man protests: *kama minasikia butamu minacheka,* when I feel the sweetness (when the play moves me) I laugh. But out of what must have looked to an outsider like total chaos flows the play in one piece, almost exactly in the sixty minutes allowed by the program director. During the shooting I keep my position under the shade tree, except to move along when the scene changes to the fields. My cassette recorder is on and I take some still photos, but I am too far away. The photos are mediocre and the sound recording evokes the atmosphere; only some of it is good enough for transcription.

When the show is over, the villagers disperse and the crew begins to stow away equipment. Around 5:00 P.M. we all get together at the chief's compound. The troupe poses as does the chief's family; I take a few pictures. Food and drinks are brought out and we are having our June 30 picnic after all. An hour later, it is getting dark, and the caravan gets moving. The villagers have gone back to their chores. In front of almost every house, women and children huddle around a *babula,* the charcoal brazier that also serves as a cooking stove. I see no men, they must have gathered elsewhere to discuss the events of the day. Kachelewa and others have talked to the villagers and tell me that the people are immensely proud that their village was chosen for a play to commemorate Independence. Some wondered whether the president himself had made the choice. *Le pouvoir se mange entier* will be talked about for months and years and will take shape in memory. I make a mental note: If I ever have the occasion, I should go back to Kawama and ask the villagers about their recollections.

It is dark when we arrive in Lubumbashi. The TV crew park their vehicles; Kachelewa's truck continues to the outlying parts of the city, where most of the actors live. Finally, there are just the two of us. When Kachelewa drops me at my friends' place I ask him in for a last drink. He is exhausted and does not talk much but obviously enjoys the calm and the bourgeois decor.

Tuesday, July 1. Today is another public holiday, the seventy-fifth anniversary of the city of Lubumbashi. I visit an exhibit prepared for the occasion, but I learn much more from a walk through town with an old Zairean friend who can recall the history of almost every house and building. My mind, however, is still on *Le pouvoir se mange entier*. It is to be broadcast tonight. In the evening, at my friends' place, I am comfortably settled in an armchair, with my notebook ready. My host and his two sons, who grew up in Shaba and are fluent in Swahili, are with me. Nothing happens at 8 P.M. when the play should have been on the air. Finally it begins more than an hour later. The French title has been retained, the credits give the TV program director more prominence than he deserves, especially in view of the result: the film is in black and white, the camera work is erratic, the sound simply awful. No wonder, the equipment dates from the early seventies (bought in, or donated by, Germany). But technical shortcomings cannot kill the piece; it moves, the story holds together. There are a few lengthy parts due to dramaturgical necessities, such as moving the scene. Only now I discover that I make a Hitchcock-like, two-second appearance when Mufwankolo, the chief, praises progress in the village: they even have a clinic and a doctor. I am seen for a moment fumbling with recorder and camera. Then we come to the point when the scene moves to the fields. The villagers have corrupted all the chief's emissaries and are defying his orders, dancing and drinking. Back in the village, Mufwankolo declares that he is tired of his peoples' disobedience. As a final move, he sends his wife to spy on them. At this point, without an announcement or even the slightest transition, the broadcast is interrupted for the evening news from Kinshasa station.

What a moment! The powers that be, for whom the troupe had to sacrifice the initial plot that was to have ended in chaos, have moved, thoughtlessly as often are the ways of power, to restore the play's artistic integrity. The broadcast is not resumed later. More than that, by another coincidence, part of the news inadvertently becomes a commentary on the play. A rather long documentary is shown of the demise of a local politician in upcountry Shaba accused of corruption and antiregime machinations.[19] A camera team traveled to the region and recorded interviews with the population and several traditional chiefs. Last among them is an interview with the Yeke paramount chief Mwami Munongo at his residence in Bunkeya. He acknowledges some responsibility. This man, he says, *est notre enfant*, is our child, one of us. But, *le pouvoir est un*, power is one. *Nous devons soutenir le pouvoir de notre chef Mobutu*, we must uphold the power of our chief Mobutu.

The news is followed by *Les montagnes russes*, the movie *Roller*

19. Kibasa Maliba, from Lukafu in Sanga country.

Coaster, dubbed in French. I keep taking notes about the significance of this aborted broadcast of *Le pouvoir se mange entier*. Armchair ethnography, perhaps, but to me one of the most exciting moments in this story.

A few days later, at the Cercle Makutano, the troupe discusses the broadcast at length (after protest from the population it was repeated in full on July 2). There are complaints about the sound and about some scenes that were not sufficiently clear. But it is apparent that the popular response, as always, was great; they say the whole town is talking about the play. I carefully bring the discussion to the interrupted first broadcast and the unintended comment made by the political documentary shown during the news. This causes much debate, everybody knows the politician involved and some are from the region and have more background stories. No one, however, makes an explicit connection with *Le pouvoir se mange entier*. It is as if such links were not made upon reflection, they have to happen. And when they happen their significance is appreciated without reflection.

So far, the story of the experiment. I continued to attend meetings of the troupe until the end of July. The play on mission history was being developed and the process was equally fascinating. Conflict in the group finally came out in the open. Some of it was generational, some sheer competition for leadership, some, to my great surprise, tribal. In order to keep control, Mufwankolo had to come out of his favorite position as one actor among others and insist on being the founder and honorary president. Although all this has a lot to do with "le pouvoir se mange entier," it is a different story, to be told elsewhere.

5

Interlude: The Missing Text

Now would be the time to let the play speak for itself, through the recorded texts and their translations. After much reflection, however, I decided to put this off until a few questions are cleared up. Even if the texts were now to be offered without much comment, they would still be presented in a form that "speaks for," above all, the ethnographer. In ethnographies that pretend to give naked texts or data, nakedness is but another costume. As a writer, the anthropologist fashions and forms his material. He differs from the writer of fiction, not in that he presents, but in that he needs to justify his presentations as contributions to a body of knowledge.

Ethnographic Texts as Protocols

Ethnography's task is to produce knowledge by transforming experience into writing. At all times, one may presume, anthropologists have felt (with varying degrees of apprehension, depending on that ineffable quality called "a talent for writing") that this is not only a difficult task, not just an aesthetic problem, but that writing also involves epistemological assumptions, or positions, and methodological decisions. Only in recent years has this aspect of ethnography become a matter of sustained public debate. Themes and positions in this debate vary a great deal, but an area of consensus seems to have developed regarding the central importance of *texts*. This is still a vast field, extending between global epistemological recommendations to regard societies/cultures as texts (Geertz 1973; see also Ricoeur 1979) and consequently to adopt a hermeneutic approach, and a critique of anthropological texts in terms of a theory of literary genres (including experimentation with "new" genres such as poetry, autobiography, dialogue, and so forth).[1] Contrary to what one might expect, this new critical awareness has only in exceptional cases focused on that vast body of texts on which anthropologists base their writing.[2]

Let us call these texts, for lack of a better term, ethnographic texts. They consist above all (but not only, as we shall see) of protocols made of actual communicative (mostly verbal) exchanges, as well as of "performances," ranging from storytelling, to poetic or mythical recitations, to rituals, records of transactions, and litigation. Other types can of course be added to this list, such as autobiographic accounts, descriptions and instructions relating to labor and production, and the lyrics of songs. In earlier times, texts acquired physical existence in notebooks; today, notebooks tend to be supplements to audio and video recorders. These technological developments made possible vastly more accurate (and just vastly more) protocols; in no way did they make the task of writing easier, let alone redundant. It was Ray Birdwhistle, I believe, who spoke of tape recordings as "corpses" of speech, a warning against the illusion that recordings can, as it were, substitute for events. On the other hand, corpses have been of great help to anatomists and recordings are a tremendous advancement in anthropological research, provided they are used to reconstruct events and processes, and are not passed off as pieces of "objectively" stored reality.

Precisely those anthropologists who have set their methodological bets on texts (and I have been one of them) have been taught lessons of humility by a linguistic approach, which at one time promised to take the place of discarded "scientific" methods. When, where, what, and how much to record asks for decisions that can be hellishly difficult. Working with recordings in languages with a complicated phonetic structure or with a great degree of tolerance for phonetic variation (the latter being the case in Shaba Swahili), not to mention changes in speed and volume of oral delivery and the absence of all those extralinguistic cues that help comprehension in a live event, make the goal of a perfect transcription utopian. In twenty years of struggle with recordings from Shaba I have never had a text which, upon listening to the tape once more, did not require corrections.

And then comes the equally vexing problem of how to convey to the

---

1. A survey article by Marcus and Cushman (1982) has become a point of reference in the debate on "ethnography as texts" (which see for further references; also Clifford and Marcus 1986). Geertz's much-cited pronouncement—"The culture of a people is an ensemble of texts"—was made at the end of his essay on the Balinese cockfight (1973: 452). Ricoeur's paper "The Model of the Text" was reprinted in Rabinow and Sullivan (1979).
2. One such exception is Tedlock (1983).

reader what tends to get lost in transcription due to the simple, linear typographic conventions we must follow if our books are to remain readable. Speakers pause for breath, reflection, or effect; they shout or whisper; they miss and make repairs; they convey irony, mockery, parody, and other modes through intonation; some of their utterances may be outright incomprehensible without non- or paralinguistic information. Anthropologists have devised typographic conventions to transmit at least some of this wealth of information to the reader,[3] but at a price. Such transcriptions become scores or scripts for performance destined for a public that is necessarily limited (at least as limited as that of serious readers of poetry). At any rate, as we know from the struggle with notation in other fields (dance, proxemics), any graphic system can only be an approximation. Search for perfection, in fact, tends to cancel the initial purpose in that notations become so complicated as to be impractical.

Even if we have solved the technical tasks to our satisfaction, we are still faced with epistemological questions, which in turn have practical consequences. As I see it, these questions arise somewhere on a continuum between two positions unacceptable to me: on the one hand, the naïve empiricist's belief that recordings-made-into-texts are objective representatives of reality, and, on the other, the equally naïve structuralist belief that a text's, any text's, objective content can be distilled by decomposition and recomposition according to formal models and logical schemes. Both, the empiricist and the formalist, can maintain their positions because they usually do not bother to raise the problem of *text production*. They are interested in givens, results, shapes, and constellations. Taken to their logical extreme, such approaches to text not only have little interest in process and performance; they must ignore performance because their methods only work with texts that "hold still." Because, as we have just seen, empiricism and formalism share what I should like to call a certain textual fundamentalism, an epistemological position I would consider more adequate cannot be reached as a superficial compromise between the two.

It may nevertheless seem—given all the time and energy devoted to transcription—that I have come out on the empiricist side. I would deny this; all that attention to, and struggle with, the sometimes minute detail of recorded speech I consider a necessary moment of a dialectical approach. To work dialectically is to move from particularity to totality and back and to make that movement visible. This has nothing to do

3. See Tedlock 1983, first formulated in Tedlock 1972, adopted and adapted by Seitel 1980.

with the contentment the empiricist, or rather his caricature, may feel when he backs up questionable generalizations with occasional illustrations from his data.

Then there are questions which touch on the politics of writing. In the course of our discipline's, indeed of our civilization's history, "reduction to writing" of spoken language became an instrument of power and domination.[4] This forms a sort of general background of which we must keep ourselves critically aware. Specifically, at this moment in history, it confronts the ethnographer with situations that did not obtain during periods when our discipline's founders and exemplary thinkers studied cultures "without writing." The image that the anthropologist who, armed with notebook and tape recorder, works on one side of a literate/oral divide with people who are on the other is no longer accurate (if, in fact, it ever was). At any rate, the people who populate this account share literacy with the anthropologist. Nor is employing devices for electronic recording any longer the researcher's privilege or something he brings along from the outside. The Troupe Mufwankolo is very much aware of the use and usefulness of sound recordings in the process of working out a play and *Le pouvoir se mange entier* would not have happened except as an event to be recorded and broadcast.[5]

These considerations, which I evoked rather than examined in any detail, are so many reasons to regard ethnographic texts as protocols. Not that this is a neutral concept (with its connotations of juridical procedure and a certain kind of language philosophy), but it has the advantage of keeping us aware that our transcribed recordings are above all *aides-mémoire*. They tie experience to memory, therefore to time, therefore to events and processes. A text-centered, hermeneutic approach in anthropology is only remotely and obliquely related to traditional hermeneutics with its orientation to sacred scriptures and literary texts. To borrow methods of interpretation from the latter is anything but nonproblematic.

But is all this not unnecessarily complicated and theoretical? After all, we are dealing here with a piece of theater and the term and concept

4. Anthropologists, some of them under the influence of writers such as Ong and Derrida, have begun to study, not just denounce, grapho-centrism, the politics of literacy, and the invention of "orality" as a counterworld to our own (see Fabian 1983; Goody 1977, 1986; Harbsmeier 1989; Lemaire 1984; Schousboe and Larsen 1989; Street 1984; Tannen 1982; Tedlock 1983; to name but some examples from a growing body of writing).

5. The general point made here was brought home to me recently when I visited one of the leaders of a group of charismatics in Lubumbashi. When I faced him during our conversation I could not help but notice a cupboard behind him which was filled with cassettes—some two or three hundred of them. These were recordings of his own speeches and of sessions of his group.

of a "script" ought to be perfectly adequate to designate the kind of text that will serve as ethnographic material. There are several reasons that speak against this. First of all, "script" would have to be used figuratively, even before we consider extensions of its meaning. Apart from the *conducteur* and a few notes jotted down here and there, no written document played a role in *Le pouvoir se mange entier*. An "oral script" is, strictly speaking, a contradiction in terms and to assume something like a mental script would be inappropriate and useless because we have no intention to move to the cognitive scientist's level of interpretation. We are not looking for templates, formal models, or neural structures; we are in search of a document.

I have already noted on one or two occasions my apprehensions and anxieties regarding the formidable difficulties I anticipated for the transcription of my recordings. Most of the recordings I had brought back from Shaba in the past—teachings of a religious movement, conversations with workers and artists, descriptions of work, tools, machines, and production process, and several sketches by the Mufwankolo group taped under optimal conditions—had eventually resulted in reliable transcriptions. In theoretical reflections on that material I had argued that success in having obtained a text should not distract from the fact that anthropological interpretation must not get fixed on such texts. Our main task is to comprehend and reconstruct events and processes—in short, to study the production of texts. Yet, in the case of *Le pouvoir se mange entier* I am faced with what looks like the ultimate irony: *Never before did I have the chance to witness and document text production in such detail. But there is no hope ever to come up with a definitive text of the play.* In the formulation of a definitive text of the play it is the play as well as the text that is problematic. It would be arbitrary to isolate one event from the process to which it belongs and to declare the filmed performance the definitive play. For that reason alone a definitive text cannot be exhibited.

It took me some time to realize that what looks like a failure may in fact help to advance our thinking about the significance of ethnographic texts. To work this out we must first clear away some relatively trivial problems. Why look for deeper significance, one could object, if failure is due simply to technical reasons? During the filming of the play I could not get close enough to the scene with my own recorder; the sound equipment of the television unit and the handling of the microphones by the crew were bad. At any rate, background noise and lack of discipline among the actors made it impossible to get clear recordings of the principal speakers.[6] True, but with a lot of effort and help from members

6. That certain communicative exchanges or events simply cannot be recorded

of the group, enough of the final recording could probably be reconstructed if such a text were vital for this project. I shall now argue why a "finished" text is not vital and why, had it been possible to obtain one due to extraordinary circumstances, it would have distracted from some of the insights to be gained in its absence.

Protocols of What?

The temptation to regard an ethnographic text as a lasting objectification of a fleeting event is strongest when one considers one text by itself, or even a collection of texts, each of which has been lifted from its context. When necessities, such as the imperfect, fragmentary character of a text, force us to search its "environment" for material that could fill the gaps and throw light on obscure passages, it is easier to realize that what the text is *about* is not contained in any given text; it can only be reconstructed from a process that becomes accessible to interpretation through a series of text protocols. Concretely speaking, whatever meaning the Troupe Mufwankolo has been able to tease out of "le pouvoir se mange entier," was obtained through action, through a series of communicative events, each of them up to a point complete in itself. It was not done through collecting propositions, ordering and classifying them, and finally assembling them in a play.

As a matter of fact, one of the first things I noticed when I gave the matter some thought, was that in the course of the rehearsal process *discourse,* in the sense of propositions, verbal accounts and descriptions, discussions and reflections, became less and less important. That this had something to do with time constraints, which are quite different in a group meeting and in a rehearsal or performance, seemed obvious. More important, this observation confirmed the idea of an extended process (rather than a mere diachronic sequence). Differences which were revealed by comparing single events could be conceived as changes with a certain direction.

In order to follow up on these hunches I prepared a synoptic summary of the entire series of events between June 17 and June 30. I listed what happened on each occasion in nine columns (one of them empty, because I was not present at the June 29 rehearsal). It then occurred to me that a development or transformation could be made to appear more clearly if three tentative generic distinctions—I opted for discussion, plot (construction), and play—were plotted as rows onto the schema. The result is shown in figure 1.

---

and therefore do not produce texts is an altogether different problem that need not occupy us at this point. I have addressed this issue in Fabian 1974.

Dates and Forum

Genre	17 G	19 G	20 C	23 C	25 G	26 G	27 G	29 G	30 V
Discussion	+++	+++	++ R	+	+	+	+	X	
Plot	+	+	+++	+++ R	+++ R	++	+	X	
Play						+++ R	+++ R	X	+++ RR

Figure 1. Development in the rehearsal process
(Symbols: G = group, C = committee, V = village; +−+++ = relative predomi-
nance of genre; R = event partially recorded; RR = entire event recorded; X = not
present at event)

Without pretending to be a theoretical model, figure 1 nicely illustrates the emergence of the play from first discussions, through plot
construction and assignment of parts, to rehearsal and filmed performance. As I reported before, notes were taken on all occasions; excerpts
were recorded starting on June 20, just about in the middle of the
process.[7] Only the performance of June 30 was recorded without any
interruption (save for turning the tape and changing the scene). But
precisely this final recording is only partially usable.

We are, then, still left with the question that started these reflections:
Where will the text come from on which we can base a presentation of
Le pouvoir se mange entier? It will have to be assembled from excerpts
and fragments. This need not mean that we capitulate and settle for an
empiricist approach after all (data is what is there) as can be shown by
considering once more some of the transformations plotted in figure 1,
this time with special attention given to two aspects of change. This is
shown in figure 2.

It is proposed, in other words, to consider the progressive transformation from one activity, discursive talk or discussion, into another,
theatrical performance, along two variables (no statistical claims intended).

7. Neither notes nor recordings were taken on June 29, nor was the dress rehearsal on June 30 taped.

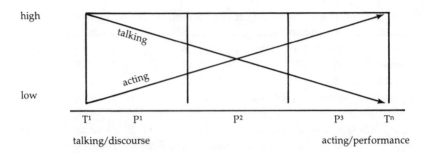

Figure 2. Verbal expression and temporal constraints showing changes during the rehearsal process
(Symbols: T^1 = begin, T^n = end of process; P^1, etc. = periods within process; $\rightarrow$ = direction of transformation)

The first one I shall simply call "talking," or perhaps "talking about" because the emphasis is on discursive, referential use of speech. One of its characteristics is verbosity, the sheer amount of talking, the length of turns taken by participants in the discussion, the explicitness of descriptive or narrative detail, and other indicators of discursiveness, down to the length and complexity of sentences.

The other variable I am tempted to call "timing." I feel that the kind of activity it designates is primarily geared toward delivery, toward creating events, and subevents, whose outer boundaries are temporal (marked by turns, pauses, or other breaks and constrained by limited duration—sixty minutes for the entire play) and whose inner structure is provided by acting rather than talking, that is by movement in space, gestures, facial expression, voice modulation, and so forth.

Figure 2 illustrates changes that occur, sometimes gradually, throughout the rehearsals. Only at a few points in our presentation of texts does the difference between timing and talking appear as a clear contrast. This is shown in chapter 6 by the two versions of the plot: Bwana Cheko's is narrative, Mufwankolo's performative (taking these terms in a more restricted sense). Both, however, are embedded in the same event and communicative setting. This should be taken as a theoretical reminder not to confuse a processual perspective with notions of linear development or evolution from talking to timing. Our model is not meant to suggest that there is somewhere a mysterious quantum leap whereby talking is left behind in the past. Rather, the relationship is to be conceived as dialectical; talking and timing are copresent determinants throughout the entire process.

Of course timing is involved whenever talk occurs, but there is at least one major difference which justifies our distinction of variables.

Discourse/talking is directed to the world; anything can become its subject. Even when the topic is specified—"le pouvoir se mange entier," for instance—content remains for all practical purposes inexhaustible. Therefore the need, observed again and again during the discussions in the group and committee, to cut talk short, to direct, select, limit; therefore also the conflicts of power that erupted occasionally, not to speak of the irruption of mundane politics; therefore also the necessity to establish authority and control. Timing/acting is teleological, geared toward performance, toward an artistic form. True, it needs artistic direction, and the director is even more conspicuous now than in the discussion phase. His authority, however, is part of the play (or should I say, part of the game). This is why almost any actor can take that role temporarily, provided he or she makes a contribution that is recognized as artistically significant. Ideas for changes that are proof of imagination, exemplary acting-out which improves a scene, establish this sort of authority, not rank in the group or the ability to convince by argument.

Keeping this contrast in mind, we can now return to figure 2. If we take the rehearsal process as a whole, we see that its movement from T^1 to T^n can be characterized in terms of an inverse change along the two variables. Before I specify what the change entails I should like to note that I did not start out with a distinction of variables as a sort of analytical device.[8] What made me eventually take that direction were two observations noted down on June 26, the last meeting that was still in a transitory phase between discussion and play. I had noticed (for the first time on June 23, I believe) that it became increasingly difficult to determine whether the verbal exchanges I was recording were still talk about the play or already part of the play's dialogue. And when the actual rehearsal started it was not through a slow transition but, as I called it, by the whole group "bursting" into action.

Figure 2 allows us to locate these observations graphically at a point where the lines which mark the variables cross. As the rehearsal process develops, talking/discursiveness decreases while timing/acting increases in importance. Because the movement is inverse there must be a point where the two tendencies converge. The point is that it is a point, a brief moment, not an extended phase; hence the impression of oscil-

---

8. Nor do I intend to "operationalize" this hypothetical model of a rehearsal process. Perhaps this is also the moment to state that I have neither the competences nor the ambitions of R. Schechner, some of whose writings on the rehearsal process I have read with interest (1982, 1985, 1986). The schematic reductions that I call models were suggested to me by the specific sequence of events which led up to *Le pouvoir se mange entier*. The question of the limits of validity of the model does not preoccupy me at the moment.

lation between talking and acting and the experience of a sudden burst into action.

It will now take one more step to bring these reflections back to our question: Where will our ethnographic text come from? Also marked in figure 2 is a rough distinction between three phases or periods within the overall process (P^1 and P^3). Assuming I had started recording the meetings right from the beginning, and also assuming that I decided to select texts only from phase 1, I would have impressive, detailed documentation of the search for the meaning of *Le pouvoir se mange entier*. There would be much information of linguistic interest (remember the problems with translation) and also detailed material on the interference of politics with artistic creativity. But these texts would convey little of what this experiment was all about: search for an answer to my questions about a cultural axiom through performance. Conversely, were I to select texts only from phase 3, even setting aside the problem of a poor final recording, I would wind up with mangled tokens, with transcribed words that are incapable of conveying the power of performance; and with documents that would show no traces of a process.

Conclusion: Events during phase 2 ought to produce texts that will be of the greatest ethnographic value. Recordings made in that phase still contain elements of discursiveness but already take the shape of dramatic dialogue. Traces of the cultural and political reflections characteristic of the initial period are still to be found during the last group meeting on June 25 and the first two actual rehearsals on June 26 and 27. Then the time constraints of performance begin to assert themselves but are not actually observed until the dress rehearsal on June 30. Although some scenes are already together (that is, more or less verbally fixed, the way they appear in the final recording; this can be demonstrated by comparing passages), most exchanges are still more verbose, more explicitly narrative and informative than in the final performance. In short, a presentation of the text of *Le pouvoir se mange entier* which meets the criteria of a processual approach cannot be but an assemblage of texts, with phase 2 recordings as its core.

Such an assemblage will be presented in the following manner:

- The last stage of plot construction will be documented by Bwana Cheko's second *conducteur* in Swahili, followed by Mufwankolo's version.
- The play will be assembled from recordings and transcriptions, made during the rehearsals and the final performance. Both are treated as textual documents of the entire process.
- In each case a transcription in Swahili will be followed by a translation into English.

- The sequence of the texts will be determined by the sequence of scenes in the filmed performance.
- Whenever useful and feasible, recordings of brief discussions, directions, and comments will be included in the presentation.
- Brief descriptive passages will situate each text in its context during rehearsal and performance.
- For reasons of space, and because my competences are limited in these matters, the text does not contain transcripts of musical performances, which make up an important part of the play.[9]
- Notes will be of two kinds: (a) Whenever the transcription requires justification or explanation, a note will be made in the Swahili text. In many cases this will regard lexical or syntactic peculiarities of Shaba Swahili (in contrast to East Coast Swahili, ECS). (b) Whenever the translation needs to be commented on, or when elements of the play's content require ethnographic or other kinds of information, these will be given in notes to the English version.

Remarks and Apologies on Transcription and Translation

Transcriptions of the Swahili recordings follow conventions and standards that have proved practical during years of working with recordings in Shaba Swahili. A common sense method has been adopted as regards phonology. It is justified by several considerations: a definitive phonological analysis of Shaba Swahili is not yet available, in spite of some useful attempts. Moreover, because Shaba Swahili is characterized by a high, sometimes extreme, degree of variation on all levels (phonetic, morphological, syntactic), a definitive description may be impossible in principle. Since there is no "official" literacy in this variety of Swahili there is also no standard orthography. However, a certain degree of standardization developed spontaneously in Shaba Swahili written by its speakers. What I called my "commonsense method" attempts to meet these standards.[10] Inevitably this involves filtering out some of the variability that could be conveyed by a cumbersome phonetic transcription. This also regards the difficult problem of the

---

9. Here are some statistics that can also be read as an illustration of our point about progression from talking to timing: The videotaped performance takes 62 minutes, of which 27.5 are "music" (i.e., nondialogue, drumming, singing, taped music). That this tendency increases within the play is shown by the following breakdown: Up to the change of scene to the fields (see chapter 12), 32 minutes elapse, of which 7.5 are filled with "music." Of the remaining 30 minutes, 20 are music.

10. See on this also Schicho 1981: 7–14.

phonic integration of loans (mostly from French). With some exceptions (where phonetic particularities convey important information about the speaker or his/her part in the play) I have side-stepped this issue by rendering these items according to orthography of the source language.

The next problem is that of segmentation of morphemes. It is not uncommon for writers of Shaba Swahili to separate prefixes from each other and from the stem. Because this does not happen according to (known) rules I opt for an approximation of standard Swahili conventions. For example, the simple verb-form translated as "I want," is sometimes written *mi nataka* or *mina taka*. I opt for *minataka*. The problem of segmentation is much more difficult on the level of the phrase or sentence. Shaba Swahili written by its speakers is notoriously difficult to read because of the erratic use of punctuation. The compromise I have adopted is based on a combination of nonsegmental signals such as intonation, pause, and semantic indicators. In the following I will employ, instead of our system of punctuation, a minimal set of signs: a colon marks a sustained clause, a slash a full clause; a question mark indicates the end of a question; occasionally the conventional mark follows brief exclamations. The last two pose few problems. The colon and slash correspond ideally to a sustained versus a falling sentence tone. In practice this is not always easy to determine (nor do these two varieties exhaust the intonation patterns in Shaba Swahili). Still, according to my experience, anything more complicated would not serve our practical purposes. Other kinds of pertinent information (such as a mocking tone, volume/loudness, speed, length of pause, in short, many of the things that Tedlock's proposal tries to cover) will occasionally be added in parentheses or notes. The same goes for nonlinguistic information such as gestures, posture, position of speaker, and so forth.

But that is not all. In varying degrees—less so in discussion, more so in performance—the exchanges which the following texts document also include what one might call verbal gestures. For instance, the participants exchange formulae of greeting, exclamations, sounds marking assent, surprise, and questioning. Some of these (audible, recorded) utterances are part of the lexicon and have specifiable semantic referents (although it is not always the referential function of these utterances that determines their communicative significance). The meaning of other elements of this kind can only be rendered by indicating their functions (such as assent or negation). Because Shaba Swahili and English agree in this respect only in a few exclamations (possibly "mm" for assent, "oh" for surprise), most of them are here translated: as "yes" or "no"; as "really?" or "no way"; as "all right" or, worse but unavoidable, as "ululation"; and so forth. This is done with the understanding that most of the flavor and much of the meaning get lost in a procedure which really amounts to attaching English labels to Swahili utterances (and thereby classifying them in a system familiar to us) rather than translating (carrying over) meanings from one language into another.

The point about verbal gestures is that they may be recorded and transcribed with more or less accuracy and thus become parts of a text, but they cannot be translated except by some sort of performative recreation—as verbal gestures. All this should be kept in mind when reading the texts that follow. Occasionally, descriptive statements are added to the dialogue or to some utterances that would otherwise not be comprehensible at all or lose more of their meaning than necessary. Words or phrases that I have been unable to transcribe are indicated either by a remark in square brackets or by a question mark preceded and followed by several dots.

Finally, a remark on the method of translation. To begin with, I attach the greatest importance to presentation of both the transcribed text and the translation. Quite likely, few readers of this study will be fully able to appreciate the Swahili texts. One may wonder whether the inclusion of original text justifies the effort and costs. But I consider the mere physical juxtaposition of Swahili and English version to be of capital epistemological importance. A translation can never claim to have accomplished the transfer of meaning from source to target language. Translation is a process; the texts we call "translations" are but documents of that process. They, too, are produced through contingent events—in fact, they may in turn be regarded as rehearsals and performances—and are therefore never definitive. If it is accepted that a text's meaning can only be ascertained fully in a context of performance, then it follows that the same must apply to all versions of that text.

While the present book was being considered for publication, I completed another project based on a text not recorded or transcribed by myself but written and typed in Shaba Swahili.[11] Paradoxically, struggling with a "literate" text made me realize more clearly than before that producing an ethnographic text does not come to an end (even provisionally) with a successful trans-scription. The reason is elementary, once one thinks about it, yet it may have consequences regarding our conceptions of the ethnographer's task. Writing ("scription") is inseparable from reading. The kind of writing that occurs in transcribing recorded speech from tapes is never just a straightforward transposition from acoustic signals to graphic signs. It is an activity geared to, guided, and constrained by the aim to make the transcript readable according to criteria that are always relative to culturally and historically specific

---

11. Fabian 1990. The interested reader may consult that study for more thoughts and information on the idea of "ethnographic reading."

situations (of both the source and the "target" text).[12] In this regard, there is little difference between the efforts and competences required to transcribe a recorded text and those one needs to read a text written in a kind of literacy which speakers of Shaba Swahili—a language that during its colonial history has been denied access to official literacy—employ when they write their language. Even though one may be seen as graphic encoding, the other as decoding, both kinds of activity require an ability to recreate the oral performance of speech. A special kind of ethnographic work, namely discussing and conversing about what is written or read is therefore required no matter whether the task is transcribing and thereby producing a text or understanding/translating a text.

When I worked on the final version of the texts presented in this study I had the privilege (and luxury) to have my friend Kalundi Mango literally at my side. His contribution was not only to help me fill gaps and correct errors (this affected perhaps less than 5 percent of the work previously done by myself), but more important, the conversations and occasional heated disputes we had about "correct" transcriptions and translations made me realize that both acts, establishing the text and translating it, are dialogical to the core. Such an insight may be obscured by the fact that this phase of ethno-graphy is usually carried out in the absence of informants with whom we can negotiate signs and meanings. To be carried off successfully, making and translating ethnographic texts in the absence of interlocutors still calls for (the substitute of) an inner dialogue in which the anthropologist who writes ethnography matches recorded sounds and graphic symbols with communicative competences, memories, and imagination.[13] In this sense all ethno-graphy is ethno-logy—recuperation of the spoken word *(logos)* through reading as "recollecting" *(legein).*

12. Perhaps this is prejudice; it was nicely confirmed to me, however, by the dismal performance I saw recently of an experimental voice-recognition computer. I imagine that if such a machine should ever work it would have to be because someone succeeded in binarizing whatever governs writing and reading in the culturally specific and historically contingent ways in which this seems to happen. To my mind such an undertaking is inherently contradictory, which does not mean that it could not reach a low, "practical" level of usefulness.

13. And, of course, with that body of knowledge which gets deposited in lexica and other ethnographies. Good dictionaries are always both.

6

Plot and Players

From Saying to Play: Developing a Plot

In earlier years, I seem to remember, it was usually Kachelewa who prepared the only kind of script used by the Troupe Mufwankolo, a short outline, usually in French, called a *conducteur*. For *Le pouvoir se mange entier* it was the group's secretary, Bwana Cheko, who took this task upon himself. First he submitted to the committee a version written and typed in French.[1] It was received without much enthusiasm. But it became a starting point for discussions and several amended versions had been proposed, some of them recorded. On June 25 the group listened to the recording; Bwana Cheko kept taking notes. But a number of other items were talked about before he took the floor and recited this version of the plot:[2]

Power Is Eaten Whole: Bwana Cheko's Version (Text 1)

1. *Bwana Cheko: pièce* inaanza: namna hii/
banakamata: mutoto wa *deuxième:* muto: mu: muntu[3] wa mugini/

---

1. See the report on June 20 in chapter 4. Why this minimal written guideline for an oral performance in Swahili should be in French is open to speculation. Is it symbolic of a higher status of French corresponding to the function of the *conducteur* as a directive document? Is it simply more practical for speakers of Swahili who are multilingual and who are used to literacy in French? Or is there a historical link to the times when French plays were translated and adapted? At any rate, the *conducteur* is a document for the director to read; as soon as it is verbalized, put up for discussion, or applied in directing, it will be transposed into Swahili.
2. For purposes of reference, texts will be numbered consecutively as they occur in this study. Each text is divided into numbered paragraphs (with original and translation corresponding). This, too, is for reference only; as a rule, divisions follow cues from the text (such as turns, change of topic) but are not based on a thorough analysis.
3. This is an example of a "repair": the speaker starts out with a more specific term *(mutoto,* child) and then changes to the more general *muntu,* person. In these texts

ule ni nani? nawaza mutaangaria jina pale . . .
Actor: Katolushi/
Bwana Cheko: Katolushi/ banamukamata/ kama aliiba: kama alifanya nini: tutachagua: ni kitu gani: kile alifanya/ banamukamata
na kumupeleka mbele ya: ya chefu/ *chef* anatoka ndani ya⁴ nyu-
mba/ na bibi/ na ba*notables* bengine: beko pale karibu/ banaanza
kumu*juger:* Katolushi/ lakini kwa kufwata na mambo alifanya
Katolushi: mambo yake alifanya: haikuwa kosa munene hapana/
lakini *premier notable:* Bwana Cheko: akakankamana tu: ya kama
inapendeza kabisa kabisa huyu Katolushi afungwe/ ao awawe/
*bon*⁵/ lakini: sultani hakufwate ile neno hapana/ akamuhurumia
kidogo: nakumupatia kosa ya kidogo/

2. kiisha siku kidogo: ule *premier notable:* mutoto yake Manyeke:
anakwenda kuharibisha kitu kikubwa sana/ anafanya kosa moya
munene sana/ basi: bakamuleta: ya kupita ile ya Katolushi⁶/
bakamuleta: vilevile mbele ya sultani/ na mwisho: kwa kuona: ya
kama Bwana Cheko: ule mutoto yake alifanya kosa mukubwa: ata-
fungwa: Bwana Cheko akaanza kuji*opposer*/ ku*défendre* mutoto
yake/ ile wakati: kukaanza ubishi/ na wa*notables* wengine/ ni
namna gani? ule mutoto: wa kwanza: alikamatwa: hakufanya kosa
munene: tulimufunga/ lakini kwa huyu mutoto wa sasa kwa sababu ni mutoto yako: basi unatafuta kumuponyesha/ paka pale:
hakukuwa tena masikilizano: katikati ya wa*notables*/

3. maneno yote ilikuwa inasemewa na *chef* Mufwankolo: wao
wa*notables:* kwa kuona: fitina inaingia katikati yao: kila muntu alianza: kwenda ku: kueleza ku watu wa mugini: namna yake/ kila
muntu: aka*créer*⁷/ kila *notable* alikuwa na *groupe* yake/ kwenda

---

many such repairs occur but will not be further commented on unless they make a
particularly interesting point. Nor did I think it useful to try to mimic "exact" equiva-
lents in the English translation.

4. An unusual form; *kutoka mu nyumba* would be usual.

5. As will be seen, Bwana Cheko uses the interjection *bon* quite frequently. This
is an example of the "grammatical" function of many French loanwords (especially of
those that occur most frequently). In this case, *bon* appears to be the lexical equivalent
of the *-ka-* affix. Both mark narrative sequence. See Fabian (1982) on this stylistic
function of borrowing from French in Shaba Swahili.

6. Here the sentence is interrupted by an afterthought taking up and elaborating
on the preceding one.

7. A subtle but important transformation occurs at this point. The speaker begins
to use the *-ka-* affix marking the "narrative" tense (of an action that follows another). In
ways that cannot be rendered in translation, this changes the generic status of his
account. Up to this point, Bwana Cheko told the scenario in the present and unspecified
past (marked by *-na-* and *-li-* respectively); this, one may assume, has been appropriate

ku*déformer:* mamambo[8]: kadiri ule: mule banawazia/ ingine ya kweli: na ingine ya bongo: na ingine ya kuharibisha/

4. siku moya: muntu moya wa mugini/ na ule tulisahau: kumupa jina/ yee ni *chasseur/* alienda: tutaangaria kama ni kwenda kulopola samaki: ao kama ni kuua nyama/ ule *chasseur:* kiisha: akakuya na nyama ao kama ni samaki/ akafika nayo: mbele ya sultani/ Mufwankolo/ na kule kwa sultani: akaleta mulambo/ na sultani: na sultani: akaanza kuita: ba*notables* moya kwa moya: na kubakabuliako ile: nani: nusu ya mulambo: ile alipata/

5. bale ba*notables:* kwa kuona kama hakukuwa masikilizano katikati yao: bakaanza: bawili bakaanza kushimanga ule moya/ *premier notable/* bakamushimanga/ ya kama: oh: ule naye: anapitishwa/ unaona jana: balimupatia kamunofu kaloko tu/ lakini she tulipata bya mingi/ maneno: lubanga lunamupita[9]/

6. *bon/* mwisho: ya ile: kukaonekana ya kama kunakuwa *laissez aller:* ku ngambo ya chefu/ juu ya nini? kwa sababu chefu alishinda namna gani? ya kutafuta: kuwakokota kila muntu/ na kila muntu: alianza kwenda kudanganya: kwa *chef:* mambo: ya mbalimbali/ mais *chef* alikuwa naweka mpaka ndani ya roho/ *au lieu* ya kubaconvoquer: kwanza kuba*corriger: chef* alikuwa anaangaria paka na: na macho/ eko anabasikia haya/

7. *bon/* siku ingine: sultani akasema *non:* inapendeza: tufanyeko kwanza kazi ya mashamba: tulimeko mashamba kwanza ya mugini yote muzima: tupate chakula: kawaida/ kwa ile fasi: bale ba*notables:* bakaenda: kupeleka ile habari: mu ma*groupes* yao: na kila moja: aka*déformer* ile ilisemewa: na chefu/

8. *bon/* kiisha: kesho yake: kukawa kazi ya mashamba/ bakaenda ku mashamba/ fasi ya kwenda kutumika kazi ya mashamba: ao: kufanya vile *chef* alisema: lakini kule: hakukuwa ginsi hapana/

---

to an outline summarizing procedure. Now he switches from description to storytelling; it is as if the plot were taking over (at least for a moment, because he later reverts to the other tenses). One may infer that narrative, a story, is in fact the starting point for the play rather than a scenario. This seems to be confirmed by the fact that earlier the account is already interspersed with dialogue. I therefore use "plot" rather than "scenario" in the heading of this chapter.

8. A form that may seem strange but is typical for developments in Shaba Swahili. *Mambo* is no longer analyzed as plural prefix plus stem; hence, to stress the plural, the *ma-* prefix is added (once again).

9. *Lubanga* (Luba; see Van Avermaet and Mbuya 1954: 51) means "the big chin," *kupita,* "to surpass." *Lubanga lunamupita* would be something like: his big mouth ran away with him.

mambo yote ya *chef:* iligeuzwa mu namna ingine/ bakaanza kunywa pombe: bakaanza kucheza mangoma: kuimba: na byote/

9. sultani akaona vile: anasema: ahah/ namna gani hivi? tangu
bantu balikwenda na saa hii: bo bado kurudia/ akatumako *notable*
wa kwanza/
Kachelewa: alisikia makelele/ . . .
Bwana Cheko: alisikia ma: makelele ku pori: ku mayani/ alisema:
ohoh: alafu ngoma iko inalia kule: ku mashamba tena bo wanali-
lishako ngoma? *notable* wa kwanza: wee wende ukaangarieko/ *notable* wa kwanza: alienda mpaka kule: kufika kule: kukuta:
mmmmm: kuko kivumbi inayasha[10]/ bantu baliisha kuwa kopo/
anaanza kusema: na kutafuta kubafokea/ basi: kukatokea mama
moya: kumuzunguka tu na kopo: oh: kumukunyika ku kinywa/
notable asema acha nimezeko mara moya wee/ *notable* mu kuingilia
mu kunywa wawa: ilikuwa kopo moya: inakuwa kopo mbili/ kopo
mbili: kopo tatu/ nayee chori[11]: anaikala/ mu ngoma sasa: anakufa
muchezo/

10. kiisha: *chef* akaangaria asema *tiens*/ saa inapita: huyu *notable*
nilituma: na sasa: eko paka kule? banatuma mwengine/ ule mwengine: kwenda kufika kule: namna moya/ banamuweza/ banatafuta asema afanye manani yote: banamuweza/ anaikala kule/ mu
chezo/ kopo/ kulewa ovyo/ weee: na vile ba*notables* bote: balienea
bote tatu kule/

11. mwisho: *chef* akasema *tiens*/ ba*notables* bote tatu: hakuna hata
moya anarudia kwa kuniletea *rapport*? *bon*/ kumbe nitatumako *policier*/ njo kutuma *policier*/
Actor: Shebele/
Bwana Cheko: beba bwayoo[12]/ beba nkamba/ ule muntu atacheza
kule: huyu umulete hapa/ Shebele kwenda kule: bo kwa kumuona
tu hivi: ah: anakuya: anakuya: anakuya/ bana*utiliser* paka nani:
manani: ma: yabo vile banafanyaka: Shebele mu kopo/ bwayoo yo
chini/ *chapeau* chini/ ki: kikwembe mu kivuno[13]/ muchezo na nani/
eh? weee kopo/ Tolushi: anasahabu na fasi gani poka *chapeau*/
nayee anaandamana mu kunywa/ analala pa mayani/

12. alaah/ kiisha: bana: sultani anasema: mm/ haba bantu bote
beko banakwenda kule: *mais:* niko nasikia makelele paka kule/ ni

10. Another possible reading could be: *kivumbi na yasho* (Standard Swahili *jazo*),
dust and sweat. The change in metaphorical meaning would be minor.
11. Shaba Swahili has the expression *kulewa chori*, to be completely drunk. The
derivation of *chori* is uncertain.
12. From the French *boyau*, rubber hose, rubber stick.
13. The Shaba Swahili form of ECS *kiuno*, waist.

makelele ya namna gani? wee inamfumu[14]: Salima/ wende kwanza:
wende ukaangaria kwanza ni kitu gani kiko kule/ mangoma:
mimbo: iko inakuwa: iko inakuwa inaleta makelele paka huku/
Kachelewa: na bantu nilituma . . .
Bwana Cheko: na bantu nilituma benyewe: hakuna hata moya ana-
rudia/ ni namna gani?
Actor: bibi wa sultani . . .
Bwana Cheko: njo inamfumu/ *donc* sawa vile nani?
Actor: wa mu *cour* . . .
Bwana Cheko: mm/ bwa mu *cour*/ eh/ *donc* yeye: anakwenda:
lakini kwa kwenda ku: asema: anashimamia pale: anaangaria: ana-
kuta bantu kule: ahah/ beko balevi sana/ anafichama/ anarudia/
anakuya/ sultani naye: tangu alisimama ku njia: eko anamuangaria
juu ya kutafuta kuya *rapport*/

13. kipande kidogo: Salima anafika/ asema sultani Mufwankolo/
huku ku nani: huku: hakuna tena mashamba kule kuntu kule/ beko
kopo boote/ na wampolushi/ na banani: ba*notables:* na bantu ya
mukini bote: beko kopo/ njo ile unasikia bikelekele kule/ kuna-
kolea: haina bure hapana/

14. *donc:* njo Mufwankolo yee moya anafunga safari: anakwenda
kule/ Katolushi mpolushi: mu kuona: paka: eeh nani?
Actor: Shebele/
Bwana Cheko: Shebele mpolushi: mu kuona tu mbali: sultani eko
anakuya: asema mama yake na mama/ kulamuka pale kulokota
ka*chapeau* yake: mioto[15]/ kipande kiloko: *chef* anafika/ anakwenda
kufichama/ *bon*/ chefu anafika/ kuya kukuta bantu bote kopo/
chefu anaaanza kubaelezea mambo: eko anabaelezea mambo:
kwanza kufoka: bo beko banazomea: mmmmm[16]: m/ aseme hivi:
banazomea mmmm/ aseme hivi: banazomea mmmm/ kipande
kiloko banaanza kutokapo moya kwa moya: moya kwa moya: moya
kwa moya/

15. chefu anabakia paka na ba: *trois notables*/ na kwanza kuba-
fanya ma: ma*remarques*/ mwee bantu niliwekea roho/ sasa namna
gani munafanya bintu ya nanma hii? hm? kumbe gani kwenu niko

---

14. *Inamfumu* comes to Shaba Swahili from Luba and means the chief's (first)
wife. In Kiluba the phrase consists of *ina,* mother, and *mfumu,* chief, and its meaning is
more specific: "femme jouissant d'un certain pouvoir; elle est une notable, mais pas du
chef indigène; elle tient son pouvoir d'étrangers, elle se promène avec une lance" (Van
Avermaet and Mbuya 1954: 194).
    15. A plural form of *moto,* fire, heat. Here used to indicate speed.
    16. An example of a phonation—not a word, nor just a sound—difficult to
transcribe and impossible to translate except by some paraphrase, such as "making
noises."

nasikia? wee siku fulani ulikuyaka: unasema hivi na hivi/ eh? juu ya huyu/ semaka basi: mwenzako mwenyewe ulikuwa kuchonga: yo yee eko hapa/ eleza/ ule kimya/ *bon*/ na wee ile siku ulisemaka juu ya huyu/ sasa yo yee iko hapa: semaka/ kimya/ nini? wapi? bote baliikala paka kimya/ njo chefu akabakia pale: anasema *voilà:* unaona sasa: ni juu ya nini? hivi: kuiko fujo: ndani ya mukini/ na bantu habapende tena kusikia sauti yangu: na batu habapende tena kutumika kazi/

16. basi: *chef* akafunga safari: anarudia ku mugini: na bo bale ba*notables:* na bo kulamuka: banafunga safari: banaenda/ nawaza: njo pa mwisho pale: munasikia: *mais:* sasa kunabakia: namna gani: ya kuweza kutengeneza muzuri na kuweka chumvi/ aksanti kwenu/

Power Is Eaten Whole: **Bwana Cheko's Version (Translation)**

1. *Bwana Cheko:*   The piece starts like this.
They pick up the son of the second [in rank], that is to say, of a person from the village. Who is this? I think you'll see about that. The name [of the actor in that scene] will be . . .
Actor: Katolushi.
Bwana Cheko: Katolushi. So they pick him up. Whether he stole [something] or whatever, we will have to choose what he committed. They pick him up and bring him before the chief. The chief comes out of his house. And his wife and other dignitaries are nearby. Then they begin the trial of Katolushi. But as they examine what Katolushi did it turns out not to have been a serious offense. However, the first *notable* set his mind on it and insisted that by all means this Katolushi should be thrown in jail, or executed. All right. But the chief did not accept this indictment. He felt some pity and ruled that Katolushi's crime had been minor [literally: he gave him a small fault].

2. A few days later, Manyeke, the son of this first *notable* Bwana Cheko, got into a real mess. He committed a serious crime and was going to be locked up. Bwana Cheko began to oppose this and to defend his son. That was the time when discord began [between him] and the other *notables*. How come? The first young man [they said] who was picked up did not commit a serious offense; but we put him in jail. Now this young man, because he is your son, you try to clear him. That was the point where there was no more mutual understanding among the *notables*.

3. Because everything was eventually told to the chief Mufwankolo, they, the *notables*, when they saw that there was discord among them, each of them went to explain to the people of the village his own point of view. Every *notable* formed his own group. They went and twisted matters according to their way of thinking. One [told] the truth, another lies, yet another things that were divisive.

4. One day, a person from the village—we forgot to give him a name, he was a hunter—went off, let us see, either to catch fish or to kill an animal. Afterward, this hunter came [back] with fish or with game. With it he came before chief Mufwankolo and brought the chief his share. The chief began to call the *notables,* one by one, and gave them each a portion of the share he had received.

5. The *notables* saw that there was no mutual understanding among them and two of them began to taunt the first *notable:* Oh, [they said] that one, he was given short shrift. Did you see, yesterday they gave him a tiny piece of meat whereas we got a lot. This is because he talks too much.

6. All right, the end of it was that it became obvious that, as far as the chief was concerned, things were out of control. Why? How did the chief fail? He did not try to convoke [literally: to pull] them one by one. Everyone began to mislead the chief in all directions. But the chief kept all this to himself. Instead of calling them together and putting them right he kept watching with his eyes. He felt shame for them.

7. All right. Some other day the chief said: No [this cannot go on], work needs to be done in the fields. Let us first cultivate the fields of the whole village so that we get the food we need. At that point the *notables* went to spread the news, each to his group, and each of them twisted what had been said by the chief.

8. All right, then, the next day, work was going on in the fields. They went to the fields, to the place where there was work, to carry out what the chief had ordered. But there—it was impossible to describe. Everything the chief had said was changed. They began to drink beer, play the drums, sing, everything.

9. When the chief saw this he said: Ah, how is this? Ever since the people went away up until now, they haven't come back yet. So he sent out the first *notable.*
Kachelewa: [prompting] He heard the noise . . .
Bwana Cheko: He heard the noise outside the village, in the bush. He said: Oh, so the drum is calling there, in the fields? They play the drum? You, the first *notable,* go and see. So the first *notable* went there. When he got there, well he found [everything] in a cloud of

dust. The people were already in the cups. He began to talk and tried to scold them. So one mama[17] came forth, turned [his head] to the cup, so that his mouth was on the cup. The *notable* said: Oh well, I am going to take just one sip. So the *notable* got into drinking, one cup, then two, then three, and he, too, got totally drunk and stayed. Now he grabbed the drum and played it like mad.

10. Then the chief looked [around] and said: What is this? It is getting late. Is this *notable* I sent out still there? So they sent out another one. This other one went away and when he got there it was just the same. They were stronger than he. They tried to talk him into doing all these things, and they succeeded. He stayed there, dancing, raising the cup, getting stupidly drunk. So it went on and on, the same thing happened to all the *notables*; in the end, all three of them were there.

11. Finally the chief said: What is this? All three *notables*, not one of them comes back to give me a report. All right, I'll send a policeman there. So a policeman was sent.
Actor: [suggesting someone for the part] Shebele.
Bwana Cheko: Carry that stick [said the chief], carry a rope; you catch a person dancing there, bring him here. Shebele went there. When they saw him coming closer and closer they used the same trick on him and Shebele got drunk. His stick and cap fell to the ground, he was showing off with a cloth tied around his waist, dancing and carrying on until he got drunk. The other policeman, he forgets where he left his cap, he, too, gets drunk and falls asleep on the green.

12. What is this, the chief said finally, all those people went there but I still hear noise in that place. What kind of noise is this? You, the chief's wife, Salima, go there now and see first what sort of thing is going on there; drums, singing, the noise can be heard here.
Kachelewa: [prompting] And the people I sent . . .
Bwana Cheko: And the people I sent, not one of them came back. How is this?
Actor: The chief's wife . . .
Bwana Cheko: That's *inamfumu*. So, like who?
Actor: The people at the court . . .
Bwana Cheko: Yes, the people at the court; in other words, this one went away and [when she got there] she stopped there. She looked

---

17. A polite term of address for a woman (*baba* for a man), which will be used untranslated.

and saw that the people were there, totally smashed. She kept hidden, then she turned and walked back. The chief, ever since he[18] stopped on the road, had been looking out for her to get his report.

13. After a little while Salima arrived. Chief Mufwankolo, she said, there are no fields anymore; this thing there—all of them are drunk; the policemen, the *notables*, and all the villagers, they are drunk. Those are the cries of joy [ululations] you hear from there. Things are sizzling over there, this is not just a little party [literally, there is spice over there, it is not something unimportant].

14. So, Mufwankolo himself got on the way and went there. When Katolushi, the policeman there, saw—or what is his name?
Actor: Shebele.
Bwana Cheko: Shebele, the policeman, when he saw the chief coming from far away he cried "mother of my mother," got up and looked for his cap and was gone in a flash. He went to hide himself when the chief arrived a little later. All right, the chief arrived and found everyone drunk. So the chief began to explain things to them. First he hollered at them. They scoffed at him, making noises. He said this, they jeered; he said that, they mocked him. After a little while they began to leave the place, one by one, one by one, one by one.

15. The chief was left alone with the three *notables*. He began to tell them off: I put my confidence in you people. And now you behave in this way? So, who among you should I listen to? You [turning to one of them], one day you came and said this and that about this person here. Speak up now. The very person you came to denounce, your fellow *[notable]*, he is here. Speak up. He kept silent. All right. And you, on that day, you talked about this one. Now he is here, talk. He said nothing. What? Where? All of them kept silent. So the chief stopped there and said: Now you see? Why [has it come that far]? Because there is discord in the village. The people don't want to listen to what I say, and the people don't want to work anymore.

16. So the chief left and went back to the village. And the *notables*, they got up and left. I think this is where it ends, you understand. But there remains [the work of figuring out] how to put this into order and add salt to it. Thank you.

Things were left at that point at the June 25 meeting. Actual rehearsal began the following day. The first scene was played out with few

18. Or "she." One problem of translation throughout is that in Swahili pronominal references (pronouns and pronominal affixes) are not marked for gender.

directions and little discussion. Then Mufwankolo begins to set up the second scene but he gets carried away and once again summarizes the plot. There are some differences in detail between the two scenarios but the most striking contrast is in the form of delivery. Bwana Cheko's version is a narrative; Mufwankolo does not so much tell the plot, he acts and directs. He uses gestures profusely, modulates his voice, and often, in the rush of "timing," resorts to "meaningless" fillers[19] and phonations.[20] In short, although the recording is of a good quality and there are not many unsolved problems of transcription, this text exemplifies almost painfully the limits of textual documentation based on sound recordings. In no conceivable way could it be said that it adequately documents the event during which it was recorded. Recording and text are, sometimes more, sometimes less so, only tokens, reminders, clues for the reconstruction of an event. This is one reason, incidentally, why in cases such as this one only a participant in the event can come up with a satisfactory transcription[21] and why, furthermore, a transcript is always part of a process of interpretation and translation. Translation in the narrow sense of the word—fashioning a text in English which actually renders the original—becomes increasingly, in fact hellishly, difficult as we move from discursive to performative texts.

Power Is Eaten Whole: Mufwankolo's Version (Text 2)

1. *Mufwankolo:*   . . . banatokatoka/ *après:* mu bale bantu ya sultani: bale mwenye bantu ya mukini: sasa kunakawa sasa kusema sawa *dis:* unasikia vile sultani alisema? asema: ah: basi sultani alipita na ku mambo ya kusemasema: ah: ya nani . . . . .

---

19. For example: hivi na hivi: *mais tout ça:* hivi (2,8), literally "such and such, but all that, such." These utterances differ from mere phonations in that they have a recognizable morpho-syntactic form and, with some effort, a specifiable semantic function. Still, they do not manifestly convey propositional information. They serve to fill gaps or, to use a less spatial image, to pass time until a new thought is, as it were, ready to succeed its (incomplete) predecessor.
20. Examples from this text are: *tititi* and *pà.* Earlier we had *mmmmm: m.* In case such a precision is needed: phonations are not random. Often they are onomatopoeic (i.e., mimetic) and are understood across languages. It is my impression that in Shaba Swahili (which in this respect seems to draw heavily on autochthonous languages) phonations occur with some predictability. When they appear to be made up on the spot they probably are made up according to certain rules.
21. In fact, transcription is always also description. The idea that a transcript is, as it were, an authorless, objective record and that just any native speaker may do the job for the ethnographer is theoretically naïve (although it may sometimes be the only practical compromise). I have always sensed this and have done my own transcriptions first and then consulted native speakers for specific difficulties.

Actor: na banazungumuza . . .

Mufwankolo: na bale banazungumuza sawa bantu/

Bwana Cheko: . . . . bana*braquer* kule: kuko bale ba*population*/ ma*critiques* inaanza/

2. *Mufwankolo:*   sasa ma*critiques* inaanza sasa: ma*population* asema: aah: lakini vile alisema: ndiyo: kazi ya kulima nayo: *mais* si hivi na hivi: *mais tout ça* hivi: *donc:* bengine beko *pour:* bengine beko *contre:* ni toka ma*critiques* panakuya pa nani: ya kusema tu: banasemasema: ile: nani: ile inaisha/

3. *bon*/ kiisha inaisha: pale inaisha: njo sasa munaona ba*notables de retour:* kwa chefu: banakuwa sasa pamoya *ensemble* na: bale banani: ba*villagois* sasa/ ni nani? kwa kwanza ule: kama ni Ntala Ngai: *tout ça:* eko *contre* ya . . . ? . . . eko anamiambiaambia ingine asema *bon:* unasikia ile maneno asema *bon*/ siye njo tulikuwa tunamuambia byote bile: *est-ce que* sultani ataweza kutosha byote mu kichwa yake? shee *ça:* lakini na hivi anafanya: shi tunamubeba: shi tunamubeba bintu tatu bule/ sasa yee anakwenda kufika na kusemasema kwa kuwa bulozi: kwa kuwa hivi na hivi: munaisha kuona pa mukini pasipo mulozi? mwee munaisha kuonapo mulozi/ mwee munaisha kuona pasema ku: ku tri[22]: *jugement* inyewe ya kizungu[23] asema banafungaka mulozi? hivi na hivi *tout ça*/ ah: anakwenda *contredire* na ile ba: sultani alisema/ tuko tunasikilizana pale?

Actress: mm/

4. *Mufwankolo:*   njo Tala Ngai: pale eko ana*contredire* vile/ aah: ni kweli: ah: basi: ah: hivi na hivi *tout ça:* tena bulozi: njo kukankamisha: yee pale sultani: hana na bulozi? si eko na bulozi? si eko na malawa hivi na hivi? *tout ça/ donc* ana*contre:* anafanya *contredire*/ *bon*/ pale bantu pale: banasikiasikia manani: bale: kunaisha/

5. *bon*/ sasa/ pale bantu banakuwa: bengine banakuwa ba*entêté:* bengine banakuwa namna gani: *tout ça:* si inakuwa sasa: habasikilizane mu namna ingine ingine/ *bon*/ hapa na hapa sasa: ile ma*lois:* njo banakwenda kubamba: *parce que* sultani haitangula kuse-

---

22. Mukwankolo begins to say *ku tribunal*, at the court, then changes.

23. *Kizungu* may be translated as "the world, the ways of the whites." But the term *muzungu* for white man or European is not a color term; North or South American blacks are *bazungu*. Nor is the principal meaning simply "foreigner" because, as in this instance, *kizungu* refers to the world of the city even one generation after independence. Therefore, possible translations of *kizungu*, depending on context, could also be "modern," or "urban." Yet another connotation of the term may be "a foreign accent" or a foreigner's way of speaking Swahili.

ma ile ma*lois*/ balibamba *voire: voire même* mwizi: ao wamakozi[24]/
munasikia? mwizi ao makozi/ anatokea/ banamubamba/ pam pa-
mpampam: namna gani: tuue banamuzika asema *non:* ile mambo:
tunafika kwa: paka kwa sultani/ njo *premier notable:* anakuya kwa
sultani/ kwa sultani/ sasa pale pa kuya sultani: hatakuya tena na:
na *officiellement* hapana/ atatoka ni ku nyumba: sasa batamufwata
ni ku nyumba yake kule/

6. *bon* batamu*annoncer:* anatoka inje: na ba*notables* banafika/ bantu
ya mukini tena ile saa: habanako/ ni paka ba*notables:* na ma*gardes
de corps* bake bale: beko kule/ na ule muntu mwenyewe balibamba/
bon/ banamuleta/ banamusambisha kwanza: weee tititi ku mecho
ya sultani: sasa beko naongoya sultani kwa ku*prendre décision* ya
mwisho/ *bon*/ kama anamu*punir:* itakuwa namna gani: anaacha/

7. *tout un coup:* tena banabamba muntu mwengine/ munasikia tena
makelele mu mukini? kunakuwa tena makelele kule mu mulemule
mu mukini/ wee njo uliona nani: waliloka mu nani: mu na: muntu:
nani? wee njo hivi na hivi? banafanya hivi na hivi: ni kweli njo
pale. . . .
Actor: mulozi sasa/
Mufwankolo: mulozi sasa eh/ banakubamba leo? si unaona sasa
leo banakubamba? eh: kumbe njo hivi na hivi/ shee tulikwenda
kulaguisha: tulikwenda kufanya vile vile: makelele pale: eh: sultani:
bamwetu humu: na *gardes:* nani: muna: muna*dire attention*/ hapa na
hapa: nani anasema eh fulani: pup: unabamba/ kipukip uu: nani
huyu? mutoto wa *premier notable*/ tikitik: . . . ? . . . *notable*/ tikitik:
kumuleta: pà/

8. sultani: ule mutoto tulikuwa tunatafutaka mu nani mu *chose*/
balimujendula: kumbe njo ule alijendulaka mutoto? mutoto tangu
aliendaka: tangu: itakuwa miaka bifulani: mwee mwenye . . ? . . ni
mambo ya mukini: baliisha kuiyuaka: balijendulaka mutoto basi ile
majende inapitayo: inafanikaka kila siku/ leo: tunavumbulayo/
sikiasikia yee mwenyewe mu kusema mu kinywa yake/ hivi na hivi:
tout ça: hivi/ kweli asema: eh . . . ? . . . /

9. ahh *bon: bon: bon*/ sasa njo kusema weye sasa: mi sitaki kumuona
tena macho/ mwee mwenyewe kanuni: munaisha kusikiaka kanuni
vile balisemaka/ haina miye: haina nani: ni bankambo: ni kanuni ya
bankambo/ huyu muntu anapashwa kufanya namna gani? sitake:
ende mbele akasumbulie na bankambo/ kusema tu ile: asema aende

24. In Shaba Swahili *makoz(s)i* means "adulterer(ess)." The derivation is not clear;
it does not seem to be of Swahili origin.

mbele akasumbulie na bankambo: *notable* anakuwa *contre/* ah:
maneno hivi na hivi: *tout ça/* anaanza kusemasema sababu ya ule:
hakumusemeaka hapana/ sasa inakuwa sasa kwake yeye: inakuwa
nani/ . . . ? . . . fanyafanya pale wee: wee wee wee: kufika kule sasa:
si munakuwa ma: ma: mafitina mafitina *tout ça/*

10. *bon/* yee: sultani: ananawa mayi: sababu yee anaisha kusema/
anatafuta kintu kimoya: bantu basikilizane: baikale kimya: mu *tran-
quilité:* na mu *paix/ bon/* mu kwenda pale wee: banaenda/ kule ule
muntu vile anakuwa kufanya ile *scène* nayo: inapita paka vile/
bantu banayua tu asema: banakwenda kumu*punir* ule: bintu gani/

11. hapa na hapa: sultani: anabakia yee peke na: na bibi yake: na
mutoto yake ya *garde de corps:* njo sasa *scène* inafika: kuleta milambo wa nyama/ kweli anasema: anatuma *garde de corps* kwenda
kuita ba*notables:* ba*notables* banakuya: *bon:* anakuwa . . . ? . . . *voilà:*
eh: kakipande anaenda kukabula: banaenda kukabula . . . ? . . .
ba*notables* . . . ? . . . banaenda/ kiisha kwenda: sultani anabakia peke
lakini/

12. *bon/* njo kubatuma sasa ba*notables/* twiko wakati wa nani? wa
kulima/ munapashwa sasa kwenda: kufanya maa . . . ? . . : kazi ya
kulima/ mubaambie bantu yote: sawa vile tulibaambiaka wakati
hivi: sasa mwende mubaambie bantu yote/ *bon/* bale banakwenda
asema tunakwenda kubaambia bantu yote: si bantu yote ni kule
kubaambia: bo banaenda na ku mashamba: kimya/ *scène* ya sultani
inabakia: inaisha: sasa inabakiako *scène:* ya: ku mashamba/

13. kule ku mashamba munaenda: hakuna tena kulima: maimbo
munaimba tu *bien/* munaji*concentrer* mwee bote: asema munakwenda huyu wabibi: wanani: wajembe wanini: *tout ça* munakwenda
ku mashamba/ kufika kule ku mashamba: kule sasa: kwiko: wa
kwanza atafika kule: yeye anaikalaka paka kule ku mashamba/
mais anakuyaka mu mukini: paka kama mwiko *manifestation: quelle
manifestation/* kazi yake ni kuikala paka ku mukini/ kufika kule:
anakuwa sawa hivi bantu banakuya asema *bon:* anakutana na
pombe *déjà* kule/ pombe ile: tunaanza kunywa nitachagula ni
pombe gani: nitakunywa kule: paka ya kishenzi yetu paka kule . . .
Feza: munkoyo/ tutaenda kuuza mu *six/*

14. *Mufwankolo:* kule *déjà* anaanza kuba: kuba*servir* bale beko
kule/ lisulu[25] inaanza/ huyu anasema: ah shiye: ah . . . ? . . . ya

---

25. *Lisulu,* of uncertain derivation (French *souler?*), is current in Shaba Swahili for
the kind of talk and noise that go together with drinking. The verb is *kusulula.*

kulima: namna gani? maneno ya nini? hivi na hivi *tout ça* . . . ? . . .
sasa makelele kule/ njo sasa sultani anasikia asema *tiens?* ni mantu[26]
gani: mangoma gani iko inapigwa kule? asema oh mangoma iko
natoka ku mashamba/ iko natoka ku mashamba? kuko bintu gani?
allez/ wende kwanza ukaangarie/

15. kufika kule: eh: mweye/ balituma huku ku sultani hivi na hivi
tout ça na . . . ? . . . kuya kwanza mbele huku/ . . . ? . . . kumupa
lupanda kà: kuikala/ kihapa na hapa: kikwembe/ pà/ kwiko: kuto-
kea mama moya kumu: ku*entrainer* bote bale/ ni Feza/ Feza kazi
yako ni ku*entrainer* bale bantu/ kubabembelesha kabisa/ kama anakuya tu anakuya: aaah hivi na hivi: unamupoka na nani: unamupa
kwanza lupi[27]: unamuchezea kwanza: unapoka ile: ah kunywa
kwanza mbele: . . . ? . . . hata uko na wamambo/ wamambo hauku-
nywake/ ao wamambo hakulyake/ si tunasikia: si mbele uku-
nyweko mbele kiloko? yee mu kunywa kakakakaka/ si ukale
kwanza? mukuikala/ banaweka mwimbo: ah yee njo wa kwanza
sasa kucheza/ njo sasa banaanza kucheza: Feza yee ni kuchezesha
bote/ bale bote bale beko banakuya/
Feza: mm/

16. *Mufwankolo:*   nyi Shebele: nyi bale bote: bale beko nakuya kule
beko napaka kubachezesha kabisa/ munaweka malisulu: mansu-
nko[28] beko banafuta: banani beko banafanya nini: *tout: vraiment*
inakuwa tu *sensationnel* kule ku mashamba/ *naturel/*

17. *bon/* sasa: njo pale sasa: inamfumu: anakuya/ *mais:* yee hatafika
karibu na mwee hapana/ ataangaria tu mbali: anaangaria asema:
aah: anarudia/ njo ku: sasa kuleta *rapport* kwa chefu/ sasa pale
chefu anapata ile *rapport:* njo chefu yee mwenyewe: anaanza kuya/

---

26. The form *mantu* (plural prefix *ma-* + *ntu*) is quite unusual; the regular plural
would be *bintu*. It exemplifies the kind of things a skillful speaker can do with prefixes.
The plural *ma-*, agreeing here with *ma-gnoma* and *ma-shamba* conveys the sense of an
unspecified multitude of things. *Ma-* prefixed to persons expresses an attitude of
contempt or disrespect: *mabibi*, for instance, means: a "heap" of women—or women
who can be imagined to be part of a heap, that is, worthless.

27. The meaning of *lupi* seems to be "a pat," or, possibly "a shove," according to
explanations I heard. The derivation is not clear. One possibility is that it combines the
Luba prefix *lu-* (connoting something big) and the Swahili interrogative particle *pi*
meaning "who? which one?" (see Lenselaer 1983: 413). In that case, *kumupa lupi* would
mean to give a person a big shove while calling "what about you?"

28. *Nsunko*, of Bemba or Luba origin (Van Avermaet and Mbuya: 1954: 653),
means snuff. To inspire it through the nose is called *kufuta* (ECS *kuvuta*), the same term
as for smoking tobacco; to apply it to the gums is *kubuya*. Chewing (*kutafuna*) is
apparently not associated with tobacco.

Shebele mu kuona vile asema: eh: chefu anakuya: anafichama/ muli*faufiler*/ kiisha kufichama: *bon:* njo chefu anakuya: anakamata sasa maelezo ingine: sasa mupya/
Actress: autorité/

18. *Mufwankolo: autorité* sasa/ njo sasa *autorité* ya chefu: inaingia ile wakati: na vile anasema: mwee *desormais:* mwee bote banani: ba*notables:* muko munatoka sasa: kuacha bu*notable* bwenu/ nita*remplacer* ba*notables* bengine: na: ule tena muntu nitaona namna gani? yote: nitafanya hivi: na bubaya: anasema tu yote na: yote kabisa kabisa sawa vile alito: mu nani yake: mu tumbo[29] yake wa kwanza: bantu yote kimya mu mukini pà: banarudia banaanza ku: kutengeneza makazi yabo: na bokaboka[30] na muzuri: nini: michezo yote hivi *tout ça*/

19. *bon*/ sasa: sasa chefu: anakuya tena mara ingine ya pili/ kuba-ambia yote na kubaambia asema *voilà:* kuwa*présenter: dévant la population: que* haba bote: tena leo: kazi yabo: inaisha/ banatoka na kutoka mu *scène:* anabaambia asema: mwee bote sasa mubakie hivi na hivi na hivi: kesho nita*remplacer* ba*notables* bengine bale tuta-tumika nabo kazi muzuri ya kuendesha: inchi yetu muzuri: kuende-sha mukini yetu muzuri/ munasikia: hivi na hivi/ kunaisha: njo *fin*/ ile kesho: inabakia paka kesho/

Power Is Eaten Whole: **Mufwankolo's Version (Translation)**

[The recording picks up Mufwankolo's directions at the point when the actors leave scene 1]

1. *Mufwankolo:*   . . . they go on filing out. After that there begins talk among the chief's people, the villagers: Say, did you hear the way the chief talked. Oh well, the chief went too far, he got into all sorts of things, what not . . .
Actor: And they discuss.
Mufwankolo: And then those people discuss.
Bwana Cheko: . . . there in the population, they are taking aim: criticism begins.

2. *Mufwankolo:*   Now criticism starts. The people say: Ah, the way he talked. Fine, work in the fields, [we accept that] but all the other

---

29. *Kusema ya mu tumbo* (literally: to speak what is in the belly), is a current expression for "to speak one's mind, to say what one has been wanting to say for some time."

30. From *woga*, in Shaba Swahili often pronounced *boga* or *boka*, fear.

things . . . So, some are for, some against [the chief], criticism comes up in this place, they keep talking and talking and that is the end of that.

3. All right, when this ends you see that the *notables* are back at the chief's place. They are now together with the villagers. Who will it be, the first one? Maybe Tala Ngai, he is against and he talks to you [the villagers] at length: You hear this? We [the *notables*] are the ones who told [him] all this. You think the chief can pull everything out of his head? We told him, we made the laws, and so on, now [look] what he did. We only brought up three points. Now he gets into sorcery and goes rambling on, this and that; you ever see a village where there was no sorcery? Did you ever hear of a sentence in a court in town where they put a sorcerer in jail? And so on, and so on. So he begins to contradict what the chief said. Do we understand each other so far?
Actress: Yes.

4. *Mufwankolo:*   So this is how Tala Ngai is going to contradict [the chief]: Sure, but . . . and so on. And then about sorcery, that really fixes it. The chief, over there in his place, is he not involved with sorcery? Doesn't he have sorcery? Doesn't he have magic charms, and so forth and so on. So he speaks against [the chief]. All right. Then the people keep listening to them [the *notables*] and that is the end.

5. All right, now the people are in all sorts of states, some are pig-headed, others are—what do I know? So what we have now is that there is no more mutual understanding among the people, also in other matters. All right, now they are going to apply the laws and arrest [offenders] because the chief will not give up pronouncing these laws. So they picked up either a thief or an adulterer. You understand? A thief or an adulterer, he is discovered, they pick him up, they beat him; let's kill him, they say, and then bury him. But no—this is a matter we must bring before the chief. So the first *notable* comes to the chief. However when he comes to the chief this is not official. He will go directly from his house to the chief's and the others [the plaintiffs] will follow him there.

6. All right. They announce the [chief], he comes outside and the *notables* arrive. At that moment the villagers are not yet there, just the *notables* and the bodyguards, and the person they arrested. All right, they bring him and they accuse him at length while the chief watches. Now they wait for the chief to take the final decision. All right, whether he punishes him, or whatever, he finishes [the case].

7. Suddenly, they pick up another person. You hear the noise in the village? There is again noise right in the middle of the village: Did you see what's his name, they put a spell on whoever, and so on and so on, really then . . .

Actor: Now it's the sorcerer.

Mufwankolo: Yes, now it's the sorcerer. Did they pick you up to-day? You see, today they [finally] picked you up? So [they say] this and that, we went to the diviner, we went to do this and that, there is an uproar. Chief [they say] you must tell the guards to watch things here in our village. [You must look] here and there [and listen] who said this. [When you know] it was such and such, you make the arrest. Who is this? The son of the first *notable*. You beat him and drag him [to the chief]: here he is.[31]

8. Chief, we were looking for this young man—wherever he was. They put a spell on him.[32] [Now we think] this is the one who put the spell on the young man. Ever since he left, ever since, who knows which year, you who . . . ? . . . those are affairs of the village they knew about: They bewitched the young man, there are too many magic spells and [this sort of thing] happens every day. Today, we found it out. Just listen to him tell it in his own voice, and so on and so on. Truly, he says . . .

9. Ah: all right then, all right then. Now, I don't want to see you anymore. You have heard long ago the rule that was pronounced. It is not me, or whoever, it is the ancestors; it's the law of the ancestors. What must this person do? I don't want [to have anything to do with it], he may go and talk with the ancestors. As soon as [the chief] says this—that he should go and talk with the ancestors—the *notable*

31. The preceding passage is an example for problems of translation that arise when the speaker, as it were, switches from discourse to verbal gestures. The many brackets used show how much of such a translation is really reconstruction. The translator can do little more than recreate the images and ideas that the speaker had in his head and tried to evoke (but did not really describe) for his listeners.

32. In the original the verb *kujendula* poses a problem. ECS has the term *zindua*, with two connotations that are relevant here: "to remove something fixed firmly or set firmly," or "to set free from a spell, disenchant." Both meanings express the "conversive" verb form whereby the verb *kuzinda*, to be firm, is converted into its opposite by inserting a *u* between the stem and the suffix. However, in this text, *kujendula*, almost certainly a cognate of *kuzindua*, must be translated as "to put a spell [on a person]." This is how it works: *kujendula*, with the help of *majende*, magic charms employed for this purpose, is considered a specialty of the "Kabinda" (Songye) and refers to the act of removing a person or thing from its visible form (and, in that sense, changing the form). A person under that spell may look his usual self but he has in fact been transported elsewhere with the aim of making him do some work or otherwise serve the sorcerer's purposes.

opposes [the chief]. Ah, he says, it's because of this and that, and he begins to talk a lot because [the ancestor] did not speak for [the accused].[33] So now he is what? And [the palaver] goes on and on to the point where there is discord and all that.

10. All right. He, the chief, washes his hands because he has given his verdict. He wants one thing only, that the people get along with each other and live in calm and peace. All right. After having gone through this they leave. This is how the scene with this person goes. The people know that he will be punished, whatever.

11. Now the chief remains alone with his wife and the young man who is his bodyguard, and now comes the scene where the tribute of game is brought. Truly, he speaks and sends his bodyguard to go and call the *notables*. The *notables* come: *voilà* they give a small piece to each of them and the *notables* go away. After they have left, the chief, however, stays alone.

12. All right. Now comes the moment when he sends out the *notables*. We are in the season of cultivating the fields. You must go and do the work of cultivating. Tell all the people about it, as we told them earlier, now go and tell all the people. All right. So they go and say we will tell all the people and this is what they do. The people go to the fields, and there is calm. With that the scene with the chief ends. There remains now the scene in the fields.

13. When you get to the fields, there is no working but good singing. You will concentrate, all of you. You'll go to the fields, the women, people with hoes, all that sort of thing. When you get to the fields there, now the first to get there just stays in the fields. He is supposed to go back to the village only in case there is some kind of unrest. The order he has is to stay in the fields.[34] When he arrives there [in the fields] he already finds the people drinking beer over there. That beer, the one we are going to drink, what kind of beer am I going to choose for drinking? Our native beer, [we will find it] there . . .

Actress: Munkoyo [maize beer]. We are going to buy it in the market.[35]

---

33. It is implied here that the *notable* went along with the accused when the latter "talked" to the ancestors. "Talking to the ancestors" refers to divination and other ritual means (such as applying *pemba*, white clay, kaolin) apt to set things right, to lift the spell and to accept punishment if necessary.

34. The original text has *mukini*, the village, but this is obviously a mistake: it should be *mashamba*, the fields.

35. The original has *six*, referring to *quartier six*, a subdivision of a township where native beer is sold.

14. *Mufwankolo:*   There she already begins to serve the people who
are there. General merriment begins. There is one who says, ah we,
about working the field, how is this? What for? And so on. . . . So
there is noise there. Now the chief hears this and says, what is this,
what crowd of people, what are the drums that are beaten over
there? [Someone says] Oh, the drums, that comes from the fields. It
comes from the fields? What is going on over there? Go and look.

15. When he [the person who was sent] gets there [he is greeted]:
Eh, you, did the chief send you, and so on and so on . . . . . come here
already. They give him [?] something to sit on, he sits down. Then
they tie a cloth around his waist.[36] There will be one woman who is
going to lead all the others. That is Feza. Feza, your work is to incite
those people, really seduce them. When someone comes you receive
him [and start talking to him], you make him dance, you tell him,
have a drink first, [don't worry] about your people who have a case
pending. People who have a court case, don't they drink and eat?
We understand. Don't you first want to drink a little? He drinks and
drinks . . . Won't you sit down? He is already sitting down. Then
they begin the singing and he is the first one to get up and dance.
Now they begin the dancing. Feza is going to make all of them
dance, all those who come [from the village].
Feza: Yes.

16. *Mufwankolo:*   You Shebele, and you all the others, all those
who come, she will really get them dancing. You begin having a
great time, some take snuff, others do whatever they do. Really, it is
going to be sensational there in the fields, really natural.

17. All right. Now the chief's wife comes. But she is not going to get
close to you. She will just watch from a distance. She will say, so
that is it, and then she returns. Then she reports to the chief. When
the chief has heard her report he himself goes and approaches [the
scene]. Shebele sees this: Eh, the chief is coming. He hides. [By the
time he arrives] you have crept away. All right, after that the chief
arrives and now he makes another speech, a new one.
Actress: [about] Authority.[37]

18. *Mufwankolo:*   Now it is authority. Now the chief's authority
comes into the play. So he says, from now on, all of you *notables*,
you leave now and give up your rank. I will replace you with other

36. This refers to girding a dancer, especially the one who is supposed to lead, a
custom kept alive in urban Shaba.
37. The original uses the French term *autorité*, echoing the discussions reported in
chapter 4 about the problems of translating "power."

notables. And if I ever see a person who is evil, this is what I am going to do; all this he says once again very clearly everything he had on his mind from the beginning. The villagers are quiet, they go back and see to their work, some out of fear, others for good reasons, others dance [with joy], and all that.

19. All right. Now the chief appears one more time to tell them everything and to announce before the population: all those *[notables]*, today their work is finished. They go away and as he is about to leave the scene he tells them: You all stay such and such, tomorrow I am going to appoint other *notables.* With them I am going to work together well so that we bring progress to our country, progress to our village. You understand? And so on and so on. And that is the end. This is for tomorrow['s rehearsal].

So much for working out the scenario. Although both Bwana Cheko's and Mufwankolo's versions are delivered as monologues, they are in fact dialogical: the other actors present are addressed, occasionally they respond or intervene. As the scenario is expounded the distribution of parts begins.

The Players

To compile a list of characters and players would seem to be a straightforward task. That it is in fact quite difficult has the following reasons. There had been changes in the membership of the group. In the seventies I had time enough to get acquainted with almost every actor and actress;[38] in 1986 time was too short to remember all the names and, in some cases, to put names and faces together. Although the plot, by the time it was discussed in the group, prescribed most parts, the list of characters was not definitive until the final performance (and even then, as we shall see, there were last-minute impromptu additions).[39] Most confusing was the casting of the principal parts (other than the chief and his court); during the rehearsal process actors and actresses walked, as it were, in and out of characters. Often this happened too fast for me to note down. Occasionally, therefore, a voice in a recorded piece of dialogue can only be designated as "actor" or "actress." Add to this some minor complications, such as the fact that neither most names nor

38. For a list of principal members of the troupe at that time and a series of biographic interviews see Schicho 1981: 21–115.
39. The theoretical implications of such a fluent conception of plot and casting were alluded to in chapter 4 and are discussed in some detail in chapter 14.

pronominal references are gender-specific and that there was some switching from stage to real names, or from one stage name to another, and it becomes clear that a definitive list of characters cannot be established.

Fortunately we have a point of departure in a document that gives the group's members in 1986 by stage name (with the exception of the "president").[40] With the help of Tala Ngai, who acted as the principal director in the production of *Le pouvoir se mange entier*, I was able to add gender and real names. Here is the result:

Stage Name	Name	Gender
Kachelewa	Wazenga Linga	m
Mufwankolo	Lyembe Kaswili	m
Bwana Cheko	Mbuyu Darabo	m
Tala Ngai	Kabeya Mutumba	m
Malisawa	Bumba Ilunga	m
Shebele	Kandayi Mabisi	m
Amunaso	Ilunga Kalongo	f
Mashimango	Muteba wa Mweba	m
Sondashi/Kalwasha	Mawej'a Kabwiz'	m
Salima	Muyumba Mauwa	f
Kamwanya	Ilunga Kasongo	f
Manyeke	Ndala Tshisola	m
Feza	Mukadi Binene	f
Sinanduku	Kabedi Kasongo	f
Mukosayi	Tshibanda Kamishi	m
Katolushi	Kayembe Mboyi	m
Sakina	Nshima Kitumbika	f

(continued on following page)

40. This is a mimeographed form. Under the troupe's letterhead it is titled LISTE DE PRESENCE DU MOIS DE . . . . 19 . ., and has the following entries: NOMS:, JOUR:, DATE:, POINTAGE:, PARAPHE DE L'INT.[ERESSE]:, REMARQUES:. On the bottom it has VISA DU PRESIDENT and a list of abbreviations called NOTATION with the following categories: "P = présent, A = Absent, E = Empêché ou Excusé, D = Déserteur ou Démissionnaire, C = En Congé, R = Retard, O = Remarques divers." Obviously this document is inspired by bureaucratic lists of presence as they are kept in offices and other work places. The copy I have was not actually used (and it is quite possible that it rarely ever is). It signals the troupe's efforts to set up some kind of formal organization, which, as far as I can tell, did not get beyond assigning offices such as president (Kachelewa), vice-president (Mufwankolo), and secretary (Bwana Cheko). Nevertheless, the listing itself is interesting. Up to a point it reflects a hierarchy within the group. This has something to do with gender and seniority (most of the females and the youngsters are listed in the second half). That some actors who belonged to the core in the seventies now occupy a low position may indicate that they are frequently absent or considered "deserters" (an example of this being Kalulu).

Stage Name	Name	Gender
Muke/Coco	Banza Mulombo	m
Kalulu	Mbambu Katuba	m
Loko	Kamuikete Sowoya	m
Foloko	Kisiamba Mayoyo	m
Shambuyi	Kamba Munsense	m
Shindano	Shebele Kabumba Mato	m
Sikuzani	Katoka Kayembe	f
Zaina	Mutwale Bileo	f
Kato	Mukwapa	m

Not all of the actors on this list participated in the events described in this study. Those who did, and their parts during rehearsal and the final performance, can be summarily indicated as follows:

Name	Part in Rehearsal	Part in Final Performance
	The Chief and His Court	
Mufwankolo	chief	same
Amunaso	?	chief's wife
Salima	chief's wife	—
Bwana Cheko	*notable*	same
Tala Ngai	*notable*	same
Masimango	*notable*	same
Shebele	guard	same
Mukosayi	?	guard
Shambui	?	guard
	The Case of the Thief	
Feza	plaintiff	same
Manyeke	accused	same
Kamwanya	second woman, witness	—
	The Hunter's Visit	
Kalwasha	hunter	same
	The Case of Adultery	
Foloko	cheated husband	—
Kamwanya	accused wife	same
Katolushi	adulterer	same
Feza	second woman	—
Kalwasha	—	cheated husband

(continued on following page)

Name	Part in Rehearsal	Part in Final Performance
Villagers: Contesting the Chief		
Feza	woman	same
Kamwanya	woman	same
Sinanduku	?	woman
Malisawa	man	same
Foloko	man, drummer	same
Kato	man, drummer	same
Muke	?	boy
Loko	man	man

Some general information on the social background of members of the troupe was given in chapter 3. More could be added based on my own notes and the texts provided by Schicho and Ndala (1981). I first considered including a biographic sketch on each of the actors. In the end, I decided against this. What I know about them was obtained indirectly through Mufwankolo or directly in private conversation. What I found out is interesting but, given the small number of persons involved, sociologically hardly relevant. Still, a few generalities may be helpful.

Bwana Cheko, the oldest as far as I know, was around sixty; the youngest, Coco, about thirteen. Mufwankolo and a few of the men were in their late forties to early fifties; the rest, including all the women, were in their twenties and thirties. Except for the young boys and some of the women all are married and have children. Kachelewa is socially and economically best off; his standing, in fact, no longer permits him to act. Three or four of the actors work under him in the company he manages. Bwana Cheko, Tala Ngai, and Malisawa seemed the most educated and have office jobs, so do some of the women (Feza, for instance, works in the laboratory of a tobacco company). Mufwankolo and one or two others are employees of Radio Zaire. I doubt that it would make sense to the troupe to be classified as either amateur or professional actors. Some of them have been acting for decades and have achieved fame locally and beyond. None of them has profited economically or, as far as one can tell, socially. Mufwankolo is treated with affection and respect even by persons in power; he still lives in a miserable little house in a crowded township, twelve kilometers from the center of town. Things are different for some of the young women, a category in which the troupe has had the highest turnover. As Mufwankolo reminded them in one of his moralizing speeches, many a former actress now has a desirable husband or career because of the fame she acquired when she played with the troupe.

Upon reflection, it seems likely that being socially nondescript, and therefore politically and economically not exposed, is an advantage for actors who need to portray stock characters in radio sketches and occasional dramatic plays, which are appreciated as running commentary on the vicissitudes of daily life. Being part of *la population* gives them and their creations credibility.

7

Scene 1: The Law of the Land

Scene 1 was adumbrated in Bwana Cheko's typed *conducteur:* "The drum, accompanied by a song,[1] announces the beginning of the play. The chief appears in full regalia, accompanied by the queen. The *notables* and villagers assemble in the chief's court. A folkloric dance to the rhythm of the drum is performed before the chief. The chief rises and speaks . . ."[2] Significantly, this opening was not part of his second *conducteur* in Swahili, which has the piece start with the first of the court cases. The reason why it could be omitted or remain implicit is perhaps that scene 1 does not yet belong to the action. It serves to formulate the premises of the play. Elements described by Bwana Cheko himself as "folkloric" (drumming, song, the chief's procession) frame the scene. In the June 26 rehearsal, to which we now turn, an opening song is intoned by Bwana Cheko, without prior announcement or discussion, and taken up immediately by the group. It is a kind of praise chant to the chief Mufwankolo and his entourage. At the same time it introduces the troupe; the actors' names are called out between repetitions of the refrain. Here is a fragment from the first version recorded during rehearsal:

Introductory Song: Rehearsal Version (Text 3)

Muite muite:	Call, call
Mufwankolo wa mitenga	Mufwankolo and his 'plumes'
eyee: muite:	eyee, call
Mufwankolo wa mitenga/	Mufwankolo and his plumes.

[repeated three times]

---

1. This is no slip. The drum leads; singing (and dancing) is accompaniment.
2. See chapter 4, p. 71, and Appendix, p. 291.

Salima: Kamwanya:	Salima,[3] Kamwanya,
Mufwankolo wa mitenga	Mufwankolo and his plumes
eyee: muite	eyee, call
Mufwankolo wa mitenga/	Mufwankolo and his plumes.
Sondashi: Tala Ngai:	Sondashi, Tala Ngai,
Mufwankolo wa mitenga	Mufwankolo and his plumes.
	[etc.]

In actual performance, the song will go on, as Mufwankolo puts it, until it is just right.[4] Now the singing stops after a few more verses and Bwana Cheko backs up one more time to give directions for the scene.

Last Directions (Text 4)

1. *Bwana Cheko: bon/* ile wakati: she bale ba kuimba: tuko tunaitikia: lakini: beko napika ngoma: eh: batasikia paka masauti/ na bale ba*batteurs de cuivre/ directement* banaona: Mufwankolo anatoka/ si beko namuita? atokee/ njo banaona: Mufwankolo sasa mu nani: mu nyumba yake/ mu nyumba pale: na *reine* wake *à côté:* muko munanifwata huku?
Actors: tuko tunakufwata/

2. *Bwana Cheko:* kiisha banaona: Mufwankolo . . .
Kachelewa: pardon kule . . . ba*notables* iko hapa?
Bwana Cheko: tuko hapa/ sasa mi niko na *cravate* mushingo/
Kachelewa: donc: wee: njo *premier des notables?*
Bwana Cheko: mi niko *premier notable/*
Kachelewa: bon/ deuxième notable/ weye [speaking to Tala Ngai]/ *troisième notable* iko nani?
Actor: Masimango/
Kachelewa: Masimango?
Bwana Cheko: eyo/
Kachelewa: bon/ déjà: tuiko naimba mimbo/ weye muko na*préparer déjà* fasi ya kuikala *chef/*
Bwana Cheko: chef/ voilà/
[Short passage skipped]

3. *Mufwankolo: . . . premier notable* na inamfumu: eeh . . .
Bwana Cheko: na bibi mwenyewe . . .

3. At this point the leader of the song begins to recite the names of the cast (see chapter 6 for a list).
4. The expression he uses is *inakolea*, from *kukolea*, to be properly seasoned, have a flavor. Later, the verb is also used in its causative form, *kukolesha wimbo*, make the song sound really good.

Mufwankolo: na bibi mwenyewe . . .
Bwana Cheko: na sultani . . .
Mufwankolo: na sultani mwenyewe/ sasa mimbo inakolea/ pale
mutaona: inamfumu anatoka: wa kwanza: grrrr: bikelekele: binapi-
kiwa sasa/ kusema sasa: busultani: anakuya/
Bwana Cheko: anatafuta kutoka/
Mufwankolo: anatafuta kutoka/ hapa na hapa: njo kule banatoka
sasa banakuya/

4. *Bwana Cheko:*   saa ile bale bantu bote baliisha kuya: banaikala
mpembeni . . .
Mufwankolo: banaikala mpembeni/
Bwana Cheko: banani? ba*notables* bale mbili: eh?
Mufwankolo: eeh/
Bwana Cheko: weye na yeye: muko pale mbele yabo/ bale bantu
bote banani*entrer* kule ku mukongo: kunakuwa sawa nani:
muvringo/
Mufwankolo: eeh/ nakuita pale/ sasa pale: sasa kutoka na nkundi
kabisa kabisa: bikelekele na nini: kabisa: mu ma: wee munene kabisa: pale kiii/ na vile sultani: anafika mu kiti: *premier notable* ana-
mukalisha/ karibu/ na yee anaikala/ kiisha munakolesha mimbo/

5. kiisha kolesha mimbo: kimya inakatika: njo sasa bote: mwee
ba*notables:* munafukama[5]: munamulamukia: kiisha na bantu yote:
banafika sasa: banamulamukia sasa: napika tu mamna moya [claps
his hand] twakwimuna vidyee mfumu[6]/ eh? banapika mikono:
kwaa kwaa kwakwakwa/ musultani ana*répondre: salut* yabo/

6. kiisha: eeh: *premier notable:* analeta *parole* sawasawa vile kama
ra: nani: *rapport/* anamupatia *rapport* weee: muzuri/ ile: kubakia
rapport: bintu biko: ba: ba: bamukini beko na: banatumika: beko
banabilia: *tout ça* hivi na hivi na hivi/

7. kiisha: njo sultani nayee ana*prendre parole* sasa: kwanza kubaelezea bantu ya mukini/ kiisha kubaelezea ile weee: *après:* [claps his
hands]: njo sasa bantu ya mukini: banaanza kwenda: na anawa-
ambia na anawa*confier* nawa*confier* asema *voilà:* minawa*confier*

---

5. *Kufukama* comes from Luba (see Van Avermaet and Mbuya 1954: 161, where
the meaning is given as "to kneel"). It refers to the proper way of greeting a chief: eyes
cast down, back and knees bent, while clapping one's hands. The latter is called
kupopwela (ibid., 536), which is distinguished in Shaba Swahili from clapping hands as
a sign of applause (*kupiga mikono*).
6. The verb *twakwimuna*, first person plural, is probably of Tshiluba or Songye
origin and means "we greet you." *Vidyee* is a honorific term for the chief. The phrase is
a case of code switching to be commented on later.

ba*notables* bangu haba: kila mara: bataenda kuni*aider:* ku ma*paroles* itaanza kutoka kwangu: na matata yote itaanza ku: ya mukini: bataenda kunielezea: ma*messages* yote bataenda kui*passer* ma*messages/ alors* mu ile ndani mule mabunga mule: njo mutaanza kunyungulula mabunga/

8. *Masimango: pardon vice-président: est-ce que* pale penyewe mutatoka: mutatoka/ *normalement:* tukifwata *coutume:* tunapashwa kuikala chini/
Mufwankolo: bien sur: ni chini/ ile ni chini/ hamuna mu biti hapana/ ni chini/
Tala Ngai: njo kusema minawaza: ni mu *français/* tupite *directement/* ku *action . . .*
Bwana Cheko: . . . voilà: . . . na ma*explications* eh?

Last Directions (Translation)

1. *Bwana Cheko:*   All right. At that moment we who are singing follow, but the drummers will listen to the voices of the *batteurs de cuivre.*[7] Right after that they see Mufwankolo appearing—haven't they been calling him to appear? So now they see Mufwankolo appearing from inside his house there, together with his queen at his side—you follow me?
Actors: We follow you.

2. *Bwana Cheko:*   Then they see Mufwankolo . . .
Kachelewa: Excuse me, let me interrupt here: are the *notables* present?
Bwana Cheko: We are here. [I am] ready, with a tie around my neck.[8]
Kachelewa: So you are the first of the *notables?*
Bwana Cheko: I am the first *notable.*
Kachelewa: All right. [addressing an actor] You are the second *notable.* Who is the third *notable.*
Actor: Masimango.
Kachelewa: Masimango?
Bwana Cheko: Yes.
Kachelewa: All right. Meanwhile we are already singing and you are getting the place ready where the chief will sit down.
Bwana Cheko: The chief, that's right.

---

7. This refers to the famous *Chanteurs de la croix de cuivre,* a choir lead by Father Anschaire Lamoral (see chapter 3). This song comes from their repertoire.
8. Meaning: All dressed up. A witty but somewhat obsolete expression, since neckties are prohibited in Zaire as "antirevolutionary."

[Mufwankolo now gives detailed directions on where to place the chairs, where the *notables* will sit, where the chief's guards stand, etc.]

3. *Mufwankolo:*   . . . the first *notable* and *inamfumu* . . .
Bwana Cheko: the wife herself . . .
Mufwankolo: . . . the wife herself . . .
Bwana Cheko: . . . and the chief . . .
Mufwankolo: And the chief himself. Now the singing gets really going. Then you'll see *inamfumu* appearing first. Grrrrrr, now they are uttering shrill, piercing cries of joy.[9] That means that the chief comes . . .
Bwana Cheko: . . . that he is about to appear . . .
Mufwankolo: . . . that he is about to appear. That is the moment when they appear and come forth.

4. *Bwana Cheko:*   By that time all the people have arrived, they stay on the side . . .
Mufwankolo: . . . they stay on the side.
Bwana Cheko: Who now? The two [other] *notables*, right?
Mufwankolo: Right.
Bwana Cheko: You and he, you are in front of them. All those people, I want to have them enter there [from] behind, they form a kind of circle.
Mufwankolo: Right. Then I call you. That is the moment when the crowd really comes forth, cries of joy are shouted, loud and long, *kiii*. And so the chief arrives at his chair and the first *notable* helps him to get seated: Sit down please. And he sits down. You see to it that the singing really gets going.

5. After the singing gets louder it stops and there is silence. Now all of you *notables* bow and greet him [the chief]. Then all the people approach and greet him. You clap your hands once and you call: greetings to you, chief. Right? They clap their hands [indicating the rhythm]: kwaa kwaa kwakwakwa. The chief responds: Greetings to them.

6. Then the first *notable* speaks, he sort of makes a report. He gives [the chief] his report, on and on, whatever goes into that report, [how] the people in the village are doing their work, [what] they are asking for. All this goes on for a while.

---

9. A clumsy paraphrase for the expression *kupiga bikelekele*. This is a piercing, trilling sound produced (by women only) by crying in a high voice, with the mouth closed, while rapidly touching, or rubbing, the lips with the right hand (the side of the index touching the lips). From now it will be indicated by "ululation" or "ululating."

7. Then the chief takes the floor and he begins to instruct the people of the village. He does this for a while. Then [claps his hands once] they [i.e., the chief] go on to instruct the villagers and to tell them: I put my trust into my *notables* here. Always they are going to help me. When I have something to tell [the villagers] or when there is some trouble in the village, the *notables* will inform me and they will pass on all the messages. Your task will be to keep an eye on what is important in all those matters.[10]

8. *Masimango:* Excuse me, vice president [Mufwankolo], when you make your appearance, normally, that is, if we follow custom, must we not sit on the ground?
Mufwankolo: Of course, on the ground. That's on the ground, you are not seated in chairs but on the ground.
Tala Ngai: That is to say—in French[11]: Let us now directly go into action . . .
Bwana Cheko: . . . exactly, with the explanations [to be given by the first *notable*], right?

This is the moment at which the play, as it were, erupts from talk about it. Tala Ngai intones the opening song: *Muite muite . . .* More chairs have been found to substitute for drums and the singing definitely has more "spice" than during the first try. Also, in this version, more of the lyrics are partly in a local language, perhaps in order to make it more "authentic."
When the song ends chief and *notables* exchange ceremonial greetings. Bwana Cheko, as the first *notable*, addresses the villagers.

Announcing the Chief: Rehearsal Version (Text 5)

Bwana Cheko: Wamama: wababa: kule kwenu wote/ mambo yote munaelezeaka ba*notables:* ni kweli: mambo yote: banotables yenu: haba munaona hapa: banaifikishaka mu mikono ya sultani/ na ni kwa hivi/ siku ya leo: alikamata mipango: ya kusema anatafuta kuzungumuza na *peuple* yake/ na ile mipango: mutayua: ni juu ya ile mambo yote munaonaka/ ile yenye kupita mu mukini/ hapa sasa: hatuna na mingi ya kuweza kusema: tusikilize sisi wote na utaratibu: na heshima kubwa: sauti ya sultani wetu/

10. The image used in the original is that of sifting a lot of flour, *kunyungulula mabunga.*
11. Here the speaker himself announces a code switch. The reason may be emphasis (as in this case); sometimes it is meant apologetically ("sorry, but I must say this in French . . .").

Announcing the Chief: Rehearsal Version (Translation)

Bwana Cheko: Mothers and fathers, all of you over there. You always tell your *notables* everything. Truly, your *notables*, the ones you see here, they see to it that everything gets into the hands of the chief. And it is because of this that, today, he conceived certain plans. That is to say, he wants to speak to his people. Those plans, as you'll know, concern all the things you see everyday, everything that happens in the village. Right now, we don't have much we could say, let us all of us listen in good order and with utmost politeness to the voice of our chief.

Then follows another song, very brief during this rehearsal, more elaborate in the performance. The chief rises to speak to his people. Monologues being as a rule easier to record and transcribe than other types of disocurse, both the rehearsal and the final performance yielded usable texts and both versions can be presented.

The Chief's Speech: Rehearsal Version (Text 6)

1. *Mufwankolo:*   Bamama: hamujambo yenu/
All: yambo sana/
Mufwankolo: bababa: hamujambo yenu/
Women: [ululating]
Mufwankolo: watoto wa mukini yote: hamujambo yenu/
All: yambo sana/
ni kweli: tokea: nilikuwa pa kichwa ya usultani ya mugini yetu hii: ni paka mweye hawa/ muliniweka hapa/ na busultani bwangu: ni juu yenu mweye/ sina na busultani: juu ya miti: hapana/ niko na busultani: juu ya mwee bantu/

2. hapa sasa/ natafuta kumiambia neno moya hii/ kazi munapa-shwa kufanya kabisa kabisa: kuwa maendeleo ya mugini yetu: na kwa mikalio muzuri ya wakaaji: na batoto bapate kuendelea vizuri: kintu ya kwanza: ni mulimo wa mashamba/ [ululating]

3. kitu ya mpili/ natafuta: mutoto: ule mwenye kuwa na miaka kumi na munane: haizuru mwanaume: haizuru mwanamuke: akuwe na yake nyumba/
[ululating]
maneno: kama mutoto wa miaka kumi na munane: eko analala mababa yake: eko analala makaka yake: eko analala madada yake: iko mubaya/ anapashwa na yeye: akuwe na yake nyumba/

4. kitu tena ingine ya tatu/ ule mutoto mwenye kuwa na ile miaka kumi na mbili: eh: kumi na munane: na kumi na munane: watoto

mwanaume na mwanamuke: anapashwa nayee vile kuwa na yake
shamba/
[ululating]
lakini kwa kula: anaweza kula kwa mama yake: ao: kwa ndugu: ao
kwa kaka: ao kwa rafiki/

5. neno ingine ni hii/ tunapashwa kufwata kanuni: ya wankambo/
kanuni ya wankambo: na bizila byake/ sababu: njo kyenyewe:
kunatuletesha na sisi wa hawa: tufike hapa/ kwa siku ya leo/ inchi
yetu: nyini wamama/ mangaribi yua anafika pa miti: hakuna mwanamuke moya: wa kuweza kwenda kushota mayi ku mutoni/ tena:
hakuna mwanamuke wote: wa kuweza kutwanga/ bunga/ tena:
hakuna mwanamuke wote: wa kuweza kusemasema: mi paka bui-
ingie kabisa bushiku: njo nipige chakula/ yua kama munaona inakuwa mwekunda: bote beko nakula chakula/ panakuwa peusi: hata
uko na njala namna gani: hakuna namna ya kula/ njo vile bankambo: balikuwa banafanya/ na njo vile kanuni: inapashwa kuwa/

6. neno ingine/ mugeni atatu: anatufikia ku mukini: hapana
kumuangaria pa nsula/ muangarie mu ntumbo/ [ululations] sababu
ya nini? kama unamuangaria pa nsula: mugeni atalala na njala/
umutafutiaka tubui[12]: umupatie/ nayee ile saa: ataona namna gani:
nguvu: ya kukuambia: namna gani anakuya: na eko naenda wapi/

7. neno ingine/ mukini yetu humu: hakuna muntu yoyote wakuwe
na choyo/ furaha ya mukini ni nini? furaha ya mukini? minami-
achia: pumuziko: kila: wa muntu yoyote mwenye kuwa na namna:
ya kufanya kazi yake: ya chuuzi/ ama: kuwa na *boutique*: ama:
kuuzisha bitu fulani: anapashwa kuendelesha na ile kazi yake/
muntu yoyote: mwenye kuteka pombe yake ya kuuzisha: anapashwa kuuzisha: sababu ya nini? kwa sababu ya kupatamo kitu:
namna ya kuendelesha mukini/

8. mulozi/ na mwizi/ muko munasikia?
All: ndiyo/
njo banini? baadui/ mulozi: narudia tena bingine: na mwizi: njo
baadui ya mukini/
All: mm/
Mufwankolo: tutamuvumbula/ lungulungu: *kelulele*[13]/ tukamate

12. *Tubuyi* consists of the plural form of the diminutive prefix *ka-* and *buyi* (ECS
uji), a porridge or soup of cereals.
13. A formula of condemnation, in Luba (Kiluba or Tshiluba). The underlining
here (and in few other places) marks a characteristic feature of oral rhetoric: A speaker
frequently seeks and gets response from the audience in the form of completion of
words or sentences pronounced. This need not involve turn-taking as the speaker's

mwizi: tukamubamba hapa: lungulungu: *kelulele/* [ululation, Feza alone]
Tala Ngai: [to the other women] njo kazi yenu: mweye/ kama munachoka/

9. *Mufwankolo:*   mulozi: hata ni alikuwa mutoto wa nani? hata mutoto wa *notable/* hata mutoto yangu miye/ hata mutoto wa yee: wa mwee bote/ paka lungulungu: *kelulele/* [ululation]
Bwana Cheko: [about the women] murudisha pale bote baanze kuitikia namna moya/ bote baanze kuitikia namna moya: eh/ na ma*gestes* namna moya [he gives directions . . .]
Mufwankolo: Namiambia ya kama: mwetu mu mukini: tunachu-kia: mulozi na mwizi/ kama tunakamata mulozi: na mwizi: kazi yake paka: lungulungu: *kelulele/* [ululations] muko nasikia? sababu ile njo kanuni ya bankambo baliachaka/

10. tena bamama nunayua asema miye iko shimpundu[14]/ unasikia kwanza kiloko/ munayua: tunaheshimu manyumba/ na bamama nabo banaheshimu manyumba/ kuheshimu nyumba ni nini? kuyua paka ule wako/ hapana kutankatanka/ kutankatanka kuangaria ku milango ya benzako/ nasikia vile/ asema: aliingia kule/ wee una-fanya vile: kinyee unaachia kwako? ni nini? si ni kuiba?
All: ndiyo/
Mufwankolo: banakubamba/ unayua asema na wee uko malipishi yako/ kama hapana: kazi yako/

11. na: ya mwisho: kusikilizana/ kupendana/ haizuru nani: mutoto: mukubwa: nyi wote/ kutumika pamoya/ vile: inchi yetu: mukini yetu: inaweza kuendelea/ na sitaki mutu wa kuleta fujo mu inchi yetu/ njo kanuni nilikuwa nayo: na njo sauti: nawachia/ aksanti/ [ululations]

This is followed by a song as accompaniment for the departure of the chief.[15]

---

utterances are joined by the audience. Intonation, context, and semantic clues enable the audience to "speak along" even longer phrases. This device is commonly used in political and religious speeches; it can also occur in all sorts of narratives, and I have observed certain speakers who seem to use it habitually.

14. *S(h)impundu* is a father, *nampundu* a mother, of twins (probably from Bemba). The twins are *mampundu*. Other expressions used are *mama/baba wawili* (Swahili) and *mampasa* (? Ndembu) or *mwambuyi* (Luba).

15. In a letter of May 30, 1988, Bwana Cheko and Kachelewa render text and (French) translation as follows:

BAFYALA BANA EPO BALILA,
KIYONGO TEBATEBA,

The Chief's Speech: Rehearsal Version (Translation)

1. *Mufwankolo:*   Mothers, greetings to you.
All: Greetings indeed.
Mufwankolo: Fathers, greetings to you.
Women: [ululate]
Mufwankolo: All you children of the village, greetings to you.
All: Greetings indeed.
Mufwankolo: Truly, ever since I have headed our village as its chief, you have been the ones who put me here. And my chieftaincy comes from you. I don't hold the chief's office for the trees. I have the chieftaincy for you, the people.[16]

2. Now I want to speak to you about one thing, which is that you must work hard for the progress of our village and for the well-being of its inhabitants, so that the children make good progress: The first thing is cultivating the fields. [ululating]

3. The second thing: I want every young person eighteen years of age, be it man or woman, to have their own house. [ululating] Because, if a young person is eighteen and sleeps at his father's relatives, or at the older brothers' or sisters' place, this is bad. He [she] too must have a house of his [her] own.

4. Then there is another matter, the third one. This young person who has reached the age of twelve, sorry, eighteen, be they young men or young women, must also have his own field. [ululating] As far as eating goes, he can eat at his mother's, or at a relative's, at his older brother's, or at a friend's.

5. Another thing is this: We must follow the law of the ancestors. The law of the ancestors and its prohibitions. Because it is only this law which has taken us to where we are today. [In] our country—

NAMI NKAFYALE, NAMI NKALILE,
KIYONGO . . . (in Shaba Bemba)
Those who have children profit from them,
Let's sing and dance,
I, too, am going to have children and profit from them,
Let's sing and dance.

16. This is a proverbial expression current in Shaba Swahili (and beyond). Sense: In everything he does or orders done a chief must consider the consequences for the people. I am told that the saying was quoted to President Mobutu some years ago when he proposed draconic measures against theft and proposed to hang everyone convicted of stealing more than 10,000 Zaire. It was pointed out to him that he would have had to hang most of the population.

this regards you women—when in the afternoon the sun touches the trees, there will be no woman allowed to go and fetch water from the river. Furthermore, not one woman will be allowed to pound flour. And there will be no woman going around saying I am going to cook the food only when it is really dark. When you see that the sun turns red everyone has to have his meal. When it is dark, no matter how hungry you are, you must not eat. This is how the ancestors used to do it. And this is the law, this is how it must be.

6. Another matter: When a visitor comes to our village, don't look at his face, look at his belly. [ululations] Why? If you only look at his face, the visitor will go to sleep hungry. See to it that you find at least a little porridge for him. Then he will have the strength to tell you how he came and where he goes.

7. Another matter: Here in our village no one is stingy. What is the joy of the village? The joy of the village? I leave you in peace so that everyone can go after his work, be it trading, keeping a little store, or selling whatever. He must make progress with his work. Every person who puts his beer up for sale, should sell it. Why? So that he may produce something, which is a way of contributing to the progress of the village.

8. The sorcerer, and the thief. You listen?
All: Yes.
Mufwankolo: What are they? Enemies. The sorcerers—I come back to this once more—and the thief, they are the enemies of the village.
All: Mmm.
Mufwankolo: We are going to expose him, and he will be convicted: lungulungu . . . *kelulele* [he be damned].[17] [ululations] We'll pick up the thief, tie him up, and convict him right here: lungulungu . . . *kelulele* [he be damned]. [ululation, one actress alone]
Tala Ngai: [to the other actresses] That is your work, are you tired?[18]

9. *Mufwankolo:* A sorcerer—even if he is the child of whom?—of a *notable*, or even my own child, or the child of anyone among you. There is only one thing: lungulungu . . . *kelulele/*
Bwana Cheko: [addressing the women] Make them go back so that they all respond in the same way. All should begin to respond in the same way, the same gestures . . . [gives directions to actors playing the villagers]

17. On the underlining see note to text 6, 8.
18. Meaning: Come on, ululate.

Mufwankolo: I tell you, here in our village we hate the sorcerer and the thief. When we catch a sorcerer or a thief, his lot will be: lungulungu . . . *kelulele.* [ululations] Do you understand? Because this is the law the ancestors left.

10. Furthermore, you, mothers, you know that I am a father of twins.[19] First listen for a moment. You know, we respect the households. And the mothers, too, respect the households. What does this mean, respect the households? To know only your own [husband]. Don't go roaming! Don't go around looking in the doors of your neighbors. If I hear about such a thing, that [a woman] went in there; if you do this [I ask] why did you leave your home? What is it? Is it not stealing?
All: Yes [it is].
Mufwankolo: They catch you and you know that you will have to pay. If you can't, it's your problem.[20]

11. And now the last thing: Understand each other, love each other, no matter whether you are a child or an adult, all of you. Work together. In this way our country, our village, can make progress. And I don't want anyone to bring discord into our land. This is the law I had [to tell you about], and that is what I had to say. Now I leave you, thank you. [ululations]

In the rehearsal, there now follows a discussion on how to make the chief's departure properly spectacular. Kachelewa and Mufwankolo make suggestions, then Bwana Cheko summarizes and gives directions to the actors. They illustrate some of the differences between the rehearsal phase and actual performance, especially the kind of oscillating between discourse and acting that was discussed in chapter 5. It is useful, therefore, to include these passages in our reconstruction of the "text."

Directions for the Chief's Departure (Text 7)

The recording starts in the middle of a remark on the role of Tala Ngai:

1. *Bwana Cheko:*   eeh/ unaona: yee si *notable*/ eh? *normalement:* eko *chargé* wa *loisirs*/ juu ya ku*animer*/ ataanza/ yee mu kwanza tuko ingia: anatupa mwimbo analamuka anaingia: Feza anaitupa

---

19. This is a title of honor, giving the chief additional authority.
20. Meaning: you will be punished otherwise.

ndani/ banachola[21]/ nani: Sondashi: kule anatokea: huku banakuya: na banakuwa kukutania na nani?
Actor: na Kamwanya/

2. *Bwana Cheko:*   na Kamwanya/ bana: banacheza: banacheza:
banatokamo/ Sinanduku nayee kule: anayeyuka/ banakuwa kukutania na Loko/
Actor: na Loko/
Bwana Cheko: *bon*/ ngoma: *accompagnateur* eko pale/ uku nasikia?
mais entretemps tuko tunaimba/ njo banaingia mu: gani: bantu tatu:
kama ni bantu bengine: batakuya pale: kwa ku*accompagner* pale/

3. kiisha: saa ile: njo: *malheureusement* Salima hanapo: inamfumu:
kama inaisha: mwimbo inaisha: mutasikia tu kule nani: wa ku*enton-
ner* pale: ataipaila[22]: mwimbo inaisha: mwee bote munaikala chini/
mukikala chini: njo sultani sasa analamuka: inamfumu anasimama:
he? munayua asema ni *tour* sasa saa ya kwenda/ *bon:* mwee pale
munabakia: munaikala chini: eh: chefu nayee analamuka: banani:
kule bote ba *gardes de corps:* banani: kulamuka na ba: banani: pamoya tunakwenda/

4. saa ile na mweye: *entretemps* yee nani: eh: *chose:* Tala Ngai: eh?
ata*former* kamwimbo kingine kale ka: sasa shee tunakwenda na
puisque yee anabakia anaingia mu nyumba/ sasa mwee pale: moya
ya kuchomoka nayo: munasambala nayo mu mukini/ muko nasikia? pa ile fasi? si unasikia?
Actress: tunasikia/

5. *Bwana Cheko:*   kale kamwimbo ka mwisho kale/
Actress: kamwimbo iko anaimba: njo shee tunasambalana/
Bwana Cheko: eeh/ hata yee kama anafanya: akitafuta kulamuka
pale pa kumifansie hivi/ *mais* mwee munafanya mwimbo *en fondu*/
Actress: tuko tunaisha kuikala chini?
Bwana Cheko: munafanya mwimbo *en fondu*/ weee: yee anasimama: akianza kwenda na mwee munalamuka: munaanza kupiga
mikono: na kuimba mwimbo/ munaanza kuimba mwimbo na
kusambalana mule mu kamukini/

___

21. *Kuchola* (ECS *kuchora*) literally means "to carve, mark, inscribe." It evokes an
expression used in talk about soccer: *kuchola* then means "to dribble, to pass cleverly"—
what it takes to make of soccer a work of art. Extending this, it can also mean "to avoid
a person or side-step something." Here, *banachola* refers to an artful performance of the
song by several persons.
22. *Kuipaila*, probably of Bemba origin, is used, like *kuchola* (see preceding note),
in soccer language, where it designates a way of skillfully stopping the ball. In other
words, its meaning here is not just to end the song but to do it nicely.

Actress: moya moya: *ou bien?*
Bwana Cheko: si tutaanza kusambalana tu polepole/ . . .

Directions for the Chief's Departure (Translation)

1. *Bwana Cheko:*   All right. You see, he is not a *notable.* Right?
Normally he is in charge of entertainment, to enliven things. He will
begin. When he begins, we join in. He comes up with a song, rises
and gets into it, then Feza joins. Together they give shape to it.
Then—who is it?—Sondashi appears over there and they come up
and meet—with whom?
Actor: With Kamwanya.

2. *Bwana Cheko:*   With Kamwanya. They dance and dance, and
then they stop with it. Sinanduku over there, she is melting away.
Then they meet Loko.
Actor: And Loko.
Bwana Cheko: All right. The drum—the musician who
accompanies the singing—is over there. You understand? But
meanwhile we are already singing, then three or more people enter
and begin to accompany.

3. Then there is the moment—unfortunately Salima who plays the
chief's wife is not here—when this song comes to an end. You will
listen to the leader, the one who intones, directing you to finish
nicely, and when that song ends all of you sit down on the ground.
While you are sitting on the ground the chief gets up, his wife is
standing, right? Now you know it is his turn to leave. All right, you
stay there, you sit on the ground, the chief gets up and who else? All
the bodyguards and everyone get up and also who? [the *notables*]
We get up and leave also.

4. Then you—meanwhile what's his name, Tala Ngai, is going to
perform that other little song. Then we leave, because he stays and
goes into the house. Then you over there, [you sing a song] one to
leave with, and with that you disperse in the village. You understand? Is this part clear? You understand, don't you?
Actress: We understand.

5. *Bwana Cheko:*   When this last little song comes . . .
Actress: When he sings the little song we disperse/
Bwana Cheko: Right. When he is about to get up he should make
you [get up], but you keep singing the song *en fondu.*[23]
Actress: Are we sitting on the ground?

23. Meaning: you keep on humming the song as you leave.

Bwana Cheko: You keep singing *en fondu* for a while. Then he stands and when he is about to leave you get up, you begin to clap your hands and you sing the song. You begin to sing the song and disperse in the little village.
Actress: One by one, or?
Bwana Cheko: We'll just begin to disperse slowly . . .

In the final performance the play opens with the villagers and *notables* arriving on the scene.[24] The *notables* sit down on the ground. The drums are played and a young boy in a raffia skirt begins the dancing. He is joined by another boy and ky Kalwasha and Malisawa.[25] Then the song is changed. The lead singer intones *Muite, muite, Mufwankolo wa mitenga eeyo . . .*, Call, call Mufwankolo and his plumes . . . The *notables* rise as the chief arrives with his wife. Shebele, playing a guard, fans the chief while he is greeted by the *notables.* Then one of the boys dances before the chief, followed by a couple. Eventually, the singing stops with a greeting called out by Bwana Cheko and a response from actors and spectators. He pauses briefly, then announces the chief.

Announcing the Chief: Final Version (Text 8)

Bwana Cheko: Wamama: wababa: wandugu wote: hamujambo kwenu/
All: yambo sana/

24. As was agreed during rehearsals, actors had to look after their own costumes. Most just brought work clothes (Malisawa wore a mining-company hard hat). Only the chief and his court had costumes to speak of. The guards had somehow assembled pieces of clothing that looked like uniforms. Two of the *notables* wore the traditional wraps instead of trousers. The chief, his wife, and the *notables* wore headdresses made of cardboard. The patterns on these headdresses differed so as to correspond to rank.

25. This was during the live performance. In the television broadcast the opening was as follows:

A song (not identified) can be heard throughout the sequence of graphics and pictures.

Graphics: *Le groupe Mufwankolo de Télé-Zaire vous présente*
Image: A take of the village road leading up to the site of filming; the party of villagers from Kawama celebrating the birth of twins is shown dancing toward the camera.
Graphics: *Le POUVOIR se mange entier.*
Image: Another view of the street, a toddler dances, then the camera pans the villagers lining the street, sitting or standing.
Graphics: *Mise en scène*   KABEYA MUTUMBA
            Producteur Délégué   WAZENGA LINGA
Image: A take of an old man (the owner's father) sitting in front of the house that served as backdrop to the scenes at the chief's court.
Graphics: *Réalisation*   SHANGO ONOKOKO.

Bwana Cheko: hapa leo: sultani: eko na sauti ya kutafuta kuzungumuza na mweeye/ aksanti kwenu/ [applause, ululations]

Announcing the Chief: Final Version (Translation)

Bwana Cheko: Mothers, fathers, all you relatives, greetings to you.
All: Greetings indeed.
Bwana Cheko: Here, today, the chief wants to make his voice heard
and talk with you. Thank you.

Mufwankolo gets up and faces the villagers. He is in full costume:
An (imitation) chief's headdress, an old dress coat over a red ankle-
length wrap, an animal skin worn like an apron, a ceremonial hatchet
over his left shoulder, a fly whisk in his right hand, beads and medals
around his neck and on his chest.

The Chief's Speech: Final Version (Text 9)[26]

1. *Mufwankolo:*   Hamujambo yenu bababa na bamama wote na
watoto na watoto . . . [applause] . . . jambo yenu/
All[27]:   yambo sana/
Mufwankolo: ni kusema: siku ya leo: niko na mambo ya kuwa-
elezea[28]/ mambo yenyewe ni hii/ ya kwanza/ ku mukini yangu hii:
minapenda watu kuwa na kazi ya kulima mashamba/ kila mutoto
wa miaka kumi na munane: mwanamuke: ao mwanaume: anapashwa kuwa na yake shamba/ [ululations]

2. tena: ule mutoto wa miaka kumi na munane: mwanamuke: ao
mwanaume: anapashwa kuwa na yake nyumba/ [ululations] haifai
analala bamama yake: ao wakaka yake/ yake nyumba/

3. wee bamama: wa mukini yote hii: kazi yote munakwenda
kufanya/ kama munaona: yua inaanza kuingia pa miti: hapana

---

26. Two recordings of the final performance are available. One I made myself
under less than optimal conditions. Most of the time I was too far away from the actors.
On the other hand, because I was in the audience, my recording contains some of the
reactions of the people around me. The other one is a copy of the soundtrack from the
video cassette. It too is of poor quality (mainly because of the placement and handling
of microphones by the TV crew). The transcription of this text has been made from
both recordings with audience response, except for general reactions recorded on the
soundtrack, left out.

27. In texts of the filmed performance "all" includes both, the audience within the
play and (in varying degrees) the people of Kawama village.

28. The proper form, addressing an audience, should be *kumielezea* (with the
second-person plural pronominal affix -*mi-*). Instead, Mufwankolo uses the third-
person *wa*. This is either a slip on his part or, more likely, it reflects a merging of the
two affixes in Shaba Swahili.

kwenda kushota mayi ku mutoni/ kama munaona: yua inalala pa
miti: inakuwa mwekunda: hapana kutwanga: kwenda ku kitwangio
kutwanga hapana/ kama munaona tena: yua yo ile: pa miti: hapana
kupika chakula ya mangaribi ya bushiku/ [pauses]

4. mukini yangu hii: mwee bote: muko munasikia? mugeni/ kama
munaona mugeni: anakuya kutembelea mu mukini humu: hapana
kumuangaria pa nsula/ [pauses] muangarie mu tumbo/ [pauses]
maneno kama munaangaria pa nsula: mugeni: atalala na njala/
kumuangaria mu tumbo: sababu mu tumbo njo: ka*mot* inasema njo
mule munaingiaka chakula/ ya mwenzako/ mumufansia hata
tubui/ mugeni anakunywa: anakulya tubui tule: na mayi ananyu-
yapo/ kiisha atakuambia kwenyewe: anatokea na kule iko naenda/
munasikia? mi niko namiambia hivi/

5. tena tunaingia mu bizila/ mu mukini yangu hii: mi sipende
bantu: sipende mulozi/ [ululations] mulozi/ mulozi/ sipende mu-
lozi/ wa kuloka batoto ya bantu/ maneno iko anapunguza bwingi
ya mukini/ kuloka benzabo/ bazazi yake ya batoto/ minakatala/ ule
tu: mulozi wa humu mu yangu mu mukini: humu: anapatikana:
namubamba: mpaka yake: lungulungu . . . *kelulele*/ [ululations]

6. tena ku: mukini yangu hii: minakatala: mutu: wa kwenda: ku
nyumba ya mwenzako/ mwiko basongakazi humu/ mwiko basongalume[29]/ banapashwa kuoana/ kila muntu na yake nyumba/
kama unatankatanka ku nyumba ya benyewe: na kulala bibi wa
benyewe: unatankatanka: kama banakubamba: banakuleta huku
kwangu: hakuna buruma: kichwa yake paka lungulungu . . . *kelulele*/

7. tena vilevile/ ngivi/ ngivi/ ngivi/ ule wa kupomona manyumba
ya benyewe/ mwenyewe hanako pomona nyumba? kuiba mali/ ku
mashamba ya benyewe: anakatala kulima: anakatala kulima: ku-
fwiya bitu ya benyewe ya mashamba: ule banamuleta huku
kwangu: tabu[30] yake *lungulungu . . . kelulele*/ [ululations]

8. munaona: miye minapenda: musikilizane/ kintu hiki: kimoya/
naomba mapendo/ mwee bote/ njo kusema hapa: muangarie batoto

29. *Basongakazi* and *basongalume*, derived from Luba, are terms occasionally used
in Shaba Swahili for unmarried women and men respectively. In Kiluba, the verb
kusonga has a more specific meaning. It refers to the right one acquires to a woman by
paying the bridewealth or some other ceremonial gift (see Van Avermaet and Mbuya
1954: 631).

30. *Tabu* is the Shaba Swahili form of ECS *adhabu*. In ECS the latter is in
phonological contrast with *adabu*, politeness. Such a contrast is not available in Shaba
Swahili, hence *adabu*, politeness, vs. *tabu*, a fine, punishment.

ya masomo/ bo bale/ bamwalimu beko hapa/ napenda bamwa-
limu/ angarie: *dispensaire:* yo hii/ iko kule/ niliomba batayenga:
banayenga *dispensaire*/ malawa bataleta/ [ululations] . . . *docteur*
mwenyewe: yee huyu iko pale/ iko na malawa/ [ululations]

9. munaona/ sasa mwee bote munapashwa kusikia kile minasema/
munasikia wee bote?
All: ndiyo/
Mufwankolo: munasikilizana?
All: ndiyo/
Mufwankolo: munasikia mwee wote?
All: ndiyo/
[ululations]

The Chief's Speech: Final Version (Translation)

1. *Mufwankolo:* Greetings to you fathers, mothers, all of you children . . . [applause] greetings to you.
All: Greetings indeed.
Mufwankolo: That is to say, today I have something to tell you.
This is what it is about: First, in this village of mine I want the people
to work the fields. Each young person eighteen years of age, woman
or man, must have his own field. [ululations]

2. Furthermore, this eighteen year old, woman or man, must have
his own house. [ululations] He must not sleep at his mother's, nor at
his older brother's. [He must have] his own house.

3. You, all the mothers of this village. [About] all the work you are
going to do. When you see the sun about to enter the trees, don't go
to the river to fetch water. When you see the sun setting among the
trees, turning red, don't work the mortar, don't get the pestle to
pound. Also, when you see the sun in the trees, don't cook the
supper when it is almost night. [pauses]

4. This village of mine: all of you, are you listening? When you see a
stranger visiting here in the village, don't look at his face. [pauses]
Look at his belly. [pauses] Because if you look at his face: the visitor
will go to sleep hungry. Look at his belly because, as a little saying
has it,[31] it is the belly where the food goes, [the belly] of your fellow

---

31. Here Mufwankolo marks his statement as a quotation, that is, a proverbial
expression (diminutive *ka* plus the French *mot*). However, that food goes into the belly
is hardly an "expression of conventional wisdom," it is a fact. Perhaps the reference is
to the phrase above: Don't look at a stranger's face, etc., which is current in Shaba
Swahili.

man. Prepare a little porridge for him. The visitor drinks, he eats that little porridge and drinks some water on top of it.[32] Then he'll tell you where he came from and where he goes. You understand? This is what I am telling you.

5. Now let us take up the matter of prohibitions. In this village of mine, I don't like people who are sorcerers. [ululating] The sorcerer! The sorcerer! I don't like the sorcerer. He is the one who puts a spell on the children of people. Because he is the one who reduces the village by [killing] his fellow men through sorcery, [killing] parents who have children. [This] I do not allow. A sorcerer from here, from my village here, this is what he gets: I catch him and his lot is lungulungu . . . *kelulele* [he be damned] [ululating]

6. *Mufwankolo:*   Furthermore, in this village of mine I won't allow anyone go to his neighbor's house. There may be young women or young men who are single; they must get married. Everyone should be with his own household. If you hang around someone else's house, sleep with someone else's wife, if you go roaming around they will pick you up, bring you before me, and there is no mercy. His head lungulungu . . . *kelulele.*

7. *Mufwankolo:*   Furthermore. A thief! A thief! A thief, he is someone who breaks into the houses of others. Does such a person not destroy houses? Stealing property. He does not want to cultivate. Instead he steals things from someone else's fields. If they bring him to me here, his punishment will be lungulungu . . . *kelulele.* [ululating]

8. *Mufwankolo:*   You see? I want you to get along with each other. Just one thing: I ask for love, all of you. Look here, the school children, over there, and their teachers are here. I love the teachers here. Look, the clinic, there it is. I asked them to build one, they built the clinic. They will bring medicines. [ululations] . . . ? . . . and the doctor himself, there he is.[33] He has medicines. [ululations]

9. You see now? All of you must listen to what I say. You understand, all of you?
All: Yes.

---

32. Adding "on top of it" is to convey something of the original phrase: *na mayi ananyayupo.* Normally one would say *na mayi anakunywa. Po* is a demonstrative locative particle which would be redundant, except if the speaker, as is the case here, wants to give the phrase a comical turn—a sort of grammatical exaggeration.

33. This is the moment when, in the television broadcast, I appear for a few seconds on the screen.

Mufwankolo: You understand each other?
All: Yes.
Mufwankolo: You understand, all of you?
All: Yes. [ululations]

After this the chief and his immediate entourage leave. The villagers begin a song: *Twamuleta lelo* . . . Some of them dance.

8

Scene 2: Trouble Brewing

In the broadcast the camera now sweeps the village and the main road while the chief leaves the scene. There is drumming and shouting and the village audience is carried along. Before members of the television crew have managed to calm them down the actors, in a way using the situation, embark on scene 2: As they walk away from the court the villagers comment on the chief's speech. The first exchanges are covered by the general din. When, on the recording of the filmed performance, the dialogue becomes intelligible again we are in the middle of a revolt. However, there is much commotion and little text. What the exchanges may have been like we can reconstruct by turning again to the June 26 rehearsal. On that occasion it became clear that there are some dramatic problems with the scene. The plot does not provide for a concrete incident or occasion that would make the rebellion plausible. Instead, "contradiction" and "criticism" are invoked, not as a description of what happens, but as motives. To translate this into action and dialogue required some discussion and several starts. Tala Ngai takes on the role of the principal troublemaker.

Contesting the Chief: Rehearsal Version (Text 10)

1. *Tala Ngai:*   banduku wee/
Others: eeh/
Tala Ngai: banduku wee/
Others: eeh/
Tala Ngai: mwee bote: munatoka munasikia mambo sultani ana-sema/ si munaisikia?
Others: tunaisikia/
Tala Ngai: *mais* lakini: inanipa sawa sikitiko. . . . / sultani: mambo anapashwa kusema ni paka mambo shee ba*notables* tunamuelezea njo kumielezea mweye/
Others: ndiyo/

2. *Tala Ngai:*   shee hatumuelezea kusema vintu vingivingi/ tuna-
mulelezea asema kintu hiki . . . *kimoya/*
Kalwasha: paka nwe: nwe njo balisema/
Tala Ngai: ni: eh: sasa yee anafika pale anamielezea ooh: muntu
asikwende ku benyewe: ku nyumba ya benyewe: ooh: muntu asi:
muntu ende karibu mu mashamba/ kama muntu yee hapana ku-
lima mashamba: analala na njala: ni mambo yake hii?
Feza: haimuangarie/
Tala Ngai: ile mambo inamuangaria sultani?
Feza: haimuangarie/

3. *Tala Ngai:*   kama utaanza kulala na njala weye: *est-ce que*
inamuangaria sultani?
Feza: ah: asitakuwapo[1]/
Tala Ngai: munielezee/
Feza: asitakuwapo/
Tala Ngai: ah: wee mwenye tu unasikia njala/
Feza: nitakulya *bien* sana/

4. *Tala Ngai:*   unasikia njala/ ile saa: yua inaisha kuingia/ muta-
kulya bukari ao hautakulya?
Others: utakulya/
Feza: hata mu nyumba unapiga bukari unakulya/
Kamwanya: . . . hata muhogo utatwanga busiku/
Tala Ngai: hamuone asema sultani bintu anaanza kufanya: bina-
anza kutoka mu mbalambala/
Feza: anaanza kutoka mu njia ya kanuni ya bankambo/
Tala Ngai: shiye: tuko namupa akili ya kusema: angarie namna ya
kuongeza . . .
Feza: inchi/
Kamwanya: inchi/

5. *Kalwasha:*   angarie: angarie baba/
Tala Ngai: eh
Kalwasha: wee kilolo[2]: njo wee/
Tala Ngai: eeh/
Kalwasha: umuambile sultani/
Tala Ngai: mm/

---

    1. An unusual negative form (*hatakuwapo* would be regular), which in Shaba is
often cited as an example for *ki-Union Minière*, that is, characteristic of the dialect
spoken in the workers' camps. It is most likely one of the few grammatical survivals of
Kikabanga ("Kitchen Kaffir" or Fanagalo, which used to be the workers' language until
World War I).
    2. A Luba term for *notable*; see Van Avermaet and Mbuya 1954: 360.

Kalwasha: ile *réunion* ile anafutafuta mu: humu mukini: atabakia
na hii mukini yee mwenyewe/
Actress: tutamuachiayo mukini/
Kalwasha: hapana kutafuta mambo ingine ya bantu/

6. *Tala Ngai:* anaanza kusema na mambo ya busiku/
Feza: asema kama jua inakuya: inakuwa mwekunda . . .
Tala Ngai: jua inakuwa mwekunda . . .
Feza: haipashwe muntu kutoka inje: paka tu mu nyumba kimya/
haipashwe tena. . . .
Tala Ngai: hee: sasa: hii inakuwa ni *couvre le feu?*
Feza: ah!
Tala Ngai: ya kusema: paka yua inaingia bantu balale busingishi?
Actor: sawa inatoka mu tauni/

7. *Tala Ngai:* njo kusema: hatutaimba tena tu mimbo: tunapigaka
tena kengele hapana?
Kalwasha: mu hii mugini hamuna mutoto wa kukomea kisungu[3]/
hatutaimba mangaribi? mu hii mugini hamuna tena muntu wa ku-
sema kunakuwa kamuchezo kafuraha?
Tala Ngai: oooh: bamuyamaa[4]/ munasema tutaikala paka hivi?
Others: hapana/
Tala Ngai: njo hivi tutaikala?
Others: hapana/
Feza: shi tunakatala bile byote. . . .

[Mufwankolo now intervenes with directions, then the recording
resumes]

8. *Tala Ngai:* asema kama mugeni anakuya munapashwa kumu-
angaria mu ntumbo: hapana kumuangaria mu nsula/ njo kusema
yee anamikabulaka chakula kupatia bageni?
Feza: ya wapi/
Kamwanya: njo bankambo benyewe balisemaka vile?
Tala Ngai: oh: kama bageni banakuya: munabatuma kwake/ yee
habalishe/
Feza: tukaanze kubatuma kwake/
Tala Ngai: habamila . . . ? . . . peleake na kintu gani?
Feza: shee kwanza kulya: bantu bale banakuya mu mugini/
Tala Ngai: aah: bamuyamaa he/

---

3. This is the Shaba Swahili form of Bemba *chisungu*, the girls' rites of puberty
(described by Richards 1956).
4. *Muyamaa* means "friend, buddy." The derivation is not clear; possibly from *ba-
mu-jamaa*, those in the family, members of the same family.

Others: he/
Tala Ngai: bamuyamaa he/
Others: he/

9. *Tala Ngai:* munaitika hii mambo anasema?
Others: hapana/
Tala Ngai: ya kusema: mweye mwanzie kupigia bageni?
Others: hapana/
Tala Ngai: yeye: njo anapataka milambo/ yeye njo anapashwa kwanza kupikia banani?
Others: bageni/
Actor: si yeye? tusha tote[5]: paka yee/ samaki yote: paka yee/
Actress: na bapombomfuko[6] bote/

[Now the other two *notables,* Bwana Cheko and Masimango, arrive; greetings are exchanged, there is ceremonial handclapping]

10. *Feza:* inafaa mbele kumiulizako hii mambo wa sultani alitoka mu kusema hapa: mwee munaona nje?
[Bwana Cheko and Masimango laugh]
Bwana Cheko: mwee ba: mwee bamama/ bantu banaisha kukomea/ na bababa: namna hii mwiko hapa: njo bampyana[7]/
Kalwasha: shi ni mwili alikomela? alafu ni loho alikomela?
Bwana Cheko: sultani alitoka kusema bintu waziwazi/ bile binapendesha kuendesha mukini mbe . . . *mbele/*
Kalwasha: oho: oho/

11. *Feza:* kweli? ni ile alisema sultani na mwee munaitika mwee?
Actor: kuendesha mbele?
Feza: mugeni kama anakuya: haipashwe kuangaria pa uso . . .
Tala Ngai: . . . asema unakuwa kumuangaria pa ntumbo/
Feza: haipashwe kulya bukari mangaribi/ kweli?
Bwana Cheko: mugeni wote kama anafika/
Feza: eh/
Bwana Cheko: hauyue ni wapi eko nakwenda: na ni fasi gani kule anatokea/
Feza: eeh/

---

5. A typical Shaba Swahili form. ECS has *nsya* for "small antelope" (Lenselaer 1983: 366). In Shaba the term is *kashia* (in French as well as Swahili and Luba; see Van Avermaet and Mbuya 1954: 236). The prefix *ka-* has *tu-* as its plural form, hence *tushia,* antelopes.

6. *Pombomfuko* is a small rodent considered a delicacy. It is often sold stretched and dried, resembling dried fish. I have been unable to identify either term or animal.

7. A term, apparently not known in ECS, meaning "successor" (see Lenselaer 1983: 321).

Bwana Cheko: kwetu hapana kuwa: hii mukini yetu hatupende
bale bantu wa kwenda kulya bukari chini ya kitanda/
Feza: kweli? na yee anasema ...
Bwana Cheko: ukiwa kaloko: kukiwa kaloko: kukiwa kaloko:
umukatie kaloko: akulye: akunywe mayi: afunge safari: ende lwake:
atakwenda na kavumu ya: ile mukini/

12. *Feza:* kama minapenda kavumu kaloko: mi nitaenda kutosha
wapi ingine ya kutolea ile mugeni anakuya huku? nitaitosha wapi?
mwee haba: hamuna bantu bazuri/ kama ulikuwa sawa Tala Ngai
huyu ...
Kamwanya: Tala Ngai ni muntu: muntu wa zamani. ...
Actor: mukubwa/
Kalwasha: eh!
Actor: mukubwa Tala Ngai/
Kamwanya: mukubwa ya kweli kweli/ Tala Ngai eko muntu mu-
zuri sana/
Masimango: tusikilizane mbele ...

13. *Kalwasha:* acha kwanza: acha kwanza mama/ munyamashe
mwee wote?
Feza: eeh/
Kalwasha: niye: muko ba*notables* ba namna gani? sultani anakuya:
eko nanu*nominer*[8]/ ananuambia asema: nuangarieko muntu: paka
mu ntumbo/ oh: shee tumuangarie mu ntumbo she njo twalikuya
naye?
Actress: hata/
Feza: semeni mbele/

14. *Masimango:* mwee bababa: banduku yetu. ...
Feza: ... kuona tu muntu anakuya sasa kufungula mbele *chemise*
tuone mu ntumbo ...
Masimango: mwee: wee munazania asema kintu alisema sultani ni
kibaya?
Feza: aah: ile anasema bya mingi ya kusema kama mu: jua ina-
kuwa mwekunda ...
Masimango: tusikilizaneni ...
Feza: ... kila muntu anapashwa kuwa mu nyumba/ asitoke inje/
Masimango: mama Feza: munisikie mbele/
Kalwasha: eheh?

---

8. Here and in the following verb forms Kalwasha uses -*nu*- instead of the
expected -*mu*- or -*mi*- as pronominal affix. This is one of the many ways in which he
marks his speech as old-fashioned, with much interference from a local language.

15. *Masimango:*   sultani alisema bintu bya: binyewe ya kabaila
bintu hibi: bitatu/
Kalwasha: eh: bitatu/
Masimango: bulozi/
Kalwasha: eheh/
Masimango: bwizi/
Others: eeh/
Masimango: busharati/
Others: eeh/
Tala Ngai: banani balozi humu?
Masimango: mwee kwanza: mwee bote mwenye kuikala hapa/
Manyeke: tozala[9] je? [others laugh]

16. *Masimango:*   kama wee: bana: bana: banakamata bibi yako:
unakamata bibi yako makozi: utapenda?
Kalwasha: mi shitapenda apana . . .
Actor: hata/
Masimango: weye mama weye: kama banakuwa kukolokea muto-
to yako asema: mwenzako njo analoka mutoto: utapenda?
Feza: mi sitapenda/
Kamwanya: hata/
Feza: kwa ile: tutasikilizane hapa . . .
Kalwasha: acha kwanza/ mulo: sul: sultani: si njo muloshi wa
kwanza?
Feza: tusikili: tusikilizane/ tusikilizane . . .

[Here Mufwankolo intervenes again with some directions]

17. *Kalwasha:*   . . . ah sultani njo muloshi wa kwanza. . . .
Masimango: muangarie/ mwee bote munayuaka basultani/ sulta-
ni: wee unasema sultani ni mulozi/ sultani anaikalaka na macho
inne/ hapana bulozi/ sultani anaikalaka na macho inne/
Feza: hii macho inne alipata wapi? si njo bulozi?
Masimango: sultani anaikalaka na macho inne: haina bulozi/ kwa
kuyua asema huyu muntu anakuwa na kintu kibaya: ni sultani
anapashwa kuyua ile mambo/
Kamwanya: macho ile ya kizalikio/
Bwana Cheko: iko vile/

18. *Feza:*   [to Tala Ngai] chefu Muteba/ anasema muzuri: bintu
biko hii bitatu sultani alisema binene/ alafu ile ya jua ya kutoka
huku ile: ilo njo kama inakuwa mwekunda mwee bote mu nyumba?
Bwana Cheko: ifike hapa pa mangaribi/

---

9. For comical effect, Manyeke uses the Lingala verb for "to be," *-zala*.

Kamwanya: musikulye/
Feza: ... ni namna gani? kama jua inaingia mutoto asifike mu nyumba yake? ni kufanya namna gani?

19. *Bwana Cheko:* hakusema vile?
Feza: si vile alisema? ...
Others: alisema/
Bwana Cheko: ... chakula: inafaa: inafaa kutayarisha chakula: hapana kuongojea paka bushiku/
Feza: alafu kama ile saa ...
Kalwasha: kama tunaanza kucheza ngoma bushiku/ mwee: mwee wote bamama na bababa: nukatale chinywa[10] yabo/ nuitike paka ya Tala Ngai/
Others: Tala Ngai/

Now all talk at once and leave the scene; Mufwankolo gives directions for scene 3.

Contesting the Chief: Rehearsal Version (Translation)

1. *Tala Ngai:* You, my relatives.
Others: We're listening.
Tala Ngai: You, my relatives.
Others: We're listening.
Tala Ngai: You all have just heard what the chief had to say. Did you understand it?
Others: We did.
Tala Ngai: But what he said makes me sort of sad. When the chief speaks he should talk only about those matters which we, the *notables*, told him to tell you.
Others: Right.

2. *Tala Ngai:* We did not tell him to mention a lot of things. We told him to speak only about this one ... *one thing.*
Kalwasha: Only you, you told [him what to say].
Tala Ngai: Now he comes and tells you: Oh, a person cannot go to someone else's house, a person can't—a person should go and stay in the fields. If a person does not cultivate the fields and goes to sleep hungry, is that his business?
Feza: It's none of his business.
Tala Ngai: Is that the chief's business?
Feza: It's none of his business.

10. *Chinywa* (that is, *kinywa* with a local accent) means "language." Here: "what they say. . . ."

3. *Tala Ngai:*   . . . if you begin to go to sleep hungry, is that the chief's business?
Feza: Ah, he won't be there.
Tala Ngai: You tell me.
Feza: He won't be there.
Tala Ngai: Ah, you are the one who feels hungry.
Feza: I am going to eat well [anyway].

4. *Tala Ngai:*   If you feel hungry at the time when the sun has set are you going to eat your *bukari* or not?
Others: You are going to eat it.
Feza: Even if it has to be inside the house, you cook the *bukari* and eat it.
Kamwanya: . . . you are even going to pound manioc at night.
Tala Ngai: Don't you see what the chief is about to do, things that leave the main road?
Feza: He begins to leave the path of the ancestors' laws.
Tala Ngai: We explained to him: This is the way to make strong the . . .
Feza: . . . country.
Kamwanya: The country.

5. *Kalwasha:*   Look here. Look here, *baba*.
Tala Ngai: Yes?
Kalwasha: The *notable*, that's you.
Tala Ngai: Right.
Kalwasha: Tell the chief.
Tala Ngai: Yes.
Kalwasha: About this meeting he has been trying to have here in the village—[if he goes on with that sort of thing] he'll be left behind alone with this village.[11]
Feza: We are going to leave him his village.
Kalwasha: He should not look for things other [than the ancestors' laws to impose] on the people.

6. *Tala Ngai:*   He begins to talk about that business with the evening.
Feza: When the sun turns red . . .
Tala Ngai: The sun turns red . . .
Feza: It is not permitted for a person to go outside, he is to stay in the house and keep calm. And he may not . . .
Tala Ngai: What is this now, a curfew?

---

11. Kalwasha's speech is elliptical; a translation is impossible without adding some of the connections between parts of his statements that are implied but not expressed.

Feza: Really!
Tala Ngai: That is to say, when the sun sets the people should be sleeping?
Actor: As it happens in town?

7. *Tala Ngai:* That is to say, we are not supposed to sing a song and beat [?] the rhythm on a bottle?
Kalwasha: Is there no girl in this village that has grown up to go through the rites of puberty? Are we then not going to sing at night? Is no one in this village going to put on a little dance to celebrate the occasion?
Tala Ngai: Ooh, friends. Are you saying we are just going to hold still?
Others: No way.
Tala Ngai: Is this how we are going to be?
Others: No way.
Feza: We refuse all this.

[Mufwankolo now intervenes with directions, then the recording resumes]

8. *Tala Ngai:* He tells us: when a visitor comes you must look at his belly, not at his face. Does that mean that he [the chief] will distribute food among you to give to the visitors?
Feza: No way.
Kamwanya: Did the ancestors say this?
Tala Ngai: Oh, when visitors come you send them to him, he can feed them.
Feza: Let's send them to him.
Tala Ngai: [incomprehensible]
Feza: First we eat, then the people who come to the village.
Tala Ngai: Greetings, friends.
Others: Greetings.
Tala Ngai: Greetings, friends.
Others: Greetings.

9. *Tala Ngai:* Do you accept the things he tells you?
Others: No.
Tala Ngai: That you ought to cook for visitors?
Others: No.
Tala Ngai: He is the one who gets tribute, he is the one who ought to cook first for whom?
Others: The visitors.
Actor: Is it not him—all the antelopes are for him, all the fish for him.
Kamwanya: And all the rodents called pombomfuko.

[The other two *notables*, Bwana Cheko and Masimango, arrive; greetings are exchanged, there is ceremonial handclapping]

10. *Feza:*   First I must ask you about the things the chief brought up in his speech here. What do you make of it?
[Bwana Cheko and Masimango laugh]
Bwana Cheko: You women, you are grown-up persons and so are you, the men who are here, you now take the place (of the old ones).
Kalwasha: Is it not the body that grew up? But what about the spirit, did it grow up?[12]
Bwana Cheko: The chief came forth and spoke clearly about the things that need to be done to bring progress to the village.
Kalwasha: Oho, oho.

11. *Feza:*   Is that so? Do you accept what he said?
Actor: Bring progress?
Feza: If a visitor comes, one must not look him in the face . . .
Tala Ngai: . . . you must look at his belly.
Feza: That one must not eat in the evening. Is that true?
Bwana Cheko: Whenever a visitor arrives . . .
Feza: Yes.
Bwana Cheko: . . . you don't know where he is going nor where he is coming from.
Feza: Yes.
Bwana Cheko: Here it must not get to the point—here in our village we don't want people to eat their *bukari* under the bed.[13]
Feza: Is that so? And then he said . . .
Bwana Cheko: Even if there is very little left, cut a little bit off for him. He should eat and drink some water, then set out on his trip and go back to his place. And he should leave with something good to tell about this village.

12. *Feza:*   I am all for it that we get a little bit of a good reputation but where am I going to get [the food to give] to the visitor who arrives here? Where am I going to get it? Come on. You [to Bwana Cheko and Masimango], you aren't decent people. If you were like this Tala Ngai . . .
Kamwanya: Tala Ngai is a man. A man like in the old times.
Actor: He is a great one!
Kalwasha: Isn't he?

---

12. Kalwasha throws this into the debate just for the sake of annoying Bwana Cheko. It is clear that he is on the side of those who criticize the chief.
13. This is a proverbial expression current in Shaba Swahili. Hiding food from (possible) visitors violates the rule of hospitality.

Actor: Tala Ngai is a great one.
Kamwanya: He is indeed great. Tala Ngai is a very good person.
Masimango: Let's understand each other first . . .

13. *Kalwasha:*   Hold it, hold it, mama. Be quiet, all of you.
Feza: All right.
Kalwasha: You are *notables*. What does that mean? The chief comes and appoints you. He tells you to look only at the belly of a person. What now? We are supposed to look at the belly? Did we bring it [to the village]?
Actress: No way.
Feza: Talk first.

14. *Masimango:*   You, men, our relatives. . . .
Feza: . . . are we supposed to look at a person who arrives and tell him to open his shirt so we can look at his belly?
Masimango: Do you think that what the chief said is bad?
Feza: Aah, all this stuff—when the sun turns red. . . .
Masimango: Let's understand each other . . .
Feza: . . . every one must be inside the house. A person may not go outside.
Masimango: Mama Feza, first listen to me.
Kalwasha: You hear that?

15. *Masimango:*   The chief named three things in this order:
Kalwasha: Ah, three.
Masimango: Sorcery.
Kalwasha: Yes.
Masimango: Theft.
Others: Yes.
Masimango: Fornication.
Others: Yes.
Tala Ngai: Who are the sorcerers here?
Masimango: You, to begin with, all of you who are sitting here.
Manyeke: What [do you say] we are? [laughter]

16. *Masimango:*   If you, if they, if they take your wife, if you catch your wife fornicating, are you going to like this?
Kalwasha: I am not going to like it.
Actor: Not at all.
Masimango: And you mama, when they come and put a spell on your child, your neighbor puts a spell on the child, are you going to like that?
Feza: I am not going to like it.
Kamwanya: Not at all.

Feza: About that we are going to agree here.

Kalwasha: Wait first, the chief, is he not the first sorcerer?

Feza: Let us understand each other, let us understand each other.

[Here Mufwankolo intervenes again with directions]

17. *Kalwasha:*   Ah, the chief is the first sorcerer.

Masimango: Look here, you all know what chiefs are like. You say the chief is a sorcerer. A chief has four eyes. That is not sorcery. A chief has four eyes.

Feza: Where did he get those four eyes from? Isn't that sorcery?

Masimango: The chief has four eyes, that is not sorcery. If a person is planning something bad, the chief needs to know this.

Kamwanya: Was he born with those eyes?

Bwana Cheko: [But] it is like that.

18. *Feza:*   Chief Muteba [i.e., Tala Ngai] put it well as regards the three points about which the chief talked at length. But this business about the sun that came up here—when it turns red, all of you should be inside?

Bwana Cheko: When it gets this far in the evening . . .

Kamwanya: You may not eat.

Feza: How is this? When the sun sets a young person may not go to his house? How is this to be done?

19. *Bwana Cheko:*   He did not say this.

Feza: Didn't he say this?

Others: He said it.

Bwana Cheko: About the food, the food must be prepared in time, [you] must not wait until it is dark.

Feza: But if at that time . . .

Kalwasha: When we begin to play the drum at night—you, all of you, women and men, don't accept what those people say. Just listen to what Tala Ngai says.

Others: Tala Ngai!

Now all talk at once and leave the scene; Mufwankolo gives directions for scene 3.

In the filmed performance, the dialogue, as far as it is comprehensible from the recording, follows the pattern set during rehearsal. At first, several actors take turns to recall the major points of the speech obviously in order to incite disagreement. There is no argument, simply enumeration greeted by angry exclamations such as *bongo,* that's a lie, or *hapana,* no way. Then one of the actors takes the line of social contestation.

Contesting the Chief: Final Version (Fragments; Text 11)

1. *Tala Ngai:* ... mambo ingine na miye/ mweye munaweza kui-
tika/ mutoto ya muntu asema/ asema muntu asikwende kulimba-
limba ku nyumba ya benyewe/
Actor: bongo/

· ·

2. *Feza:* chefu eko nasema hivi: busiku bukiingia: mama: kama jua
inakuwa mwekunda: asipigie bukari/ ni bya kweli?
Others: hapana/ bongo ...

· ·

3. *Tala Ngai:* asema kama mugeni anakuya: umuangarie mu
tumbo/ kama iko vile: hatunamupeleka kwake?
Others: kweli/
Tala Ngai: kama mugeni anakuya tunamupeleka wapi?
Others: kwake/

· ·

4. *Kalwasha:* yee ule *chef:* alafu ile: kwanza ile yee alisema: minasema: weeye endake kulima mashamba/ oh sheye tukalime paka
mu mashamba/ yee iko nakulya bukari kwake ku mulango: shee
tuko nakwenda kuikala paka ku mashamba/ bilonda bitoka mu
mikono ...
Others: hapana. ...

Contesting the Chief: Final Version (Fragments; Translation)

1. *Tala Ngai:* ... and I have something else; you can listen. It was
said that a person may not go around to some one else's house.
Actor: That's a lie.

· ·

2. *Feza:* This is what the chief said: When the evening comes and
the sun turns red, the women are not to prepare food. Is this true
[acceptable]?
Others: No way, it's a lie.

· ·

3. *Tala Ngai:* He said, when a stranger comes, look at his belly. If it
is to be like this, should we not take the stranger to him?
Others: Right.
Tala Ngai: When a stranger comes, where are we going to take
him?
Others: To his [the chief's] place.

· ·

4. *Kalwasha:*   Oh, that chief! But above all he said: You go work the
fields. Oh, we are just to work in the fields! He has his meal at home
while we go and stay out in the fields. Sores come out on our
hands. . . .
Others: No way.

Then Bwana Cheko, who had left the scene earlier in the chief's
company, comes back and tries to calm the villagers by addressing them
formally with an exchange of greetings. They respond, but when he tries
to remind them of the chief's speech general dissent breaks out again.
Once more they comment on his orders point by point. The real villagers
join the general shouting and merriment. Meanwhile there is a change
of scene. Some of the actors who play the villagers leave.

9 _____

Scene 3: The Case of the Thief

That the chief's power should be shown in action was agreed upon very early during the preparations. From the beginning, a court case was thought to be a suitable example. However, by the time discussion got around to determining what kind of crime should be tried, the plot had acquired a complexity which could no longer be satisfied by simply demonstrating the chief's role in litigation. After the fact, it seems possible to name several reasons why, when it came to the first rehearsal, three scenes were required to make the point.

First, there was a need to meet a problem which poses itself whenever the group stages a play and which, although it is obvious upon reflection, never became an explicit topic of debate. Each actor occupies a rank in the hierarchy of the troupe, based on a number of factors such as age, sex, seniority; his or her rank is expressed in a stock of characters he or she usually plays. Therefore, distributing parts is not simply a matter of casting, of finding suitable actors for predetermined roles. Rather, it requires tactful negotiations to achieve agreement between the rights of actors who are currently available and the requirements of the play. In the Troupe Mufwankolo the rule seems to be that the plot will be modified rather than bench an actor. That solution may also be adopted if an actor does not show up, although the alternative, to assign more than one part to an actor, may also be chosen. At any rate, in the case of *Le pouvoir se mange entier* it was clear that the element of drama could not be limited to a confrontation between the chief and his villagers. Additional scenes had to be invented to provide an outlet for some of the senior actors.

Second, moving from general to specific reasons, it had been decided that, in this play, the collapse of law and order should not appear to be the chief's fault alone, nor the villagers. Above all it should be the result of conflicts of interest among the *notables*. This could have been achieved by disagreement among them when their opinion was sought regarding the case on trial. The element of self-interest was introduced by making the accused the child of one of the *notables* who would then have to set his kinship obligations above his impartial judgment. A way to bring this point home (and to call on more actors) was to introduce a second court case in which the culprit had committed a more serious offense (adultery) than the petty theft of the first case. This made it possible to add another element of tension and development to the play by having the theme of self-interest appear even more dramatically in the second case. The first *notable*, to whom this part was assigned demanded severe punishment for the thief while he tried to argue that the adulterer, his child, was just a victim of circumstances. Judging by the public's response, scene 5, in which this happens, turned out to be perhaps the most successful scene of the play.

Third, although I cannot recall any explicit discussion on the reasons, another scene at the chief's court was eventually sandwiched between the two trials. This is the visit of a successful hunter who comes to tell his tale and offer the chief his share of game. The scene has several functions. Implicitly, it adds to the authentic flavor of the play. Hunting is a traditional activity; in Luba-Lunda cultures, great hunters are not only respected but powerful people. Rendering tribute to the chief makes the power of the latter visible as something more than judicial authority. Furthermore, the chief then decides to distribute parts of the tribute among his *notables*. The shares he hands out are not equal (perhaps another demonstration of his power). This causes envy and further deepens discord among the *notables*. Thus scene 4 makes a major contribution to the play. Yet, it is not unlikely that it was added above all to provide a part for Kalwasha whose specialty is, as Mufwankolo put it, *sauti ya buzee*, the voice of old age. He plays the folksy type characterized linguistically by one or another regional accent or by certain exaggerated phonological peculiarities of Shaba Swahili.

Scenes 3 to 5 belong together, in terms of their topic, their function in the play, and their setting in the chief's court. They could be presented under the common heading "Law, Custom, and Conflict." For practical reasons, the length of the texts among them, each scene will be given a separate chapter.

In scene 3, the case of the thief, the actor Manyeke is the center of attention. He is small enough to look like a pygmy, and although he is no longer young, he is very agile. His voice is resonant, but he speaks very rapidly and tends to stutter. He is the troupe's clown; most of his appearances are all gesture and action and few words. Manyeke is decidedly not an ideal producer of transcribable texts. In rehearsal everyone had great fun with his portrayal of a petty thief caught stealing a few bananas. Feza, playing the woman who owns the field, accuses him before the chief while the guards have trouble restraining Manyeke. They literally "picked him up," lifting him up and carrying him while he tries to wriggle free from their grip, loudly protesting his innocence. His line of defense is laconic: *paka njala,* I was just hungry. To no avail, he is punished, because, as Bwana Cheko puts it, *mwizi ni nduku ya mulozi,* the thief is the sorcerer's brother.

This summary contains the outlines of the scene as it was eventually performed; it fails to convey an impression of the work that went into the final shape, which, as we shall see, was reduced to bare essentials in the filmed performance. Meanwhile we can turn to a recording of scene 3 made at the June 26 rehearsal. The transcript/translation presented here is abbreviated. Left out are a group discussion about how to set up the scene and the first part where Manyeke is accused by Feza, arrested by the chief's guards, and first brought before Bwana Cheko. The latter then calls for his fellow *notable* Tala Ngai. Feza and Manyeke exchange accusations and defense. The *notables* decide that this case must be submitted to the chief.

As we shall see, the text that follows documents what I called a kind of oscillating between doing the play and talking about it (a crucial transitional phase in the overall process). Bwana Cheko first makes a report to the chief.

The Case of the Thief: Rehearsal Version (Text 12)

1. *Bwana Cheko:*   Chefu/ tunaona tu: tulikuwa: na *notable* wangu pale Masimango: tushitukie tu: mu mukini makelele/ beko hapa na muntu/ ah: ah: kunakuwa lufu: kunakuwa bintu gani: nini: mm/ tuangarie: ba*gardes* yako: bo haba/ mama Feza: ku mukongo/ na mutoto huyu bataunga banamunyonga nkamba/ ni nini anfanya? asema oh: anaiba maboké[1] mu mashamba/

2. *Mufwankolo:*   liboké?
Bwana Cheko and Feza: maboké/
Mufwankolo: bya mingi?
Feza: byo hibi baba/
Bwana Cheko: tatu/ tatu/ njo tunaangaria tunasema ah: ah: paka hapa? sauti ya sultani: alitosha paka hapa sauti yake: kumbe twende tukafike kwanza: kule/ tukafike na huyu mutoto kule: nawaza: Masimango iko pale: ataungapo sauti: ya mambo/

---

1. *Maboké* (stress—or high tone?—on the last syllable; singular *liboké*) is the term for large bananas used for cooking (plantains). The general term for all sorts of bananas is *ndizi.* Of the sweeter varieties that are eaten uncooked, the larger ones are called *ndizi* (now in contrast with *liboké*), the smaller ones *kitika* (plural *bitika*).

3. *Masimango:*   sultani/ ile nani: sauti ile ulisemaka ile: tunakwenda na: na mukubwa pale: Bwana Cheko/ tunaeleza paka
mambo yako hii/ asema mu mukini sultani alikataza kuiba/ mama
hapa: aliniambiaka: mukubwa Bwana Cheko . . .
Bwana Cheko: asema: asema: buizi: kama muntu anakuibia: ni
muzuri/
Masimango: bile bi[ntu] sultani alisema ni bibaya/
Bwana Cheko: bibaya/
Masimango: mama nayee tuko hapa/

4. *Feza:*   [asking for direction] *est-que* hapa tunaweza kubisha? *ou*
bien munaenda kusema vile . . .
Masimango: wee kyako ni kilio . . .
Kamwanya: wee: wee tu ni kusema . . .
Masimango: mama leo tuko wapi?
Feza: [goes on talking, not comprehensible]
Tala Ngai: hapana kujibu wee/

[Scene continues]
5. *Masimango:*   njo mambo ya sul: sultani: ya huyu mama: na huyu
mutoto/
Mufwankolo: mama huyu umukutanisha mashamba anabeba na
mihogo: nani: maboké yako?
Feza: baba: maboké inyewe yo hii/ minaisha ya kusema/
Manyeke: chefu/ chefu: mi nilimuomba/
Feza: ah/ ulinilomba wapi baba?
Manyeke: ku mashamba/
Feza: njo nikwende kuleta ku bachefu?
Manyeke: uko mazimu?
Feza: aaah baba/

6. *Guard:*   [restraining Manyeke] sss: *tu as tort/ qu'est-ce que ça?*
Feza: baba ananilandia[2] huyu mutoto mwanaume huyu/
Actor: mm/ mm/
Manyeke: tatu bule tu mwizi?
Others: eee/
Feza: alafu iba ulinilomba?

7. *Mufwankolo:*   ni mutoto wa nani huyu?
Masimango: wee/ sultani eko nakuuliza/
Mufwankolo: baba yako ni nani?
Masimango: [asking for direction] ba: baba: mi: chefu: wa nani?

---

2. The verb is *kurandia* in ECS (to get something by slyness). Synonyms more
frequently used in Shaba Swahili are *kulongofea* or *kudanganya*.

Feza: Kafwankumba/
Manyeke: baba yee huyu/ [points to Mufwankolo, the others laugh]
Mufwankolo: he?
Manyeke: si huyu baba: si ni baba? sasa?
Others: [laughing, partly incomprehensible] baba yake yee huyu/ baba yake ni sultani/
Guard: sema muzuri wee/
Tala Ngai: bababa ni Kafwankumba/
Masimango: [laughing] *no no:* ni mutoto wa sultani/
Kamwanya: ni mutoto wa sultani . . .
Feza: mutoto wa muloko yake wa sultani/
Masimango: ni mutoto ya sultani/
Feza: mutoto ya muloko yake ya sultani/
Masimango: eeh/ *parce-que* ni. . . .
Manyeke: [trying to go back to the scene] baba ni: baba ni njala tu/
Bwana Cheko: ni mutoto wa Bwana Cheko/
Feza: ni mutoto yake/
[There follows general discussion, largely incomprehensible because all talk at once]

8. *Tala Ngai:*   *ne vous perdez pas*/ huyu mutoto wa kwanza: huyu mutoto wa kwanza batabamba: hana mutoto wa muntu hata moya ya ku *cour*/ njo maana wee uta*insister* bamu*punir*/
Bwana Cheko: *oui*/
Feza: kumbe hawezi kuwa yee/
Tala Ngai: ule mutoto wa pili batabamba: njo mutoto yako/
Bwana Cheko: huyu mutoto ni Katolushi/
Tala Ngai: baba yako ni Kafwankumba/
Bwana Cheko: ni Katolushi kumbe/
Feza: eeh/ Katolushi
Kamwanya: kama banaisha kumubamba Katolushi: yee. . . .
Masimango: . . . ni paka *imaginaire là:* Kafwankumba/
Actor: bon/ bon/ njo yee lamuka Katolushi . . .
Tala Ngai: non: non: non/ *ce n'est pas ça*/ huyu njo vile wa kwanza: munabamba/ mutoto wasipo kupashwa kumuteswa huyu. . . .
[several talk together; incomprehensible]

9. *Feza:*   wa kwanza ilikuwa ni Katolushi: huyu ni wa Manyeke . . .
Tala Ngai: hivi namielezea: hivi namielezea: njo vile/ huyu wa kwanza: *premier notable* ata*insister:* njo kusema . . .
Feza and Tala Ngai: . . . bamu*punir*/
Tala Ngai: sasa kule bataleta mutoto yake: njo *deuxième tour*/ tu *comprends?*

Feza: si si/
Tala Ngai: njo *carte* ita*changer* sasa mu ngambo yake/

10. *Masimango:*   na mi lakini nitafanya *intervention* kwa adisi basi: basi*punir:* vile: vi: *punition/*
Tala Ngai: non non/ mi njo nita*intervenir:* njo kusema usimu*punir* yeye/ *parce que* mi njo wa leta *desordre* mu mukini/
Mufwankolo: hapana: Bwana Cheko atasema?
Kamwanya: Bwana Cheko ata . . .
Feza: mu *deuxième tour/*
Tala Ngai: angaria/ hapa munafanya hivi/ Bwana Cheko . . .
Mufwankolo: . . . atakankamana/
Tala Ngai: . . . anaisha kusema: weye unasema/ sasa wee njo ulikamata *parole/*
Mufwankolo: njo anatafuta kukamata *parole/*
Tala Ngai: hapa sasa wee utamu: kama unakamata *parole:* uta: utapima kuuliza: utauliza ba*notables: avis* ya kusema tumu*punir* je? njo mita*intervenir* mi njo ya ku: kuomba ya kusema bamuhurumie/ yee atakatala sana: anasema *non non non non:* ulisema kama muntu mwizi anafanya longolongo[3] . . . *wooo/*
Tala Ngai: njo pale tutamu*condamner* mutoto/
Mufwankolo: *bon/*
[A few more remarks are exchanged]

11. *Mufwankolo:*   [continuing with the scene] bazazi yako weko paka mukini humu?
Manyeke: ba: ba: chefu: bazazi beko mbali sana: ni baba: baba balimufahamu wa zamani sana humu . . . eh . . .
[Manyeke gets stuck]
Feza: baba yake ni Kafwankumba/
[Some more direction given in the background]
Mufwankolo: baba yake ni Kafwankumba/

12. *bon/* eh: ba*notables/* Bwana Cheko/
Bwana Cheko: [clapping hands] vidyee/ vidyee/
Mufwankolo: Masimango/
Masimango: chefu/
Mufwankolo: Tala Ngai/
Tala Ngai: ndiyo/

3. This appears to be a variation on the *lungulungu-kelulele* formula used so far. But the pronunciation is different as is the response to the call. This makes possible a different interpretation. In colonial times the prison in Elisabethville used to be called *mwalongolongo,* that is, the place of *Longolongo,* the latter being the (nick)name of a European director. So the translation might be: "He/she goes to prison."

[The women react to this as an improper way of acknowledging the chief.]

Feza: eh!

Kamwanya: [mocking] ndiyo/ ndiyo/

Mufwankolo: [to the *notables*] munawaza nje: mambo ya hii mambo/

Manyeke: [interrupting] chefu: ni njala tu/

Tala Ngai: lakini . . .

[Manyeke's response again causes laughter]

Masimango: [to Manyeke] yee [i.e., Tala Ngai] njo ya kwanza mbele/

Tala Ngai: [continuing with the scene] . . . minaona miye: ku mambo ya huyu mutoto/ hivi: alikwenda kuiba: na: anasema mbele yetu ya kama: ni juu ya njaa: tunaweza juu ya mara ya kwanza: kumuhurumia: sultani: nazania njo yangu akili ile/

Feza: eyo/ ni yako/

13. *Masimango:* sultani/ mu mukini: turudie ku: ku mukongo: mukini wasiyo kiwelewele: . . . ? . . . ile haina mukini/

Feza: ooh/

Masimango: mukini wasiyo mwivi: ile haina mukini/

Feza: aah/

Masimango: mukini wasiyo busharati: ile haina mukini/

Feza: eyo/

[Manyeke moves again, is called to order by the guards]

14. *Bwana Cheko:* eh/ eh: eh: eh/ uliona wapi? fasi gani? bantu batatambuka sauti ya sultani?

Feza: eeh: baba/

Bwana Cheko: bantu gani batatambuka sauti ya sultani? mwizi ni nduku yake na mulozi/

Feza: eyoo/

Actor: mama!

Bwana Cheko: mwizi ni nduku yake na mulozi/ pale anakwenda kubiiba: byakulya bya ule: ule alilimiabyo juu ya nini? si juu ya kuponesha batoto yake ku nyumba na bwana pamoya?

Actor: na si bote/

Bwana Cheko: mwizi/ benzake: saa ya kwenda kulima: yee analala macharichari[4] mu nyumba/ byakulya binaivya: anaanza kufunga njia ya kwenda kule/ ana: inapendezwa paka: anakamata masiku yake/

---

4. This is the Shaba Swahili form, with reduplication for emphasis, of ECS *chali*, on the back, prone.

Feza: [clapping hands] eyoo/
Bwana Cheko: hata miaka tatu/ ku buloko/

15. *Mufwankolo:*   Tala Ngai/
Tala Ngai: vidyee/
Mufwankolo: Bwana Cheko/
Bwana Cheko: vidyee/
Mufwankolo: Masimango/
Masimango: vidyee/
Mufwankolo: kanuni ni kanuni/
Feza: [clapping hands] eyoo/
Mufwankolo: buivi bwa namna hii: sawa hivi anaiba ni chakula:
tutaipa malipishi yake/ mumupeleke: ku kisukulu ya bankambo:
atapata malipishi/
[Manyeke starts clowning again, the others laugh; he is removed]

16. *Mufwankolo:*   mama/ ni kweli mama tunasikia/ sawa vile tunasema: mwivi wa kuiba: tunakatala kabisa/ ni hivi tunamupa malipishi kule ku bankambo: ni sababu ni chakula/ ingekuwa makuta:
ingekuwa viti ya mu nyumba: ingekuwa bintu gani: byote: lakini
njo kule kunaanziaka na byote bile/ yee mwenyewe anakwenda
kupata malipishi ku bankambo: nawaza kama: atabadirisha mioyo
yake/
Feza: [clapping hands] wafwako/
Mufwankolo: mama/ kamata bintu yako ende mama: hapana kusi-
kitika tena hapana: eh mama?
Feza: wafwako/ wafwako/
Mufwankolo: aksanti sana mama/
Feza: wafwako sultani: wafwako/
Mufwankolo: eyo/

17. *Bwana Cheko:*   sultani/ mama huyu: juu ya mambo: alikatalayo
kabisa sauti leo unakuwa nasema/ huyu mama: Masimango yee
huyu/ ziaka mbali[5]/
Masimango: alikatala/
Bwana Cheko: yee alisema buizi ni kintu kimoya kizuri/ lakini leo
juu ya maboké: analia/ utaangaria: juu ya maboké analia/ Masi-
mango/
Masimango: yee: si yee anakuwa anakatala asema oh: nani: sultani
aliitikia mambo ya buivi/ sasa juu ya nini alileta huyu mutoto huyu:
asema ananiiba bintu mu mashamba?

5.   An expression current in Shaba Swahili. The verb form *ziaka,* from *kuzia* plus
the affix *-ka-,* marking continuation or repetition, could be related to ECS *mzaha,* or
masihara, joke.

[This is followed by a short discussion among the actors who play the *notables*]

The Case of the Thief: Rehearsal Version (Translation)

1. *Bwana Cheko:*   Chief, my fellow *notable* Masimango and I were together over there when all of a sudden we were startled to hear noise in the village. There they are [dragging along] a person. We were surprised, has someone died, what was going on? Then we look and see your guards, followed by mama Feza. And this young person all tied up with a rope around him. What did he do [we asked]? Oh, he stole bananas in the fields.

2. *Mufwankolo:*   One banana?
Bwana Cheko and Feza: Bananas.
Mufwankolo: Many?
Feza: Here they are, baba.
Bwana Cheko: Three. three. So we looked at this and said: This happens now and here where the chief has just given his speech? So let us go there first, let us go there with this youngster. I think Masimango over there will add what he has to say about the matter.

3. *Masimango:*   Chief, about the speech you made. Together with Bwana Cheko, the dignitary, we went [to the villagers] to explain your intentions, such as: In the village the chief has forbidden to steal. The woman here told me—you go on, Bwana Cheko.
Bwana Cheko: [She said] about theft that if someone steals from you this is all right.
Masimango: [And she said] the things the chief said are bad.
Bwana Cheko: Bad [she said].
Masimango: Now we are here with this mama.

4. *Feza:*   [asking for directions] Can we have a dispute about this, or are you going to go on talking . . .
Masimango: You, your role is to complain.
Kamwanya: You just keep talking . . .
Masimango: Mama, where are we today?[6]
Feza: [goes on talking, incomprehensible]
Tala Ngai: Don't you answer back!
[Scene continues with a new start]

5. *Masimango:*   Chief, this is the dispute between this woman and this youngster.

6. Meaning: Just remember what your role is.

Mufwankolo: Mama, did you actually catch him in the fields carrying away your manioc, [correcting himself] your bananas?
Feza: Baba, here are the very bananas. I have no more to say.
Manyeke: Chief. Chief, I asked her [for the bananas].
Feza: Ah, where did you ask me, baba?
Manyeke: In the fields.
Feza: This is why I bring you before the chief?
Manyeke: Are you crazy?
Feza: Come on, baba.

6. *Guard:*   [restraining Manyeke] It's your fault. What is this?
Feza: Baba, this young man has cheated me.
Actor: Really!
Manyeke: Just three, does this make me a thief?
Others: Of course.
Feza: So you asked me for permission to steal?

7. *Mufwankolo:*   Whose child is he?
Masimango: [to Manyeke] You, the chief is asking you.
Mufwankolo: Who is your father?
Manyeke: [asking for directions] My father, chief—who is he?
Feza: Kafwankumba.
Manyeke: He is my father [points to Mufwankolo, the others laugh at this turn].
Mufwankolo: What?
Manyeke: Isn't he the father? What now?
Others: [laughing, partly incomprehensible] He is his father. The chief is his father.
Guard: Speak to the point, you.
Tala Ngai: The father is Kafwankumba.
Masimango: [laughing] No, no, he is the chief's child.
Kamwanya: He is the chief's child . . .
Feza: The child of the chief's younger brother [or sister].
Masimango: He is the chief's child.
Feza: The child of the chief's younger brother.
Masimango: Yes, because . . .
Manyeke: [trying to go back to the scene] Baba, it is only because I was hungry.
Bwana Cheko: He is the child of Bwana Cheko.
Feza: He is his child.[7]

7. This passage nicely illustrates how the group works in rehearsal. They begin the scene with just a general idea in their minds. When Mufwankolo introduces the additional dramatic element agreed upon earlier—but only in the most general terms—

[There follows some general discussion, largely incomprehensible because all talk at once]

8. *Tala Ngai:*   Don't get lost. This first youngster, the first youngster they are going to pick up is not the child of someone at the [chief's] court. This is how you can insist that he be punished.

Bwana Cheko: Yes.

Feza: So it cannot be him.

Tala Ngai: So the second youngster they are going to arrest, he is your child.

Bwana Cheko: That youngster is going to be Katolushi.

Tala Ngai: [to Manyeke] Your father is Kafwankumba.

Bwana Cheko: [continuing the other line] So it is Katolushi.

Feza: Yes, Katolushi.

Kamwanya: As soon as they have arrested Katolushi, he . . .

Masimango: Kafwankumba is present only in imagination.

Actor: All right, all right, so now Katolushi should get up. . . .

Tala Ngai: No, no, no, that's not it. He is the first one, you pick him up without being too severe with the youngster . . .

[Several talk at once; incomprehensible]

9. *Feza:*   The first [case] was Katolushi, this one is Manyeke's . . .

Tala Ngai: I tell you how it goes. It goes like this: About this first one the first *notable* will be insistent . . .

Feza and Tala Ngai: . . . that they punish him.

Tala Ngai: Now, when they bring his child, that is the second turn, you understand?

Feza: Yes, yes.

Tala Ngai: Then the cards change [so that the problem is] on his side.

10. *Masimango:*   And I am going to intervene to the effect that they should not punish him . . .

Tala Ngai: No, no, I am going to intervene, saying don't punish him, because I am the one who brings disorder to the village.

Mufwankolo: Isn't Bwana Cheko going to speak?

---

and asks the accused who his father is, it turns out that this has not been determined so far. That does not stop the dialogue, though. Manyeke immediately comes up with an answer calculated to amuse the group. This is acknowledged as a joke but then the collective search begins and two potential fathers are suggested: the chief's younger brother (a part that doesn't exist so far) and Kafwankumba (one of the actors from the crowd of villagers). Finally Bwana Cheko's name comes up. This is closer to the target, and, as the following shows, the complication of a kinship relation between one of the judges and the accused will be left to a later scene.

Kamwanya: Bwana Cheko will speak . . .
Feza: . . . at the second turn.
Tala Ngai: Look, here is how you do it: Bwana Cheko . . .
Mufwankolo: . . . [who] will be adamant . . .
Tala Ngai: . . . will speak first, then you [Masimango] speak.
[to Mufwankolo] Then you speak.
Mufwankolo: This is when he tries to get the floor.
Tala Ngai: When you speak your turn, you are going to try to ask
the *notables* for their opinion how he should be punished. Then I
intervene, begging that they should have mercy with him. He is
going to reject this altogether: No, no, you said if a person is a thief
he will condemn him.
All: Indeed.
Tala Ngai: This is when we condemn the youngster.
Mufwankolo: All right.
[A few more remarks are exchanged]

11. *Mufwankolo:*   [continuing the scene] Your parents are here in
the village?
Manyeke: Baba, chief, my parents are very far away. The old peo-
ple here used to know my father . . .
[Manyeke gets stuck]
Feza: His father is Kafwankumba/
[Some more direction given in the background]
Mufwankolo: His father is Kafwankumba.

12. All right, let's see. *Notables!* Bwana Cheko.
Bwana Cheko: [clapping hands as required by politeness]
vidyee, vidyee.
Mufwankolo: Masimango.
Masimango: Chief.
Mufwankolo: Tala Ngai.
Tala Ngai: Yes.
[The women react to the "yes" as an improper way of acknowl-
edging the chief]
Feza: What is this?
Kamwanya: [mocking] "Yes, yes."
Mufwankolo: [to the *notables*] So what do you think about this
affair?
Manyeke: [interrupting] Chief, it's just hunger.
Tala Ngai: But . . .
[Manyeke's response again causes laughter]
Masimango: [to Manyeke] He [Tala Ngai] comes first.
Tala Ngai: [continuing with the scene] This is how I see the case of

this youngster. He went to steal and said before us that it was
because of hunger. Therefore, also because it is the first time, we can
have mercy with him, chief. I guess, this is my opinion.
Feza: So, that is your [opinion].

13. *Masimango:*   Chief, in a village—let us go back—a village with-
out insanity is not a village.[8]
Feza: Oh?
Masimango: A village without a thief is no village.
Feza: Ah?
Masimango: A village without adultery is no village.
Feza: Really?
[Manyeke moves again, is called to order by the guards]

14. *Bwana Cheko:*   Stop it, stop it. Where did you see this? Where is
the place where the people go above the chief's word?
Feza: That's it, baba.
Bwana Cheko: What kind of people are going to go above the
chief's word? The thief is the sorcerer's brother.
Feza: Right.
Actor: [telling her off] Mama!
Bwana Cheko: The thief is the sorcerer's brother. When he went to
steal those things to eat, what did she grow [that food] for? Was it
not to do something for her children at home, as well as for her
husband?
Actor: That's what we all do.
Bwana Cheko: The thief—when it is time for his fellow villager to
go and work the fields he just sleeps in his house, flat on his back.
When the food plants get ripe then he is on his way there. He picks
his days.
Feza: [clapping hands] Yes indeed.
Bwana Cheko: Three years prison!

15. *Mufwankolo:*   Tala Ngai.
Tala Ngai: Vidyee.
Mufwankolo: Bwana Cheko.
Bwana Cheko: Vidyee.

---

8. This sounds like a proverb. Crazy and stupid people are to be found
everywhere; no wonder that there is trouble in every village. There is a corresponding
proverb, asserting, as is often the case, the contrary: *Mu mugini hamukosake muzee*
(literally: In a village you won't be without an old person), meaning: Wisdom and
sound advice to counteract *kiwelewele* are to be found in every village. The possibility
that Masimango's pronouncement may mock a proverb which states "A village without
a chief is not a village" will be discussed in chapter 14.

Mufwankolo: Masimango.
Masimango: Vidyee.
Mufwankolo: The law is the law.
Feza: [clapping hands] Yes indeed.
Mufwankolo: Theft of this sort—since what he stole was food—we
will set his fine accordingly. Bring him to the termite hill of the
ancestors, there he will get his fine.[9]
[Manyeke starts clowning again, the others laugh; he is removed]

16. *Mufwankolo:*   Mama. Truly, mama, we understand. As we said,
we are strictly against the thief who steals. So we gave him his fine
there at the ancestors' place, because it was food. Had it been
money, had it been some chairs [stolen] from a house, or what not,
anything else—but it is there [with food] that everything always
starts. He himself goes to get his fine at the ancestors' place and I
believe he will change his heart.
Feza: [clapping hands] Thank you.
Mufwankolo: Mama, pick up your things and go and don't be upset
any longer. Right, mama?
Feza: Thank you, thank you.
Mufwankolo: Many thanks, mama.
Feza: Thank you, chief, thank you.
Mufwankolo: All right.

17. *Bwana Cheko:*   Chief, but this woman is the one who was all
against what you said today. This woman—Masimango, isn't that
her? All joking aside.
Masimango: She refused to accept [your orders].
Bwana Cheko: She said there is nothing wrong at all with theft. But
today she cries about some bananas. You will see, because of the
bananas she complains. Masimango [you tell him].
Masimango: Wasn't she the one who opposed [you] saying the
chief has nothing against theft? Now, why did she bring this youngster telling [us] he stole from her fields?

In the final performance the plaintiff is not played by Feza. Manyeke is dragged by the guards onto the scene, followed by his accuser
and other "villagers." Everybody laughs; one of the real villagers calls
out *mwizi ya kwelikweli,* a real thief, to show his appreciation for the
acting. Otherwise the scene is pared down to the bare essentials; both

9. This takes up something Mufwankolo proposed in his version of plot, see text
2,9. Often the shrines where one "speaks with ancestors" are placed next to a termite
hill.

accusation and interrogation are very brief. General noise and merriment make most of the recording incomprehensible. Here is a fragment of the chief's summing-up and decision.

The Case of the Thief: The Chief's Verdict, Final Version (Text 13)

Mufwankolo: minasema kila siku/ mi siwezi kurudia ku mukongo hata kiloko/ unaenda mashamba ya benyewe/ *au lieu:* pahali pa kwenda ku: kuomba mama: unamuomba: anamupatia chakula unakulya/ *mais* wee unakwenda kuiba/ anafanya nguvu yake yote: yee hapana kukulimia wee hapana/ analimia bantu wote? wa mwema anakwenda kuuzako/ bintu gani sawa hivi?
Manyeke: mais/
Mufwankolo: bon/ angarie/ *allez*/ minakuhurumia kabisa pale/
Manyeke: mais: mais/
Mufwankolo: mara ya kwanza: lakini kama unarudisha mara ingine: utaukumiwa[10]/ unasikia muzuri? *bon*/ mukamupeleke kwanza mpembeni kwenda akalipe mu kale kanyumba ya malipishi kule/
Bwana Cheko: anapashwa paka kutengeneshwa huku/
[Manyeke is dragged away]

The Case of the Thief: The Chief's Verdict, Final Version (Translation)

Mufwankolo: This is what I have always been saying. There is no way I can go back on it. You go to fields that belong to someone else, instead of asking the woman—you ask her, she gives you food, you eat. But you go and steal. She worked very hard but she did not work the fields for you. Did she cultivate for everyone? Someone with good intentions would go [to her] and buy [from her].
Manyeke: But . . .
Mufwankolo: All right. Look here, I am going to be very mild with you.
Manyeke: But, but . . .
Mufwankolo: It was the first time. But if you do it once again I am going to punish you. All right, now bring him away; he should pay his fine at the [ancestors'] shrine over there.[11]
Bwana Cheko: He must be taken care of here [? and now].
[Manyeke is dragged away]

10. Shaba Swahili form of ECS *kuhukumu,* to give an official pronouncement, pass sentence.
11. In the text it says "at the little house"; some shrines look like miniature huts.

In the final performance the scene ends with a walk-on appearance by the woman who owns the house and yard that serve as the setting for the chief's court. She gathers the evidence (bananas and some sweet potatoes) in a basket which she carries away on her head. The *notables* keep discussing the case.

10 _____

Scene 4: The Hunter's Visit

In scene 4 the hunter, played by Kalwasha, visits the chief's court. In the filmed performance Kalwasha arrives, greets the chief and offers him game. He delivers a short speech. He recounts the hunt and cites the chief's order to "look at the belly, not at the face" of visitors. Mufwankolo accepts the tribute and orders his guard to cut the meat into pieces. While this is done there is some animated conversation, the hunter's exploits are recalled and praised. Then the chief distributes portions of the game among his *notables* and, with much ceremonial handclapping and greeting, the hunter leaves.

It has been difficult to make a complete and viable transcription of this scene from the sound recording of the filmed performance. In addition to the many problems already noted, Kalwasha, who plays the hunter, chose a "folksy" register of Shaba Swahili (with a recognizable accent and some lexical admixture from one of the regional languages). As a matter of fact, in an earlier phase of this study, before I was able to consult the soundtrack of the video recording, I had decided to write this part off as a "missing text."

Matters are different with the recording made during rehearsal (on June 26). On that occasion, conditions for taping a transcribable version were much better. There was none of the general background noise from the people of Kawama village who, in the final performance, responded with great enthusiasm to this scene and all but covered the dialogue. On the other hand, already in rehearsal Kalwasha had assumed the "old age" register of speech and his example was followed by Mufwankolo. Both of them swing through the dialogue; delivery is at times very rapid and the use of language is often elliptic when prosody and gestures seem to take over. Also, this scene had an even more tentative character in rehearsal than some of the others. Several actors contributed their opinion about its dramatic construction. As in the rehearsal version of the case of the thief, this lead to backtracking and numerous interruptions. For all these reasons, the texts and translations that follow are even more tentative than some of the others.

The Hunter's Visit: Rehearsal Version (Text 14)

1. *Kalwasha:* [bowing to the chief and clapping hands throughout this exchange of greetings] kalombo/
Mufwankolo: wafwako[1]/
Kalwasha: kalombo/
Mufwankolo: wafwako/
Kalwasha: kalombo/ ·
Mufwankolo: wafwako/
Kalwasha: nalikwenda mu pori chefu/
Mufwankolo: eheh!
Kalwasha: angaria angaria minasema: nitakulya mi moya? hoho/ acha nifanye kwanza mayele: nipelekea hata sultani nayee awekele kwanza kiloko mu ntumbo/
Mufwankolo: [laughing] wafwako: wafwako/
Kalwasha: kalombo/
Mufwankolo: wafwako/
Kalwasha: kalombo mfumu[2]/
Mufwankolo: nakwimuna[3]/
Kalwasha: kalombo/
Mufwankolo: wafwako/
Kalwasha: kalombo/
Mufwankolo: nakwimuna/
Kalwasha: kalombo/
Mufwankolo: nakwimuna/
Kalwasha: eyo/

1. Of the greeting formulas with which this text begins (and is liberally interspersed) neither *kalombo* nor *wafwako* is part of the "standard" Swahili lexicon. Both are, however, in the repertory of every speaker of Shaba Swahili. The terms are of Luba origin. *Kalombo,* a shorter form of *vidye kalombo* (originally used in addressing the deity), is the proper way to acknowledge a chief (see Van Avermaet and Mbuya 1954: 362). *Wafwako* is derived from the Luba verb *-fwa,* to die; literally it means "I die for you" and is used either as a greeting or an expression of gratitude (Van Avermaet and Mbuya explain that derivation, ibid., 152).
2. Kalwasha now changes the formula. Strictly speaking, *kalombo mfumu* is a pleonasm (*mfumu* means "chief"). Perhaps it is explained by the fact that *kalombo* has lost a specific reference to chief and can therefore occur, as a kind of epithet, together with *mfumu.*
3. Possibly as a response to Kalwasha's changed greeting, Mufwankolo now switches the code: *nakwimuna,* in Kiluba (and probably in related Luba languages), from the verb *-imuna,* to greet (see Van Avermaet and Mbuya 1954: 192f.).

2. *Mufwankolo:* mm: hii nyama yote: iko inaonekana ya mingi kabisa?
Kalwasha: eeeh/
Mufwankolo: eeh/
Kalwasha: njo nilikwenda mule mu mihulu ile ya kule ya samani ile ya bankambo: njo kule nalipata huyu lupenge[4]/
Mufwankolo: eh eh/
Kalwasha: eyo/
Mufwankolo: banaikala kama ya mingi sana?
Kalwasha: eeh: wa mingi/

3. *Mufwankolo:* wee mukwetu mu fu: wee: bu*chasseur* bwako mule mu fundi bwako hautabwachaka hapana/
Kalwasha: eeh/
Mufwankolo: unazekela nazekea paka kule?
Kalwasha: eeh/
Bwana Cheko: anakawiya nayo kabisa/
Mufwankolo: eeh/ anakawiya nayo/
Bwana Cheko: mm: mwanaume wa kweli/
Masimango: . . . anenda pale mu ile matongo ile/
Bwana Cheko: eheeeh/

4. *Mufwankolo:* angali/ na batoto yake banamufwata/ ule mutoto mwenyewe ule aliuaka tembo: eko wapi mutoto yako?
Kalwasha: huyu mutoto?
Mufwankolo: eh/
Kalwasha: sijue mwenyewe nayee anaikala kamukini ka: ka: kufwatana na hii mukini yetu: anakuwa: anayengala pale pa kiwanza: pale pa masanga njila[5]/
Mufwankolo: nitamupa bu*notable*/ mutoto wa kweli/
Masimango: yeye?
Mufwankolo: nitamupa bu*notable*/
Masimango: ule mutoto nayee iko na akili kabisa/
Mufwankolo: mutoto wa kweli/
Bwana Cheko: muko naikala na ule mutoto mu mukini: hamuna wa kulala njala/
Mufwankolo: mm/
Masimango: tena nayee: iko na mashauri muzuri/

---

4. *Mpenge* is a Luba term for "warthog" (*phacochère* in French); the *lu*- prefix indicates something big (see Van Avermaet and Mbuya 1954: 512).

5. The corresponding ECS term is *njia panda*, for crossroads or a fork in the road. *Masanga* probably comes from the Luba verb *-sanga*, to meet (Van Avermaet and Mbuya 1954: 572). It is possible that Kalwasha mentions the crossroad to allude to a place that was traditionally of great significance in the hunters' society, called *buyanga*.

Mufwankolo: unazala bantu wa kweli/
Bwana Cheko: oh! kweli/

5. *Mufwankolo:*   eh eh eh/ eeeeh: Shebele/
Shebele: [kicks his heels saluting] *chef/*
Mufwankolo: kuya huku/
[Shebele the guard is given directions]
piga magoti/ [pretending to whisper instructions in Shebele's ear]
waziwaziwazi . . . [then turns to the others] huyu *notable* Tala Ngai
iko hapa? unafanya paka vile unafanya? ba*notables* beko tatu/ kila
muntu unamupatiako ya kale ka kuenea/

6. [Shebele misunderstands his orders and Mufwankolo gives
directions]
Mufwankolo: hapana/ ni ile banaleta kule nyama: una: unakuya na
bifulusi tatu/ pale minakuambia ni ile/ unakuwa na bifulusi tatu:
komoya unaumpatia: unamuwekea hapa *directement:* ule . . .
Tala Ngai: *Je pense que c'est bien* vile: nani: vile mukubwa
aliingia . . .
Mufwankolo: *c'est ça/*
Tala Ngai: njo kusema nyama baliipokelea: banaisha na kubeba
kule/ [to Mufwankolo] unasema vile: unamutuma Shebele kwabo/
. . . ? . . . anakwenda: anatuletea nyama/
Mufwankolo: eeh/
Tala Ngai: bifulusi binakuwa ya kuaachana/ kya *notable* moya
kinakuwa sawa kinene: kya mwengine: kengine/
Bwana Cheko: ya kaloko/
Tala Ngai: kiisha kuleta bile: shiye tutafanya nini: tunazambalana/
Mufwankolo: eeh/

7. *Tala Ngai:*   bon/ *c'est qui fait que:* juu ya: nirudie sasa: *parce que*
minaanza kuona sawa kazi inataka kuwa butamu hapa/ njo kuse-
ma: hapa tunasambisha huyu mutoto hapa/ minamiuliza mbele
mwee mwenye kuyua ku mukini muzuri/ *est-ce que* bibi ya chefu
anapashwa kuwa pale?
Masimango and Bwana Cheko: *normalement: non/*
Tala Ngai: *normalement non/ parce* muko *conseil des sages/*
Bwana Cheko: ndiyo/
Tala Ngai: bibi hanako/
Bwana Cheko: eeh/
Tala Ngai: bon/ pale si tutabakia tena kufanya *conseil des sages:*
bibi hanako/
Mufwankolo: eeh/

8. *Tala Ngai:*   pale bataleta milambo: bibi ataiona kule bataenda
kuipeleka: *parce que* ni: ah: inapitia kule/
Mufwankolo: *c'est ça/* inapitia kule/
Tala Ngai: pale batakuwa kuleta: pale utakuwa kuleta manyama
ile: bibi nayee anaingia mule ndani mule tu/ inatu*permettre* kila
muntu anabebe kifulushi yake: tunazambala/ *vous comprenez?*
Bwana Cheko: *donc:* munabakia na mbili . . .
Tala Ngai: weye unabakia kwako ku nyumba: na: . . .
Bwana Cheko: na Shebele: na inamfumu . . .
Tala Ngai: bale babwana bale batakuya na ule bwana wa makozi:
bakuye bakukutanische wee ku lupango yako na polushi wako/
utume *police* sasa kwa: tuite sasa *conseil* ingine . . .
Bwana Cheko: na inamfumu/
Mufwankolo: *c'est ça: oui oui/*
Tala Ngai: njo *conseil* ingine kule/ *okay?*

9. *Mufwankolo:*   *bon/* nani aweza kutaniapo?
Actor: nani?
Bwana Cheko: inamfumu/
Mufwankolo: na: nani sultani: eh: *chasseur/*
Bwana Cheko: inamfumu/
Mufwankolo: *chasseur:* kiisha kumuambia tu vile na nani: nayee
chasseur anakwenda/
Others: eeh/

[There is a passage which is incomprehensible because several talk
at once]

Tala Ngai: . . . anakwenda: *alors:* eeh: banatumatuma eeh . . .
Bwana Cheko: Shebele . . .
Tala Ngai: Shebele/ anakwenda kuletakaletaka: sasa: tuko nasu-
mbulia shee benyewe pale mambo yetu moya mbili tatu/
Mufwankolo: aah/ *c'est ça/*

10. [Now the scene resumes where it was left off: the *notables'*
shares of game are distributed]
Bwana Cheko: kalombo/ eyo vidye/
Mufwankolo: eh/ Bwana Cheko/
Bwana Cheko: eyo vidye chefu/
Mufwankolo: na wee kwanza ukaangarieko muzuri/ Masimango/
Bwana Cheko: eyo vidye chef/
Mufwankolo: na wee kwanza ukaangarie muzuri/
Masimango: . . . kalombo/
Mufwankolo: Tala Ngai/
Tala Ngai: kalombo/

Mufwankolo: na wee kwanza ukuangaria muzuri na bamama na
batoto/
Notables: eyo: aksanti sana/
Masimango: wafwako: wafwako/
Mufwankolo: eyo/

11. *Bwana Cheko:*   chefu/ tunakupikia aksanti mukubwa sana/
Mufwankolo: aah: namna gani?
Masimango: [insisting] chefu: baba . . .
Bwana Cheko: nabeba kwanza kakifulushi ya kanene nikafikische
ku nyumba: nikafikische ku nyumba . . .
Mufwankolo: eeeh/
Masimango: sultani wee . . .
Mufwankolo: sawa ni *authenticité* ya kuweka na mama akaweke
mu moto/
Bwana Cheko: eeh basi: basi shee bantu wa mambo/
Mufwankolo: eeeeh/ bale bakwetu bale: ba kuendesha mukini:
kwanza bakabuleko buningi[6]/
Bwana Cheko: eyo chefu/
Mufwankolo: eyo: umusalimie kwanza bakwetu ku mulango/
Notables: eyo wafwako/ wafwako mulopwe[7]/
Mufwankolo: Tala Ngai umusalimie kwanza bakwetu ku
mulango/

12. *Tala Ngai:*   [interrupting the scene] *j'ajoute encore*/
Bwana Cheko: *oui*/
Tala Ngai: miye nitatokea na ngambo yangu: mwee mbili muta-
enda: mwee benyewe/
Bwana Cheko: eeh/
Tala Ngai: kule mutaenda sasa munishimange: munasema:
unaona Tala Ngai kwa kusemasema mingi: yee njo iko naharibisha
mukini: ni yee mulipatia kifulushi munene/
Bwana Cheko: eeh: njo vile itakuwa vile . . .
Tala Ngai: chefu . . . kifulushi munene: bo basiyue asema: Tala
Ngai njo anaharibisha mukini: angaria sultani/ bintu ya kutupatia
shiye bakubwa: eeh/
Bwana Cheko: uliona kifulushi yake vile kiko?
Tala Ngai: ni bakutengeneza: yeye: anamupatia yeye: iko anahari-

---

6. Literally: They should distribute *buningi*. But what is *buningi*? The best guess,
after consultation with Kalundi Mango, is that it is an obsolete expression derived from
English [good] morning. I translate it as "greeting."
7. *Mulopwe* is a Luba term (already encountered in some of the proverbs quoted
in chapter 2), yet another synonym for "chief" (others being, so far: *chef(u), sultani,
mfumu, vidye, kalombo*).

bisha mugini/ mutafanya ile *commentaire*/ bo banapashwa kuone-
kana mafanya ile *commentaire:* ku ile fasi bo nakwenda kule/
Bwana Cheko: mm/
Tala Ngai: kiisha njo barudishe *caméra:* ongoya pale beko nakuya
na ule: muntu/

13. [Without transition, the scene resumes]
Bwana Cheko: *c'est ça/ dis:* Masimango/ Masimango/
Masimango: mukubwa/
Bwana Cheko: unaona kwanza hii mambo hii?
Masimango: eeh/ si: si ile bitu ya kushangaa?
Bwana Cheko: Tala Ngai: siyue kama atapelekesha hii mukini
fasi gani/
Masimango: haukuona kwanza kifulushi ile yee anabebaka: iko
sawa na yako?
Bwana Cheko: [laughs] sijue/
Masimango: na muntu njo mwenye kuharibisha: mwenye kuleta
potopoto mu mukini . . .
Bwana Cheko: *fujard*[8] mwenyewe wa kwelikweli: minakuambia
bantu humu siku ingine batauanaka tu/ batauanaka/
Masimango: mu hii mukini si: mukini: si mutasambala tu/
Bwana Cheko: sultani eko nasema bitu bingine: yee eko anafanya
bintu ingine: na bantu kufanya bintu ingine . . .
Masimango: hii potopoto: si iko inaingia mu mukini: si Tala Ngai
huyu?
Bwana Cheko: ni nani mwenye kwanza: paka yee moya tena
alimuchagulaka/
Masimango: alafu sultani: mi siyue ile mambo ya sultani . . .
Bwana Cheko: twende [they walk away]

The Hunter's Visit: Rehearsal Version (Translation)

1. *Kalwasha:*   [bowing to the chief and clapping hands throughout
the exchange of greetings] Chief!
Mufwankolo: Thank you.
Kalwasha: Chief!
Mufwankolo: Thank you.
Kalwasha: Chief!
Mufwankolo: Thank you.
Kalwasha: I went into the bush, chief.

8. *Fujard* is, as it were, a remigrant loan word. From Swahili *fujo*, disorder,
trouble, a French calque is formed (on the model of *vantard, soulard*, etc.) to mean "a
troublemaker."

Mufwankolo: You did?
Kalwasha: Look here, I said, am I alone going to eat? No way. No, I am going to see to it so that I can bring something along for the chief to put in his belly.
Mufwankolo: [laughing] Thank you, thank you.
Kalwasha: [clapping] Chief!
Mufwankolo: Thank you.
Kalwasha: Greetings, chief!
Mufwankolo: I greet you.
Kalwasha: Chief!
Mufwankolo: Thank you.
Kalwasha: Chief!
Mufwankolo: I greet you.
Kalwasha: Chief!
Mufwankolo: Thank you.
Kalwasha: Yes.

2. *Mufwankolo:*   All this game, it looks like there is a lot of it.
Kalwasha: Oh, yes.
Mufwankolo: Ah.
Kalwasha: So I went to the forests along the river, those of old where the ancestors used to live, that is where I caught this big warthog.
Mufwankolo: Well, well.
Kalwasha: Yes.
Mufwankolo: Are there lots of them?
Kalwasha: Yes, many.

3. *Mufwankolo:*   You, my friend, so you are not going to give up your profession as a hunter.
Kalwasha: No.
Mufwankolo: You just grow old with it.
Kalwasha: That's it.
Bwana Cheko: He really stays with it.
Mufwankolo: Yes, he stays with it.
Bwana Cheko: Yes, he is truly a man.
Masimango: And then he goes to those places where there used to be villages.[9]
Bwana Cheko: Yes, indeed.

9. By mentioning the "forests along the rivers" (the geographer's "gallery forests") Kalwasha evokes an important topos of hunting lore. Masimango now follows him when he comes up with *matongo*, places where there used to be villages. By their vegetation (shade and fruit trees, sometimes bananas) these stand out against the surrounding savanna. Both actors contribute the small detail which can have a great effect on the audience, giving authenticity to the scene.

4. *Mufwankolo:*   He is still [strong]. And his children follow in his steps. Your son, the one who is a killer of elephants, where is he?
Kalwasha: This son?
Mufwankolo: Yes.
Kalwasha: I don't know, he lives in the little village behind this one. This is where he built [his house] near the open place there by the crossroads.
Mufwankolo: I am going to make him a *notable*. He really is someone.
Masimango: That one?
Mufwankolo: I am going to make him a *notable*.
Masimango: That young man is very clever.
Mufwankolo: He really is someone.
Bwana Cheko: If you live with that young man in a village there will be no one who goes to sleep hungry.
Mufwankolo: No way.
Masimango: Also, he has good advice.
Mufwankolo: You have fathered children of value.
Bwana Cheko: Yes, indeed.

5. *Mufwankolo:*   Yes, yes, yes. [hesitating] Eh, Shebele.
Shebele: [kicks his heels saluting] Chief.
Mufwankolo: Come here. [Shebele approaches, is given directions] Kneel down. [Mufwankolo pretends to whisper instructions in Shebele's ear] pspspspsps . . . [then turns to the *notables*] Notable Tala Ngai, is he here? You just do [the distribution] the way you [always] do it.[10] There are three *notables*. Give each a small piece that will be sufficient.

6. [Shebele misunderstands his order, Mufwankolo gives directions] No [not that way]. This is the game they brought. You will have three parcels, that's what I am telling you. You will have three parcels, you give one of them directly to him, the other . . .
Tala Ngai: I think this is good that way. The way Mufwankolo[11] began to explain it . . .
Mufwankolo: That's it.
Tala Ngai: That is to say, the game was received, it was already carried over there [to the chief's place]. [to Mufwankolo] Then you

10. There is a *sousentendu* here: When meat is distributed, it is determined beforehand who receives a bigger or a smaller share.
11. In the Swahili text Tala Ngai does not name Mufwankolo but refers to him as *mukubwa*, a term of respect for a person who is either older or more important than the speaker (something that tends to coincide in a culture where seniority is important). He himself is called elsewhere *mukubwa* Tala Ngai, meaning "Tala Ngai, the *notable*."

give instructions and send Shebele to them . . . ? . . . he goes and brings us [the *notables*] the meat.
Mufwankolo: Right.
Tala Ngai: The parcels are of different size. For one *notable* it is big, for another one it is different.
Bwana Cheko: Small.
Tala Ngai: After it is distributed we each go our way.
Mufwankolo: Yes.

7. *Tala Ngai:*   All right. That makes that, regarding the—but let me back up now because I begin to see that we are getting onto something good here—what I am saying is this: We try the young man here [the case of the thief]. What I want to ask first from you people who know the ways of the village well: Must the chief's wife be present?
Masimango and Bwana Cheko: Normally, no.
Tala Ngai: Normally not, because you are the council of the wise men.[12]
Bwana Cheko: Right.
Tala Ngai: So the wife isn't there.
Bwana Cheko: Right.
Tala Ngai: Fine, when we stay and gather in the council of the wise men, the wife is not present.
Mufwankolo: Right.
Tala Ngai: When the tribute is brought, the wife will see where they carry it, because it passes there [at her place].
Mufwankolo: That's it, it passes there.

8. *Tala Ngai:*   When they carry—when you bring those pieces of meat, that is when the wife gets involved too. That will make it possible for us to have each person carry his parcel and then go his way. You understand?
Bwana Cheko: So you are left with the two of them.[13]
Tala Ngai: [to Mufwankolo] You stay in your house together with . . .
Bwana Cheko: . . . with Shebele and *inamfumu* [the chief's first wife]
Tala Ngai: Then those men are going to arrive together with the adulterer. They should come and meet you here in your court

12. This is a literal translation of the French term used in the Swahili text. Referred to is the council of village elders, of which the chief's wife, although she may be called a *notable*, is normally not a member.
13. Sense not clear. Probably he means that the chief and his wife stay behind once the *notables* have each gone to his home.

together with your policeman. Then you should send the police to
call together another council meeting . . .
Bwana Cheko: . . . with *inamfumu.*
Mufwankolo: That's it, yes, yes.
Tala Ngai: So there is then another meeting, okay?

9. *Mufwankolo:*   All right, who should be there?
Actor: Who?
Bwana Cheko: *Inamfumu.*
Mufwankolo: The chief, eh [correcting himself], the hunter.
Bwana Cheko: *Inamfumu.*
Mufwankolo: So after we have talked to the hunter he leaves?
Others: Yes.[14]

[There follows a passage which is incomprehensible because several
talk at once]

Tala Ngai: He leaves and then they send around [hesitates] . . .
Bwana Cheko: . . . Shebele.
Tala Ngai: Shebele. He goes around to bring [the presents]. Mean-
while we [the *notables*] talk about our business, point by point.
Mufwankolo: Yes, that's it.

10. [Now the scene resumes where it was left off: the *notables'*
shares of game are distributed, the chief talks to his first *notable*]
Bwana Cheko: Chief. Yes, chief.
Mufwankolo: Eh, Bwana Cheko.
Bwana Cheko: Yes, chief.
Mufwankolo: You will first have a good look [at the case].
Masimango.
Bwana Cheko: Thank you, chief.
Mufwankolo: [to Masimango] You too, take a good look.
Masimango: [Yes] chief.
Mufwankolo: Tala Ngai.
Tala Ngai: Chief.
Mufwankolo: You too go and see how your wives and the children
are.[15]

---

14. Here is an example of an exchange whose meaning cannot be reconstructed
from the recording. That it is about the transition from one scene to another seems
clear. The literal rendering of this passage here must be incomprehensible to the reader
and should perhaps be omitted. But if this is done once it would have to be applied
systematically to dialogue of this type. The problems this would cause (e.g., how to
distinguish between utterances that are still somehow comprehensible and others that
somehow no longer are) may be more serious than an occasional obscure passage.

15. There is a change of reference in the chief's injunction "to go and look" that

Notables: Thank you, thank you very much.
Masimango: Thank you, thank you.
Mufwankolo: Thank you.

11. *Bwana Cheko:*   Chief, we are really grateful to you.
Mufwankolo: [being modest] Ah, don't mention.
Masimango: [insisting] Chief, baba . . .
Bwana Cheko: So I am going to take the big parcel and have it
brought to the house.
Mufwankolo: Right.
Masimango: [admiring] Really, chief . . .
Mufwankolo: As it is our custom, [the meat] is to be given to your
wife to put it on the fire.
Bwana Cheko: [laughing] Yes, well, we are people who must keep a
lot in mind.
Mufwankolo: Yes. [Now] the people who run our village should
take greetings to everyone.
Bwana Cheko: Yes, chief.
Mufwankolo: Right, so give my greetings to the people at home.
Notables: Thank you, thank you chief.
Mufwankolo: Tala Ngai, greetings to the people at home.

12. *Tala Ngai:*   [interrupting the scene] I am going to add some-
thing.
Bwana Cheko: Yes?
Tala Ngai: At the place where you go you are going to taunt me.
You say: Do you see Tala Ngai, the one who brings discord to the
village with all his talking. But the big parcel was given to him.
Bwana Cheko: Yes, that is how it is going to be. The chief . . .
Tala Ngai: . . . [gave] the big parcel [to him]. [This is done] so that
they should not know it is Tala Ngai who ruins the village.[16] See
what the chief does now. [He gives to him] what he should have
given to us who are [Tala Ngai's] seniors.
Bwana Cheko: Did you see how [big] his parcel was?
Tala Ngai: [speaking for Bwana Cheko and Masimango] There are
people who see to it that there is order, but he bestows his favors on
the one who ruins the village. [Addressing the two] This will be your

---

might be confusing. Masimango and Bwana Cheko are told to look into the matter put
before them; Tala Ngai is told to see how his family is.

16. This is an unexpected turn. On the other hand, it illustrates the deviousness of
politics where the troublemakers may receive special favors so as to keep them obliged,
all this behind the back of the people.

commentary. [Now addressing the group] They must be seen making [critical] comments in the place where they go to.[17]
Bwana Cheko: Yes.
Tala Ngai: After that they are going to turn the camera back [to the scene and] wait for them to come with this person [who is accused of adultery].
Mufwankolo: That's it.

13. [Without transition the scene resumes]
Bwana Cheko: That's it. Say, Masimango. Masimango.
Masimango: Bwana Cheko.[18]
Bwana Cheko: Do you see what is happening?
Masimango: Yes. Is it not something to be surprised at?
Bwana Cheko: I don't know where Tala Ngai will get this village.
Masimango: Didn't you see the parcel he carried away, was it as big as yours?
Bwana Cheko: [laughing] Ah, this chief.
Masimango: But what did the chief have in mind when he did this?
Bwana Cheko: [laughing] I don't know.
Masimango: He [Tala Ngai] is a person who destroys things, someone who brings confusion to the village . . .
Bwana Cheko: He really is a troublemaker, I tell you, one day the people here in the village will be killing each other. They will be killing each other.
Masimango: In this village, everyone will go in a different direction.
Bwana Cheko: The chief says one thing, he does another, and so do the people . . .
Masimango: If all this confusion now enters the village, is it not because of this Tala Ngai?
Bwana Cheko: And who started [this]? [The chief] himself chose Tala Ngai.
Masimango: But—I don't understand the chief. . . .
Bwana Cheko: Let's go. [they walk away]

---

17. The necessity to intersperse this passage with remarks specifying who is being addressed illustrates one of the most difficult problems with translations of this kind: the indexical function of pronouns, which cannot be grasped from lexical or syntactic information alone. During the event itself the ethnographer can observe clues such as direction of gaze, body posture, etc. The sound recording may preserve some of these clues (as changes in volume or tone) but essentially the translator must rely on memory and imagination in reconstructing the event.

18. The original has *mukubwa*, a respectful term of address marking seniority.

The Hunter's Visit: Final Version (Text 15)[19]

1. *Kalwasha:*   kalombo mfumu/ kalombo/ [Mufwankolo's response is not audible. A pause follows before Kalwasha continues] sultani wangu: nalikwendela kule: ku kamuhulu kule/ minasema niangarie tu hivi: lupenge kabisa/
Mufwankolo: eh/
Kalwasha: minasema eeh/ leo paka hapa niliona: nalikamata pale nalisimamaka buyana pale/
Mufwankolo: eheh/
Kalwasha: namuntenteka/ njo minasema hapana: habakulyake: unasahabu sultani siku yote banasema unaangaria pa ntumbo?
Mufwankolo: [laughs]
Kalwasha: hapana kuangaria pa nsula/
Mufwankolo: mukwetu mwanamulume/[20]
Kalwasha: eeh/ njo vile nilisemaka acha kwanza nikamupelekee nayee sultani: kiloko hata kalupenge/ nayee asikie muzuri/
Mufwankolo: wafwako pale/ wafwako/
Kalwasha: eyoo/

2. *Mufwankolo:*   Shebele/
Shebele: kalombo/
Mufwankolo: utakatakata utakatakata bipande bipande: uta: utajuako na ba*notables*/ *dis:* ingisha mu nyumba/

3. [to Kalwasha] wee mukwetu bulumba bwako bule haiyasahabu na sasa?
Kalwasha: eeh/
Mufwankolo: ukingaliki nalumbata/
Bwana Cheko: ni mwanaume wa kweli huyu/
Mufwankolo: alafu ule *garçon* wako ule? we hamuna na *garçon*?
Bwana Cheko: kale katoto kanaume kako ka mbele kale/
Mufwankolo: ni kale kale kale/ njo mwenyewe/ namuna kake keko kalumbatayi/
Kalwasha: hapa tuko tunasema eko na mwenzake mu masimbiliki/
Mufwankolo: eh/ anapenda paka kulumbata pa . . . ? . . . ya baba yake/

---

19. This transcript is based on the soundtrack of the video recording, which, on the whole, is of very bad quality. Quite accidentally, speakers were in a better position with regard to the microphone than in other scenes. In my own recording of the filmed performance, made from my place among the audience, this scene is all but covered by noise and the spectators' comments.
20. Here Mufwankolo switches to Luba.

Bwana Cheko: ...? ... wa baba yake/
Masimango: paka mukulukulu ya baba yake: na mutoto anafwatako/
Bwana Cheko: eh/ eheh/

4. *Shebele:*   hamufu mwana[21]/ njo kusema: hapa sasa tungaliki na ma: na makazi mingi: nitabeba ma: manyama kiloko kiloko ile nitapeleka ku ba*notables*/
Mufwankolo: eeh/ Bwana Cheko/
Bwana Cheko: vidyee/
Mufwankolo: eh: batakupelekea kwanza mbele/
Bwana Cheko: aksanti chefu: aksanti: sultani wetu aksanti/
Mufwankolo: Tala Ngai/
Tala Ngai: eeh baba/
Mufwankolo: batakupelekea/
Tala Ngai: aksanti baba [clapping his hands]/
Mufwankolo: Masimango/
Masimango: mfumwa/
Mufwankolo: ku nyumba kule/
Masimango: wafwako [clapping his hands]/
Mufwankolo: batakupelekea/
Masimango: wafwako/
Mufwankolo: utasikia kwanza muzuri mbele/

5. *Kalwasha:*   eeeh/ wafwako/
Mufwankolo: eyo/
Kalwasha: kalombo/
Mufwankolo: aah/
Kalwasha: kalombo/
Mufwankolo: mukwetu/ wafwako mukwetu/ endelea paka vile na kazi/
Kalwasha: eyoo/
Mufwankolo: eeh/ salimia mama/
Kalwasha: eyoo/ [walks away with his bow and arrows]

6. *Bwana Cheko:*   sikie: si ni mwanaume ya kweli huyu. . . .
Tala Ngai: sultani/ nakuacha kwanza/
Mufwankolo: eeh/ wende kwanza ukumulamukie mama kwanza . . .
Tala Ngai: kalombo . . .
Mufwankolo: . . . akuwekee mu chungu mule/

---

21. I am told that this is an expression in Luba corresponding to Shaba Swahili *mutoto wa mama* (literally: child of a mother). It expresses appreciation and respect.

Tala Ngai: kalombo/
Mufwankolo: eeh/ salimia bakwetu bale/
Bwana Cheko: sultani/
Mufwankolo: eh/
Bwana Cheko: nawaza na mi tunatangulia kwanza kiloko tuka-
pumuzike/
Mufwankolo: eeh/
Bwana Cheko: tukapate nguvu/
Mufwankolo: muzuri/ vidyee/
Bwana Cheko: kalombo/
Mufwankolo: nakwimuna/
Bwana Cheko: vidyee/
Mufwankolo: nakwimuna na mi/

The Hunter's Visit: Final Version (Translation)

1. *Kalwasha:*   Greetings chief, greetings. [Mufwankolo's response is not audible. A pause follows before Kalwasha continues] My chief! I went to this little forest over there. I told myself, let's just look around [and what do I see?] Some real big warthog.
Mufwankolo: Really.
Kalwasha: So I say, today, when I was looking around, I caught [some warthog] at a place where I used to stop when I was still young.
Mufwankolo: That's so.
Kalwasha: And I hit it right. Then I said to myself, no, one should not eat [alone]; are you forgetting that the chief always says: Look at the belly?
Mufwankolo: [laughs]
Kalwasha: Don't look at the face.
Mufwankolo: You, our friend, are a man.
Kalwasha: Yes, well, this is why I said [to myself] let me first bring a little of the warthog to the chief, so that he may feel well.
Mufwankolo: Thank you for that, thank you.
Kalwasha: Thank you.

2. *Mufwankolo:*   Shebele!
Shebele: Chief!
Mufwankolo: Get busy cutting [the meat] into pieces [so that it can be distributed among] the *notables*, you know [how].[22] Say, get it into the house.

---

22. This is another difficult passage. The original contains, on the one hand, morpho-syntactic information that cannot be rendered with equal ease in English (these

3. [Then to Kalwasha] So, my friend, you haven't forgotten how to hunt, up to this day?
Kalwasha: Right.
Mufwankolo: You go on hunting.
Bwana Cheko: He is a real man, this one.
Mufwankolo: But what about that boy of yours? Don't you have a boy?
Bwana Cheko: That little one, the boy who came first.
Mufwankolo: That's the one, that little one, that's the one. He is some little hunter.
Kalwasha: That is to say he is with his friends after bamboo rats.
Mufwankolo: [parts of the following exchange incomprehensible] So, he likes to go hunting . . . ? . . . [just like] his father.
Bwana Cheko: . . . ? . . . like his father.
Masimango: He is a chip of the old block,[23] that child just follows [his father].
Bwana Cheko: Yes, yes indeed.

4. *Shebele:* Chief! That is to say, we still have a lot of work to do now, so I am going to carry the little pieces of meat to the *notables'* [houses].
Mufwankolo: Right. Bwana Cheko!
Bwana Cheko: Chief!
Mufwankolo: They will bring it to your place first.
Bwana Cheko: Thank you, chief, thank you, thank you, our chief.
Mufwankolo: Tala Ngai!
Tala Ngai: Yes, baba.
Mufwankolo: They'll bring you [some].
Tala Ngai: Thank you, baba [clapping his hands].
Mufwankolo: Masimango!
Masimango: My chief.
Mufwankolo: [You will get it brought] to your house over there.
Masimango: Thank you.
Mufwankolo: Above all, you will feel well [after eating].

5. *Kalwasha:* [taking leave] Thank you.
Mufwankolo: Thank you.

---

are reduplications pronounced extremely rapidly; I try to indicate the sense by "get busy . . ."); on the other, it is elliptical and needs knowledge of the context to be reconstructed with some accuracy (knowledge, e.g., of the fact that the chief intends to divide the portions unevenly and that he wants this done out of sight).

23. The original has the term *mukulukulu* (see Lenselaer 1983: 310) and says something like: He is the same kind of bastard as his father; "bastard" being used in a joking fashion, in this case even to express admiration.

Kalwasha:　[I greet you] chief!
Mufwankolo:　Greetings.
Kalwasha:　Chief!
Mufwankolo:　My friend, thank you, my friend. Just go on with your work.
Kalwasha:　I will.
Mufwankolo:　Yes, and greetings to your wife.
Kalwasha:　Thank you. [walks away with his bow and arrows]

6. *Bwana Cheko:*　Listen, isn't he a true man . . .
Tala Ngai:　Chief, I am leaving you now.
Mufwankolo:　Right, just go and greet your wife . . .
Tala Ngai:　Chief!
Mufwankolo:　. . . she should put [the meat] in the pot.
Tala Ngai:　Chief!
Mufwankolo:　Right, greetings to our friends.
Bwana Cheko:　Chief!
Mufwankolo:　Yes.
Bwana Cheko:　I think we'll take a while to rest a little.
Mufwankolo:　Right.
Bwana Cheko:　So that we get [our] strength [back].
Mufwankolo:　That's good. Greetings.
Bwana Cheko:　Chief!
Mufwankolo:　I greet you.
Bwana Cheko:　Chief!
Mufwankolo:　I, too, greet you.

The *notables* leave the chief and this is where the scene ends in the filmed performance. The part where, in the rehearsal version, Bwana Cheko and Masimango complain about the chief favoring Tala Ngai is left out. Instead, the play continues with the second court case.

11 _____

Scene 5: The Case of Adultery

In scene 5 a second culprit is brought before the chief. Earlier I suggested some of the reasons why another court case was introduced into the play. Already during rehearsal it was clear that this one would be an especially entertaining and successful scene. Unlike the trial of the thief, which relied for effects mainly on Manyeke's clowning, this one has a spicy topic—debauchery and fornication in the fields. Apart from the young man who is treated as the principal culprit, it involves three more persons: the woman and her husband and the adulterer's father. The recording of the rehearsal version shows that the work is still in a phase which admits discussion and suggestions for improvement (most of which will only be summarized in English). But some of the dialogue already resembles that of the performance version: exchanges are brief, delivery is rapid, verbal gestures are prominent.

The Case of Adultery: Rehearsal Version (Text 16)

[Two guards bring the accused man, the woman, and her husband before the chief]

1. *First Guard:* vidye kalombo/
Mufwankolo: vidye vidye/
First Guard: mambo: tunabamba: huyu baba huyu Katolushi: na huyu mama Kamwanya: bibi yake ya: Foloko/
Second Guard: [clapping hands] vidye kalombo *tatu*[1]/
First Guard: tunababamba kule ku ngambo ya kule ku kinani: kyetu kile tunawekeaka ma: mapamba kule . . .
Second Guard: . . . mutoto ya kisukulu/
First Guard: kule chini ya bisukulu/

---

1. The Luba term *tata* or *tatu*, corresponds to Shaba Swahili *baba*, father, here used as a polite term of address.

Second Guard: balikuwa bawili/
First Guard: *chemise* yake yo hii/ bilatu biko hapa/
Villager: bupuluzi ya huyu mutoto/ mutoto tunakomeshamo mu
mukini . . .
Second Guard: *dis/*
First Guard: njo mambo ile *chef/*
Second Guard: wee ukafunge kinywa/

2. *Mufwankolo:*   Shebele/
First Guard: sultani/
Mufwankolo: ita Bwana Cheko: Masimango: na Tala Ngai/
First Guard: sasa sultani/
Mufwankolo: mama/
Kamwanya: abé[2] baba/
Mufwankolo: bwana yake iko wapi?
First Guard: yee ule *chef/*
Foloko: ndiyo *chef/*
First Guard: *dis* uikale chini/

[*Notables* arrive]

3. *Bwana Cheko:*   vidye kalombo/
Mufwankolo: eyo/
Bwana Cheko: vidye kalombo/
Mufwankolo: eyo/
Notables [clapping hands]:   vidyee kalombo/
Mufwankolo: eyo vidye/
Notable: vidye kalombo/
Mufwankolo: wafwako/ [pause]

4. mm/ eh: baba/
Foloko: *chef/*
Mufwankolo: njo bibi yako?
Foloko: wangu Kamwanya huyu/
Mufwankolo: muko naye miaka ngapi?
Foloko: hii miaka njo inakuwa kumi mbili na tano/
Mufwankolo: miaka kumi mbili na tano?
Foloko: makumi mbili na tano/
Mufwankolo: batoto ngapi?
Foloko: batoto tano/

2. This is how women acknowledge a call; men often use the French term
présent (as in a roll call at school or in the army). The latter, however, is considered
foreign and not really polite. The preferred answer is a term of address for the caller
(e.g., *baba, mukubwa*). As to the derivation of *abé* (stress on the second syllable), see
Lenselaer 1983: 253, where it is related to ECS *labeka*.

Mufwankolo: hamulishake?
Foloko: *chef:* tuko tunakulya tu/ muzuri sana/
Mufwankolo: munalima sana?
Foloko: kulima sana/ sawa mwee mwenyewe mulisemaka/
kulima tu/
Mufwankolo: kumuvwika hamuvwikake?
Foloko: kuvwika kabisa/

5. *Masimango:* wee: hapana muzuri/ tosha ule muti kule/ uko
nasema na sultani na uko na ule muti humu?
Mufwankolo: wee uko na bibi?
Katolushi: ndiyo *chef*/
Mufwankolo: uko na bibi?
Katolushi: ndiyo/
Mufwankolo: na batoto ngapi?
Katolushi: batoto mbili/
Mufwankolo: uko naye miaka ngapi?
Katolushi: tuko naye miaka: sasa njo mwaka ya kumi/
Mufwankolo: mwaka ya kumi?

6. [pause, then to Kamwanya] mama/
Kamwanya: abé baba/
Mufwankolo: bile binasema ule bwana yako ni kweli? muko naye
miaka makumi mbili na batoto tano?
Kamwanya: ni bya kweli baba/
Mufwankolo: bya kweli?
Kamwanya: ndiyo baba/
Mufwankolo: sasa: huyu: haunamufahamu huyu? huyu haunamu-
fahamu?
Kamwanya: minamuonaka tu/
Katolushi: *chef:* niko na sauti ya kusema/
Guard: *dis*/
Mufwankolo: muna: muna: munaonanaka tu eh?
Kamwanya: mi minamuonaka tu . . .
Foloko: njo wake abala[3] *chef*/
Guard: eh *dis*/
Kamwanya: namuonaka tu/
Mufwankolo: munaonanaka tu ku macho: ao munaonanaka tu?
Kamwanya: minamuonaka tu pa kushota mayi iko anapita/

7. *Mufwankolo:* ku macho/ ku macho/
Masimango: mulopwe/

---

3. *Abala* is the Shaba Swahili form; in ECS it is *hawara*, mistress, lover.

Mufwankolo: bon/
Masimango: mutoto ya nani?
Mufwankolo: eh?
Masimango: mulopwe umuulize mbele ni mutoto ya nani?
Mufwankolo: wee mwenyewe baba yako ni nani?
[There is a short interruption for directions]
Mufwankolo: baba yako ni nani?
Katolushi: Bwana Cheko/
Mufwankolo: Bwana Cheko?
Bwana Cheko: sultani/

8. *Mufwankolo:*   Bwana Cheko/ ni mutoto yako? njo wa ngapi?
Bwana Cheko: ni mutoto yangu: huyu njo wa tatu/
Mufwankolo: njo wa tatu/
Bwana Cheko: lakini minazania mutoto hapa: pa hii fasi hapa: hana
na kosa/ huyu mama njo anaoa wabwana mbili/ [laughter from the
others]
Tala Ngai: aaah: Bwana Cheko sema muzuri/ nani anaharibishia
nyumba?
Mufwankolo: Tala Ngai?
[more laughter from the audience]
Bwana Cheko: mutoto yangu hana na kosa/
Mufwankolo: Masimango?
Masimango: [clapping his hands] wafwako/

9. *Mufwankolo:*   mutoto wa Bwana Cheko/ njo wa tatu: anaoa:
bibi: wa: Foloko/ yee na yeye: eko na babibi: na batoto mbili/
Masimango: bibi yako iko mu *congé?*
Katolushi: hapana *chef/*
Tala Ngai: eko paka humu?
Katolushi: ndiyo/
Mufwankolo: saa ulikwenda kwa yee: bibi yako ulimuacha ku
nyumba eh?
Katolushi: *chef* niko na sauti moya ya kusema/
Mufwankolo: aah: iko na neno moya ya akusema/
Katolushi: ndiyo/
Mufwankolo: banakulongofea? semaka/

10. *Katolushi:*   *chef* ilikuwa ni hivi/ mama anapikiaka lutuku kule
ku mashamba/
Mufwankolo: anapikiaka lutuku?
Katolushi: ndiyo/ minafika minauza chupa hii: *moya/* nakunywa
ver/ nakunywa: nakunwya: nakunywa/ nasikia: bulevi inanika-
mata/

Mufwankolo: eh/
Katolushi: njo mina: minalamuka pa mituta[4]/ mama nayo si njo kutosha kikwembe yake kunitandikia: mi kulala pale/ bwana yake kuya kunikutana kupita pale asema: ah: minabamba makozi/
Kamwanya: njo vile sultani/

11. *Masimango:* sultani/ sultani/
Mufwankolo: mm/
Masimango: hii mambo: iko nguvu/ hii mambo ni bukari bwa nyama:[5] bunakabulaka mwenye bukari/
Mufwankolo: semaka/
Masimango: njo kusema: mambo hii: mwenyewe wa . . .
Mufwankolo: wa mutoto . . .
Masimango: mwenyewe wa mutoto: akabule mboga ya: ya mwe-nyewe ya bukari/

12. *Bwana Cheko:* sultani/ nawaza kama mulisikia sauti inatoka mu kusema: mutoto huyu/ anasema huyu mama huyu: anafansiaka pombe yake kila siku/ ku mashamba/ mama: hapana vile?
Kamwanya: njo vile/
Bwana Cheko: mutoto alikwenda kule: kwenda kufwata pombe ya: ya kunywa/ bulevi bunamukamata: anaangukia pa mututa/ lakini mama huyu alisikia buruma . . .
Kamwanya: minasikia buluma eeh/
Bwana Cheko: juu ya: *client* wake/ na vile kwiko baridi: na vile . . .
[Interruption for directions and discussion]

13. *Bwana Cheko:* minawaza: sultani: ulifwata sauti inatoka mu kusema mutoto/ huyu ni *client* wake wa siku yote/ na anaisha kuzobelea kupikakaka pombe kule: ku mashamba/ mutoto ana-sema: alikunywa: anaisha kunywa analewa: anashinda nguvu ya kwenda/ anaanguka: anaangukia pa mututa/ bon/ huyu mama:

---

4. The ECS form is *tuta,* a term with a complex meaning that can only be rendered by a paraphrase: "a raised bed for planting, a long ridge of earth with deep furrows on either side" (Standard Dictionary). As we shall see, that very complexity will be exploited in this scene. Because it would be awkward to repeat the paraphrase I opted for the one element that seems to be salient in this case: furrow (with groove or ditch as possible alternatives).

5. Although the two terms are connected by *bwa,* the translation must be "*bukari* and meat" (not: *bukari* made of meat, a contradictory expression because *bukari,* ECS *ugali,* is the staple food made from corn or manioc, or a mixture of both). The term *boga,* which occurs a little later, is often translated as "vegetables." This corresponds to European categories whereby vegetables is what "goes with" meat and potatoes. Here *boga* is everything that goes with *bukari,* hence also meat or fish.

alikuwa na kikwembe yake: anaangaria asema *client* atakuwa kufa
na baridi ya: ya hii wakati hii/
Mufwankolo: yee muntu anakunywa lutuku anasikia baridi?
Bwana Cheko: tena: amufunike/ kuko baridi/ njo sawa ile bana-
kaukaka ba kunywa lutuku/

14. *Masimango:*   mukubwa Bwana Cheko/
Bwana Cheko: vidyee/
Masimango: muu: tuangarie mu kanuni yetu kabisa ya ba: ya
bankambo/ kama muntu anakunywa lutuku: anakunywa pombe:
lawa ya: ya kuisha pombe ni nini?
Actor: baridi/
Masimango: hapana mayi na baridi?
Bwana Cheko: mayi na baridi? nawaza/
Masimango: [to Tala Ngai] ongeze/

15. *Tala Ngai:*   [claps] kalombo/ minazania: mukubwa Bwana
Cheko eko anaenda mbali kabisa/ sultani wee ulisema mambo
hapa/ banauliza mutoto mwanamuke: anasema/ pake vile bwana
yake: halibakutanisha?
Others: eyoo/
Tala Ngai: bwana utaelezea mbele? wee: ulibakutanisha yee iko
anamularika pa kikwembe ao ulimukutanisha vile tu ndani?
Mufwankolo: beko banakombana? [general laughter] unamukuta-
nisha anaisha kulala pa kikwembe ao munamukutanisha paka
banakombana?
[Interruption: general mirth]

16. *Foloko:*   sultani wangu/ sultani wangu/ minafika tu mu
mashamba: minaona paka machupa mwa lutuku/ iko kwiko/
namukutanisha . . ./ beko nakombana ile ya . . ./ wee mwenyewe
unayua . . .
Katolushi: hapana/
Foloko: mi: bongo/ kuniona paka hivi: analamuka pale/
[Interruption for directions]

17. *Mufwankolo:*   pale unabakutana: ulibakutanisha: beko banakombana: ao: unabakutanisha: analala: beko namularisha? ao una-
mukutanisha: beko nakombana? mbo mbili?
Foloko: nafika mule mu mashamba mule: kufika tu paka hivi:
kuniona: kulamukapo tu: na mbio: kwanza kurugaruga: na mi paka
pale: kukimbia njo kabisa pale: kumubamba/ njo kumukamata
kumutosha *chemise* hii/

18. *Feza:*   [intervening here because she still does not like the way
the scene goes] hapana: hautamutosha/ asema anaisha banakimbia:

minafika pale balikuya: nakutanisha *chemise* inabakia pale: na bilatu: na kikwembe/ njo vile nabibeba/ njo unaanza kubafukuza sawa
mbio/

19. Mufwankolo: [making another start] ulibakutanisha: beko nakombana: ao: ulibakutanisha: beko namularisha?
Foloko: ndiyo *chef*/ ile wakati minatoka mu mashamba: nabaona
pale: mi kufika tu karibu: huyu kuchamoka mbio: huyu kuchamoka
mbio/ nafwata bwana kule ku kashamba yangu ya mihoko ya kule
chini kule/ namubambia mule mu ma: mandizi mule/
Mufwankolo: ku lutuku kule/
Foloko: kule ku lutuku/ njo minarudia naye nakuwa kulokota bilatu na shimisi hii/
Mufwankolo: paka pale?
Foloko: pake pale ile fasi balikuwa na kikwembe ya bibi yangu
ilibakia paka pale/

20. Tala Ngai: sultani/ nataka kusemako kintu moya/ banasema
hivi/ kama tunda: yenye kuivia: iko ku muti: wee unaifka unai-
angaria/ ile tunda ile: kama ni ya kula: si utaichuma naye kula?
haiko vile? sasa kama tunda: we unaona inaanguka chini/ kunapita
masiku/ muntu yee hapana kupita pale/ ile tunda kama ni ya kuo-
za: minazania: itaoza/ alafu juu ya nini: huyu kiyana: mwenye
kuyua asema hii tunda: ni ya benyewe iko yulu ya muti/ ya lelo
kefwatene nakaikule?[6]
Bwana Cheko: mm/
Tala Ngai: yee njo alipanda ili muti/ minazania mambo iko: iko . . .
Others: wazi/
Tala Ngai: iko wazi/
Masimango: iko wazi kabisa/
Tala Ngai: na kanuni: wee mwenyewe unajua: ni kintu gani tuna-
weza kufanya na huyu kiyana/

21. Masimango: sultani: naongeza pa mambo ya Tala Ngai/ bakubwa walisema: mwanamuke: ni kangozi ya kabundi/ [laughter from
the others]
Feza: alafu unaona huyu . . .

---

6. This phrase is partly in Luba and the transcription and translation are
approximate. Van Avermaet and Mbuya list *dya lelo* as an interjection, "allez donc,
voyez" (1954: 346). Why does the speaker switch to Luba at this point? He started out to
give his opinion on the case by quoting a saying, if not a proverb, then some sort of
sententious wisdom. He does this as a way of appealing to traditional authority. The
code switch to Luba could then be understood as an additional linguistic signal marking
this episode as "quoting behavior" (see chapter 2).

Masimango: kanakalaka muntu huyu . . . *moya/*
Masimango and others: habikalaka wawili/

22. *Bwana Cheko:*   sultani/ mufwate sauti ya mutoto/ mutoto alisema alikwenda kunywa pombe/ analewa: anaangukia pa mututa/
Katolushi: ndiyo baba/
Bwana Cheko: bon/ munaweza kuyua namna gani nako hakukuwa
témoin/ kulikuwa paka bwana na bibi/ pa kuona mutoto yangu:
anaisha kulewa: banamumvula mu semishi/ pengine alikuwa yee
bado kulipa/
Katolushi: voilà baba: njo vile bilikuwa mambo/

23. *Mufwankolo:*   Bwana Cheko/ minasikia mambo yako/ njo
kusema pale anaanguka pa mututa: si kwa mututa si njo yee ule?
[points to Kamwanya] si njo mututa?
Feza: njo yoo *idée/* [the others laugh]
Bwana Cheko: ni vile/
Katolushi: hapana *chef/*
Mufwankolo: si njo mutoto ule haiangukia pale?
Foloko: kabisa *chef/* kabisa *chef/*
Guard: [to Foloko] wee/ tss/

24. *Masimango:*   pale: sultani iko nakuuliza mambo kiloko/ pale
huyu bwana alifika mu mashamba/ alikukutanisha fasi gani? na
alikubambia fasi gani?
Katolushi: alinikutanisha mwenye kulala/

25. *Guard:*   chefu/ naweza kusema kidogo?
Mufwankolo: semaka/
Guard: sababu huyu mutoto: anataka kuleta bongo hapa/ ile
wakati tunamubamba na baba pale: alisema hivi/ tunamuuliza
mbele yee: hii mambo bwana huyu eko nasema ni ya kweli ao ni ya
bongo? unasikia? yee akasema hivi/ asema mi nilikuwa sawa mi
natelemuka huku/ sema nipite: asema nishuke: sawa nipande hivi:
namukuta huyu mama aliisha kuikala chini/ asema niko natokea ku
mutoni: nilienda kuilobeka mihogo mayi/ njo swahili huyu bwana
alileta/ [to Katolushi] na wee unataka kuleta bongo hapa?
Masimango: swahili mbili ile si sultani?
Guard: sasa pale: akasema: namukuta huyu mama/ eko natoka
mu kulobeka mihogo mu mayi/ na muchoko nilikuwa nayo: nika-
muomba muhogo mubiti: ile muhogo: sababu nilianguka mule mu
matope mule hatukuwa ngisi ya kuingia mule hapana/ alikuwa na
muhogo kipande eko mufuku: eh: ya kula hivi/ ile wakati sasa huyu
mama asasema: tunamuuliza: anasema: *non:* nilikuwa nilikala niko
namuuliza habari ya mashamba sababu minatafuta kamatia

mashamba kule ngambo/ *mais* balikuwa chini/ sauti yake/
nikisema bongo: nduku yangu iko pale/
Second Guard: mm/ *okay*/ . . . [others laugh]

26. *Mufwankolo:*   mambo ya mwisho: ni: Bwana Cheko/
Bwana Cheko: sultani/
Mufwankolo: Masimango/
Masimango: sultani/
Mufwankolo: Tala Ngai/
Tala Ngai: kalombo/
Mufwankolo: kama uko nakwenda kya mbele: utarudia kya
mukongo?
All: hapana/ hata/
Masimango: sultani anatoka ni kuitokelele/
Mufwankolo: kunaisha/ mikulu iko pa mayi: wee uko nalia haumu
ya mayi?
All: hapana/
Mufwankolo: njala mu tumbo: uko sawa inaniingia pa mufupa?
Actor: mm mm/ mm mm/
Mufwankolo: wee uko unalia njala mu tumbo/ ile mambo tulise-
maka: tulisemaka ni humu mu mukini yetu . . .
Tala Ngai: kama muntu anafanya mambo ya hivi: yee longolongo
. . . *kelule yooo*/

27. *Bwana Cheko:*   sultani/ sultani/ nawaza: ya kama: sauti: ulisemaka: ulisemaka bintu bya mingi sana/ turudie: tuangarie mambo
ya ule muntu mwengine/ eko namna moya na mwizi: na mulozi: na
musharati/ beko namna moya/ namna gani habakumufanya longolongo: wooooo?
Mufwankolo: angaria: mambo: ya kiashiri ni kiashiri[7]/ kanuni ni
kanuni/ kanuni: minaisha kusemea/ kila makosa ya watu: iko na
malipizi yake/ mwizi wa kuiba makuta: kupomona manyumba:
kufanya kintu gani: ule: eko pamoya na ule muntu musharati na
muntu mulozi/
Masimango: muaji/
Mufwankolo: mwizi: ndiyo: kama anakwenda ku mashamba: ana-
kulyako kachakula nayee banamukamata kule: eko na malipizi ya-
ke/ atarudishiako tena lingine na yeye lungulungu: kelulele/
Others: ahah/

28. *Mufwankolo:*   sawa hivi/ mwizi munene ni yee/ anaangukia pa
mututa ya muntu/

---

7. *Kiashiri* is derived from *asili*, origin.

Masimango: anaua nyumba/
Mufwankolo: na anapomona nyumba/
Masimango: ni kuvunja kule/
Katolushi: ni mututa ya muhogo/
Mufwankolo: yeye hapa iko na batoto tano: miaka makumi mbili
na tano/
Masimango: na bibi yake/
Mufwankolo: sasa kichongwakazi[8] huyu: munsongwalume huyu/
akatoka tu kwake lokutalokuta: tiketiketik: kufika tu pa mututa ya
benyewe: mama anaisha kulima: angukiepo: na kwanza kufuru-
mafuruma? uliona wapi? tena mu pori/ kama yee alikatala: si
anamualiua?[9]
Masimango: sultani/
Mufwankolo: kama yee alikatala: wee kufwataka kumuua/
Masimango: sultani/
Mufwankolo: semaka/

29. *Masimango:*   naongeza sauti yako/ kama huyu baba alikuwa
na lawa yake: ya kusema: bibi yake . . .
[Interruption; the microphone was switched off accidentally]

30. *Mufwankolo:*   mutoto yako: hakuwatunza kanuni/ maneno
yee: kanuni: haina mi peke nilileta: hana we ulileta: hana nani
alileta: ni kanuni ya tangu zamani: ya wankambo/ na kila muntu
mu kazi yote wa mugini: anafaa kusikia ile kanuni: na kusikia
kanuni vema/ *alors:* mutoto yako: juu alikosa kanuni: anapashwa
kupita ku wankambo na kupata maliphishi yake/ kunaisha/
Bwana Cheko: vidye kalombo/

[End of scene, directions for the following]
Actor: . . . *jugement* haina butamu/
Tala Ngai: no/ haiyakuwa butamu/ ni ya kutengeneza/

The Case of Adultery: Rehearsal Version (Translation)

[Two guards, played by Shebele and Shambui, bring the accused
man, the woman, and her husband before the chief]

---

8. This looks as if Mufwankolo had started out to use the Shaba Swahili term
kijana, youngster (which is not marked for gender) and then switched to Luba
nsongwakazi, nubile girl, young woman (see Van Avermaet and Mbuya 1954: 632).
    9. In this passage Mufwankolo is at his best (and the translator at his worst).
Lokutalokuta and *tiketiketik* are phonations describing, respectively, the gait of a person
who takes himself importantly and the way someone runs who is in a hurry. *Furuma-
furuma* (see ECS *vuruma* under *vuru*) describes in Shaba Swahili the gasping and
snorting noises of sexual exertion, to put this delicately.

1. *First Guard:*   I greet you, chief.
Mufwankolo: Greetings, greetings.
First Guard: Chief, we arrested this man Katolushi and this woman Kamwanya, the wife of Foloko.
Second Guard: [clapping hands] Greetings, father.
First Guard: We picked them up over there where we store the cotton . . .
Second Guard: . . . at that small termite hill . . .
First Guard: . . . there below the termite hills.
Second Guard: It was the two of them.
First Guard: Here is his shirt, and here his shoes.
Villager: [Imagine] the foolish behavior of this young man, a child we brought up in the village . . .
Second Guard: [to a villager who has been talking] Listen, you!
First Guard: This is what happened, chief.
Second Guard: [to the villagers] You shut up!

2. *Mufwankolo:*   Shebele.
First Guard: Chief.
Mufwankolo: Call Bwana Cheko, Masimango, and Tala Ngai.
First Guard: Right away, chief.
Mufwankolo: [to Kamwanya] Mama.
Kamwanya: Yes, baba.
Mufwankolo: [to the guards] Where is her husband?
First Guard: That's him over there, chief.
Foloko: Yes, chief [I am here].
First Guard: [to Foloko] You sit down.

[*Notables* arrive]

3. *Bwana Cheko:*   Greetings, chief.
Mufwankolo: Thank you.
Bwana Cheko: Greetings, chief.
Mufwankolo: Thank you.
Notables: [clapping hands] Greetings, chief.
Mufwankolo: Yes, thank you.
Notable: Greetings, chief.
Mufwankolo: Thank you. [pause].

4. [to Foloko] Mm, eh baba.
Foloko: Chief.
Mufwankolo: Is this your wife?
Foloko: It's her, my Kamwanya.
Mufwankolo: How many years have you been together?
Foloko: It's been twenty-five years.

Mufwankolo:　Twenty-five years?
Foloko:　Twenty-five.
Mufwankolo:　How many children?
Foloko:　Five children.
Mufwankolo:　[pauses] Don't you feed her?
Foloko:　Chief, we eat, very well.
Mufwankolo:　Do you work hard in the fields?
Foloko:　We work hard, as you said yourself [we should do]. We just work the fields.
Mufwankolo:　Don't you give her clothes?
Foloko:　I clothe her very well.

5. *Masimango:*　[? to Katolushi] You there, that's no good. Put away that stick of yours. Are you going to speak to the chief with that stick?
Mufwankolo:　[to Katolushi] Do you have a wife?
Katolushi:　Yes, Chief.
Mufwankolo:　You have a wife?
Katolushi:　Yes.
Mufwankolo:　And how many children?
Katolushi:　Two children.
Mufwankolo:　How many years have you been with her?
Katolushi:　We have been together for years, now it's the tenth year.
Mufwankolo:　The tenth year? [Pauses, then to Kamwanya] Mama.

6. *Kamwanya:*　Yes, baba.
Mufwankolo:　The things your husband says, are they true? You have been together with him for twenty years [Mufwankolo makes a mistake] and you have five children?
Kamwanya:　It's true, baba.
Mufwankolo:　Is it true?
Kamwanya:　Yes, baba.
Mufwankolo:　Now, this one [the accused], don't you know him? Don't you know this person?
Kamwanya:　I see him around, that's all.
Katolushi:　Chief, I have something to say.
Guard:　[to Katolushi] Listen, you.
Mufwankolo:　So you just see each other, eh?
Kamwanya:　I just see him . . .
Villager:　She is his lover, chief.
Guard:　Hey, you!
Kamwanya:　I just see him.
Mufwankolo:　You just see each other with your eyes, or do you "see each other"?

Kamwanya: I just see him when I fetch water and he passes by.
Mufwankolo: With your eyes. With your eyes.

7. *Masimango:*   Chief.
Mufwankolo: All right.
Masimango: Whose child?
Mufwankolo: What?
Masimango: Chief, ask him first whose child he is.
Mufwankolo: You, who is your father?
[There is a short interruption for directions]
Mufwankolo: Who is your father?
Katolushi: Bwana Cheko.
Mufwankolo: Bwana Cheko?
Bwana Cheko: [intervenes] Chief.

8. *Mufwankolo:*   Bwana Cheko. He is your child? Which one?
Bwana Cheko: He is my child, this one is the third.
Mufwankolo: He is the third one.
Bwana Cheko: However, I think this child is in this case without
fault. This mama is the one who is married to two husbands. [The
others laugh.]
Tala Ngai: Aah, Bwana Cheko, speak so that you make sense. Who
is the one who breaks up the household?
Mufwankolo: Tala Ngai?
[More laughter from the audience, covering his response]
Bwana Cheko: My child is not guilty.
Mufwankolo: Masimango?
Masimango: [clapping his hands] Yes, chief.

9. *Mufwankolo:*   Bwana Cheko's third child married Foloko's wife.
He himself has a wife[10] and two children.
Masimango: [to Katolushi] Is your wife away on vacation?
Katolushi: No, sir.
Tala Ngai: So she is here?
Katolushi: Yes.
Mufwankolo: When you went to her [Kamwanya] you left your
wife at home?
Katolushi: Chief, I want to say something.
Mufwankolo: Ah, he has something to say.

---

10. The original has *babibi*, technically a plural form. Translation as a singular
(one wife) is justified by context and by the fact that the plural prefix *ba-* is often used
to mark polite address or reference. I have heard *baFabian banafika*, meaning "Fabian
arrives."

Katolushi: Yes.
Mufwankolo: Did they accuse you falsely? Speak.

10. *Katolushi:* Chief, this is how it happened. Mama [Kamwanya] was making moonshine[11] there in the fields.
Mufwankolo: So she was making moonshine?
Katolushi: Yes. So when I got there I bought one bottle. I had a glass, then another one, and another one, and another one. I felt that I was getting drunk.
Mufwankolo: Eh.
Katolushi: I woke up lying in the furrows. Mama had taken off her wrap and spread it; so I went to sleep [on it] there. Then her husband came by and saw me there and said: I caught an adulterer.
Kamwanya: That is how it was, chief.

11. *Masimango:* Chief. Chief.
Mufwankolo: Yes?
Masimango: This is a difficult affair. This case is *bukari* and meat; it is dealt out by the one who has it.
Mufwankolo: Explain.
Masimango: As far as this case is concerned, the one to whom the . . .
Mufwankolo: . . . the child . . .
Masimango: . . . to whom the child belongs [i.e., the husband of this young woman] may distribute the food.

12. *Bwana Cheko:* Chief, I think you heard what this young man has had to say. He said that this mama is brewing beer in the fields everyday. Mama, isn't that right?
Kamwanya: Yes, it is.
Bwana Cheko: The young man went there to get beer and drink. Drunkenness took hold of him, and he fell into a furrow. But this mama had pity on . . .
Kamwanya: Yes, I felt sorry for him.
Bwana Cheko: . . . pity on her customer. And because it was cold there . . .
[The others find this hilarious and cannot refrain from laughing. Tala Ngai calls for order: the actors are responding too much, intervening in the scene. He also makes an important dramatic point: Kamwanya should not defend Katolushi; she should keep in the background, "just make a noise like a car that is running." The play needs a culprit, so Katolushi must be guilty. If you get him acquitted,

11. The term used here is *lutuku*, Shaba Swahili for alcohol distilled (in Shaba) from corn. Making alcohol is illegal and therefore often done somewhere in the fields.

she is told, the scene is finished and there is no way to link it to the chief's speech in which he announced that adulterers would be punished. Others join the discussion; then Bwana Cheko resumes the scene.]

13. *Bwana Cheko:* I think, chief, you followed what the young man had to say. He is a regular customer of hers. And she always is brewing beer there in the fields. The young man declared that he drank and finally got drunk and that he did not have the strength to leave. He fell down in to the furrow. All right, this mama was wearing her wrap. She looked [at him and told herself] that her customer was going to die of the cold we have in this season.
Mufwankolo: Does a person who drinks alcohol feel the cold?
Bwana Cheko: [ignoring the chief's question] Then she [thought] she ought to cover him because it was cold. This is how drinkers of moonshine usually die.[12]

14. *Masimango:* *Mukubwa* Bwana Cheko.
Bwana Cheko: Yes.
Masimango: Let us look carefully at our laws that came from the ancestors. When a person has been drinking moonshine, or beer, what is the medicine against beer?
Actor: The cold.
Masimango: Isn't it cold water?
Bwana Cheko: Cold water? I think so.
Masimango: [to Tala Ngai] Add [your opinion].

15. *Tala Ngai:* [clapping hands] Chief. I think, *mukubwa* Bwana Cheko is really going too far. Chief, you got to the point. The young man was questioned and he responded. Nevertheless, did her husband catch them?
Others: Of course he did.
Tala Ngai: Let the husband explain first. [Turning to Foloko] When you caught them, was it that she had made him lie down on the wrap or did you catch him inside her wrap?
Mufwankolo: Were they fighting? [General laughter] Did you catch him when he was already asleep on the wrap or did you catch him when they were "wrestling"?
[Interruption: general mirth]

16. *Foloko:* My chief. My chief. I came to the fields and I just saw bottles of *lutuku*. And I caught him . . . They were wrestling in . . . You know it yourself . . .

12. In the original it says literally: This is how drinkers of moonshine usually dry up. The term *kukauka,* to dry, is also used to designate rigor mortis.

Katolushi: No.
Foloko: I—that's a lie. When he saw me there he got up.
[Interruption for direction: This is a difficult point. We have to justify why he was arrested—not for just lying there. At this point the actors go back and forth between rehearsal and discussion. Scene resumes]

17. *Mufwankolo:*   When you found and caught them, were they embracing, or did you find him asleep because she had made him lie down? Or did you catch them embracing, the two of them?
Foloko: I arrived in the fields. When I got there he saw me and quickly got up and he began jumping up and down. [He saw that] I was there and then wanted to run away. This is when I stopped him. I grabbed him and pulled off his shirt here.

18. *Feza:*   [intervening here because she still does not like the way the scene goes] No, you are not going to pull it off. They had run away, and when I got there [you say] I found that the shirt was left there, together with the shoes and the wrap. This is [how you can say] I carry them with me. Then you begin to go after them, running.

19. *Mufwankolo:*   [making another start] Did you find them embracing each other or did you see that he had been made to lie down?
Foloko: Yes, chief. When I left for the fields I saw them there. When I got close, each got up and ran away quickly. I followed the man there to my little manioc field, down there and I caught him among the bananas.
Mufwankolo: Where they make the moonshine.
Foloko: Where they make the moonshine. Then I went back [where I had surprised them] and picked up his shoes and the shirt.
Mufwankolo: So it was there?
Foloko: Right there, where they found my wife's wrap that had been left behind.

20. *Tala Ngai:*   Chief, I want to say one thing. There is a saying: There is a fruit, it is ripe and on a tree. You come by and look at it. If this fruit is edible, are you not going to pick and eat it? Isn't that so? Now, [let's assume that] you saw that the fruit has fallen to the ground. Days go by and no one passes the place. If this fruit is perishable, then, I think, it will rot. What is this about? This young man here knew that the fruit on the tree belonged to someone else— why would he not go after it and eat it?
Bwana Cheko: Mm.
Tala Ngai: He climbed that tree. I think the case is . . .

Others: . . . clear.
Tala Ngai: It is clear.
Masimango: It is quite clear.
Tala Ngai: And as to the law, you yourself know what we can do with this young man.

21. Masimango: Chief, I want to add something to what Tala Ngai said. The old people used to say: A woman is like the skin of *kabundi*.[13] [Laughter from the others.]
Feza: [laughing] Look at this one!
Masimango: [continuing with the saying] There is room in it for . . .
All: . . . one person.
Masimango and others: Never for two.

22. Bwana Cheko: ˌ Chief, follow what the child said. He said that he went to drink beer. He got drunk and fell into the furrow.
Katolushi: Right, father.
Bwana Cheko: All right then, how can you know [how it really happened], there was no witness. Only the man and the woman were there. When they saw that my son was drunk they took off his shirt. Maybe he had not paid yet.
Katolushi: That's it, father. This is how things happened.

23. Mufwankolo: Bwana Cheko. I hear your view of the matter. [But] when he fell into the furrow—"in the furrow," isn't that her [pointing to Kamwanya], wasn't she the furrow?
Feza: That's an idea. [The others laugh]
Bwana Cheko: Right . . .
Katolushi: No, chief.
Mufwankolo: Isn't that where this young man fell into?
Foloko: Of course, chief, of course, chief.
Guard: [to Foloko] You, be silent.

24. Masimango: [to Katolushi] Now the chief is asking you just one small thing. When this man, her husband, came to the fields where did he see you and where did he catch you?
Katolushi: He found me asleep.

---

13. Here we have an expression of conventional wisdom in the form of a riddle, even though the saying is not quoted as a question. But the way it is completed and "solved" by the speaker and the audience is characteristic of this genre. The translation of *kabundi* poses some difficulty. It is a small tree-dwelling animal, something like a squirrel (see Van Avermaet and Mbuya 1954: 96), and a major figure in traditional animal stories. As to the meaning of the riddle/proverb, its point seems to be the tight fit between this animal and its skin.

25. *Guard:*   Chief, can I say something?
Mufwankolo: Speak.
Guard: Because this young man now wants to tell a lie. When we caught him together with this baba there [Foloko], this is what he said. We first asked him: What this man accuses you of, is it true or is it a lie? You understand? This is how he spoke: I was just getting down here. I told myself, shall I just go by, shall I go down, shall I go up? I found this mama sitting on the ground and she said, I came from the river where I went to soak manioc. This is the version[14] this man gave us. [to Katolushi] And you want to give [us] a lie here?
Masimango: Aren't those two versions, chief?
Guard: So then he said, I met this mama. She came from soaking manioc. And because I was tired I asked her to give me a piece of fresh manioc because I had fallen into a morass and there was no way to get to [the field]. She had a piece of manioc in her bag, the one that is edible. At that time, when we asked her, this mama said: No, I was sitting there and asked him about the fields because I wanted to take some field over there. But they were on the ground. This is what she said. If I am lying, my brother [fellow guard] is there [to correct me].
Second Guard: [clearing his throat] Mm, okay . . . [preparing to speak. The others laugh]

26. *Mufwankolo:*   To bring this matter to an end—Bwana Cheko!
Bwana Cheko: Chief.
Mufwankolo: Masimango!
Masimango: Chief.
Mufwankolo: Tala Ngai!
Tala Ngai: Chief.
Mufwankolo: When you go forward, are you going to go back?
All: No, no way.
Masimango: The chief will now come up with a decision.[15]

---

14. The term "version" is here a translation of *kiswahili* used in the original. In the original it says literally: That is the Swahili this man gave me. In Shaba Swahili *kiswahili* covers a complex semantic domain in a manner that is at first surprising and even improbable to the outsider. *Kiswahili* can be the name of a language; it can also designate a variety, dialect, or register of that language (regional, social); and finally, it can refer to the content of that which is said. In the last two cases the term can occur in a plural form *(biswahili)*. What seems to make such polysemy possible is the fact that (in this culture) a (terminological) distinction is made neither between language as form and speech as its realization nor between how one speaks and what one says. There is much food for thought—philosophically and sociolinguistically—in this peculiar use of *kiswahili*.

15. This is but an attempt to render the meaning of the idiomatic expression used in the original (which plays with nuances of the verb *kutoka*).

Mufwankolo: That's the end of it. When you have a foot in the water, are you going to complain for want of water?
All: No.
Mufwankolo: The hunger you feel in your stomach, are you going to say it is in the bone[s]?
Actor: No, no. No, no.
Mufwankolo: You are going to complain about the hunger in your stomach. About this case we have said here in our village . . .
Tala Ngai: When a person does a thing like this, he be damned.
All: He be damned.

27. *Bwana Cheko:* Chief. Chief. I think, you have talked about a lot of things. [But] let us go back and look at the case of this other person. The thief, the sorcerer, and the fornicator are just the same. Why didn't they condemn him?
Mufwankolo: Look here. What has been valid of old, must remain valid. The law is the law. I have talked about the law. Every offense a person commits has its fine. A thief who steals money and breaks into houses, or whatever he does, he is just the same as this fornicator or a sorcerer.
Masimango: [He is] a killer.
Mufwankolo: A thief, all right, if he goes to the fields and eats a little and they catch him there, he gets his fine. If he does it again then he too will have his verdict.
Others: Aha.

28. *Mufwankolo:* [But] in this case, he is a big thief. He fell into the furrow that belongs to someone else.
Masimango: He killed a household.
Mufwankolo: And he broke into a house.
Masimango: This is breaking in.
Katolushi: It was a furrow in a manioc field.
Mufwankolo: [about Foloko] This one has five children, twenty-five years . . .
Masimango: . . . with his wife.
Mufwankolo: [now very angry] Now this young woman, or rather this young man. He leaves his home walking big and then running fast.[16] Then he comes to someone else's furrow, the woman who has finished working in the field, he falls down on her and starts pumping away. Where did you see a thing like this? And all this outside the village. If she had refused would he not have killed her?
Masimango: Chief.
Mufwankolo: If she had refused you would have tried to kill her.

16. Meaning: First openly, then surreptitiously.

Masimango: Chief.
Mufwankolo: Speak.

29. *Masimango:*   I am going to add something to what you said. If this baba had had his magic protection, that is to say, his wife . . . [At this point something went wrong with the recording; probably the microphone was switched off accidentally when the tape had to be turned. About ten minutes were lost. During this time the scene was interrupted. It was getting toward the end of the rehearsal and concentration was slacking. There was some discussion back and forth, including small changes. Finally the chief ends the litigation, and the culprits are sentenced to work in the fields. Bwana Cheko still protests, but the chief insists.]

30. *Mufwankolo:*   [to Bwana Cheko] Your child did not respect the law. Because I did not put down the law by myself, nor you, nor anyone else. It has been the law from times of old and it came from the ancestors. And every person, whatever he does in the village, must obey the law and obey it well. Therefore, your child, because he broke the law, must go to the ancestors and get his fine. That is the end.
Bwana Cheko: Thank you, chief.

The scene ends. Tala Ngai begins with directions for the next one. Someone tells Tala Ngai: The part with the judgment is not right. He answers: No, it isn't right yet, it has to be improved.

The Case of Adultery: Final Version (Text 17)

In this version there has been a change of casting. Not Foloko but Kalwasha plays the husband of the accused woman. Two guards bring the culprits before the chief. They are made to sit down and one of the guards removes the shoes of the accused young man. Kalwasha stands.

1. *Mufwankolo:*   Baba Kalwasha/
Kalwasha: présent chef/[17]
Mufwankolo: ni mambo gani tena?
Kalwasha: hehe/ hii mambo hii: huyu mutoto huyu: eh: ey: nali-mukutana na bibi yangu/
Mufwankolo: Shebele/
Shebele: kalombo mufumwami/
Mufwankolo: ita ba*notables*/
[While this is being done, the chief begins the interrogation]

---

17. Actually he says something like *pélésent*. About forms of acknowledging a call or being addressed, p. 194, n. 2.

2. *Mufwankolo:* ni mambo ingine/ mu nyumba?
Kalwasha: eh?
Mufwankolo: mu nyumba?
Kalwasha: eeeeh: he: si nalibakutana tu paka pa mututa? ya bilazi/
Audience: [laughter][18]/
[Now the *notables* arrive and the evidence, the woman's wrap, is placed before the culprits.]

3. *Bwana Cheko:* vidyee kalombo/
Mufwankolo: nakwimuna/
Bwana Cheko: vidyee kalombo/
Mufwankolo: nakwimuna/
Bwana Cheko: vidyee kalombo/
Mufwankolo: nakwimuna/
Masimango: vidyee mfumwami/
Mufwankolo: wafwako/
Masimango: vidyee mfumwami/
Mufwankolo: wafwako/
Masimango and Tala Ngai: vidyee mfumwami/
Mufwankolo: wafwako/

4. *Mufwankolo:* mambo yoo hii/ huyu mutoto mwanamuke: ni mama huyu ya baba Kalwasha: na huyu nsongwalume huyu/ huyu nsongwalume nayee iko anatafuta kuoa/
Kalwasha: aoe bibi wa benyewe?
Mufwankolo: njo bale beko naye/ eh: mama/
Kamwanya: abé baba/
Mufwankolo: ni bwana yako huyu?
Kamwanya: ndiyo: bwana yangu/
Mufwankolo: uko naye miaka ngapi?
Kamwanya: makumi mbili na tano/
Mufwankolo: makumi na mbili na tano miaka?
Kamwanya: eeh/
Bwana Cheko: wee mwenyewe hausemake nguvu?
Guard: makumi mbili na tano: sema nguvu/
Mufwankolo: batoto ngapi?
Guard: sema nguvu/
Kamwanya: niko na batoto kumi/

5. *Mufwankolo:* [now turning to Katolushi] eeh/
Katolushi: ndiyo *chef/*

---

18. It was at this point when, upon being told by the technicians to be quiet, one of the Kawama youths said: *kama minasikia butamu minacheka* (literally: when I feel the sweetness I laugh).

Mufwankolo: wee uko na watoto ngapi?
Katolushi: mutoto moya: bibi sasa na mimba/
Mufwankolo: iko na mimba?
Katolushi: ndiyo *chef/*
Mufwankolo: *bon/* sasa unakamata bibi wa mwenyewe namna gani? baba yako na wee ni nani?
Katolushi: baba ni Bwana Cheko/
Actor: Bwana Cheko njo baba yako?
[The audience acknowledges this turn with laughter.]

6. *Masimango:*   sultani/ vidyee mfumwami/ vidyee mfumwami/ vidyee mfumwami[19]/ mambo hii sultani minaona ni bukari wa nyama/ bukari bwa nyama bunakabulaka paka mwenyewe ya bukari/

7. *Mufwankolo:*   baba ulibakutana nabo namna gani kwanza mbele?
Kalwasha: sultani wangu: bibi yangu anafanyaka pombe ku pori/
Mufwankolo: eeh/
Kalwasha: mi niko nakuya tu polepole/
Mufwankolo: polepole/
Kalwasha: kiyana ananisikia na pale niko nakuya/
Mufwankolo: eh/
Kalwasha: maneno niliacha muketo: kama nalimutekula[20]/
Mufwankolo: kama ulimutentekayo/
Kalwasha: alinisikia pale iko nakuya/ si tshikwembe hiki? iko nake mu shingo/ si njo tshinyewe balimutandikila pa mututa?
Mufwankolo: pa mutata wa bilazi? [general laughter]
Kalwasha: ni hii kikwembe hii/
Mufwankolo: eeh/

8. *Kalwasha:*   anaanza mbio/ mwizi munikamatile munikamatile/ bantu muzuri asema ni: ni ule/ banamulintama na kumulintama[21]/

19. The greeting formula is repeated by Masimango alone three times in this transcription because this is what the sound recording retained. In reality it was an exchange whereby Mufwankolo acknowledged the greeting nonverbally.
20. *Muketo* is Luba for "arrow" (Van Avermaet and Mbuya 1954: 249). *Tekula* corresponds to ECS *tegua*, to trigger a trap, to let off an arrow.
21. The form used here suggests a verb *lintama*, which does not seem to exist in Shaba Swahili. A native speaker, however, understands the sentence, hearing the verb *tantama*, to jump on someone, to overpower someone. It is possible that Kalwasha simply got carried away in his effort to produce quaint and old-fashioned speech (the *munikamatile* in the preceding sentence is an example of plausible "accent," which situates the utterance more closely to Luba than to Swahili; the same goes for *anasangila* a few exchanges further, which should be *anachangia*).

Tala Ngai: hii manguo ni yake hii?
Kalwasha: yake ilibakia paka pa tshikwembe.
Tala Ngai: hii ni yako?
Kalwasha: na bilatu byote/
Mufwankolo: kwake ilikuwa ni bushiku anaanza kuvwula binani?
Kalwasha: eh/ sawa anaisha ku: kuona na mpombe: na bibi yangu vile anasangila ku moya/

9. *Mufwankolo:* [to Katolushi, partly incomprehensible] . . . ? . . . sema mbele/
[Here follows a passage impossible to transcribe, several persons talk at once]
Katolushi: Kamwanya ni *client*[22] wangu wa zamani nilimukutani-sha ku pori/ minafika pale: natula kifulusi nilikuwa naye/ namu-omba unipatie chupa moya nikunywe/ anatosha chupa ya lutuku moya: ananipatia/ minakunywa polepole: kunywa polepole/ hapa na hapa: sasa ile chupa mi: minaisha/ pale minaisha ile chupa: *c'est fini/*
Mufwankolo: unalewa?
Katolushi: minalewa/ asema nilamuke hivi: minaanguka/
Mufwankolo: pa mututa?
Katolushi: naunguka/ asema nilamuke hivi: naunguka paka na mututa/
Mufwankolo: wa bilazi?
Katolushi: tena mama Kamwanya pale anaangaria asema ahah/ baba sawa vile unalewa: kumbe uache nikutandikie ulale/
Mufwankolo: akutandikie?
Katolushi: nidyo/
Mufwankolo: eeh/
Katolushi: njo kutosha kikwembe yake anatandika/
Mufwankolo, Notables: pa mututa?
Katolushi: pa mututa pale/ napinduka nao/
Mufwankolo: sasa yee anasimama?
Katolushi: yee anafanya kazi yake/
Mufwankolo: wee unakuwa nalala?
Katolushi: ndiyo/

10. *Katolushi:* minasikia paka: baba [hesitates] Sondashi? yee ana-fika paka hivi/
Masimango: yee anakuwa Sondashi: hana tena Kalwasha hapana?

---

22. When the French loanword *client* was incorporated into Shaba Swahili it underwent an interesting change. It now designates a mutual, reciprocal relation and can mean customer/buyer as well as purveyor/seller.

Mufwankolo: munaona mwee batoto wa sasa vile munaikalaka mukululu[23] mubaya/
Katolushi: basi . . .
Tala Ngai: ubape heshima: ukote[24] heshima/
Kalwasha: maneno ya baba yake: njo ile mi: ana: anataka kufanya/

11. *Bwana Cheko:*   minatafuta kwanza kujua: ile makozi yenyewe/ balimukamata saa gani? ule mama: eko anapigaka pombe: ile pombe banakatazakayo: ni pombe moya ya mubaya/ lutuku/ ya kuua muntu/ . . . ? . . . anakunywa chupa moya: kipimo yako hii: kumupa chupa moya: ya *cinq cent:* atakuwa namna gani?
Mufwankolo: sasa ile mambo yee anasema: wee unakatalayo/
Bwana Cheko: ile minazania: ni kumulongofea kwa sababu ali-kuwa kwa yee peke/
Masimango: vidyee mfumwami/
Bwana Cheko: analewa: banakuwa kumuvika kikwembe: kiisha banayua asema baba yake ni muntu mukubwa: tutapata kwa kwenda kuwinia/
Mufwankolo: unasema: ya: ya: ya bongo ile unasema/. . .
Masimango: kalombo vidye/
Mufwankolo: . . . unasema mambo ya bongo/

12. *Masimango:*   kalombo mufumwami/ *bon/* mama uniambie: ile kiswahili nasema bwana yako: ni ya bongo: ni ya kweli: ao nasema huyu abala yako: njo ya kweli?
Kamwanya: ile anasema bwana yangu njo ya kweli/
Mufwankolo: ya kweli ya mututa?
Kamwanya: eeh/
Kalwasha: alimukutanisha pa mututa/
Mufwankolo: pa mututa: banatandika na kikwembe pa mututa/
[General noise from the audience, thus making the following partly incomprehensible]

13. *Bwana Cheko:*   . . . na bwana na bibi/ na bwana na bibi wana-unga kanuni/
Tala Ngai: sultani/ minazania hapa ulileta mipango bantu bote balisikiliza/ huyu mutoto: wee mwenyewe kamataka mipango/
Mufwankolo: njo kusema: hapa sasa: weye unaletesha haya mu mukini yangu humu/ unaleta haya/ nililetaka mipango: njo kuse-

23. Mufwankolo may be mispronouncing *m[u]kulukulu;* see Lenselaer 1983: 310.
24. I am told that *kukota* is a Bemba verb synonymous with Shaba Swahili *kukomea,* to grow up, to age.

ma: weye unatafuta kuvunja mipango? tokea hapa sasa wee/ lwako
lwunaena/ bampolushi/
Guard: chef/
Mufwankolo: mutamubeba: wende mukamuache lungulungu . . .
kelulule/

14. *Katolushi:* chef: munihurumieko/
Guards: telema[25]/ telema/ telema . . .,
Katolushi: acha mbele niseme: acha mbele niseme/
Guard: telema/
[general confusion; the accused keeps pleading]
Katolushi: muniache: niko na batoto . . .
[The accused man is dragged off by the guards]

15. *Mufwankolo:* Kalwasha/
Kalwasha: présent/
Mufwankolo: bibi yako/
Kalwasha: mfumumwami/
Mufwankolo: namufunga miezi mbili/ atakwenda kulima masha-
mba ya mi sultani kule/
Kalwasha: ahe/
Mufwankolo: mama: pita kule/
Kalwasha: mupeleke yee/
Mufwankolo: tosha na manani yake ile/ unaleta haya mu mukini
wangu/
Guard: allez twende mama: kujiheshimia/ si unasikia we moya/
twende mama/ twende/
Mufwankolo: makozi/ kya makozi/
[short passage incomprehensible]
Mufwankolo: bibi yako namufunga miezi mbili/
Kalwasha: eyoo/
[short passage incomprehensible]
Kalwasha: kalombo mfumwami/ wafwako/ wafwako mfumwa-
mi/ eyoo/ hehe/ alafu huyu bibi alinikalisha matako pembeni/

16. *Tala Ngai:* sultani: mambo iko paka nadani ya mukini/ hivi
wiko unaimaliza kiloko kiloko: na bale benyewe beko naangaria:
beko banasikia boga/ banasema hapana/ sultani sasa anawaka mo-
to/ nawaza hii mugini itakwenda paka muzuri kabisa/ hivi tuna-
maliza mambo/

---

25. *Telema* is a (military) command in Lingala, corresponding to Shaba Swahili
simama, get up, stand up.

Bwana Cheko: ita: itaendea muzuri paka pa mutoto yangu/
Masimango: Bwana Cheko mi nilikuambia ni bukari wa: wa: wa
nyama/ bunakabulaka mwenyewe ya bukari/

17. *Mufwankolo:*   eeh/ minaona bapolisi beko fasi gani? tangu bali-
kwenda habayarudia hapana/
Masimango: bado sultani/
Mufwankolo: natafuta kwanza mbele kubatuma/

18. *Bwana Cheko:*   [his voice breaking] sultani/ tunakwenda/
Mufwankolo: eyoo/
Bwana Cheko: sina ya kusema: mutoto basi: anaisha kufwa/ . . . ?
. . . anaisha kufwa/
Masimango: [clapping his hands] vidyee mufumwami/ vidyee
mfumwami/ vidyee mfumwami/ [to Bwana Cheko as they go
away] acha kushirika/

The Case of Adultery: Final Version (Translation)

1. *Mufwankolo:*   Baba Kalwasha.
Kalwasha: Here I am, chief.
Mufwankolo: Now, what's the matter?
Kalwasha: Well, this is what it is about: This young man here, how
shall I say, I caught him with my wife.
Mufwankolo: [calling a guard] Shebele!
Shebele: Greetings, my chief.
Mufwankolo: Call the *notables.*
[While this is being done, the chief begins the interrogation]

2. *Mufwankolo:*   So this is another case. [Did you catch them] in the
house?
Kalwasha: What?
Mufwankolo: In the house?
Kalwasha: Well, don't you know I caught them in a furrow, in [a
field] of sweet potatoes.[26]
Audience: [laughter]
[Now the *notables* arrive and the evidence, the woman's wrap, is
placed before the culprits]

---

26. Compared to the rehearsal version, Kalwasha here adds detail that fits the
image. Unlike corn, sweet potatoes require planting in such a way that there is space
for the vines to spread. *Mututa* is not so much a straight furrow (plows are not used) as
a depression between mounds. That makes plausible the idea that one can hide in a
mututa; it also favors the *double entendre* that contributed greatly to the success of this
scene.

3. *Bwana Cheko:*   Greetings, chief.
Mufwankolo: I greet you.
Bwana Cheko: Greetings, chief.
Mufwankolo: I greet you.
Bwana Cheko: Greetings, chief.
Mufwankolo: I greet you.
Masimango: Greetings, my chief.
Mufwankolo: Thank you.
Masimango: Greetings, my chief.
Mufwankolo: Thank you.
Masimango and Tala Ngai: Greetings, my chief.
Mufwankolo: Thank you.[27]

4. *Mufwankolo:*   So [these are the facts] of this case: This young woman is the wife of baba Kalwasha. And this young man, he wants to get married.
Kalwasha: Should he take a wife that belongs to someone else?
Mufwankolo: [But] now she is with him.[28] [Addressing the woman] Mama.
Kamwanya: Yes, baba.
Mufwankolo: Is this [i.e., Kalwasha] your husband?
Kamwanya: Yes, he is my husband.
Mufwankolo: How many years have you been with him?
Kamwanya: Twenty-five years.[29]
Mufwankolo: Twenty-five years?
Kamwanya: Yes.

27. This translation does not convey the fact that the entire exchange of greetings is in what one might call "generalized" Luba. Some elements clearly belong to a Shaba variety (such as *vidyee kalombo*); others, I am told, sound more like Tshiluba or Songye *(mufumwami)*. This could be determined more exactly, but the point here is that this passage illustrates a kind of emblematic use of langauge. The whole passage is marked as "traditional" (or "folkloric") without being linked to a specific context. Notice that it is not in Bemba/Lamba, a choice that would seem to have been indicated by the setting in Kawama village.

28. Literally, the original says "they are the ones that are with him." But it is clear from the context that the reference is to the one woman that was brought before the chief.

29. This response would seem to contradict the designation of Kamwanya as a "young woman." Kamwanya, the actress, is a young woman and what appears as a contradiction illustrates the processual nature of this performance. The transformation from a real person into a character in a play is in this case still incomplete. The "twenty-five years" are required to show that this is a particularly serious case of adultery; that the role is being played by a young woman is acknowledged but not permitted to interfere with the requirements of the plot.

Bwana Cheko: Can't you speak up?[30]
Guard: Twenty-five. Speak up.
Mufwankolo: How many children?
Guard: Speak up.
Kamwanya: I have ten children.

5. *Mufwankolo:*   [now turning to Katolushi] Yes, you.
Katolushi: Yes, chief.
Mufwankolo: How many children do you have?
Katolushi: One, and my wife is now expecting.
Mufwankolo: She is expecting?
Katolushi: Yes, chief.
Mufwankolo: All right then. How come you now take the wife of someone else? Who is your father?
Katolushi: [My] father is Bwana Cheko.
Actor: Bwana Cheko is your father?
[The audience acknowledges this turn with laughter]

6. *Masimango:*   Chief! Greetings, my chief [clapping his hands] Greetings, my chief. Greetings, my chief. As I see it, this case is *bukari* with meat. It is the owner alone who [has the right] to distribute this food.

7. *Mufwankolo:*   Baba, how did you catch them in the first place?
Kalwasha: My chief, my wife was making alcohol in the bush [outside the village].
Mufwankolo: So that is it.
Kalwasha: I just walked up slowly.
Mufwankolo: Slowly?
Kalwasha: The young man heard me coming.
Mufwankolo: I see.
Kalwasha: I had left my [bow and] arrow [at home]. If not, I would have shot him.
Mufwankolo: You would have shot him.
Kalwasha: He heard me coming. This here is the wrap which he had around his neck. Isn't that the same which she spread for him in the furrow?
Mufwankolo: In the furrow of a [field of] sweet potatoes? [general laughter]

---

30. Kamwanya's response was barely audible. She had a bad cold on this particular day. Bwana Cheko makes part of the dialogue what is in fact an instance of directing the actress. This sort of extemporizing occurred several times during rehearsal as well as in the final performance.

Kalwasha: It is this very wrap.
Mufwankolo: I see.

8. *Kalwasha:*   He began [to run away] fast. A thief! [I cry] catch him
for me, catch him for me. [There were some] decent people there
who said: He is the one. So they jumped him and overpowered him.
Tala Ngai: The clothes here, are they his?
Kalwasha: His [clothes] were left there with the wrap . . .
Tala Ngai: [to Katolushi] Are they yours?
Kalwasha: . . . and his shoes and all.
Mufwankolo: So he thought it was night and he began to take off
his whatever.
Kalwasha: Yes, because he had seen strong drink and my wife and
made a mixture of both.

9. *Mufwankolo:*   [to Katolushi, partly incomprehensible] . . . ? . . .
speak first.
[Here follows a brief passage impossible to transcribe; several persons talk at once]
Katolushi: I have been Kamwanya's customer for a long time and I
met her there outside the village.[31] When I got there I put the bundle
I was carrying down. I asked her to give me a bottle so I could have a
drink. She brought a bottle of moonshine and gave it to me. I kept
drinking slowly. Suddenly I had finished that bottle. When I had
finished that bottle, that was it.
Mufwankolo: Were you drunk?
Katolushi: I was drunk. I told myself I must get up but I fell down.
Mufwankolo: In the furrow?
Katolushi: I fell down. I told myself I am going to get up, but I just
fell into the furrow.
Mufwankolo: Among the sweet potatoes?
Katolushi: And then, when mama Kamwanya saw this she said:
This is no good. Baba, since you are so drunk let me spread some-
thing out for you to sleep [on].
Mufwankolo: She was going to spread [something]?
Katolushi: Yes.
Mufwankolo: I see.
Katolushi: Then she took off her wrap and spread it.
Mufwankolo, Notables: In the furrow?

---

31. The original has "in the bush" *(ku pori)*. *Pori*, however, is a term whose
meaning depends on the context. As "bush" it is in opposition to the cultivated land
(shamba). Here it contrasts with the village (and therefore includes the fields).

Katolushi: Right there in the furrow. I wrapped myself with it.
Mufwankolo: Now, was she standing?
Katolushi: She did her work.
Mufwankolo: You were asleep?
Katolushi: Yes.

10. *Katolushi:*   I hear this baba [hesitates] Sondashi? He was just then coming.
Masimango: So now it is Sondashi and no longer Kalwasha?[32]
Mufwankolo: You see, you young people nowadays, you are up to nothing good.
Katolushi: Well . . .
Tala Ngai: Be polite to the people here; behave politely like a grown-up.
Kalwasha: It is because of his father that he tries to make [up excuses].

11. *Bwana Cheko:*   First I want to know [the facts] about this case of adultery. When did they catch him? This mama has been making alcohol; this is prohibited, it is a very bad sort of alcohol, moonshine. It can kill a man. . . . ? . . . he drank one bottle; you gave him one bottle measure of the grade called "five hundred proof,"[33] what do you expect he will be?
Mufwankolo: Then you deny what he says.
Bwana Cheko: I believe he is being falsely accused because he was alone.
Masimango: [trying to get the floor] Greetings, my chief.
Bwana Cheko: [ignoring Masimango] He got drunk, they put the wrap around him and then, because they knew that his father is a person of importance, they said we are going to profit from this.
Mufwankolo: You are talking—what you are saying is a lie . . .
Masimango: [trying again] Greetings, chief.
Mufwankolo: . . . you are telling things that are false.

12. *Masimango:*   Greetings, my chief. All right mama [to Kamwa-nya]. Is the version which your husband tells [us] false or true; or is what your lover tells [us] true?
Kamwanya: What my husband says is true.
Mufwankolo: About the furrow, is that true?

---

32. What happened is that Katolushi forgot for a moment which stage name (Kalwasha or Sondashi) the actor was using. Masimango corrects him, but in such a way that this becomes part of the dialogue.

33. This is the translation of a term used in Shaba Swahili, *cinq cent,* to designate a twice-distilled alcohol.

Kamwanya: Yes.
Kalwasha: They got together in the furrow.
Mufwankolo: [mocking] In the furrow, they spread the wrap in the furrow.
[General noise from the audience, thus making the following partly incomprehensible]

13. *Bwana Cheko:*   ... husband and wife; husband and wife had an agreement.[34]
Tala Ngai: Chief, I think you put down the rules and all the people heard them. As far as this young man is concerned, you yourself ought to apply the rules.
Mufwankolo: That is to say, you have brought shame on this village of mine. You bring shame. I set the rules, and now you seek to break the rules? From now on I have had enough of you. Guards!
Guard: Chief!
Mufwankolo: Take him away, go and leave him to be . . .
All: . . . damned.

14. *Katolushi:*   Chief, have pity with me.
Guards: Get up, get up, get up . . .
Katolushi: Let me speak first, let me speak first.
Guard: Get up.
[General confusion; the accused keeps pleading]
Katolushi: Let me go, I have children . . .
[The accused man is dragged off by the guards]

15. *Mufwankolo:*   Kalwasha.
Kalwasha: Here I am.
Mufwankolo: As far as your wife is concerned . . .
Kalwasha: My chief.
Mufwankolo: I am going to lock her up for two months. She is going to work in the fields over there that belong to me, the chief.
Kalwasha: So be it.
Mufwankolo: Mama, get over there.
Kalwasha: Take her away.
Mufwankolo: Take away her things. You bring shame on my village.
Guard: Come on, let's go mama, have some respect for yourself, you heard it yourself. Let's go, mama, let's go.
Mufwankolo: Adulteress, adulteress.

---

34. This statement is incomplete (because partly inaudible) as well as elliptic. Bwana Cheko tries a sort of last defense, maintaining that Kalwasha and Kamwanya had an agreement regarding her relation with Katolushi.

[Short passage incomprehensible]
Mufwankolo: I am going to lock up your wife for two months.
Kalwasha: So be it.
[Short passage incomprehensible]
Kalwasha: [leaving] Greetings, my chief. Thank you. Thank you, chief. Yes, indeed. This wife of mine really gave me trouble.[35]

16. *Tala Ngai:*   Chief, this case [has to do with problems we have] in the village. The way you deal with them, little by little, you will be watched by the villagers and they will experience fear. They will say no [we can't go on] the chief has put fire [in his orders/rules]. This village is going to do all right. So we have finished the case.
Bwana Cheko: [The village] will do all right at the expense of my son.
Masimango: Bwana Cheko, I told you this is *bukari* and meat. Only its owner has the right to give it away.
[*Notables* begin to leave]

17. *Mufwankolo:*   Eeh, where are the guards? Since they went away [to take away the accused] they haven't come back yet.
Masimango: Not yet, chief.
Mufwankolo: I want to send them out.

18. *Bwana Cheko:*   [his voice breaking] Chief, we are leaving.
Mufwankolo: Yes.
Bwana Cheko: I have nothing to say anymore. My child, he is already dead. He is already dead.[36]
Masimango: [clapping his hands] Greetings, my chief, greetings, my chief, greetings, my chief. [To Bwana Cheko as they go away] Stop being angry.
[The *notables* leave, then the chief and the guards]

The ceremonious departure of the *notables*, Bwana Cheko's bickering, and the amused reactions of the public all help to extend this scene so as to give the other actors and the TV crew time to get to the setting for the next one. On the soundtrack of the video recording the change of scene is bridged by playing a popular old record in Bemba.

35. This is a pale rendition of a colorful idiom: *kukalisha matako mpembeni*, to make someone sit down on one buttock; meaning: to make someone uncomfortable.
36. In a manner of speaking. The verb *kufa*, to die, lends itself easily to this sort of exaggeration. One "dies" whenever he feels pain or disappointment or is being treated unjustly; a car "dies" when it breaks down. Because its meaning is so inflated, reference to actual death must often be ascertained by specifying *kufa lote*, to die completely.

12

Scene 6: Revolt in the Fields

Up to this point the play has shown the chief's power. His speech in scene 1 established him as the guardian of the law laid down by the ancestors. Scene 2 prepared the audience for trouble in the form of disobedience and selfish pursuit of conflicting interests. After that, everyone expects the balance between order and chaos to be precarious. This is shown in scenes 3 to 5 at the chief's court. They exemplify his authority and impartiality as a judge, as well as his privileges and generosity as a receiver of tribute. At the same time they are occasions to bring into the open not only breaches of the law but also conflicts among the *notables*, who are shown to fail in their role as spokesmen both for the chief's authority and the legitimate interests of the villagers. But, in a way, all this is routine. Scene 6 introduces a new dramatic element into the play. It no longer parades cases that illustrate the workings of power, but creates an *event* which leads to a breakdown. Significantly, the action of the play itself, not only of implied or reported activities such as in previous scenes, now shifts to the fields outside the village or, to be exact, to movement back and forth between the chief's court and the fields.

At the same time, another displacement takes place. The challenge to authority that is now presented no longer regards a breach of law by individuals whose culpability can be determined and settled in litigation. The villagers rebel as a group against a specific command given by their chief. They had been ordered to carry out communal work. On one occasion during rehearsal this was referred to as *salongo*, the term used for general clean-up and other work which the president of Zaire made obligatory for every citizen (to be carried out each Saturday, supervised by the Party). In other words, scene 6 definitely moves from the judicial, ceremonial, and perhaps economic aspects of the chief's position to his political power.

Given this dramatic turn there would still have been several possibilities to enact it. One of them was at least adumbrated in rehearsal (but eventually not developed): The most renitent among the *notables*, Tala Ngai, might have mobilized the villagers into accepting him as a contender for the chief's position. This would have amounted to an organized rebellion with a clear objective. But there was agreement already in the first preparatory discussions that the great "catastrophe" should be an orgiastic happening, a feast of dancing, drinking, and corruption.

As regards textual documentation, scene 6 confirms the expectations that were formulated in our model of the rehearsal process. It is in the nature of a communal feast that it be mostly action and little discourse. Constant singing, drumming, and moving about put limits on obtaining a transcribable audio recording, not only of the final performance but also of the rehearsals. The latter were complicated by the fact that it obviously took a special effort, several starts and many revisions, to "plan" an event whose effect depends on being playful, spontaneous, and above all entertaining.

The textual yield of recordings made of the preceding scenes was varied but on the whole quite plentiful. This is not so with scene 6, not only for the technical reasons just mentioned but also because the rehearsal on June 27 seemed to require more working and reworking than had been the case so far. There were at least ten takes or repetitions before the acting and dialogue were felt to be satisfactory. Dialogue, the one thing that seems to come easiest to the troupe, is less important in this scene and what there is of it consists of brief exchanges, many exclamations, and even more drunken bragging. Drumming and dancing are almost continuous and singing took up more than half of the rehearsal time. All this required more direction than other scenes, especially also because there was more need for choreographing movement. Accordingly, the audio recording made on June 27 was discontinuous, with most of the attention given to instructions and dialogue; recording of much of the singing (almost all in languages other than Swahili) was cut short. The transcriptions/translations that follow begin at a point when Tala Ngai and Mufwankolo come to a first agreement on how to structure the scene, including the change from the chief's court to the fields.

Revolt in the Fields: Rehearsal Version (Text 18)

1. *Mufwankolo:*   . . . banamu*accuser* wa makozi/ bote bana: sultani anaenda: sasa we wote munaanza ku: kunywa kiloko: na vile: munaanza kwenda/ *bon: dis* Kabeya: eh: Tala Ngai: eh: hakutakuwa: eh: wa kubatuma kwa kwenda ku mashamba? *ou bien* batafwata paka ile ya sultani alibaambia/

Tala Ngai: *c'est à dire:* eh: eh: *scène* iko *continue/* njo kusema *scène*
iko *normale* vile tulianza: uliezea bantu banapashwa kwenda ku
mashamba . . .
Mufwankolo: *c'est ça/* ndiyo/
Tala Ngai: *bon/* ile tunaweka *entre* nani: ile *majugements* mbili/
c'est que ambiance ya *village* iko . . .
Mufwankolo: iko *continue/*
Tala Ngai: *une ambiance parfaite, quoi/*
Mufwankolo: *c'est ça/*

2. *Tala Ngai:*   *bon/ après seulement jugement* njo tunasema bale
bantu: kule ku kazi kule balikwenda: banaanza kuharibisha kazi:
suite ya bile Tala Ngai alibasemasema kule/ *c'est qui fait après* tu
scène yako: kama tunakata *scène* yako: *la caméra est branchée déjà*
sur: eh . . .
Mufwankolo: . . . bamashamba/
Tala Ngai: bale bamashamba/ *alors on pourra faire:* tunaanza kufanya nani: sawa vile tunafanyaka: tunafanya ka: ka*écriteau* kamo-
ya: banasikia paka tamtam: kiisha banabaona sasa *ambiance* ku
mashamba: kila muntu na jembe yake: na mupanga: eko nalima:
eko: eko nacheza: nakunywa pombe: ulevi vile . . .

3. *Mufwankolo:*   *bon/* tufanye sawa/ mutakuwa ka: *en rond* hapa/
eeh? *bon/* mama moya hapa: njo ataenda ku*servir:* bale bote/ *bon:*
tutafanya kinawapi?[1] mukate itakuwa moya: ao itakuwa mbili/
banaku*servir* weee: unakunywa mu upesi/ unafanya: na wee
unamu*servir* tena mungine bwana paka vile/ eeh? sawa mama
anasafisha: unasema *servir* mwengine: *à la Zairoise/* eh? *bon/* sasa
pale mutaanza kupata bale benyee ba sultani alituma: bataanza
kuya: ule mama moya nayee: kwa ku: kwa kuwapokelea kabisa
kabisa: eh? kuwalarisha bushingishi: anabapokelea: ah: banasikia
kwanza sauti: anasema: ooh kuya kwanza mbele: yee anababembe-
lesha: anakala: sawa vile tulisema jana/ eh? *bon/* tufanye kwanza ile
scène: ya kuikala mwee mbele pamoya/ mukale tu hivi/ *tout ça/*
cercle moya hivi/
[Several starts are made but not recorded here; then Mufwankolo
gives the following directions]

4. *Mufwankolo:*   muikale kwanza mbele hapa/ *déjà* atamikutana
mu *rythme* ya ile mimbo ile/ he? haba wote bawili banakuya: muko
naimba *déjà/* mwee munabaona: muna*continuer/* tena mwee muna-

---

1. *Kinawapi* is an expression of uncertain origin, synonymous with *namna gani,*
in what manner? how?

ona: muna*continuer* tu kipande: njo banami*faire stopper:* eh: habari gani tena huku? njo kazi munaikalia? munaikala kwanza kimya/ munabasikia vile batasema/ banasema papapapapa: ule mama wa kuba*entrainer:* ooooh: tunayua: karibu kwanza kukaribu: eeh: weewe: karibu: kiti munamupokea kiti: bana*assoir/*

5. *Tala Ngai: est-ce que . . . ? . . . paka moya moya?*
Mufwankolo: voilà/ eh/ munaikala/ *donc c'est: c'est la femme qui doit dire ça/* muni: amewakalisha: banaikala: banakamata na nani: unona tu hivi na hivi/ mwee vile *tout ça* banafanyafanya: *non:* eh: mambo hata mambo inakuyaka: basi yee . . . ? . . . munaibashukia pale: banaanza kunywa/ kiisha kunywa: mimbo ina*continuer/* mukisha *continuer:* mama moya anakwenda mu ngoma/ anaimba na anachezacheza nachezacheza weee: na bale banakuwa *tentés:* nabo banaanza kutafuta kucheza: ule mama mwenyewe anakamata kikwembe: anavwika moya kati yabo/ ana: nayee anatambuza[2] mu ngoma/ banapiga bikelekelekelekele: banaikala/ *entretemps:* habaseme tena kintu hapana/ *bon/* kiisha tena: mwingine anakuya wa kutoka kwa chefu: *notable/* anafika: *mêmement/* eh? tunasikilizana vile? munaweza ku*changer* hata mimbo moya: mimbo munaweza *continuer* paka na ile mimbo: *je ne sais pas quoi/* eh? . . . . .
[The rehearsal continues; here is a sample of the kind of dialogue that was tried out]

6. *Feza:*   yambo yenu baba/
Tala Ngai: heya: yambo/
Villager: yambo yenu/
Tala Ngai: yambo/
Kamwanya: hamujambo[3] baba/
Tala Ngai: jambo/ sasa ni: eheh: munafansia *fête* leo huku? ku mashamba?
Villagers: eeh baba/
Kalwasha: baba shiye . . .
Tala Ngai: juu ya nini?
Kalwasha: mukongo: baba: mukongo walikunjama mubaya: njo twalisema[4] acha kwanza leo tunyoroshe[5] mukongo/

---

2. The verb *kutambuza* could be an ECS form (not used in Shaba Swahili) meaning "to forge, to beat the iron," hence, by extension, "to beat the drum"; but then the locative *-mu-* would be incomprehensible. Or it is simply a "mistake" for Shaba Swahili *kutambuka,* to stride, step over (see Lenselaer 1983: 515). In the translation I opt for the latter.
    3. By using the ECS form of the greeting (seldom heard in Shaba), Kamwanya switches to a "higher" register, in this case as a mocking exaggeration of politeness.
    4. Kalwasha here (and elsewhere) mixes morphemes; *twa-* is the Bemba equivalent of Shaba Swahili *tu-,* the verb-prefix marking first-person plural. In other words,

7. *Tala Ngai:* pale haukuwa kunyoroshea mu mugini: juu ya nini munakuya kunyoroshea ku mashamba?
Kalwasha: aah baba: si unayua asema: kazi kama inanichokesha ni kukala kwanza ku mashamba/ alafu kwanza: wee mwenyewe baba: acha nakuwa nakuulishe musuri musuri/
Tala Ngai: eeh/
Kalwasha: sultani njo anasema namna kani?
Tala Ngai: eeh: ananituma asema nikuye angaria/ ni ngoma tu tulisikia kule/
Woman: eyo/
Kalwasha: ngoma eh?
Tala Ngai: eeh: njo yee anasema ni kintu gani kule banacheza. . . .
Villager: karibu *chef*/
Tala Ngai: . . . angarie kwanza/
Kalwasha: ana: anaanza kutufokela? ao?
Tala Ngai: hapana: alikuwa asema wende ukaangarie mbele niyue ni kintu gani: njo mi nitamupatia lwapolo[6]/
Kalwasha: umupatie lapolo?
Tala Ngai: eeh/
Villager: eeeeh baba/

8. *Tala Ngai:* lakini na mi mwenyewe minakuya tu/
Feza: regezako kwanza kiloko/ jua yoyote natembea nayo baba?
Villager: eh: chunga kwanza kiloko/
Tala Ngai: na mi: namna tunamikutanisha/ njo ile bantu bana- pashwa kuikala mu mugini/
Villagers: [acclaiming and applauding] eeeh. . . .
Tala Ngai: [shouting] munatumika kiloko: munapata nguvu kiloko: munakunya na mutama/
Villagers: eeh/
Tala Ngai: hivi munabakia tena na nguvu ya kutumika kazi tena ingine ya kesho/
Villagers: hoo baba . . . [appplause; ululations]

---

apart from using phonological ("accent") and lexical elements, he also plays with morphology in order to achieve the desired effect of an old-fashioned, peasant way of talking.
    5. *Kunyororosha* means to stretch (see ECS *kunyorora*, to become thin).
    6. Here a French loan appears phonologically fully integrated: *rapport*, heard as something like *lapoo*, becomes, with an intervocalic *l* and a further "Luba" touch in the form of an *lw* cluster, *lwapolo*. The point is, though, that this is no longer done "naïvely" but in a manner calculated to get a laugh. It is another question why Tala Ngai uses this form although it would be more appropriate for the character played by Kalwasha. This is one of several examples I observed during rehearsal where actors could not resist pulling a gag or joke even if it did not fit the character.

9. *Kalwasha:*   munaona mwee bote? njo nalimiambia asema pale
sultani anakatala kuya mu mukini: atatuma kanyamba/
Woman: eheh/
Kalwasha: kanyamba atakuya kutufwata/ *sinon:* kanyamba
anakuya/
Woman: eyo/
Kalwasha: njo ule nalimiambia/

10. *Tala Ngai:*   lakini: hii: hii pombe: inakuwa butamu sana/
Feza: nitaongezee kingine?
Tala Ngai: [pretending to hesitate] eh *non non non:* leta kwanza
lupalo[7]/...
Woman: muanzeko na kamwimbo...
Tala Ngai: ...si ni...?... kubolo: bolomosha[8] pa mulibo kwanza/
Man: umuache kwanza akunwye/

11. *Tala Ngai:*   [drinks] eyoo/ mmm/ eh [shouting] munasikia/
Feza: mm/
Tala Ngai: tshintu nilikuwa namielezea ile shiku ile?
Villagers: eeh/ mm/
Tala Ngai: sulutani: na bale bantu yake mbili/ Bwana Cheko naaa
... [hesitates]
Actor: Masimango/
Tala Ngai: Masimango.
Feza: eeh/
Kalwasha: ndyo mubaya: muwaya: muwaya: muwaya
Masimango/
Tala Ngai: zaidi Masimango/
Kalwasha: eh/
Tala Ngai: na jina yake inafanana paka na bubaya bwa mambo
yake yoooote/
Actress: ... wa chuki sana/
Tala Ngai: kama bantu wa mugini bataikalako muzuri/ bawazeko
muzuri vile banawaza/ ah: yee anakatala asema hapana chefu: paka
vile unasema: njo vile bo banaitikaka?
Villagers: hata/ hapana/ [ululations]

12. *Tala Ngai:*   ... nani mwenyewe anapiga hutu tumpombe/
Kalwasha: ...?... mama Fesa huku/

---

7. *Lupalo* or *lupao* means "a spoon"; in this case it refers to a cup with a handle
made from a gourd, resembling a large spoon or a ladle. Synonyms are *lukata* (see ECS
kata) and *lubaya* (Luba, see Van Avermaet and Mbuya 1954: 41, a long-stemmed
calabash, cut in two along its length).
8. A form of ECS *poromosha*, knock down, cause to fall.

Tala Ngai: eh eh eh mama/ tumpombe twako tuko makari: karibu nikatale na ile mampombe ingine ile/
Feza: eeh baba/ shi kintu unasema: na baone paka ba*clients* bote haba banayalaka hapa/
[All begin singing and dancing. Eventually, the other two *notables*, Bwana Cheko and Masimango, arrive and the scene continues.]

13. *Tala Ngai:* [drunken] ah: aaah/
Feza and Kamwanya: [greeting the *notables* who arrive] jambo yenu baba: hamujambo yenu/
Tala Ngai: aaaah/ *oh lal[ā]/* [laughing] mukubwa/
Bwana Cheko: [to Tala Ngai] toka na bulevi/ toka na bulevi/
Woman: *notable/*
Tala Ngai: hapana mukubwa/
Bwana Cheko: kwende kala kule/

14. *Tala Ngai:* sikia nakuelezea/ mambo iko hapa iko hii/ bantu banasikia fulaha sana/ banasema hivi: banasikia fulaha . . .
Bwana Cheko: ya mashamba ya kulima?
Tala Ngai: mbele yabo: banalima nguvu/ nilifika kule chini kote minaangaria/ mashamba ni paka kutoka kufika katomena[9]/
Villagers: [laugh]
Tala Ngai: kutoka hapa kuingia paka katomena/ njo banasema . . .
Masimango: mwee muntu . . .
Tala Ngai: njo banasema . . .
Bwana Cheko: mwee muntu mukubwa unalewa mbele ya bantu ya mukini/
Masimango: ni mutoto kiloko hivi/
Tala Ngai: hapana: hapa tuko ni mu fulaha/ [laughs] bantu ya mugini banapashwa kufulahi na bamfumu yabo/
Villager: eeh/
Tala Ngai: kama mfumu anafurahi: nabo nafanya nini? . . .
[Interruption. The following is a sample of Kachelewa's approach to directing]

15. *Kachelewa:* tusikilizane: eh? tukamata hii *scène* [to Tala Ngai who is not listening] *dis:* Kabeya: *je parle/* kamata hii *scène:* tuweke kama ilikuwa *réalité/* eh? pale unaenda ku mashamba: uko moya alikuwa sasa asema *bon:* [aside] mi sione banafanya ile/ banamuke batangulia na: na bibuyu ya pombe juu mukaufichame kule/ eh? *parce que* hanipende tena ku nani: ku: kufanya nani: *ça on va voir/*

9. Derived from Luba -*toma, tomena,* to drink (Van Avermaet and Mbuya 1954: 708).

sasa hii saa: bale bantu si muko munapiga ngoma/ banakuya/ [clap-
ping hands] ooh: *voilà* banakuya/ *donc pour vous:* munaona asema
na bale banakuya: batafanya sawa vile shee tuko nafanya/ *donc*
hamuji: hamuji*soucier* asema bo banaanza kufoka juu ya sultani: *ou
bien* kufoka: *non*/ bale banakuwa na bo batafanya vile tunafanya/
donc: pour vous muko *conscient* asema na bo batakunywa/ *bon*/ pale
banafika: banaanza nani: kukatala kunywa/ *alors c'est en ce moment
là que* wee unatuma nani: ile saa banafokea unatuma nawaza/
uwapatie nabo/ he? yee anakuya: anakutanisha pale: hamujambo
yenu/ he: toka kule/ weye Tala Ngai: sultani aliisha kushirika kule/
kumbe wee njo unaleta bantu huku? he? paka vile tu analeta bantu
huku/ bale banaona banaona banaona asema *bon:* analeta bantu
huku/ *pourquoi?* banakunywa: habatumike: *tout ça*/ na vile unamupa pombe: anaitikia: anaikala kuikala/ hawezi mbele kuikala/
parce que kama anaikala: *du fait* anaikala yee bado kunywa: *c'est
que:* ana*accepter* ile nani: muko nafanya/ ni ile pombe anakunywa:
pour lui sasa pale anakunywa: butamu ya pombe njo inamu*decider*
ende kaikale/ he? muanze vile pale . . .

Revolt in the Fields: Rehearsal Version (Translation)

1. *Mufwankolo:* . . . they accuse the adulterer. They all [go]. The
chief leaves and then you all begin to drink a little and leave. All
right. Listen, Kabeya, eh, Tala Ngai,[10] is there not going to be a [short
scene] where [the chief's representatives] are sent to the fields? Or
are they simply going to follow what the chief has told them?[11]
Tala Ngai: That is to say, well, the scene is continuous. In other
words the scene develops normally according to the way we
began it: you had explained to the people that they had to go to the
fields . . .
Mufwankolo: Right, that's it.
Tala Ngai: All right. We are going to put this[12] between the two
court cases such that the village ambience is . . .
Mufwankolo: . . . continuous.

10. Mufwankolo corrects himself here; Kabeya is Tala Ngai's name in real life.
11. The sense of these questions is: Should the change of scene to the fields and
the necessity to move back and forth between fields and court require a separate scene
or should the action simply go on and explain itself (by orders presumed to be given by
the chief)?
12. What "this" refers to is not clear. Were the chief's orders to be sandwiched
between the two court cases (taking the place of the scene with the hunter)? Be that as
it may, the remark suggests that it was a function of the hunter's visit to create a
"continuous village ambience." In Shaba Swahili *ambiance* is integrated as a loan and
has a positive connotation, roughly "having a good time."

Tala Ngai: [We are looking to create] a perfect ambience.
Mufwankolo: That's it.

2. *Tala Ngai:*   All right. Only after the judgment will the people
who have gone to work begin to spoil the work because of all the
things Tala Ngai had told them. Therefore, after your [Mufwa-
nkolo's] scene is finished we will cut and meanwhile the camera is
already on, eh [hesitates] . . .
Mufwankolo: . . . the people in the fields.
Tala Ngai: On the people in the fields. Then one could do as we
always do, that is, we insert a little notice [on the screen]; one hears
the drumming and then they see them celebrating in the fields.[13]
Everyone either has a hoe, or a machete; one person works, another
one dances, or drinks. In this way drunkenness . . .

3. *Mufwankolo:*   All right. Let's do it that way. You will be here in a
circle. Right? All right. One mama is going to serve all the others. All
right, how are we going to do this? There will be one bread or two.
They go on serving you[14] and you will drink fast. You go on and
serve another man, just the same way. Right? Then mama will wipe
off the cup and serve another one, *à la Zairoise*. Right? Then you are
going to get the people who were sent by the chief. They are going
to come. This one mama will give them a mighty welcome, right?
And she will make them sit down and stay. She receives them and
they will hear her say: Ooh, come here first. She will seduce them.
[And the person who arrives] stays, just as we said yesterday. Right?
All right. Let's first do this scene where you are sitting together. Sit
right there, in one circle.
[The troupe then gives the scene a try, beginning with a song *"Minakwenda no buta."*[15] But singing as well as drumming are as yet without "fire." During the half hour that follows this is repeated three or
four times. At one point Mufwankolo himself takes the drum (the
seat of a chair that substitutes for it) and shows how it should be
done. He also gives the following directions in order to assure that

13. This is how it was done in the final performance. While the move was made,
a record was played (see the end of the preceding chapter) and a legend appeared on
the screen saying *Shambani*, in the fields.
14. The "you" here is second-person singular, explained by the fact that Mufwankolo addresses the actors who will be sent out by the chief and corrupted, one after
the other, by the villagers. In the following sentence, "you" refers to the woman whose
role it is to cajole the visitors.
15. This is a song that used to be popular in Lubumbashi. At this point in the
rehearsal only the refrain is repeated, later on verses are added; both are in Bemba.
Minakwenda no buta means "I am off with my gun [to go hunting]."

one of the main points of the scene, the corruption of the chief's emissaries by the celebrating villagers, becomes clear. He delivers his instructions in a style we encountered earlier: some very rapid speech, many interjections, and even more demonstrations of movement—a delight to watch and to listen to, but extremely difficult to transcribe and translate.]

4. *Mufwankolo:*   Stop here for a moment. [When one of the chief's emissaries arrives] he will already find you in the rhythm of this song. Right? When those two come you are already singing. You see them [approaching] but you go on. You see them, but you go on for a while. Then they make you stop. What is going on here [they will say], is this work, sitting around? First you remain silent and you listen to what they are going to say. They talk, blablablabla, then the mama who is supposed to seduce them [says]: Oooh, come on, we know [all that]. Sit down first, you, make yourselves comfortable. Get a chair. You give each of them a chair and they sit down.

5. *Tala Ngai:*   Shouldn't this be first one and then the other?[16] *Mufwankolo:*   That's it, yes. You sit down. So it is the woman who has to say this. After you, or rather after she has made them sit down they stay, they take whatever, you see, and so on. You are going to insist, [someone objects] no there will be trouble. . . . You make them sit down, then they start drinking. After that, the singing continues. You go on and then one mama gets into the circle.[17] She sings and dances and dances for a while until they, too, are tempted and they begin to try a dance. This mama takes a cloth and wraps it around one of them. And he, too, gets into the rhythm of the drum. They ululate and so they go on. By that time they [the *notables*] don't say a thing anymore. All right. Finally another emissary comes from the chief, a *notable*. He arrives and things happen as before. So, do we understand each other? You can change the song, or go on with it, I don't know. Right?

[The rehearsal continues along these lines with most of the attention directed to singing and drumming. Then the following piece of dialogue was recorded. Principal speakers are Kalwasha (for the villagers) and Tala Ngai who has been sent by the chief to check

16. Tala Ngai seems to be somewhat confused by the constant switching in pronominal address in Mufwankolo's direction (a confusion shared by the translator) and asks for clarification. Are we talking about two events or one?

17. The original says literally that she "goes into the drum[ming]." This evokes the manner a dance gets started. First people sit or stand around in a circle, then one person takes the initiative, steps into the center, and begins dancing.

what is going on in the fields. Kalwasha talks with an up-country
accent and his example is followed by Tala Ngai as he gets drunk.]

6. *Feza:*   Greetings to you, baba.
Tala Ngai: Hey, greetings.
Villager: Greetings to you.
Tala Ngai: Greetings.
Kamwanya: Be greeted, baba.
Tala Ngai: Greetings. Now, what is this? Are you feasting here
today? In the fields?
Villagers: Yes, baba.
Kalwasha: Baba, we . . .
Tala Ngai: What for?
Kalwasha: It's the back, baba. They bent their backs badly. So we
said: Come on, today let's stretch our backs.

7. *Tala Ngai:*   You did not stretch [your back] in the village and
now you are doing it in the fields?
Kalwasha: Come on, baba. You know, when the work gets me tired
then I rest in the fields. But first, baba, come and let me ask you [so
that I understand it] well.
Tala Ngai: Go ahead.
Kalwasha: What did the chief say?[18]
Tala Ngai: Well, he sent me saying go and have a look. It was the
drumming we heard over there.
Woman: So that was it.
Kalwasha: The drumming?
Tala Ngai: Right. So he said what is this dancing about over
there . . .
Villager: [inviting him] Sit down, chief.
Tala Ngai: . . . to have a look first.
Kalwasha: Did he begin to scold us, or what was it?
Tala Ngai: No, he just said go and have a look first so that I know
what is going on. I was to give him a report.
Kalwasha: You were going to give him a report?
Tala Ngai: That's it.
Villager: So that's it, baba.

8. *Tala Ngai:*   But I also came on my own.
Feza: Come here, first relax a little. You have been walking under
the [hot] sun, baba.

18. Literally it would have to be "How did the chief speak?" but see the earlier
remarks on form and content, p. 210, n. 14.

Villager: Right, first rest a little.

Tala Ngai: As far as I am concerned, the way I found you [having fun] that is the way people ought to live in the village.

Villagers: [acclaiming and applauding] Right on . . .

Tala Ngai: [shouting] You work for a while, then you rest a little and have some millet beer.

Villagers: Right.

Tala Ngai: That way you will have the strength to go on working again tomorrɔw.

Villagers: Ooh, baba. . . . [applause, ululations]

9. *Kalwasha:*   You see, all of you? This is what I told you: When the chief does not want to go to the village he'll send *kanyamba.*[19]

Woman: Really?

Kalwasha: *Kanyamba* will be after us. [If the chief refuses to come] *kanyamba* will come.

Woman: So, that is it.

Kalwasha: That is what I told you.

10. *Tala Ngai:*   [interrupting him] But this beer there, it really is very tasty.

Feza: Should I give you some more?

Tala Ngai: [pretending to hesitate] Oh, no, no, no, just give me the cup . . .

Woman: Start a little song . . .

Tala Ngai: Let's have some to wet the pipe.[20]

Man: Let him drink first.

11. *Tala Ngai:*   [drinks, makes noises of contentment] Yes, indeed. Mmm. [Then begins to shout in a drunken voice] You understand?

Feza: Yes.

Tala Ngai: About the thing I said the other day?

Villagers: Yes.

Tala Ngai: The chief and the two men of his, Bwana Cheko and . . . [hesitates]

Man: Masimango.

Tala Ngai: Masimango.

Feza: Yes.

19. Kalwasha uses ("quotes") a metaphorical and possibly proverbial expression. As to the meaning, I can only offer the following guess. *Kanyamba* may be a Luba term said by Van Avermaet and Mbuya (1954: 439) to designate an animal, striped red and white, which stinks. This could refer to the chief's uniformed guards.

20. The sentence is partly incomprehensible in the original. Literally, it says ". . . cause [something] to go down the throat."

Kalwasha: He is a bad, bad, bad, bad one, that Masimango.
Tala Ngai: Above all Masimango.
Kalwasha: Yes.
Tala Ngai: His name is like the evilness in all his affairs.[21]
Woman: . . . and he is a person full of hatred.
Tala Ngai: If the people of the village should do well and be full of good intentions then he will ignore this, saying to the chief: You must stick to what you said. Will [the people] accept this?
Villagers: No way. [ululations]

12. *Tala Ngai:*   Who is the one who prepared this nice beer?[22]
Kalwasha: . . . ? . . . mama Feza here.
Tala Ngai: Ah mama, your beer is real strong. I am just about to renounce [all] that other beer.
Feza: Yes, baba, now you're saying something. Look at all the customers that are crowding this place.
[All begin singing and dancing. Eventually, the other two *notables*, Bwana Cheko and Masimango, arrive and the scene continues.]

13. *Tala Ngai:*   [drunken] Ah, aaah.
Feza and Kamwanya: [greeting the *notables* who arrive] Greetings baba, greetings to you.
Tala Ngai: Aaah. Oh lala. [laughing] [Greetings] sir.[23]
Bwana Cheko: Go away you, you are drunk. [shouting] Go away, you drunk.[24]
Woman: Notable!
Tala Ngai: No, sir . . .
Bwana Cheko: [interrupting him] Go away, sit down over there.

14. *Tala Ngai:*   Listen, I'll explain to you what is going on here. The people really are enjoying themselves. They said, because they were feeling the joy . . .
Bwana Cheko: . . . of work in the fields?
Tala Ngai: First they worked real hard. I went [to look] down there, everywhere. There are fields everywhere, from here to the place where they get water.

21. *Masimango* means "rejoicing over another's misfortune" (especially going around, telling others about it).
22. "Nice" is an attempt to render a connotation which in the original is marked by adding to *pombe* the diminutive plural prefix *tu-*. A more literal translation, with a diminutive having about the same connotation, would be possible, for instance, in Dutch or German: *biertjes, Bierchen.*
23. Tala Ngai addresses Bwana Cheko properly as *mukubwa*, older person, person of importance, chief.
24. Literally, the original says: Go away with your drunkenness.

Villagers: [laugh][25]
Tala Ngai: [All the way] from here until you get to the place where they get water.
Masimango: You are someone who . . .
Tala Ngai: So they said . . .
Bwana Cheko: You are a person who holds a high office and you get drunk in front of the villagers.
Masimango: [He behaves] like a little child.
Tala Ngai: No way, we are enjoying ourselves here. [Laughs] The villagers must enjoy themselves together with their chiefs.
Villager: That's it.
Tala Ngai: If the chief has fun, what are they going to do?
[At this point, Mufwankolo interrupts with further directions. Bwana Cheko and Masimango are sent away and then approach the group of villagers once again. They are greeted as before, Feza plays her role as the seducer, but Mufwankolo insists on yet another take. Finally Kachelewa intervenes telling the actors to avoid repetitions and superfluous dialogue. He points out that they are not rehearsing a radio sketch where the listeners have to be told what is happening. In this case they are going to see what the actors do and how they move. For instance, when Bwana Cheko tells the villagers that they are drinking and dancing, this is superfluous because everybody can see that they are drinking and dancing.[26] The following gives an example of his approach to directing]

15. *Kachelewa:*   Let's understand each other, all right? Let's take this scene . . . [to Tala Ngai who is not listening] Listen, Kabeya, I'm speaking. Let's take this scene and let's set it up as it would be in real life. Right? When you go to the fields, there is one who says—[aside] because I don't see that they are doing this—anyway, you women with your calabashes of beer you should hide over there. Right? Because I don't think it is good if they still do . . ., well, we'll see about that. At that moment, the people there—you are already drumming. They [the *notables*] arrive. [Clapping hands, as the villagers would do to greet them] Ooh, here they come. So, as far as you are concerned, you see them coming, [and you will think] they will do as we are doing. So, you are not going to worry, saying they

25. The laughter acknowledges a pun or *double entendre* based on the Luba word *kutomena* in the original. It can refer to a place where one fetches water, but also to a place where one drinks.
26. Directives of this kind should be interpreted in terms of the dialectics between talking/discourse and acting/timing which I believe operates in the rehearsal process (see chapter 5).

will scold us because of the chief['s orders] or for whatever reason. No, they come and they'll do as we do. So, you must realize that they will drink. All right. So, when they arrive they first refuse to drink. That is the moment, I think, when you [to Mufwankolo] send out the one that is to scold them [telling him]: Give it to them. He arrives and finds them. [He is received:] Greetings to you. [And the emissary says] Get off, you. You, Tala Ngai, the chief over there is really angry. So it is you who brought the people here? Right? [So he complains that] he brought the people here. The people keep looking and looking and they realize that it was he who brought the people here. What is this about? They drink instead of working, and so on. Then you offer him beer, he accepts it and settles down. He must not sit down at the beginning. Because if he sits down right away before he drinks this would mean that he goes along with what you are doing. It is the beer that he drinks, it is the taste of the beer that makes him decide to sit down. Right? So begin at that point . . .

This part of scene 6 is then repeated two more times up to the point where Bwana Cheko and Masimango have also been corrupted and have joined the drinking and dancing. Then the chief and his wife are approaching. The singing and drumming first slows down, then it dies. Some of the actors pretend to be too drunk to notice and continue. They are silenced and Mufwankolo clears his throat.

The Chief Goes to the Fields: Rehearsal Version (Text 19)

Mufwankolo: minaona sasa: njo kazi yenu hii/ ba*notables* yangu: bale minaweka kitumaini: kwa kuniunga mukono: nabo kweli: banakuwa kujitumbukiza mu hii kazi/ minabatuma: kama mwende: mukaonyeshe: *population:* bakaaji:[27] bote wa mukini kwa kuwa kuendelesha kazi ya mashamba/ hii kunywa hivi: njo kazi gani hii? munaacha kazi ya kulima: munaikalia paka kunywa/ kweli: muzuri sana/ lakini: hata wananikimbia: wanaikimbisha mwee wenyewe/ na miye sasa hapa: nitakamata mpango moya makali kabisa kabisa/ mi iko natafuta kuendelesha inchi mbele/

27. Here is an example for something one hears quite often in Shaba Swahili: a French loan is uttered together with its Swahili gloss. Is it a "doublet" (two words of different derivation but identical meaning co-occurring) or is Mufwankolo correcting himself? From my experience (Fabian 1982) I would lean toward the first possibility. Notice, that Mufwankolo later pronounces *wakahaji*. Both forms, although intended to be in "pure" Swahili (ECS *mkaaji*, plural *wakaaji*) bear traces of Shaba Swahili: the *ba*-prefix and the intervocalic *h*, a form of hypercorrection as deletion of *h* before *a* is frequent.

niko natafuta kuendelesha: ninyi wakahaji: mukuwe kweli
wakahaji wa kweli: mu umoja wenu/ mapendo: masikilizano:
kusaidiana/ lakini ile yote nilifanya: mwee yote munaona kama ni
kazi ya bure/ munanizarau[28]/ sababu ya wale watu watatu/
wanakuja kumichonga/ waiko namiambia mambo ya bongo/ wiko
namidanganya/ lakini: tutaonana nao/ na hapa sasa: hii yote:
mipango yote: inabakia yangu mi mwenyewe peke: nitakamata
uwezo na mipanga yote: nitaanza paka kufanya mi mwenye peke/
tele: vile batafanya/ kunaisha: *allez:* nyi yote wa vi: nani: wa:
wakaaji: ku mukini/

The Chief Goes to the Fields: Rehearsal Version (Translation)

Mufwankolo: Now I see, this is what you call work. I had hoped
that my *notables* would lend me a hand [to help me]; now I find that
they got themselves mixed up with this "work." I sent them out. Go,
[I told them] show the population,[29] all the people of the village,
how to get on with the work in the fields. This drinking here, what
kind of work is this? You stopped the work in the fields and you just
sit around drinking. This is very fine, indeed. But, although it may
seem that they alone abandoned me, in reality they made you run
away from me. And as far as I am concerned now, I am going to
make a truly severe ruling. Above all, I want the country to make
progress. I want you, the population, to progress, so that you may
become a population of value, one that is united. Mutual love,
mutual understanding, and mutual help.[30] But everything I have
done you seem to regard as worthless. You pay no attention to me,
because of those three people who came to work on you.[31] They tell
you lies. They cheat you. But we will face each other. As for right
now, responsibility for all orders will be with me alone. I alone am
going to assume responsibility and I alone shall give all the orders.

28. The verb *kuzarau* is current for "to ignore, to neglect." It does not seem to exist
in ECS, unless one assumes that this Shaba Swahili form is a variant of *kusahau*, to
forget.

29. Here and in the following term "population" may sound awkward but it
renders an intentional assumption, on the part of Mufwankolo, of an "official" register
in his speech.

30. Mufwankolo here uses a formula that occurs almost exactly in the same form
as a central tenet in the teachings of the Jamaa movement in Shaba (see Fabian 1971a).
It is possible that he did this consciously, for my benefit. More likely, I believe, it is
simply the kind of spill-over from Jamaa discourse into general popular rhetoric which I
have observed elsewhere (see Fabian 1979d: 182).

31. The original has the verb *kuchonga*, to carve, to work on a sculpture; the
extended meaning is: to work on someone in order to turn him around; see the
meaning of ECS *kuchongea*, tell tales about, inform against.

And you are going to see how they will act. That's it. Go away, all of you people go to the village.

The villagers take up their tools and the drums and leave. This could be the end. Tala Ngai suggests a change: if the chief now goes back to his place alone, *hakuna suite*, then there is nothing that follows. Kachelewa thinks the villagers should follow him. Tala Ngai: You get them moving right away. Tell them that all have to go home right now. You and your wife go ahead, they follow you to the court. They enter and sit down. Then you give your *morale*, the final admonition. This is agreed upon. Kachelewa makes suggestions for the *morale* (see chapter 13).

As will be recalled from the end of the preceding chapter, in the final performance the change of scene is bridged on the soundtrack of the video recording by some canned music while a sign appears on the screen, saying *Shambani*, In the fields. The villagers are shown drinking and dancing and this continues for some time. Then the camera is briefly back on the chief's court where Mufwankolo gives orders to *notable* Tala Ngai.

The Chief Sends Tala Ngai to the Fields (Text 20)

Mufwankolo: bantu bapashwa: beko nalima mashamba/
Tala Ngai: ndiyo/
Mufwankolo: ule wasipo kulima: wasipo kuwa na kazi: wasipo kuwa na shamba yake: ukuye kuniambia/
Tala Ngai: kalombo/
Mufwankolo: upite ku mashamba ya kila muntu: eh/
Tala Ngai: kalombo/
Mufwankolo: wende wepesi/
Tala Ngai: kalombo/
Mufwankolo: mbiombio/

The Chief Sends Tala Ngai to the Fields (Translation)

Mufwankolo: The people have the order to work their fields.
Tala Ngai: Yes.
Mufwankolo: [If you find] someone who does not cultivate, who has no work, who does not have his field, come and tell me.
Tala Ngai: [At your orders] chief.
Mufwankolo: Go by everybody's field, you understand?
Tala Ngai: Yes, chief.
Mufwankolo: Go and hurry.
Tala Ngai: Yes, chief.
Mufwankolo: Hurry up.

After that, the scene in the fields appears on the screen. The villagers are still singing and drumming, there is drinking and general merriment. Then Tala Ngai arrives. The soundtrack is of fair quality but portions cannot be transcribed because several persons talk at once.

Tala Ngai in the Fields (Text 21)

Tala Ngai: acha: acha: . . . alafu ni nini kwanza makelele hivi?
Villagers: [protest][32]
Tala Ngai: hii furaha inyewe ni ya nini? inapashwa hivi: inapashwa hivi/ [. . .] kila muntu analima mashamba yake/ [. . .] kuisha kulima mashamba munaweza kuikala paka hivi munakunya kakilauri: si njo . . . . ? . . . [. . .] leta mbele lubaya/
Woman: acha kwanza bakupatieko mbele kamoya/
Kalwasha: ikala kwanza pa mututa pale/
Others: pa mututa/ njo vile tunaonaka [. . .]
Woman: wimbo: wimbo: mwiko mu kucheza . . .

Tala Ngai in the Fields (Translation)

Tala Ngai: Stop it, stop it . . . but what is this noise here?
Villagers: [protest]
Tala Ngai: What is all this rejoicing about? This is what ought to be done, what ought to be done [. . . .] every one cultivates his fields. When the fields are worked you can take a rest and a little glass, isn't that . . . .l ? . . . pass the ladle.
Woman: Let them first give you a small one.
Kalwasha: He should first sit down in the furrow over there.
Others: In the furrow. That's how we see it [. . .]
Woman: Singing! Singing! Get into the dance!
[A sort of fighting song is intoned, consisting mainly of repetitions of *tuta mawila, Lumundu*][33]

---

32. Here and in the following, the villagers greet Tala Ngai's speech with protest and interjections. These are too confused to be rendered meaningfully and are therefore only marked by [. . .].

33. According to information received in a letter from the Mufwankolo group (May 30, 1988) it is in Kizela (a group east of Lake Moero):

TUTA MAWILA, LUMUNDU
KWA MWENGE I KULA
March on, Lumundu
It is still far to Mwenge's.

Incidentally, both Kalundi Mango and I "heard" *tutabawina*, we shall beat them, and thought of it as a kind of fighting song.

Then the camera is back on Mufwankolo and his court in the village.
He speaks to his guards.

The Chief Sends His Guards to the Fields (Text 22)

Mufwankolo: muangarie/ nilituma Tala Ngai: mwanzo alienda: yee
bado kurudia hapana/ mwee wende: mukapite mu kila mashamba/
tena kama munamukutana Tala Ngai eko kule: munabamba yee:
munaleta hapa/ tangu nilimutuma: kunakuwa masiku tatu muzi-
ma/ yee hapana kurudia/ mwee munakwenda hapa: mwende/
mutaangaria bantu: kama beko naanza na kazi ya kulima/ munasikia?
Guards: ndiyo *chef*/
Mufwankolo: *allez:* mwendeni bwepesi/
Guard: ...? ... *chef*/
Mufwankolo: ule hakutumika kazi munafunga yee: kuleta hapa/
Guards: ndiyo *chef*/
[Short passage incomprehensible]

The Chief Sends His Guards to the Fields (Translation)

Mufwankolo: Look here. I sent Tala Ngai. He left and has not
returned. Now you leave and go to every field. And if you find that
Tala Ngai is there, arrest him and bring him here. It's been three full
days [hours?] since I sent him and he has not come back. You leave
right now and see whether the people have started working. You
understand?
Guards: Yes, chief.
Mufwankolo: Come on, get going fast.
Guard: ...? ... chief.
Mufwankolo: Anyone who does not do his work you tie him up
and bring him here.
Guards: Yes, chief.
[Short passage incomprehensible]

After that the action is back in the fields. The villagers are singing
and dancing. The guards arrive. When they come to the villagers they
have difficulties getting their attention. Tala Ngai, now obviously drunk,
speaks for the people. Almost everyone joins him in trying to get the
guards to sit down and have a good time. They protest weakly: *chef
atashirika*, the chief is going to be angry. Then they give in; Tala Ngai
orders *piga ngoma*, beat the drum, and the festivities continue. As to
obtaining a text of this brief scene, some fragments could probably be
retrieved but they would be meaningless. In this case the sound record-

ing is of reasonably good quality, it is simply that disorder, confusion, and anarchy successfully enacted do not lend themselves to being represented in an orderly fashion.

The camera stays for a while on the people in the fields, then the action is back in the village.[34] The Chief gets more and more impatient and now sends the two remaining *notables*, Bwana Cheko and Masimango, to the fields.

The Chief Sends Bwana Cheko and Masimango to the Fields (Text 23)

Mufwankolo: Bwana Cheko/
Bwana Cheko: vidyee/
Mufwankolo: Masimango/
Masimango: kalombo/
Mufwankolo: mwendeni/ mwende mukaangarie bantu bupesi bupesi/ . . . ? . . . bwepesi/ bantu pa fasi/ mulete haba bantu betu/
Masimango: vidyee kalombo/
Mufwankolo: *toi viens ici*/ bantu pa fasi/
Masimango: vidyee kalombo/
Mufwankolo: mwende . . . [the rest incomprehensible]

The Chief Sends Bwana Cheko and Masimango to the Fields (Translation)

Mufwankolo: Bwana Cheko.
Bwana Cheko: Chief.
Mufwankolo: Masimango.
Masimango: Chief.
Mufwankolo: Go. Go and look at the people and do it fast. . . . ? . . . fast. [See to it that] the people are each where they are supposed to be.[35] And bring me those people of mine [whom I sent out before].
Masimango: At your orders, chief.
Mufwankolo: You, get here![36] [I want] the people where they are supposed to be.

---

34. I might mention at this point that on viewing the videotape one gets the impression that the movement back and forth between the chief's court and the fields was achieved by cutting. But in fact there was no interruption at all. What appears to be put together from cuts consists of sequences in real time "mixed" by switching from one camera to another. Incidentally, during this scene I was at the second location, in "the fields" (a few gardens and a stand of bananas behind the house that served as backdrop for the chief's court).

35. Literally, the command given by Mufwankolo would have to be translated as "people in place."

36. In the original this short phrase is pronounced in French, using *toi*, the

Masimango: At your orders, chief.
Mufwankolo: Go . . . [the rest incomprehensible].

Then the fields appear on the screen again. The villagers are singing and dancing; some are on the ground, overcome by drunkenness. The camera shows the two *notables* approaching through the fields. When they arrive, Bwana Cheko addresses the villagers. He scolds them and reminds them of the chief's orders. Masimango does the same. Then things happen as before in rehearsal—the two *notables* accept a drink and join the singing and dancing. Again, I had to give up making a usable transcription of this passage. The gist of it is: Bwana Cheko and Masimango stop the villagers and accuse them, above all Tala Ngai, of disobeying the chief's orders. The villagers talk back. Beer is offered and things turn around when Bwana Cheko has a taste and declares it delicious.

At any rate, dialogue is now getting less and less important. The soundtrack consists mainly of singing and drumming, providing the background to scenes of drunkenness and dissipation. The song is still the same: *Tuta Mawila,* march on. Also, something went wrong with the microphone connection and there are some gaps on the TV soundtrack. At one point the director (or a technician) switches to camera 2 (in the chief's court). There is a brief passage of (incomprehensible) "backstage" conversation between Mufwankolo and the people who are still with him. Then the mistake is noticed and camera 1 is put back on. Finally there is one more switch back to the chief's court. The chief has nothing left but to send out his wife.

The Chief Sends His Wife to the Fields (Text 24)

Mufwankolo: inamfumu/
Amunaso: mwami[37]/
Mufwankolo: minaona mambo inaanza kunichokesha kabisa/
mambo inanichokesha/ nitafanya sasa namna gani kwanza mbele?
bantu natumako: tangu balikwenda: natumako haba: tangu balikwenda: natumako haba: tangu balikwenda/ . . . ? . . . kwanza

---

impolite form of address. This is one of several instances of a code switch made for stylistic-rhetorical reasons. French is here presented as the colonial (and post colonial) command language; it demeans the speaker as well as the addressee. That the chief resorts to it shows that he is losing his countenance.

37. The terms of address exchanged here are both marked as "traditional." *Inamfumu* is Luba for the chief's (first) wife, the "queen." *Mwami* is yet another term for "chief," here probably taken from Sanga/Yeke (where it was introduced from the East). This combination of traditional terms of different linguistic and cultural background is another example for folklorization (which seems to involve generalization).

mambo gani inapita kule ku: ku mashamba kule? sasa wee mwenyewe wende kwanza ukaangarie bale bantu haba/ wende kabisa
kabisa/ unapita fasi yote/ kubaambia asema sultani anasirika kabi-
sa/

The Chief Sends His Wife to the Fields (Translation)

Mufwankolo: Inamfumu.
Amunaso: Chief.
Mufwankolo: I see that I am really getting tired with this affair. I am
getting fed up. What am I going to do now? I sent out people, again
and again, they never came back.[38] . . . ? . . . [I want to know] first
what is happening there in the fields. So now you go yourself and
look at those people there. Leave right away, and go everywhere.
Tell them the chief is really angry.

Then the action is back in the fields. *Inamfumu* approaches the
villagers and watches them from a distance, hiding among banana trees.
Then she returns to the court and tells the chief what is going on in the
fields. He now decides that he must go and see for himself. He arrives on
the scene and addresses the villagers. Tala Ngai tries to steal away.

The Chief Goes to the Fields: Final Version (Text 25)

Mufwankolo: mwee/ njo kazi munaikalia huku? wanamituma
kwenda kulima/ kufanya kazi ya mashamba/ munaikalia kunywa
mapombe/ na kucheza paka michezo wa bule/ mwee hapana
kumbuka hata na kazi hapana/ minatuma bapulisi: banakuya hu-
ku/ hata kunileta *rapport* hapana/ minatuma ba*notables:* nabo
banakuya huku/ banakimbia na kukimbia/ . . . . ? . . . ./ mwee kazi
yenu inaisha/ njo kusema: mwee bote mwiko hapa: *allez* munifwate
kwangu ku mulango/ mutasikia/ ba*notables* njo bangu kweli:
minaibatuma: banakuya kuikala paka kazi ya kunywa pombe na
kucheka michezo ya bule/ tutaangaria nabo/ pamoya na polisi/
nitaangaria: *allez:* mwee bote ya mugini: *allez* kwangu upesi/

The Chief Goes to the Fields: Final Version (Translation)

Mufwankolo: You there, is this how you are doing your work? You
had the order to cultivate, to work in the fields. Now you are sitting

---

38. Here, once more, the translation renders the sense but fails to convey the
special flavor of exasperation which the original expresses by formal means, ellipsis and
repetition. Literally translated, Mufwankolo's statement would be "I sent people there,
since they left, I sent them there, since they left, I sent them there, since they left."

around drinking and dancing stupid dances. Not for a moment do you think of your work. I sent out my guards. They got here but never gave me a report. I sent the *notables*. They too arrived here and [now] they are running away [in all directions]. [Short passage incomprehensible; then to the *notables*] Your job is finished. And all of you here, get going and follow me to my house. You will hear [what I have to say]. I sent out my *notables* and they got here and all they did was drink and have fun with stupid dances. We will look at them, as well as the guard, [and see what we do with them]. I will look [at them]. Now get going, all of you from the village, get to my place fast.

The villagers pick up their things and follow, together with a crowd of spectators from Kawama who had followed the action to the fields.

13

Scene 7: The Chief Takes Control: Order Restored

During the June 27 rehearsal, scene 6 was brought to an end when the chief, together with his wife and guards, appeared in the fields. He scolds them right there and this could have been the end of the play. Instead, it was decided that the final scene should be at the chief's court. The fields are the place for rebellion; the village is the place of order. But more about that later (in chapter 14). In the village Mufwankolo is to pronounce his *morale*, the admonition that usually closes a play by the troupe. Kachelewa himself gives directions.

The Chief's Final Speech: Kachelewa's Directions (Text 26)

1. *Kachelewa:* [to Mufwankolo] *donc* unafanya *morale* ya mwisho ile/
Mufwankolo: *d'accord:* kweli/
Kachelewa: ya: kusema/
Tala Ngai: ni bo ulielezea zaidi/
Mufwankolo: bale tatu . . .

2. *Kachelewa:* munaona: namna gani niliweka kitumaini mu: bantu bale nilikuwa natumika nabo/ eh? ni kweli banasemaka: kufanya kitu hamuwezi kufanya wee mwenyewe/ niliwekea nani: kitumaini sana: lakini bo benyewe banaharibisha ile kitumaini niliwekea/ sasa hakuna tena huruma/ sitaki tena kubaona mu nani: mu lupango yangu/ na hapa sasa nitatafuta banani: bengine ba kuweza kutumika na mi/ lakini: uwezo yote nikamate mi mwenyewe: na ile nitasema: munasikia sauti yangu: njo ile mutafwata/

3. ile ni *résumé* minakuambia: *donc* upime ku*développer* mu *morale* ya kufanya/ *bon*/ minasema vile juu ya nini? unaji*rappeler:* eh: *dernière meeting* ya *président* ku nani/ alikuwa kusema nilikuwa *patient* kabisa: eh: nili*patienter* mingi: *maintenant* kunaisha/ angaria

bantu nilikuwa nasema bataweza kutumika na mi muzuri: mina-
wawekea *confiance:* angaria vile banafanya/ banaanza kukamata na
mwee *peuple* kupeleleka njia mubaya/ kwabo sasa: kunaisha/ nitakamata: mi mwenyewe: ile itakuya: njo ile/ ile itakuya: itakuya/
sasa ni kusema *oyee* ku hii: *eyaa*/ na bantu banasema: aaaaaaaaah:
pièce inaisha/ . . .
[Some of the actors briefly comment]
juu ya bale bote ba: eh?: banapendaka ku*essayer* ku*interpreter* mubaya: banasema *non: non non ils ont bien fait/ ils ont parlé de ça et
tout ça/*

The Chief's Final Speech: Kachelewa's Directions (Translation)

1. *Kachelewa:* [to Mufwankolo] So, then you do your final
admonition.
Mufwankolo: Yes, indeed.
Kachelewa: That is to say . . .
Tala Ngai: [You begin by telling them that] you explained matters
to them at length.
Mufwankolo: [To] those three . . .[1]

2. *Kachelewa:* You see how I put my hope in those people I used to
work with. Right? It is true what is said: There is nothing that you
can achieve alone.[2] I really put hope [in them] but they themselves
have destroyed the hope I put in them. Now there is no mercy
anymore. I don't want to see them anymore in my court. And I am
going to look right away for others who can work with me. But I am
assuming all the power and what I am going to say, you will listen to
my voice and obey my orders.

3. [To Mufwankolo] What I'm telling you is just a summary, you try
to develop it in the final admonition you are going to give. All right.
Why am I talking like this? You remember at the latest rally,
wherever it was, the president was saying: I really have been patient, I had a lot of patience, but now it's over. [going back to
Mufwankolo's speech] Look at the people about whom I said that
they would work well with me, in whom I put confidence, look how

1. This is not clear without some context. The dramaturgical problem is the
continuity of action. From scolding his *notables* (to whom he has spoken enough) the
chief should go on to a confrontation with the villagers and he should make the
connection by insisting that the *notables* had all the necessary instructions.
2. Kachelewa quotes a sentence, possibly a proverb. Literally it says: "To make
something, you cannot make [it] by yourself." Applied to the chief it means that he
must rely on the advice and help of others when making his decisions.

they act. And they begin to take you people on a bad road. As far as they are concerned, it is finished. I myself am going to take over and whatever happens, let it happen, and that is it. Whatever happens, let it happen. [To Mufwankolo] this is when you shout *oyé* and the others respond *eyaa*.³ Then the people applaud and that's the end of the piece.

[Some actors briefly comment]

[We are going to end in this way] so that all those who like to try and interpret [the play negatively] will say, no, no, no, they have done well, they talked about all that.⁴

The rehearsal continues; it has now been decided that the chief's final speech will not be in the fields but in his court back in the village. Mufwankolo tells the villagers to follow him, they start moving while a song in Luba is intoned by Tala Ngai. The singing is subdued, there is no drumming. After some last discussion Mufwankolo addresses the villagers.

The Chief's Final Speech: Rehearsal Version (Text 27)

1. *Mufwankolo:*   wandugu wapenzi/ wababa na nye wamama/ twiko na mukini yetu hii moya/ kweli kweli: mu mukini: kama hamuna masikilizano: hakuna namna ya kuendelea/ mu mukini kama muko njala: hakuna namna ya kutumika kazi/

2. lakini mi sultani: navumulia mingi sana/ namiweka kitumaini/ hasa zaidi/ niliwaweka kitumaini wale wa kuniunga ku mukono/ na ninyi: wenyewe munabafahamu sasa/ ni mambo ya kushangaa: kwa siku ya leo: wale watu minatumaini: lakini leo: wananizarau neno moya munene sana/ wananikata mikulu na kichwa/ sababu: ya kuvumilia kwangu sababu ya ile kitumaini nilitumaini asema: nabawekea kitumaini: ni watu wanaweza kunisaidia/

3. munayua asema: kilole moja: hakikutake chawa/ mi siwezi kui-tuka kazi yangu miye peke yangu hapana/ kwa mufano vile nita-weza kuwa asema nakuwa *égoïste*/ na vile nilibachagula bale/ ba-anze kumiletea ma*messages* mweye/ ile inasemwa na miye/ baanze kumionyesha namna gani: hii tunafanya yetu: *organisation*/ lakini:

---

3. Kachelewa reverts to quoting the president. His speeches are interspersed with exclamations of *oyee*, hail, hurrah; *eyaa*, from the verb *ya*, is the Lingala equivalent of the *itakuya*, which precedes it in our text: may it come, may it happen.

4. Regarding apprehensions about a possible "wrong" (political) interpretation of the play see the discussion reported on in chapter 4, notes on the meeting of Friday, June 20.

kwa siku ya leo: nilibaambia kama mwee mupitepite: mu mikini mu
mikini mu mikini: miaka huu: bantu bote banapashwa kuwa na
mashamba ya kila namna/ mashamba tatu ya chakula: mashamba
inne ya chakula: wa nguvu analima hata sita/ twiko na bulongo
moya muzuri sana ya chakula/ hii bulongo: bantu bote beko nai-
kumbwa[5]/ sasa mweye: munaikala paka munakwenda: munani-
fichika: munaikwenda mu mashamba: munaikalia paka kunywa/
ile pombe muko nakunywa ile: inatoka wapi? inatoka ni ku chaku-
la/ kama hamulime mutapata pombe?

4. kwa mufano sawa ule Tala Ngai/ eh: simama/ unaona/ njo kazi
ile/ namutuma kwenda kufanya kazi yote: yee lakini: mu pale
munamuona na mwee bote munarekea/ sababu ni nini? sababu yee
njo tulitumikakaka naye: njo anaikalalaka kwangu/ na mwee bote
munarekea/ munamufwata/ angaria sawa Masimango/ simama
Masimango/ angaria/ ni kazi ile? Masimango ni mutu nilitumaini
sana sana na zaidi/ kama kweli kazi yetu tutaweza kuongoka/
Bwana Cheko: ah: unaona: anafichama: simama kule/ mutazame
kwaza/ na bale bote nilituma baende kule si bangu bote namna
moya?

5. lakini: hapa sasa niko namiambia/ mweye bote: bakaji ya mukini: byote binabadirika/ sasa hakuna huruma/ maneno nahurumia
weeee: minachoka/ haba wabwana haba bote haba: beko naharibisha mioyo ya watu: namikuwa kwa kuchonga: bya bongo: na
kuleta mambo ya bongo/ paka hapa sasa kazi yabo yote i-na-isha[6]/
shiwezi tena kutumika nabo hata kiloko/
Actor: ndiyo *chef/*

6. *Mufwankolo:* na: mutoke mu lupango yangu bende hata fasi
gani banakwenda/ sipende/ nitachagula bantu: bale nitatumika na-
bo/ bale nitaona bantu ba kweli/ bale banapenda kazi kutumika/
tosha batoshe hapa/ nitatumika nabo/ sasa: *pouvoir* yote/ ukumu[7]
wote/ yote yote inabakia yangu: mikono yangu/ nataanza kusema
paka kile minasema: mwee bote munafwata/ na tangu hapa sasa:
hakuna ule mwengine/ atajaribu tena/ kupima ama kujaribu: kuharibisha mioyo ya watu: kwenda kulongofya bongo: na kuharibu
kazi/ kama namupata: naweka ndani/ munayua ndani ni nini?
kuweka na kofiri munene/
Actor: longolongo/

5. *Kukumbwa* is a verb of uncertain origin, synonymous with *kutamani*, to desire.
6. In order to put emphasis on it, Mufwankolo pronounces the verb morpheme
by morpheme.
7. The Shaba Swahili form of ECS *hukumu*, authority, power, jurisdiction.

Mufwankolo: na kusahabu/ *ekoya: heya/ ekoya: heya/* paka vile/
Women: [ululate]
Mufwankolo: allez/
[end of recording]

The Chief's Final Speech: Rehearsal Version (Translation)

1. *Mufwankolo:*   Dear relatives. Fathers, and you, mothers. Our village is one. Truly, if there is no mutual understanding in a village there is no way of making progress. If you go hungry in a village there is no way of doing the work.

2. But I, the chief, have put up with a lot. I put hope in you, too much [hope]. And I put hope in those who should have joined hands with me. You know them very well. To my great surprise I find today that those people in whom I put hope have let me down in a very important matter. They really did everything to work against me.[8] I put up [with them] because I had this hope, saying I will put hope in them, they are people who can help me.

3. You know the saying: A single finger does not catch a louse.[9] I cannot do my work all by myself. If I were to do that, I could be called an egotist. Therefore I chose those people so they may pass on to you messages that come from me; that they may show you how we organize ourselves. So today I told them to go really everywhere in the village [and tell you:] This year, everyone must have fields of all sorts. Three, four fields to produce food; a strong person can even have six under cultivation. The soil we have is very good for growing food. Everyone would love to have a soil like that. And now you go and hide from me, you go to the fields and just sit around drinking. The beer you are drinking, where does it come from? It comes from the food. If you don't work the fields are you going to get beer?

4. For example, take this Tala Ngai. Get up, you! You see, this is how he does his work. I sent him out to do all the work but when you saw him you all became weak. Why? He was supposed to work for me because he has been living with me.[10] And you all got weak

---

8. This is a translation of an idiomatic expression which says literally: They cut off my feet and my head.

9. Mufwankolo quotes a popular proverb. Lenselaer gives a slightly different version of it under *chawa: Kidole kimoja hakivunji chawa,* one finger does not squash a louse (see 1983: 61).

10. Meaning: He was supposed to carry out my order because he depends on me, he is my subordinate.

and follow his example. Look at Masimango. Stand up Masimango! Look [at him], is this the way to do the work? Masimango is someone in whom I really put all my hope so that we might truly get our work together. Bwana Cheko—ah, you see, he is hiding—stand up there! Look [at him] first. And all my people whom I sent there [to the fields] aren't they all my people?

5. But right now I am telling you, for all of you in the village everything is going to change. Now there is no mercy. Because I have had mercy for a long, long time. Now I am tired of it. All those gentlemen here who corrupt the hearts of the people, who distort things and tell you lies, from this moment on all their work is finished. There is no way I can go on working with them, no way. *Actor:* Yes, chief.

6. *Mufwankolo:* Get out of my court. Let them go wherever they go. I have had enough. I am going to choose people with whom I am going to work, people whom I will find to be persons of value, people who love work—get those people out of here!—and I will work with them. As of now, all the power, all the authority, everything will be in my hands. And when I am going to speak all of you will obey my orders. And from now on, there will be no one to try and seduce [you] or to corrupt the hearts of the people, or to spread lies and spoil the work. If I catch such a person, I put him inside. You know the meaning of "inside." Put him behind a big lock. *Actor:* [in a low voice] In prison. *Mufwankolo:* And forget about him. What ever happens, let it happen. Whatever happens, let it happen.[11] Just like that. *Women:* [ululate] *Mufwankolo:* [Now] go away.

The Chief's Final Speech: Final Version (Text 28)

1. *Mufwankolo:* Shebele/
Shebele: kalombo/
Mufwankolo: ita banotables bakuye huku/. . . .
[does this, they arrive]

2. *allez* munaikale chini/ bapolishi iko wapi? . . . ? . . . munasikia? mweye bapolishi: mweye ba*notables* mwee njo: muliniunga mukono/ macho/ njo yangu/ mukulu: njo wangu/ pale minawekea kitumaini asema: tutatumika na mweye: kazi muzuri aendeke/ niko

11. Mufwankolo here takes up Kachelewa's suggestion (see text 26, 3) and quotes the president in Lingala.

namituma/ kwenda kubaambia bantu: mambo: ni ile minatafuta/
mwee munakwenda kuharibisha/ kwenda kusema mambo ya
bongo ku bantu/ ku bakaji bote/

3. sababu ya kusema: miye nikuwa mubaya: mi sultani/ bantu beko
nakuwa kunisimanga asema sultani ni mubaya/ mwee bo muko
nakwenda: namituma mwee asema mwende mubaambie bantu:
munafika kule munafichikayo/ munabaambiako mambo ingine/
sababu ya roho yenu mubaya/ mwee bantu tatu weye/ kuharibisha
mukini wote muzima hii/
4. lakini/ lakini/ tangu hapa sasa: *allez:* muache tumoto[12] chini
hapa/ tosha tumoto/ tosha tumoto/ weka hapa/ tangu leo: mwee
bu*notable* wenu tena: hamunako/ *allez*/ toke/ mi sitake kumiona/
na mwee bapolisi toke hapa [comments and laughter from audience
as the *notables* get up and leave] mutoke mbio/ mutoke pale/ mbio/

5. mwee bote wakaaji/ bantu yote wa mugini/ munaona bubaya ya
bale bantu haba/ bantu batatu/ na bapolushi wabo wawili/ njo
banatafuta kuharibisha mukini: kuharibisha mioyo yenu mweye/
juu ya mambo ya bongo/ ile ilikuwa balikuya kumilanda/ minasema mambo ya kweli/ bo banakuwa kumilongofya mambo ya
bongo: sababu mwee munasema asema: ah: sultani ni mubaya:
sultani ni mubaya/ mi sina mubaya hapana/ babaya ni haba muna-
ona/ si munaona bo benyewe: leo nakuwa kuwashirika[13] pa macho
yenu/ si munaona?
Audience: ndiyo/
Mufwankolo: si munanona?
Audience: ndiyo/

6. *Mufwankolo: voilà/* njo mambo ya bongo: njo bantu babaya
kabisa ka: minabatosha kazi/ hapa sasa: busultani bwangu: na uwezo wangu: bunabakia paka mi mwenyewe/ paka yangu: kunaisha/
Women: [ululations]/

---

12. What Mufwankolo pronounces here sounds like *tumoto* or *tuboto.* So far I
have been unable to identify the word but the reference is clear from the video
recording (see translation). This is one of the few cases where recourse to recorded
visual information has been necessary to ascertain the meaning of an utterance. I say
recorded because there have of course been many instances in these transcriptions and
translations in which I, often unconsciously, supplemented acoustic signals with the
visual memory I have as a participant in the events.
13. Mufwankolo pronounces *kuwashirika*, which poses a problem. *Kushirika,* to be
angry, is an intransitive verb and cannot have a pronominal affix marking an object
(-wa-). It is likely that there has been a mistake and that most speakers of Shaba
Swahili would hear *kuwashinika,* a verb (origin so far not identified) meaning "to
confront someone with a witness," for example, in a case of litigation.

Mufwankolo: batachagula ba*notables* bengine: bantu nitatumika
nabo: bale ba roho muzuri/ bale ba kuyua kazi/ bale ba akili/ wa
kuendelesha kazi/ nitabachagula ba*notables* bengine: tutatumika
nayo pamoya/ hapana sawasawa bantu wa bongo hapana/ bale ba
kucheza bule/

7. *bon:* pamoya na bapolushi vilevile: nitaanza na bapolushi bengi-
ne/ bale tutatumika nayo muzuri/ njo bale banaonaka asema sultani mubaya/ sina mubaya hapana/ mi niko muzuri: mi niko juu
yenu/ niko juu yenu/ munasikia muzuri?
Actor: ndiyo *chef/*
Mufwankolo: aksanti sana bamama/ [ululations; final song, drumming, dancing before the chief. . . .]

The Chief's Final Speech: Final Version (Translation)

In the chief's court. There is singing and drumming. Mufwankolo, in
full chiefly attire, with his fly whisk, hatchet, and headdress, dances by
himself. Then he calls his guard.

1. *Mufwankolo:*   Shebele!
Shebele: Chief.
Mufwankolo: Call the *notables,* they should come here.
[The guard does this, the *notables* arrive; there is some shouting and
ordering around until they are settled. Then the chief begins his
final admonition.]

2. Come on, sit down. Where are the [other] guards? . . . ? . . . Are
you listening? You, the guards, and you, the *notables.* You locked
hands with me. [You were supposed to be] my eyes and my feet. I
used to put hope in you saying, I am going to work with you so the
work may go well. I sent you out to tell the people what I wanted [to
have done]. You went to spoil [things]. You went to tell lies to the
people, to all those who live in the village.

3. Because you told them that I, the chief, am bad the people are
scoffing at me, saying the chief is bad. I sent you to talk to the
people, you went and when you got there you kept hiding [my
orders] from them. You told them something else. Because you have
a bad spirit, the three of you. [You want] to corrupt this entire
village.

4. But, but from now on—come on, put your headdresses down
here! Take off your headdresses, take them off! Put them here! From
today on your office of *notable* no longer exists. Go ahead, leave! I
don't want to see you. And you guards, get out of here. [Laughter

and comments from the audience as the *notables* get up and leave]
Get away now, quick!

5. You, the population, all the people of the village, you see how
evil those three men are, as well as the two guards. They seek to
corrupt the village, to corrupt your hearts. Because [they told you]
lies. What [they told you was] to turn you around. I am speaking the
truth. They tricked you with lies. Because [now] you say, ah, the
chief is bad, the chief is bad. I am not bad. The bad ones are those
that you see here. Don't you see them? Today I put them before you,
before your eyes. Don't you see?
Audience: Yes, we do.
Mufwankolo: Don't you see?
Audience: Yes, we do.

6. *Mufwankolo:* *Voilà*, there are the lies and there the people who
are truly bad. I fire them from their work. Right now, my chiefhood,
my power, are mine alone. They are mine alone, and that's it.
Women: [ululations]
Mufwankolo: Other *notables* are going to be elected, people with
whom I will work, people who have a good heart, who know their
work, who are intelligent, and [who know] how to make the work
progress. I am going to select other notables and I will work with
them, not like these liars who just play around.

7. All right, and the same goes for the guards. I am going to appoint
new guards with whom I will be able to work well. The way those
people see it, the chief is bad. I am not bad. I am good, I am here for
you, for you.[14] Do you understand me well?
Actor: Yes, chief.
Mufwankolo: [addressing the women] Thank you, mothers.

The speech is greeted by exclamations of joy from the audience, a
final song is intoned. There is dancing before the chief, the dancers pay
their respect to the chief.[15]

---

14. The original phrase *juu yenu* could also be translated as "because of you,"
"because you put me here."
15. Meanwhile on the screen there appears once more the title: *C'était "Le Pouvoir
se mange entier."* Credits for images and sound are added. Director and producers are
acknowledged once again.

14

Reflections and Afterthoughts

On Endings, Meanings, and Interpretation

The play has ended. The actors who created it declared that its end should be the beginning of "reflection." This was a term they used and when I take it up now to bring my story to an end I do so with the conviction that the anthropologist's task is not to rise above his ethnographic material but to continue the work of reflection, to widen the audience, to ponder thoughts that were formulated, to show how formulations were produced, and, perhaps, to argue with some of the statements.

Three main strands went into the composition of my story. First, I gave an account of a discovery, made while doing fieldwork on religious movements in Shaba in 1986: Much of cultural knowledge, that is, realized, objectified cultural knowledge, is performative; therefore performance may also be a mode of acquiring cultural knowledge through ethnography. In chapter 1 I tried to spell out some theoretical assumptions and methodological consequences.

The second story-line also began with an event, the quotation of a saying about power: "Le pouvoir se mange entier," Power is eaten whole. Its meaning was explored in chapter 2 with the help of lexical-semantic, generic, and sociolinguistic analysis, always with two questions in mind: Can we assume that such a saying, or the axiomatic principle it seems to state, expresses a way of thinking about power? And if so, what is involved in "expression"?

Then there was a third event, in fact, a sequence of events whose story is told in a report on work (in 1986) with a group of popular actors who, by accident more than by design, took up a search for the meaning of "le pouvoir se mange entier" by making it the topic of a popular play. Chapters 3 and 4 described this as an ethnographic experiment: I recall my first contacts with the Mufwankolo troupe and give a sketch of its earlier history and the emergence of popular theater in the region. Then the making of *Le pouvoir se mange entier*, from initial planning, through rehearsals, to the filming of the piece for local television is recounted. Preceded by an interlude on the status of texts (chapter 5), the documented results, in the form of transcribed and translated recordings, were presented in chapters 6 to 13. Throughout, but especially in this last part, I made no effort to, as it were, hold back on comments and reflections. Many of them were necessary to justify the presentation and translation of the texts. The purpose of this last chapter is to pull dispersed comments together by addressing a limited number of problems of interpretation.

All Is Well That Ends Well . . .

Not the ending as such, but a certain kind of ending was to make people think about "le pouvoir se mange entier." The *comité artistique* had to tackle a problem when it discussed the plot and the possibility of an open ending. As long as political considerations did not intervene it was agreed that the play would make its point most strongly if it were to conclude with disorder, that is, with scenes that would have been all action and little discourse. When it turned out that some accommodation was inevitable, the actors still thought that their conception could be saved if a *morale*, a discursive disclaimer, were added after the curtain had gone down, figuratively speaking.[1] But that would not have satisfied authorities who are quite sensitive to tongue-in-cheek demonstrations of loyalty. So the last scene was construed such that order was reestablished by the chief, making the play unassailable without, as we shall see, compromising the initial intention altogether.

To take all this a step further, I feel that the ethnographer trying to bring his story to an end is in a situation that resembles that of the troupe. Should I not simply leave the account at the end of the play and let readers draw their own conclusions? Or, conversely, if I now conclude with "talk," with an interpretive discourse pronounced from a higher level of reflection, am I not trying to provide a more or less happy ending where there is in fact none? Am I not about to go through an exercise calculated to satisfy expectations regarding a monograph; satis-

---

1. Perhaps this is a point that should be stressed because it is so obvious that it escapes attention: The setting of this play was such that the troupe could not work with the kind of disclaimers which theater normally provides. There was no stage that would have signaled that the action takes place in a world apart from "real life," no curtain symbolically enforcing that separation, not even a clear distinction between actors and audience, if we remember the ways in which the people of Kawama village were made part of the event.

fying readers who do not care to read the texts but want to have a vicarious understanding provided by the anthropologist? Am I not engaged in political appeasement, taking the sting out of *Le pouvoir se mange entier?* On the other hand, who am I to disregard political sensibilities (and real dangers) and to add incisiveness to expressions of critique by making explicit what is best kept implicit just because I happen, for the time being, to write from a position that is safe?

The problem boils down to this: How can this book be ended without cancelling its purpose, which was to tell the story of a process of search for the meaning of [statements about] power? It seems to me that this can be done only by taking the process into a new cycle, making room for a new story. This is one more reason why I must apply to this record of events, solidified in texts, what the troupe wanted to have applied to their play: reflection.

Following a habit we have acquired during centuries of dealing with texts, I first wanted to call this last chapter "Interpretations." I now opt for "Reflections," not because a simple terminological twist can change habits, but in order to express my understanding of the troupe's intentions. I want to find a way of terminating my account in such a way that it can serve these intentions. This involves staying clear of a model of hermeneutics where the authority of an ethnographic account is based on a static, hierarchical relation between text and interpretation (whereby it matters little whether the hermeneut places himself beneath the text—as in theological or juridical exegeses of sacred or legally binding texts—or above the text—as in the often presumptuous analyses offered by ethnologists and psychoanalysts). I have grappled with an alternative before,[2] and here is another occasion to clarify the idea of ethnography as the continuation of a search for understanding that begins with cultural performances. The theoretical benefit that is to be derived from making performance a guiding idea is a conception of relationships between texts and interpretation which is neither static nor hierarchical but processual. The burden of such an approach is to show the essential openness of that process.

Thus, rejecting a hierarchical relationship between text and interpretation implies that this last chapter will not be reserved for higher levels of abstraction (certainly nothing higher than what I offered in

---

2. When I said that a critical interpretation of religious movements would have to be carried out somehow as continuation of prophetic discourse (Fabian 1979c: 5f.). A similar point was made, more generally, by R. Fenn, who suggested that approaches to the sociology of religion tend to be of two kinds, prophetic and priestly (1982: 107–14). His priestly style corresponds to what I just called the hierarchical model of hermeneutics. See also Fabian (1990) (part 3) for elaboration of the idea of nonhierarchical interpretation.

chapter 5). I shall not employ devices—such as formalized, paradigmatic, or diagrammatic representations and rewritings in technical jargon—apt to increase the distance from the events and texts that form the core of this account. I have no interest in proving that I can move from "mere" ethnography to theory. The time that has passed since they were witnessed and recorded alone creates distance from the events, and it is by virtue of such distance that the work of reflection can continue; but that is not a device which could be switched on or off.

Does It "End Well"?

In order to get reflection going, we should first undo a number of closures that may suggest endings, or boundaries, where there are none.

To begin with, there are some questions as to how happy the ending of the play is. Scene 7 was described by the authors of the scenario as "The Chief Takes Control, Order Reestablished." At first glance the chief's final speech looks very much like a *morale*, the moralizing admonition which ends most sketches and plays of the Mufwankolo troupe (and which in fact makes most of them moralizing plays). The similarity is deceptive. In the usual epilogue, Mufwankolo steps outside the part he played and outside the play. His speech is in that case clearly marked as a meta-statement, even linguistically when he switches to a "higher" variety of Swahili (characterized by stronger interference of "standard" phonology, morphology, and lexicon). He signals solidarity with his audience by beginnings such as

Ndugu, wasikilizaji wetu watukufu . . .
(Brothers, our most honored listeners . . .)

Ndugu, wasikilizaji wetu . . .
(Brothers, our listeners . . .)

Wandugu wanainchi . . .
(Fellow citizens . . .)

Wandugu . . .
(Brothers . . .)[3]

A similar beginning appears in the rehearsal version of scene 7 (*wandugu wapenzi*, dear brothers, perhaps better translated as dear relatives; text 27, 1). The final version is quite different. Mufwankolo does

---

3. For examples of Mufwankolo's *morales*, also called *mafundisho*, teachings, from which these beginnings are quoted, see Schicho and Ndala 1981: 178f., 220f., 270f., 314f.

not leave the play; he tells his guards to call the *notables* and then addresses them with a question which really is an order: *munasikia?* You listen (text 28, 2). Later he turns to the general audience, the villagers who are also present, addressing them not as "brothers" but as *mwee bote wakaaji/ bantu yote wa mugini*, you, the population, all the people of the village (text 28, 5). Only at the very end does he make an intriguing gesture of selective solidarization when he concludes his speech with *aksanti sana bamama*, thank you very much, mothers. Neither in rehearsal, and certainly not in the filmed version, does he switch to a more refined variety of Swahili (at least not with the consistency that characterizes his usual *morale*). He acts tough, and he talks tough. There are traces of moralizing application or explanation in the rehearsal version (text 27, 1, 3); almost nothing of that is left in the final performance. Here everything is geared to action (see the dismissal and degrading of the *notables*; text 28, 4), and it is certainly not without significance that this entire last scene is preceded by the chief dancing in his regalia. He asserts his power, he does not reflect on it.

Not only in rhetorical and linguistic form but also in content, this last scene stays entirely within the structures defined by the play. *Notables* and guards are dismissed, but their offices and functions remain the same and so do the chief and the villagers. Order is reestablished by a purge of disloyal *courtiers*, not by some kind of change or movement toward new premises or values. Could it be anything else, given that the social "idiom" chosen for the play is that of a traditional village situation? Perhaps not (although we still have to ask ourselves just how authentic the chief and his village were meant to be). Those who do not stop at the ending of the play but go on thinking can only conclude that the play's "solution" is but the beginning of a new cycle of anarchy.

Closure and Meaning

With that the question of the meaning or message of the play is raised. There is no lack of methods or techniques designed to distill signification from texts. On the contrary. But more important than to embark on one or another exercise of analysis is to realize that epistemic obstacles had to be overcome before the meaning of "le pouvoir se mange entier" could be investigated. There was first and foremost the mistaken notion that, to get at the message of the saying, it should be regarded as a proverb and that proverbs should be taken to encode, in culturally specific ways, culturally specific messages. In a very loose manner of speaking they do. As soon as one tries to move beyond generalities, however, the idea of a code ceases to be helpful. Although the saying and each of its terms can be sounded for encoded "meaning" (a task that begins as soon as the sentence is being translated), its significance is not exhausted by its being a carrier of specifiable semantic meaning. A proverb or sententious statement has, as a sentence, a beginning and an end; however, it is not bounded or closed (to assume this, which seems to be inevitable in a narrowly defined semiotic approach, is an example of what I call deceptive closures). Hence the need, demonstrated in chapter 2, to proceed from semantics to pragmatics, to a praxis of "quoting behavior" that exists in fields of tension between cultural axioms—definite and definitive formulations—and an indefinite, and practically infinite, supply of expressions, situations, settings, and purposes.

Yet another epistemic obstacle may obstruct inquiry even if the task is not narrowly defined as semiotic decoding but more widely as "translation." As I see it, translation, too, presupposes a static hermeneutic model, especially if it is not taken literally as translation from one language into another, but metaphorically as translation from one culture into another. In the situation that obtains in urban Shaba, what could possibly be regarded as a culture in the sense of an (even relatively) bounded and closed system? And what would be the target culture of such translation?

For the sake of completeness I should note that the kind of problematic closure I have in mind can also be achieved by treating the events and experiences I recount as data to be explained by one or another type of sociological theory of drama. An example of this is one of the few studies of popular theater by an anthropologist, and an excellent one of its kind, James L. Peacock's book on Javanese *ludruk* plays.[4] Because, at this stage, I have little interest in comparison, I have made no use of the many interesting points of convergence that could be noted. There is, however, a major difference between his approach and the one pursued here. In the spirit of the times (the mid-sixties), Peacock starts with a clearly formulated theoretical frame: symbolic analysis and modernization theory, both being applied to clearly delimited empirical phenomena. The result is a monograph. Times have changed and I have explained at the outset that my aim was not and could not have been to write a monograph, given the circumstances of research and the kind of data on which I must base my story.[5]

---

4. Peacock 1968 (recently reprinted).
5. The reasons just given also explain why I did not make use of theories that treat social interaction as drama (see, apart from references to Turner's work given earlier, a study by Hare [1985]). Nor do I feel that our understanding of what happens in the staging of *Le pouvoir se mange entier* would be served by C. Geertz's proposal to use theater as a literal conception of power politics (see 1980: 135f.). What may work for nineteenth-century Bali could not render what is happening in twentieth-century Zaire.

Finally, we must address a further complication of matters. In this study I am not only trying to understand the significance of the play in itself. The unusual, and unusually interesting, problem has been to record how the saying "le pouvoir se mange entier" is being worked out by the play. This means that the play is approached as ethnography. If I stick to the view formulated so far, I cannot expect it to be an interpretation of a proverb (understood in terms of a static hermeneutic model or, semiotically speaking, as the decoding of a message or messages contained in a saying). The play is a rhetorical, artistic performance, an appeal to raise thought about power to the level of quoted wisdom. This view has consequences for thinking about the political significance of the play. Response to an artistic appeal is not (at least not primarily) in terms of assent or dissent to a presumed message; it is to imagination, imagery, experiment (or experiential enactment) involving necessarily a collectively shared, or sharable, form of reflection. Even though it is about power there is nothing in this performative ethnography that could be pinned down as a position for or against the powers that be.

On Performance, Folklore, and Power

Contexts of Performance

Inasmuch as proverbs and plays are statements (which perhaps should be questioned),[6] they need authors and audiences, positions to be made from and situations to be addressed to. As performances they need occasions and "repetitions." As artistic creations they require material—shared experiences, habits, images—from which they can be construed and canons according to which they may be judged and appreciated. Propositional content, event, and rhetorical form are inextricably related; temporarily to focus on one of them does not constitute it as a distinct object of investigation. Literary deconstructivism may be an approach congenial to this view but does not have to be applied as doctrine. In my view, moving in several directions at once is the only realistic way to deal with the complex context from which *Le pouvoir se mange entier* emerged (even though to invoke realism is certain to rub deconstructivists the wrong way).[7]

It will be useful to recall in this concluding chapter some of the principal elements of what I called contexts of performance. First, and

6. Certainly in the sense that statements are referential. But more about this below when we examine power as a referent.
7. For a view of multiplicity in anthropological construction, which I find congenial, see Friedrich 1988. It is masterfully exemplified in his *Princes of Naranja* (1986).

most encompassing, is the social ground from which both the saying and the play were pronounced: the urban, popular culture of Shaba.[8] In chapter 2 I explored the traditional background against which the contemporary version, in French, of what looked like a Luba proverb might be understood. In chapter 3 I recounted my first contact with the Mufwankolo troupe and gave some indications of the history of popular theater in Shaba from its beginnings in school plays and in improvised sketches performed in youth groups, through youthful, vaudeville-like, multimedia shows in bars and dance halls, to the *spectacles populaires* at the end of the colonial period and a further transformation that occurred when radio sketches became the major outlet. In the first part of chapter 4 I showed, somewhat obliquely, the place of Mufwankolo and his fellow actors in the present topography of power in Lubumbashi.

This last point deserves some further attention if the position of the troupe is to be determined more exactly. Although the adoption of theater as a genre of performance was a spontaneous act of cultural appropriation, troupes such as Mufwankolo's always accepted sponsors and, through sponsorship, a certain degree of control and integration into the local power structure. Sponsorship in colonial times was formal as well as informal. On the formal side were colonial institutions such as the Benedictine and Salesian missions (and the schools run by missionaries), the social services of the omnipresent mining company, and youth movements such as the Boy Scouts which were, at least in part, organized by both. Equally important was informal sponsorship by individual colonials who were often idealists and who felt that to support artistic expression among the Africans could humanize colonialism (and their own contributions to that regime). Some of them may even have counted on a mild form of subversiveness.

The changes that came about with independence and the Katanga secession and its end in the early sixties were important but not so much as to preclude a certain degree of continuity. On the side of formal sponsorship, affiliation of the Mufwankolo troupe with the local radio and, later, television station provided a new institutional support. As a result, popular theater came to be more thoroughly under the control of the State and political regime.[9] The mining company was nationalized

8. For an attempt to give theoretical form and cultural substance to this notion, see my essay "Popular Culture in Africa: Findings and Conjectures" (1978). See also the "state of the art" essay on popular arts in Africa by Karin Barber (1987) with an extensive bibliography. A popular account of the colonial history of Shaba is documented in Fabian (1990).

9. In colonial times the radio station of Lubumbashi (then Elisabethville) was run by the Salesians out of their *collège*. In the seventies the TV studio of "La voix du Zaire" was housed in that building and in 1986 at least some of the equipment and

and is now more closely linked to the government, but in practice this changed little as far as sponsorship of theater by its social services is concerned. It is still the most profitable "client" of the troupe. Occasional commissioned performances usually mean tours of the numerous *sièges* (principal mining towns) in Shaba as well as a source of (moderate) income. Sponsorship by the mission has lost most of its former importance but did not cease altogether as the story of the anniversary play told in chapter 4 shows. On the side of informal sponsorship we find the Cercle Makutano, a private club catering to the new bourgeoisie of which the president of the troupe is an active member. The university professor who acts as artistic advisor and, last but not least, expatriate researchers such as W. Schicho and myself, provide a kind of sponsorship whose political significance is not entirely different from that of the former enlightened colonials, whether we like this or not.[10]

I am sure that the sociologically minded reader would like to have more information (more, that is, than that which is provided in remarks and observations dispersed throughout this account) on the audience addressed by performances such as *Le pouvoir se mange entier*. An analysis of the socioeconomic profile of "consumers" ranging from the people of Kawama village to the viewers who watched the two television broadcasts was not made. As far as I can see, it could not have been made even if the research on which this story is based had been planned beforehand (which it was not and could not have been). It is fair to assume that, given the medium, more members of the elite and the petite bourgeoisie watched the play than of the urban masses (about half a million at the present time). Mufwankolo's television plays are probably many more times told and retold than actually watched by people whose expectations are formed by listening to the weekly radio sketches by the troupe (and I doubt that any person in Lubumbashi and the area covered by the regional transmitter is ever outside the reach of a transistor radio). In the absence of quantitative studies we have only three sources to go on: extrapolations from other studies of urban Sha-

---

production facilities were still located there although the organization had its headquarters elsewhere.

10. Although I do not have the information to make this a strong point I should at least mention that there have been contacts between Mufwankolo's group and more "professionally" oriented theater troupes such as the former Mwondo Théâtre (see Povey 1976), which, I am told, has now been incorporated into the National Theater of Zaire in Kinshasa. Tala Ngai used to be with Mwondo Théâtre and is still a member of the Théâtre National Mobutu Sese Seko (headed by Bukasa Oshoko). Also, the Troupe Théâtrale Mufwankolo is registered with the local office of the ministry of culture (recorded conversation with Mufwankolo, Lubumbashi, July 21, 1986).

ba,[11] my own observations during the last twenty-odd years, and above all the principal actors of our story whose articulations of the joys and vicissitudes of life in Lubumbashi have the success they have because they come from people who are socioeconomically representative of their audience.

Performance Genre

One may think that performances by a group that calls itself *troupe théâtrale* do not pose problems when it comes to identifying genre, yet the contrary is true unless we chose categories so general as to be meaningless. Yes, *Le pouvoir se mange entier* was a theatrical play; it had a plot, parts, dialogue, even a few props. But then, there was no script, no preexisting written or printed text except a rudimentary outline (which, remember, was lost just before the final performance). We may qualify this sort of theater as improvisational. However, this is not really a satisfying term because it evokes wrong ideas about the scope of the play (it is not a brief sketch invented on the spot; the Mufwankolo troupe does that kind of thing, too, but not here) and about the process of creating it from a few ideas. Even if improvisation, in the sense of on-the-spot invention, was a feature of the troupe's work up to, and including, the filmed performance the term hardly fits the concentrated efforts in discussions, direction, and rehearsals, which are documented in chapter 4.

An even more serious problem (and a shortcoming of this study of which I am aware) is the temptation to use "theater" metonymically for a performance genre which not only includes visual presentation in some general way (all theater does; even radio sketches appeal to visual imagination) but also employs music, vocal and instrumental, and dance. The suggestion itself, implicit in the categories just named, that these distinctions have some sort of universal validity is problematic. This became clear in our sketch of the prehistory of popular theater in Shaba. A team approach by specialists in the verbal, visual, musical, and movement arts would go a long way in meeting these complexities analytically; however, it would not as such solve the question how all of them contribute to making the sort of performance we witnessed in *Le pouvoir se mange entier* a specific genre.

Similar caution is in order with a comparative view which would either demonstrate connections between popular theater in Shaba and

---

11. I do not see much use in burdening this account with references to socio-logical studies of urban Shaba. To my knowledge, a recent comprehensive overview does not exist. The interested reader will have to consult relevant bibliographies such as the one produced by the Centre d'Etude et de Documentation Africaines in Brussels.

some sort of integrated theatricality in traditional ritual performances or stress similarities, noted by some observers, with a historical form such as the *commedia dell'arte*. The problem with the former is that it must presume a generalized tradition whose existence can only be inferred from contemporary forms such as this play, and that would be begging our question.[12] The second possibility suffers from being only typological—what could be actual connections between *commedia dell'arte* and the Mufwankolo troupe?[13] However, both suggestions can be used as food for thought. Later on, I will briefly come back to ritualization, and the convergences between popular theater and *commedia dell'arte* are quite striking indeed when one considers the intricate interplay between topic, plot, and stock characters which make the classical model of a separation between author, text, and performers inappropriate.[14]

Perhaps we should conclude that the problems raised by the notion of genre are so numerous that the concept ought to be dismissed as unproductive. However, this is not what I want to suggest. I do want to show that in the case under consideration here, much as in others I can think of, "genre" is of limited use if it signals a typological, classificatory approach concentrating on lists of traits that register generic *differences* instead of studying generic *differentiation*. Only if we also do the second can we be reasonably sure that our categories are more than arbitrarily imposed devices of ordering our material; only if we go beyond the results, or products, to consider process and production can we do historical justice to kinds (or genres) of performance such as proverbs and popular plays.[15]

When I examined uses of performance in anthropology (in chapter 1), I said that I felt closest to an approach that owes much to the ethnography of speaking. I proposed to bring together, in the pragmatic notion of speech event, aspects of communication that are often dealt

12. It is a different matter when the question is begged intentionally—because (African) theater "as ritual" becomes a project (see Hourantier 1984).

13. On such typological similarities see Fiebach 1986: 272. The most recent study of *commedia dell'arte* in English I have seen is Green 1986.

14. This should not be misunderstood as construing doubtful distinctions between Western and African theater. There have been conceptions of "total theater" in the West, as there were critiques of authorship and text (and experiments without either). At any rate, comparison should be made between popular forms of theater.

15. Such a processual view of genre, one that seeks to ground differences in the communicative praxis that is studied, was proposed in the late sixties by Dan Ben-Amos (1969, here cited as reprinted in 1976). In my own work on aspects of popular culture in Shaba I tried to demonstrate the uses of generic analysis as applied to religious discourse (Fabian 1974), to popular painting (Szombati-Fabian and Fabian 1976), and to the history of linguistic descriptions of Swahili (Fabian 1986).

with separately: setting, occasion, addressor/addressee, topic, linguistic channel, register, role differentiation, and so forth. Although I do not think that this approach should be reduced to a search for rules or grammars of communication (which seems to have been the aim of some of its proponents), it has proved useful as a heuristic guide.[16] Thus, I already introduced *producers* and audiences and their social setting. In the remainder of this chapter I shall return first to some features of popular play that are of a more formal nature and apt to provide insights into *process*. Then I will recall, and at times further develop, observations which were addressed to folklore as a means of production. Finally I turn to content, message, and topic considered here as the product.

Plot and Players, Talking and Acting

The plot and scenario for *Le pouvoir se mange entier*, as we recall from chapters 4 and 6, were agreed upon after intense discussion. I tried to describe how the group struggled for a compromise between their own artistic vision and political expediency. Here I want to concentrate on the plot as text and on the relation of that text to the rehearsal process. The first thing that might be pointed out is that the plot—in the form of a one-page typewritten outline called *conducteur*—was the only text (apart from the titular saying) that was "given" in the sense of being available for inspection and reference. Significantly, it was formulated in French, the official (as opposed to national) language of Zaire, which, apart from lexical interference and occasional code-switching, was not used in the rehearsal process. We speculated on some of the reasons for this linguistic choice before; now we can add another suggestion which imposes itself when we consider the external form of the *conducteur* (see Appendix): It is framed by the troupe's letterhead and a concluding formula, including place, date, and signature. These are conventions borrowed from administrative bureaucracy, which proclaim the *conducteur* as a *document*.[17]

Yet it would be misleading to conclude that this outline actually functioned as a reference which remained constant. Leaving aside the controversial issue of an open ending, a more detailed reading of the

16. Views similar to those developed in the ethnography of speaking have appeared in literary theory. For an argument that "speech genres" ought to be considered an integral part of a theory of literary genres, see M. M. Bakhtin 1986 (originally written in 1952–53).

17. Remember that in the discussions it was proposed that the *conducteur* could be the document to be submitted to the authorities for official approval. And at one point, when the troupe's version of an open ending in "disorder" came under political attack, the paper was actually "produced" in the way one shows a piece of identification.

recorded texts would show that the troupe, while keeping to a general schema, made numerous changes, additions, and emendations up to the final performance. The significance of each of them could be pondered, although I don't think that much could be gained if this story were to be burdened with a kind of exegesis that is bound to create tedium and a false sense of completeness.[18] At any rate, when Bwana Cheko, the author of the document, gives his summary of the version agreed upon in the committee in Swahili (text 1) and when this is followed by Mufwankolo's version (text 2), it is clear that the troupe keeps constructing the plot as it goes about the business of transforming ideas into dialogues, and that, when it respects constraints and responds to demands, these are not the requirements of an authoritative document. Foremost among them is the need to coordinate plotting and casting. I have tried to show how this works on several occasions (see, for instance, chapter 9). Here I should like to add a thought that will further relativize the notion of the plot as a "given text."

If we were to distinguish and weigh degrees of givenness that affect the construction of sketches and plays by the Mufwankolo troupe (and if we leave aside, for the moment, language, cultural images and habits, socioeconomic situation, and politics as givens the actors must work with), then there can be no doubt that the composition of the troupe itself constitutes a pre-text, one that precedes and significantly shapes every possible plot/text. This is inherent in their conception of acting. Each actor has developed one or more stock characters, often signaled by different stage names. This limits the pool of parts which are available for plots; it lends to the plays concreteness as well as predictability, both of which are much appreciated by the troupe's audiences.[19] It also means that every plot—even that of a commissioned play such as the one commemorating the founding of the Catholic missions—must in the end be a synthesis between text (i.e., an instance

18. Here is a problem that every hermeneutic project has to face. In the absence of a preexisting theoretical frame to be filled with data, or a catalogue of questions to be matched with answers, there can be no logical or otherwise objective end to exegesis. To propose "thick description" as a sort of canon for a complete ethnography (as it was done by C. Geertz, following Ryle, in 1973, chap. 1) has a certain metaphorical persuasiveness. Milk that curdles is thick and has thereby reached a state in which it is appreciated by some people. On the other hand, as Goethe observed, *getretener Quark wird breit, nicht stark;* there is always a point after which interpretation can only get more tedious rather than more profound.

19. Here incidentally are some striking resemblances with the esthetic appreciation of popular painting in Shaba. See the paper cited above and remarks on "repetitiveness" in Fabian and Szombati-Fabian 1980: 271ff.

of verbalizing, or discourse) and what I called pre-text, a relatively limited, closed repertoire of kinds of action, in this case acting.

A similar tension between potentially endless talk and acting oriented toward an ending was a discovery spelled out in chapter 5 where it helped to construct a model of changes occurring during the rehearsal process. With qualifications that need not be repeated here, the model provided a better understanding of the overall process; it accounted for the phenomenon of oscillation between discourse and dialogue in the middle of it (making thereby more plausible what Dell Hymes has called a "breakthrough into performance");[20] and it allayed our anxieties caused by the "missing text," that is, by insurmountable difficulties with providing accurate transcriptions/translations, or any text at all.

Incidentally, in the essay just cited Dell Hymes makes a remark which I find confirmed in our case: "Code-switching, from one language to another, is . . . , I believe a sign of 'breakthrough' into full performance" (1975: 24). Although there is no dramatic full switch from Swahili into French, there are several instances where changes from acting to directing (and back) are linguistically marked by a higher degree of code-switching in the latter (see, for instance, text 12, 8–10, and text 26). It may be argued that this simply reflects the higher degree of education of the two speakers, Tala Ngai and Kachelewa, hence their propensity to use French. But Tala Ngai uses hardly any code-switching when he acts, and Kachelewa does not act in the play.

Folklore 1: Folklore as Means of Production

There should be no need to argue that this study, in subject matter and orientation, comes close to what a folklorist might do with similar material. Yet the term "folklore" has played no role to speak of in this story. And although the absence of a term does not imply the absence of a concept, my avoidance of "folklore" does reflect doubts and hesitations on my part. These do not regard disciplinary boundaries; I could not care less whether this account will be classified as anthropological or folkloristic. Nor is this the place to invoke critical discussions in folklore studies, which often parallel those in anthropology, in order to show

---

20. See Dell Hymes's essay with this title (1975: esp. 20). If there are differences between his approach and the one taken here they are (a) in Hymes's more narrow definition of performance, restricting it to the phase after the "breakthrough," which he shares with Bauman (see p. 8ff) and (b) in emphasis, which, in his case, is on rule rather than process. Although it may seem that one cannot be had without the other, there still remains much to be argued for placing the emphasis on process, see Fabian 1979a.

that my doubts are shared by folklorists. Still, as I am now about to introduce the notion of folklore after all, I feel the need to qualify my use of it.

To begin with, I do not wish to employ "folklore" to designate either marginal survivals of a presumed tradition or colorful counterpoints to modernization. There is nothing in the practice of quoting behavior in which "le pouvoir se mange entier" was found to be embedded as a saying, nothing in the Mufwankolo play and the popular urban culture to which it belongs, which would be clarified by declaring it folkloric. In other words I consider neither saying nor play as *objects* of folkloric study. However, it is impossible to overlook that the *subjects*, the actors in this story, are themselves engaged in conceptualizing folklore.[21]

Having said this, I should immediately insist that, in this case, folklore is not perceived as some kind of archival activity. Efforts made by Africans to collect and preserve ancestral customs, stories, songs, and dances exist and are attested to since the very beginning of urbanization and the spread of literacy in Shaba (shortly after the turn of the century). The earliest African urban associations in Lubumbashi and elsewhere certainly pursued such goals. But, in my view, these efforts fail to meet two criteria that determine the emergence and definition of "folklore" in the West: First, they are not made in a situation where there has been a dramatic break with traditional rural practices. Funeral and initiation rites, the whole complex summarily designated as magic, sorcery, and divination, never needed to be revived; they are, in varying degrees of transformation, quite alive in urban Shaba. Second, preservation of custom has not been related to class differences as was the case with a thoroughly bourgeois folklore in the West. There are indications that the latter may happen as Zairean society undergoes a process of *embourgeoisement* (folklore is a discipline taught at the university and there are Zairean folklorists of international distinction).

At any rate, for the Mufwankolo troupe, although links to the academy seem to have been established through an artistic advisor from the university, folklore is not an academic subject. For them it is a means of (artistic) production. This is obvious on the level of choosing a setting, protagonists, and a plot that invoke traditional village life. Yet there is never any doubt in the minds of the actors or the spectators that the play is not about village life. Why should the troupe have worried about

21. Epistemologically speaking this means that I do not follow the customary alignment between the (Western) researcher and folklore science on the one hand, and Africans and folklore on the other. I consider it more fruitful and interesting to imagine both the researcher and the actors facing "folklore" as a mode of knowledge and expression.

political consequences if their performance had been intended as merely folkloric—colorful, entertaining, perhaps a bit nostalgic?

If I speak of folklore as a means of production, I do not want to suggest that the elements of folklore or tradition used by the troupe resemble tools or instruments which are preformed before the creative process starts or that they remain, as it were, constant throughout the process. As soon as the actors decided that it would be politically expedient to cast the play in a folkloric idiom they faced the problem of diversity among traditions. This was discussed in the meeting on Thursday, June 19 (see chapter 4). As far as I can see, the solution was found by a combination of "methods."

First, the troupe freely borrowed or assembled elements without much concern for consistency and purity. Take for example the selection of songs. Not only are they sung in several regional languages and representative of different genres, they are also performed according to canons that seem to contradict each other. In text 4, 5, the singers are directed to bring a song to an end by a sort of climax expressed by increased volume. Just before it stops, often abruptly, the singing gets (slightly) louder. As far as I know, this corresponds to traditional rules of performance.[22] In text 7, 5, the singers are told to finish *en fondu*, humming pianissimo, a sort of acoustic fade in which singing becomes background music to action or talking. This is a style or technique I encountered in Shaba only in some theatrical productions and in religious gatherings, for instance, among the Catholic charismatics. I assume that it is of Western origin.

Second, a similar kind of eclecticism was applied to elements of material culture. During preparations and rehearsals, props and costumes were discussed only in the most summary fashion. Each actor, it was said, would know what to wear. In the final performance drums were brought along that were in a condition to be played and not borrowed from some kind of stock of theatrical props. Agricultural tools, a basket, and other domestic implements, as well as a calabash and cups

---

22. This is also the case with drumming and dancing, which are such an important part of the play (filling close to one-half of the recorded performance time). These musical and dance elements could be more fully appreciated and analyzed by competent ethnomusicologists. Maybe a specialist can eventually fill this gap although current research interests, as far as I am aware of them, do not make this likely. Some ethnomusicologists have gone beyond the collection and description of "pure" traditional forms and turned their attention to popular music which, in a country like Zaire, is hard to ignore. But large areas of musical performance in contexts such as this play and especially in the hundreds of religious movements (and even in the official churches) remain to be studied. An example of an otherwise excellent collection of essays, which, in spite of the title "Music in Africa" maintains a focus on traditional music, is Simon 1983.

for maize beer (in fact the beer itself) were requisitioned on the spot, in the village. Only the headdresses of the chief, his wife, and the *notables* were fake, made of painted cardboard to resemble the intricate bead-work of the genuine objects. Incidentally, these headdresses looked Lunda to me, and most of the verbal symbols of tradition (see below) suggested Luba derivation.[23] I made some notes on the geometrical patterns decorating the headdresses from the video recording. They certainly looked authentic, but because the headdresses suddenly appeared in a matter-of-fact fashion just before the filmed performance, I had no occasion to discuss the designs or, for that matter, to find out who had made them.

Third, some of the conditions of use of traditional elements are revealed on the level of verbal performance. In commenting on trans-lation problems with a passage that makes use of traditional greetings (text 17, 3), I said that this part of the text was marked as folkloric by the use of generalized Luba. In a similar comment on a similar problem later on (text 24), I brought both notions together by suggesting that the mixture of traditional elements from several sources was made possible by folklorization, which seems to involve generalization. Remember also the generalized "up-country" accent put on by Kalwasha, the visiting hunter, who specializes in this sort of thing (chapter 10). In fact, what is at first perceived (and identified by the troupe) as an accent involves more than peculiar phonic realizations; it also includes prosody, mor-phological changes, and lexical interference. The "folksy" as a speech register exemplifies most directly what I am driving at with the idea of folklore as a means of production: *Le pouvoir se mange entier* is folklore in mood or style, affecting all levels of presentation, not just because it utilizes certain verbal and nonverbal elements that are demonstrably traditional.

There is of course nothing new about the idea that folklorization involves generalization. It imposes itself as soon as one begins to think about relations between folklore and its sources (they must involve typification, decontextualization, perhaps also reduction of complexity); the phenomenon is amply attested to all over the world, especially in situations where folklore comes to symbolize ethnicity. But that is not really the kind of generalization I believe has been accomplished by the Mufwankolo troupe in *Le pouvoir se mange entier*. Being multilingual and of many different traditional backgrounds and playing for an audience

23. To the reader not familiar with the traditions that converge in urban Shaba this may seem a pointless distinction. Local audiences, I suspect, would appreciate the political implication of references to Lunda chieftaincy, which had ascertained itself against less-centralized political entities in precolonial times, formed a core of resistance against Belgian rule, and remains a force to be reckoned with by the current regime.

that is similarly equipped, they can "quote" and refer to many sources. The effect of generalization is brought about by playful (and skillful) juxtaposition, not by inventing a streamlined "fakelore" that looks authentic only to those who are unable to judge authenticity.

Questions of the politics of folklore will be taken up in the last section of this chapter but, since I invoked authenticity, a few remarks on the famed Zairean *authenticité* are in order. As a political slogan and as policy it had its heyday in the seventies. It materialized in the imposition of such powerful symbolic changes as the prescriptive use of traditional rather than Christian names. An "African" dress code was introduced (the *abacost*,[24] a sort of Neru suit for men and the wrap, no skirts or pants, for women) and State rituals were invented. These are often folkloric in that they consist of dances and praise songs copied or derived from tradition. They are performed by quasi-professional troupes and serve to orchestrate self-presentations of the regime ranging from huge political rallies down to local occasions such as the arrival or departure of dignitaries. Up to this day, radio and television broadcasts are regularly interspersed with political songs and bits from the leader's speeches. *Authenticité* has not been limited to symbolic manifestations. It consisted, first of all, of an ideology formulated by intellectuals (not all of them supporters of the regime) and propagated by the Party (the Mouvement Populaire de la Révolution). As such it was designed to further a "return to the sources" as a means to achieve cultural independence once political independence had been gained.[25] In the perspective "from below" that we take in this account, *authenticité* was received with reactions ranging from modest enthusiasm generated by its entertainment value to skepticism and outright irony, for instance, when popular wit designs poverty and corruption as *authenticité*. It is in this field of tension between acceptance and resistance that the Mufwankolo troupe had to find its precarious position toward "authentic" folklore. In chapter 4 I noted critical reactions from the audience at Kawama village when, toward the end of his first speech during dress rehearsal, Mufwankolo as the chief presented himself (linguistically and rhetorically) somewhat like a party leader, that is, as soon as, semiotically speaking, the *signifié* intruded on the *signifiant*. Finally, there is a passage in chapter 8 where the villagers contest the chief's power, a

24. Said to be derived from a revolutionary slogan: *à bas le costume*, down with the suit.

25. For an official statement of the ideology of *authenticité*, see *Authenticité et Développement* 1982; critical assessments may be found in any of the numerous recent works on Zairean politics.

passage which was omitted from the final performance. Here the villagers insist on their right to sing and dance at night and to perform initiation rites (text 10, 6f., 19).

Folklore 2: *Cultural Axiomatics and Proverbs*

Our remarks on generalization notwithstanding, the play did utilize distinctive elements of tradition, for instance, in the form of honorific titles and greeting formulas. These items are in contrast with their linguistic environment as foreign words which are not integrated as loans. But there is more to them than their origin outside Swahili; they announce, as it were, their provenience, and to use them is to invoke (give voice to) the world from which they are taken. And that comes close to "communication with quotes" which, according to J. Penfield (and Mukařovský), is the distinctive characteristic of proverb use. Without repeating what was said in chapter 2 I should now like to note a few observations on proverbial expressions in the play that may add an insight or two.

A remarkable fact worth pondering is that the saying which gave the play its title was not once quoted in actual performance.[26] A natural place to have done this might have been the *morale* with which the group usually ends their sketches. As we have seen, this play ended with action rather than reflection. I was concerned about this conspicuous absence of the saying early on in the rehearsal process. When I reported on the meeting of the *comité artistique* on Monday, June 23 (chapter 4), I noted that I expressed my concern to the participants. Their response is worth looking at in some detail.[27] Kachelewa first declared that he saw no problem without, however, giving any reasons. At least one of the actors, Malisawa, was not satisfied and his reaction can help us now to formulate a seemingly paradoxical hypothesis: As a saying, "le pouvoir se mange entier" had to be absent from the play if the play was to be "about" it, if it was to explore and convey its meaning.

Malisawa began by insisting that the saying did not have a clear message.[28] To this Kachelewa responded by giving a translation into Swahili. He must have realized, of course, that the participants in the

26. In the television broadcast, *Le pouvoir se mange entier* appeared, graphically, as the title of the play, followed by the credits. But it was never actually pronounced.

27. The following is based on a recording made of that session but not reproduced among the texts in this study.

28. My recollection is that it was understood, but not said, that the ambiguity was above all political. Does "le pouvoir se mange entier" legitimize the existent power structure, or could it be interpreted as a challenge?

discussion were bilingual and really did not need such a translation. So his next step was to propose a different sort of translation: He sketched elements of the plot such as the dissipation of power due to conflict among the *notables* as a way of illustrating, by means of contrast, the wholeness of power. At this point, he said, we must worry about a *charpente*, a frame or supporting structure, for the play. But Malisawa insisted: How will the saying "infiltrate" the frame? Kachelewa thought that such infiltration would occur as a sort of overall effect. He stated: "We will bring it out, let them feel, that power must be eaten whole."[29] Malisawa continued to pursue his line, he wanted to see proverbial expressions used; proverbial wisdom could infiltrate the play through authoritative pronouncements made by the dignitaries and counselors. Kachelewa ignored this and came back to the plot: Instead of following all sorts of advice or, worse, giving the impression that power is to be divided, the chief must assume power alone.

The back-and-forth of this discussion reflects the artistic problem posed by the task to translate a sententious pronouncement into drama, that is, into characters, dialogue, and action. The very choice of the term "infiltration" does away with simple notions of the play as merely illustrating or exemplifying "le pouvoir se mange entier." At the same time it adds another dimension to proverb use as quoting behavior that may be missed if one were to consider only its positive and edifying aspects. Infiltration connotes subversiveness or at least surreptitiousness, an element which, as I argued in chapter 1, is essential to the concept of performance and which, at any rate, was essential for the success of the play.

With this general idea in mind we can now take a look at some of the instances of quoting proverbial expressions. There are not many of them but those that occur pose interesting problems. At one point, Masimango, one of the *notables*, says that the case of adultery before them is a difficult one:

> *hii mambo ni bukari bwa nyama: bunakabulaka mwenye bukari/* this case is *bukari* and meat; it is dealt out by the one who has it. (Text 16, 11; see also the explanatory note there)

This was in rehearsal; in the final version Masimango cites the same expression with slight variations:

> *mambo hii sultani minaona ni bukari wa nyama/ bukari bwa nyama bunakabulaka paka mwenyewe ya bukari/* I look at this case, chief, as

29. In the original: *tu: tutoshe ile nani: tufaire sentir ile asema pouvoir: inafaa kulya bote buzima/*.

bukari and meat; *bukari* and meat is distributed only by the owner of *bukari*. (Text 17, 6, which see for a more elegant translation)

This example shows, first of all, that the shared wisdom, in fact its culturally axiomatic aspect, need not be self-evident. The more elliptic first version caused the chief to ask Masimango for an explanation: *semaka*, spell it out. Masimango reacted with some hesitation until, with the help of the chief, he makes explicit that the "young person," the cheated husband's younger wife, is the one referred to by the food metaphor. As expected, this explanation was not given in the final performance; the version quoted was, however, clearer about the point of ownership.[30] It is also possible that this expression represents a merging of genres. Context and function mark it as a proverb; in its form it may approach a riddle, which is characteristically presented in two parts, a task and its solution. This also seems to happen with a pronouncement, qualified as a "saying," which Tala Ngai applies to the same case:

banasema hivi/ kama tunda: yenye kuivia: iko mu muti: wee unafika unaingaria/ ile tunda ile: kama ni ya kula: si utaichuma naye kula/
There is a saying: There is a fruit, it is ripe and on a tree. You come by and look at it. If this fruit is edible, are you not going to pick and eat it? (Text 16, 20)

As it stands it lacks the elegance of riddles by being too explicit about the application. It is further watered down in the remainder of the paragraph where Tala Ngai develops the image for his defense of the adulterer. The saying was not quoted in the final version of the scene. What a better performed riddle/proverb looks like is shown immediately following this passage when Masimango says (thereby responding to Tala Ngai in the way proverbs have been used traditionally):

bakubwa walisema: mwanamuke: ni kangozi ya kabundi/ the old people used to say: a woman is like the skin of *kabundi*. (Text 16, 21; see there a note on *kabundi*)

The other actors greet this with laughter, the culturally appropriate response to a point well made, and provide the riddle's obligatory second part:

Feza: kanakalaka muntu huyu- (raising the tone to elicit communal response) there is room in it for this person . . .
Others: -moya/ . . . one [for one person only].[31]

30. In the use of *mwenyewe* instead of *mwenye*. In Shaba Swahili *mwenyewe* alternates with ECS *mwenyeji*; see the Standard Dictionary under *-enye*.
31. Even here the performance is not perfect. To state that the riddle refers to a

That exchange, which undoubtedly would have been successful with a larger audience, is absent from the filmed version.

It is no accident that the examples cited so far have come from texts representing a court case. Sententiousness, proverbial or quasi-proverbial, goes with passing sentence. Mufwankolo, the chief, seems to feel the need to intersperse his judgment with the following condensations of wisdom:

> *kama uko nakwenda kya mbele: utarudia kya mukongo?* When you go forward are you going to go back [literally, are you going to return to the back]? (Text 16, 26)

> *njala mu ntumbo: uko sawa inaniingia pa mufupa?* The hunger you feel in your stomach, are you going to say it is in the bone [literally, hunger in the stomach, you, as if it came into me through the bone]? (Ibid.)

Again, this is from a recording made during rehearsal. The meaning is not immediately clear and no explanation is given except for the implicit assumption that these sayings, in the form of questions, support the court's sentence: We must stick to the rules we adopted and we must not be evasive when it comes to identify violations of a rule.

At one time during rehearsal for the scene with the thief, Masimango appears to poke some fun at sententiousness when he proposes three variations, one after the other:

	Kiwelewele insanity	
mukini wasiyo	*mwivi*	*ile haina mukini*
A village without	a thief	this is not a
	busharati	village
	fornication	

(Text 12, 13)

These pronouncements are based on a frame provided by well-known proverbs of this type.[32] The parody, or irony, in Masimango's way of using that frame is that he substitutes positive values (a chief, old people) with negative ones (confusion, theft, fornication). Thus he cites "proverbial" expressions that contradict the chief's orders and is immedi-

---

woman should not be necessary at all; it certainly should not be done before the riddle is recited. So the reconstructed "original" version would be: *kangozi ya kabundi: kanakalaka muntu huyu moya/.*

32. Examples cited earlier were: *Kibundji kyampikwa mukulu i kifwe,* the village without one in authority will die out (Burton 1957, 3:83; see chap. 2), and *mu mugini hamukosake muzee,* there is no village without an old person (cited by Kalundi Mango as an example of the same kind; see p. 171, n. 8).

ately stopped by his fellow *notable* Bwana Cheko, who counters with a genuine proverb:

> *mwizi ni nduku yake na mulozi*/a thief is the sorcerer's brother. (Text 12, 14)

This idea had already been used by Mufwankolo in the rehearsal version of the chief's first speech (text 6, 8; see chapter 7), where he declared both thief and sorcerer the enemies of the village. There we had an example of a proverb infiltrating a text without being actually cited. As far as I recall the proverb was not used in the final version of the scene (of which we have only a fragmentary text). As in most of the other cases, the reason may have been economy, the need to pare down dialogue to essentials; it may also have been political sensitivity. To point out that traditional wisdom equates thieving politicians with sorcerers (sorcery being the gravest accusation against a person) may have been too risky in a public play.[33]

There are a few more instances of quoted proverbs which are less problematic.[34] Only at the end, in Mufwankolo's speech, do we get one that meets expectations without needing the kinds of qualifications we have had to make so far:

> *kilole moja: hakikutake chawa*/ a single finger does not catch a louse. (Text 27, 3)

But that, too, was in rehearsal; in the final performance it was not repeated. All in all, this leaves us with the conclusion that a play which was triggered by search for a proverb and its meaning did not, with one somewhat problematic exception, use proverbs in its public performance.

Power Performed

There is drumming and singing as the villagers and courtiers assemble for the last scene to listen to the ruler's tirade which ends their rebellion. Before he actually speaks, the chief makes an astonishing

---

33. The latter possibility is also suggested by A. Roberts' excellent case study on the use of tales of survival in contemporary Zaire (in his case, among the Tabwa in northern Shaba). There he cites two variants of our proverb:

> "Theft and sorcery are twin brothers," Tabwa often say, and the narrator of the aphorism will cross index and middle fingers to show the closeness of the two. Or someone may use the familiar rhetorical form to ask, "How many paths do theft and sorcery follow?" Whereupon the listener will respond with "One." (1986: 118)

34. But not without problems entirely; see texts 18, 19, and 26, 2, with explanatory notes.

gesture: in full regalia he dances before the assembled population. It is as if he were stating what he has to say before he puts it in words: I am back, moving, and in control. For a moment, power is performed, literally.[35] And so it is when "le pouvoir se mange entier" is made true by a person of importance who eats the chicken gizzards whole.

It is tempting, as I said at the outset of this chapter, to let these fusions of power and performance speak for themselves. Yet, I must resist that temptation in order to be true to another kind of performance: to tell the story of a search for the meaning of power as best I can. Powerful images have their way of convincing us. They enhance a story, they do not make it. This is why I feel that this account, open and tentative as it may be, should be concluded with some reflections on what was given shape and expression, not only in the final product, but throughout the rehearsal process. Accordingly I shall begin summarizing what could be called major elements of a conceptualization of power, that is, of a process whereby experience and received traditions are made into knowledge that can be stated discursively.

Search for the conceptual content of power was most intensive at the beginning when the troupe faced the seemingly straightforward task of translating the French term *pouvoir* into Swahili. Our brief review of some traditional proverbs relating to power (chapter 2) led us to expect that a single gloss would not be found and, indeed, the efforts that were made during discussion produced a number of terms, not one of which was found satisfactory. In the traditional sayings that we took to be about power we have terms that refer either to political office (chieftaincy, *bulopwe, bukalenge*), or seniority *(mukulu)*. These terms came back in the discussion among the actors (chapter 4, reports on the meetings of Thursday, June 17, and Friday, June 20) and although a few abstract nouns are briefly considered (such as *uwezo*), the only full translation of the saying given eventually by Kachelewa was *busultani banakulyaka wote buzima*, chieftaincy is eaten whole (on Monday, June 23). In the rehearsal version of his final speech Mufwankolo uses a French/Swahili doublet of abstract terms: *pouvoir/ukumu* (text 27, 6). In the final version he replaces *pouvoir* with *busultani* and *uwezo* (Text 28, 6).

This invites speculation about a cognitive difficulty. Could it be that the troupe failed to come up with an abstract Swahili synonym for *pouvoir* because they are (a) intellectually incapable of thinking about power abstractly, (b) unwilling to do so, being artists rather than scien-

35. I called the chief's dancing "astonishing" because I imagined that this is how it strikes the Western outsider. But there have been dancing kings in our own tradition and, at any rate, African rulership has been associated with performers and instruments (above all the drum) not only for display and entertainment but as actual embodiments of power.

tists or philosophers, or (c) culturally programmed to conceptualize power in terms of offices and other embodiments? There was a time, not so long ago, when the first question would have been thought anthropologically interesting. Now we can dispose of it on the grounds alone that it is derived from spurious evidence. The absence of a certain kind of term, in this case an abstract noun designating power, permits no conclusions whatsoever regarding cognitive capacities.

The second possibility deserves more serious attention. It is true that the troupe was engaged in representing power in a speech genre other than scientific analysis or philosophical reflection. At the same time, our documents show that, in preparing themselves for the performance of the play, the actors discussed ideas that deserve to be called theoretical. Let us recall three of them (see chapter 4).

Among the very first reactions to "le pouvoir se mange entier" as a saying and as a possible theme for a play were reflections on its context. It was agreed that this was change and *transition*. The saying itself belongs to the kinds of statements that would be pronounced in a crisis such as the enthronement of a new chief. Both eating and symbols of wholeness were part of the rites designed to assure passage through this difficult period in the life of a community (see the remarks on ritual ingestion in chapter 2). It is precisely this element of transition as something that does not merely affect power but is essential to it which made *pouvoir* such an attractive subject for dramatic treatment. As far as I can tell, the actors never thought of "le pouvoir se mange entier" as an authoritative statement standing on its own; they always perceived it together with conflict and contradiction and this expressed itself in the structure of the play.

A second sort of abstract reflection was addressed to a theme related to transition: *mediation*. It was beautifully evoked with the help of a double analogy: a chief, like a pregnant woman, is a *kivuko*, both a ford and a ferry, a place of transition and a vehicle. Although one may approach the idea of power from one angle as if it were a substance or at least an embodiment, it nevertheless only exists in relations—*mi niko juu yenu*, I exist for you, says and repeats the chief in his final speech. But as a relationship, power, unlike the abstractions which sociologists tend to distill from behavior, needs content. It exists only inasmuch as it is revealed and proven, that is, mediated. A concrete form of mediation was invoked by one actor who pointed out that every traditional holder of office and power was linked up with his *kizazi*, his group of relatives and clients; they stood between him and the people. This prompted him to trace corruption, a practice every contemporary Zairean associates with power, back to the olden times: *kukata bidomo ilianza ku bankambo*, paying bribes began with the ancestors. The idea of mediation can be found in the importance traditionally attributed to chiefly insignia but also in the possibility of buying the office by acquiring the insignia.[36] In the play, the idea of mediation and the risks of corruption were expressed dramatically by locating the most serious threat to the chief's power in the corruptness of the *notables*, his intermediaries.

Third, there was—surprising at first but quite understandable on second thought—some discussion about the role of *information* in the conception and exercise of power (especially in the recording of the meeting on Monday, June 23). A chief, in order to exercise his power, needs to know what is going on among his people and it is the responsibility of his advisers to provide him with information and to report what they know correctly. "A chief has four eyes," says *notable* Masimango, quoting another proverbial expression (text 10, 17). Conversely, the people have a right to know the chief's mind and to receive his decisions without distortion (see text 27, 3, and 28, 2f.). This theme was developed as part of the plot; in the concluding scene, when the chief dismisses his worthless counselors, he accuses them of withholding the truth from the villagers. True, there is also the motive of self-interest (exemplified in the court cases and the hunter's visit), which sets the *notables* against each other and causes one of them to incite the villagers against the chief (chapter 8), but the more direct threat to the chief's power is seen in divisiveness caused by partiality and distortion when it comes to interpreting the chief's orders. This, I would suggest, goes beyond the threat of conflict and disorder; it goes to the core of power, which is its wholeness and integrity. "Le pouvoir se mange entier" also means that power must be based on true knowledge and supported by people of integrity. Notice that the troupe did not exploit a political theme that must have been on their minds when information was talked about in connection with power: the omnipresent intelligence network in which every citizen of the country is caught. When the villagers rebel in the fields the chief sends emissaries to check on them; his wife actually spies on them

---

36. See on this Theuws 1983: 7. Without denying its oppressive and destructive aspects it may be worthwhile to approach corruption as an all-pervasive practice with the idea of mediation in mind. To be sure, modern corruption has deeper historical determinants (such as the truly corrupting effect of colonial rule fostering bribes as a routine form of getting what you need or want); it has economic determinants (such as the necessity created by a coincidence of power and poverty—see the underpaid soldier, policeman, customs officer, etc.). But there are also cultural determinants in the very conception of relationship. Corruption, at least the small-scale daily variety is always accompanied by interpersonal claims or "demonstrations," which may—within the same transaction—range from humiliation/intimidation to friendship and tokens of reciprocity. If I pay graft to traffic police in order to avoid a ticket and, worse, a lengthy interrogation at the station, I become (in their words) their "client." Offering a bribe does not end a relationship, it starts it.

from a distance without being seen herself (chapter 12). But this is acted out and talked about in such a way that "undesirable" interpretations cannot come up.

There remains the last of the questions we raised above, about the manner in which power is conceptualized: Where does the play move along culturally programmed paths? Throughout this study, especially in notes to the texts, I have tried to point out linguistic and nonlinguistic items which pose translation problems because they presuppose knowledge of cultural specifics. Here I want to focus on one series of observations apt to clarify our understanding of conceptualization of power. When we looked at Luba proverbs in order to get an idea of how power was treated in traditional lore we found a striking importance of metaphors and analogies derived from the domains of food and eating (chapter 2). It may not be obvious—and it should not be if it is well done—but if there is one domain of experiences and metaphors that the play employs more than others for social relations in general and for the exercise of power in particular, it is food and eating.[37]

When the chief lays down the law of the land (chapter 7) his first order is to cultivate the fields (produce food; texts 6, 2, and 9, 1). Rules for proper behavior for young people above the age of eighteen prescribe that they work their own fields and have their own houses, but they may eat at their relatives' (texts 6, 3f., and 9, 1f.); women must keep to a daily schedule such that they never need to prepare food or cook a meal after dusk (texts 6, 5, and 9, 3); strangers arriving in the village should be fed first (texts 6, 6, and 9, 4); brewing and selling beer is an example for a good contribution to the welfare of the village (text 6, 7); a thief is a criminal because he refuses to grow his own food (text 9, 7).

When the villagers begin to contest the chief's orders (chapter 8) they make a statement about the limits of his power in which they declare that cooking a meal or going hungry is a person's own business (texts 10, 22f., and 11, 2). The order to feed strangers is an occasion to criticize the chief's privileges: he receives tribute in the form of game, he eats his meals without working the fields (texts 10, 8f., and 11, 3f.). One of the *notables* feels that this is going too far and reminds the villagers of the traditional rule of hospitality by quoting a proverbial expression:

hii mukini yetu: hatupende bale bantu ba kwenda kulya bukari chini ya kitanda, here in our village we don't like people who eat their *bukari* under the bed.[38]

37. Taking the term in a broad sense so as to include sources for analogies and extensions to other domains. In a study that appeared after this book went into production, J.-F. Bayart (1989) finds that the eating-metaphor is central in what he calls 'politics of the belly.'

38. Compare this to the first of the Luba proverbs quoted in chapter 2, p. 30.

In the court cases and the hunter's visit, which are designed to illustrate the chief's powers, food is again central. The thief was caught stealing food, the hunter brings food and states his motive: he does not want to eat alone (texts 14, 1, and 15, 1). The chief shows his esteem for his *notables* by distributing some of the game. In the case of adultery, drinking in the fields provides the setting, and the sententious quotation *bukari bwa nyama*, "*bukari* and meat," is invoked when the offender is about to be sentenced. A calabash of beer is the center of scene 6, where the villagers rebel in the fields. They refuse to work (produce food) and the chief's emissaries are corrupted, one after the other, by enticing them to drink beer. Finally, when the chief takes control in the last scene, he justifies his action by saying that a village must not go hungry (text 27, 1); he reminds them that it is their duty to grow food by working the fields; and that even their pleasure in drinking beer is derived from cultivating because beer "comes from food" (text 27, 3).

Aside from such linguistic and rhetorical means, which reveal how power relations are conceptualized and expressed in performance, the play gets its effects from attitudes and actions. This point can be brought into focus by taking another look at ways in which the chief's power is contested by the villagers. Rebellion was required by the plot but, as we remarked at the beginning of chapter 8, there were at first some difficulties in providing concrete motives aside from general attitudes such as insubordination and criticism. As the idea was worked out during rehearsal there was a shift from gratuitous opposition to specific complaints. Resentment concentrated on the chief's orders that restrict personal freedom (a person's right to do what needs to be done where and when he wants to do it) and impinge on traditional custom (to use the night for singing and dancing, without living under a curfew). The chief's social privileges (receiving tribute and eating without having to work for it) were criticized, and there was even an intimation of the chief being also the chief sorcerer (text 10, 16f.).

When rebellion breaks out openly it comes as a refusal to work. In accordance with the folkloric idiom in which the play is conceived, the villagers do not organize a strike (a form of resistance with which the people of urban-industrial Shaba have been familiar since colonial times). They do not stay at home and away from their workplace. Different spatial categories determine the setting of rebellion in the country, above all the opposition between the village and *pori*, the bush, uncultivated land between villages. *Pori* is the place where game and spirits roam, where sorcerers and magicians and healers obtain their licit and illicit charms and medicines; *pori* is where youngsters go through initiation rites and secret societies meet, and where the prophets of some of the new churches seek their visions. The fields, *mashamba*, appear to share more with the bush than with the village (often they are at a great distance from the village, dispersed in the bush). In the play they are the scene for theft, illicit stills, and illicit love, before they become the place of revolt.[39]

Most remarkable, however, is the form in which the villagers rebel. Verbally they grumble and complain; when they pass to action it is to drink, sing, and dance, and have a good time. Revolt becomes an orgiastic feast, and the greatest challenge to the chief's power is put up by a refusal to take his orders seriously. The celebration away from the village in the fields comes close to the traditional way of deposing a chief, which was simply to move out on him and leave him with an empty village. This was proposed in Bwana Cheko's second version of the plot (text 1, 14) and taken up in rehearsal as a threat from the villagers (text 10, 5). It was probably considered too sensitive for the final performance.

Does the fun-and-dance folklorize contestation in the sense of making it harmless?[40] In my view, the contrary could be argued. Although it denotes village lore, its connotations cannot be missed. For decades there has been a "dance on the volcano" feeling about life in the cities of Zaire; beer and music for the masses and the more refined kinds of conspicuous consumption for the *nouveaux riches* have been the counterpoint to the dreariness of poverty, bureaucratization, and oppression. The image of "rebellion in the fields" does not incite revolt but, all the more powerfully, it evokes one possible meaning of "le pouvoir se mange entier." The saying could also be read as a sedimentation of the experience of powerlessness. Power is not acquired piecemeal, with sense and moderation; under the conditions that obtain, it can not be accumulated slowly, stored away for future use, traded upon, and so forth. It must be gobbled here and now, eaten entirely.

A few decades ago, an anthropological analysis without much interest in "modern" politics or intent on containing politics in tribal contexts (M. Gluckman's "Rites of Rebellion" and V. Turner's "Schism and Continuity" come to mind) may have taken the rebellious feast as a ritualization of conflict and dissent. In fact—a point which so far I have

39. That the bush is also where the enemies of the State operate appears not to have been associated with this location. Apart from the fact that it would have been too obvious and dangerous it may have been ruled out by the logic of the imagery. Guerrillas and organized rebellion do not belong to what I call the idiom of the play.

40. In his study of theater in Mali, N. S. Hopkins came close to such a conclusion when he stated: "It is possible to argue that the players present symbolic behaviour that takes the place of real behaviour" (1972: 227).

deliberately refrained from making—the overall structure of the play corresponds exactly to the course that social drama runs according to Turner:

> A social drama is initiated when the peaceful tenor of regular, norm-governed social life is interrupted by the *breach* of a rule controlling one of its salient relationships. This leads swiftly or slowly to a state of *crisis*, which, if not soon sealed off, may split the community into contending factions and coalitions. To prevent this, *redressive* means are taken by those who consider themselves or are considered the most legitimate or authoritative representatives of the relevant community. Redress usually involves ritualized action. . . . (1982: 86)

But *Le pouvoir se mange entier* is not an icon of social drama. It is action; if anything it is what Turner calls a redressive means. To call that sort of action "ritualized" may obscure more than it reveals. How can ritual render the conscious, collective effort that went into the rehearsal process, how the power of the event taking place at that particular time in Zaire? That a dramatic performance conforms to certain generic rules does not justify the conclusion that performance which has power as its theme must inevitably be conformist.

Because writing about it can easily become part of it—"it" being the "dialectics of oppression"[41]—I feel the need to conclude now by rejecting briefly some misconceptions that may linger despite all the efforts to dispel them. (This will not remove the danger that this study may be misread and used, or read and misused; but it should make clear that what happened in *Le pouvoir se mange entier* cannot be taken as political agitation of the kind that offers a "handle" to those who feel endangered by it.)

First, it is wrong to assume that the Zairean "folk," here represented by the Mufwankolo troupe, live only in the present and, as folk are said to do, only worry about forms of power and oppression as they exist now. The village and colonial past are very much on their minds and popular reflection is capable of looking at a state of affairs in historical perspective.

Second, there are no grounds for assuming that critical reflections on power and oppression which are expressed on political occasions (such as Independence Day) and in political imagery (the chief being the central figure of the play) are aimed at the political regime only. The Zairean folk know of oppressive power other than political: economic

---

41. Thus the title of the most recent of a series of critical studies of political oppression in Zaire by M. Schatzberg (1988).

exploitation, for instance, the terror exercised by certain forms of religion, and an all-pervasive fear of sorcery.

Third, even inasmuch as critique is addressed to the regime in power it is not true that the Zairean folk are incapable of seeing beyond the limits of their country. They are very much aware that oppression is inherent in government under conditions of the current world economic system. Power is to serve well-being and progress, the play asserts repeatedly; Zairean folk know that their lot has been to be the victims of power which serves well-being and progress—elsewhere.

Appendix: Bwana Cheko's Scenario
Bibliography
Index

Appendix: Bwana Cheko's Scenario

TROUPE THEATRALE MUFWANKOLO
" T. T. M."
LUBUMBASHI.-

Vice-Président

LES IDEES MAITRESSES DE CONDUCTEUR

"LE POUVOIR SE MANGE ENTIER."
━━━━━━━━━━━━━━━━━━━━━━━━━━
(à développer)

a)- Personnage

b)- DECORS: —village coutumier

—ville moderne

—pancarte avec écrit: régner dans le désordre

—pancarte avec écrit: paix - justice - travail

c) TENUE: comme d'habitude (chaque acteur ou actrice fera le nécessaire)

D E T A I L S :

1/——le tam-tam accompagnée d'une chanson annonce le début de la pièce
théâtrale;

—le chef et la reine en costume d'apparât;

—les notables ainsi que les villageois vont se rassembler dans la cour
du chef;

—danse folklorique au rytme du tam-tam devant le chef;

—le chef se lève et prend la parole et ne contrôle pas;

—les villageois font autres choses par manque d'encadrement;

—désordre total dans le village et le chef n'a plus d'autorité;

—

2/——convocation d'une réunion mixte: chef et notables;

—mesures prises pour remettre de l'ordre au village;
(conseils et remarques)

—le chef passe en action et prend la situation en mains;

—l'ordre rétabli, le respect, la justice, la protection des biens et
des personnes, le travail pour le progrès;

—MORALE: LE POUVOIR SE MANGE ENTIER, c.à.d.: le chef est pour tout le
monde et n'a pas de parti pris, il doit servir son peuple au même pied
d'égalité mais avec autorité.

FAIT A LUBUMBASHI, le 20 Juin 1986.

M'BUYU-DARBO BWANA-CHEKO

Secrétaire Administraif.

291

Bibliography

Abedji, J. A.
1971   The Church and the Emergence of the Nigerian Theatre, 1866–
            1914. *Journal of the Historical Society of Nigeria* 6: 24–45.
1973   The Church and the Emergence of the Nigerian Theatre, 1915–
            1945. *Journal of the Historical Society of Nigeria* 8: 387–96.

Abrahams, Roger D.
1972   The Training of the Man of Words in Talking Sweet. *Language in
            Society* 1: 15–29.
1975   Folklore and Communication on St. Vincent. In Ben-Amos and
            Goldstein, pp. 287–300.

Abrahams, Roger D., and Richard Bauman
1971   Sense and Nonsense in St. Vincent. *American Anthropologist* 73:
            762–72.

Actes du Colloque sur le Théâtre nègro-africain, Abidjan 1970
1971   Paris: Présence Africaine.

African Theatre
1976   New Haven: Yale School of Drama.

Anonymous
1950   Un Théâtre de marionnettes au Congo belge. *La Voix du Con-
            golais* 6: 344–47.

Arewa, E. O., and A. Dundes
1964   Proverbs and the Ethnography of Speaking Folklore. In *The
            Ethnography of Speaking*, J. J. Gumperz and Dell Hymes. Mena-
            sha, Wis.: American Anthropological Association, pp. 70–85.

Authenticité et Développement. Actes du Colloque National sur l'Authenticité
1982   Paris: Présence Africaine.

Bakhtin, M. M.
1986   *Speech Genres and Other Late Essays*. Austin: University of Texas
            Press.

Baker, William J. and James A. Mangan, eds.
1987   *Sport in Africa: Essays in Social History.* New York: Africana Publishing Company.

Banham, M., and C. Wake
1976   *African Theatre Today.* London: Pitman Publishing.

Barber, Karin
1987   Popular Arts in Africa. *African Studies Review* 30: 1–78, 113–32.

Bateson, Gregory
1979   *Mind and Nature. A Necessary Unit.* New York: E. P. Dutton.

Bauman, Richard
1986   Performance and Honor in 13th-Century Iceland. *Journal of American Folklore* 99: 131–50.

Bauman, Richard, et al.
1984   *Verbal Art as Performance.* 2d ed. Prospect Heights, Ill.: Waveland Press.

Bayart, Jean-François
1989   *L'Etat en Afrique. La Politique du ventre.* Paris: Fayard.

Bemba, Sylvain
1984   *50 ans de musique du Congo-Zaire.* Paris: Présence Africaine.

Ben-Amos, Dan
1976   Analytical Categories and Ethnic Genres. In *Folklore Genres,* ed. Dan Ben-Amos, pp. 215–42. Austin: University of Texas Press.

Ben-Amos, Dan, and Kenneth S. Goldstein, eds.
1975   *Folklore. Performance and Communication.* The Hague: Mouton.

Bissot, L.
1952   A propos du théâtre indigène. *Zaire* 6: 623–30.

Boon, James A.
1982   *Other Tribes, Other Scribes. Symbolic Anthropology in the Comparative Study of Cultures, Histories, Religions, and Texts.* Cambridge: Cambridge University Press.

Brasseur, Jean
1957   Jacques Huisman: Pour la création d'un théâtre africain. *Belgique d'Outremer* 246: 150.

Burton, J. W.
1981   The Proverb: An Aspect of Atuot Collective Thought. *Folklore* 92/1: 84–90.

Burton, W. F. P.
1955–59   Proverbs of the Baluba. *Bulletin de Juridiction Indigène* vols. 23–27 (page nos. omitted).

Callaghy, Thomas M.
1984   *The State-Society Struggle. Zaire in Comparative Perspective.* New York: Columbia University Press.

Casson, Ronald W.
1983   Schemata in Cognitive Anthropology. *Annual Review of Anthro-
              pology* 12: 429–62.

Cauvin, Jean
1980   *L'image, la langue et la pensée.* St. Augustin: Anthropos Institut.
1981   *Comprendre les proverbes.* Issy les Moulineux: Les classiques afri-
              cains.

Cigogne Patiente (pseud.)
1951   Rallye Scout à Kimwenza. Pentecôte 1951. *La Voix du Congolais* 7:
              378–87.

Clifford, James and George E. Marcus, eds.
1986   *Writing Culture: The Poetics and Politics of Ethnography.* Berkeley:
              University of California Press.

Collard, J.
1958   Vers un théâtre congolais? *Jeune Afrique* 11: 9–10.

Colle, Père
1913   *Les Baluba.* 2 vols. Brussels: Albert Dewit.

Coplan, David B.
1986   Ideology and Tradition in South African Black Popular Theater.
              Journal of American Folklore 99: 151–76.

Cornet, C. M., M. D. Vandenbulcke, and Kalonji Mutambayi
1975   *Bantu? Proverbes africains à l'usage de l'enseignment secondaire.*
              Brussels: A. De Boeck.

Cornevin, R.
1970   *Le théâtre en Afrique noire et à Madagascar.* Paris: Le Livre Afri-
              cain.

Darkowska-Nidzgorska, Olenka
1980   *Théâtre populare de Marionnettes en Afrique sub-saharienne.* Ban-
              dundu: CEEBA.

De Clercq, A.
1911–12   Lubavolkeren in den spiegel van hun spreuken. *Onze Kongo* 2: 1–
              18, 81–101.

De Sousberghe, L.
1983   A propos d'une maxime kongo. *Paideuma* 29: 351.

Dimandja, E. Nkondo
1979   "Homme d'autrui": Étude sémantique à partir des parémies
              tetela. *Cahiers des religions africaines* 13: 109–29.

Drum, Henri [pseud., van Herreweghe]
1948   Le Théâtre des marionnettes congolaises. Dent pour Dent.
              Drame en un acte, deux scènes et deux tableaux. *Jeune Afrique* 1:
              42–46.
1950   Les Marionnettes au Congo. *Jeune Afrique* 3: 23–29.

Dundes, Alan
1981   On the Structure of the Proverb. In *The Wisdom of Many: Essays on the Proverb*, ed. Alan Dundes, 1: 43–64. New York: Garland Publishing.

East, N. B.
1970   *African Theatre. A Checklist of Critical Materials*. New York: Africana Publishing.

Eastman, Carol M.
1972   The Proverb in Modern Written Swahili Literature: An Aid to Proverb Elicitation. *African Folklore* 193–207.

Eister, A. W., ed.
1974   *Changing Perspectives in the Scientific Study of Religion*. New York: Wiley Interscience.

Elisabethville 1911–1961
1961   Brussels: L. Cuypers.

Epskamp, Kees P.
1987   Historical Outline of the Development of Zambian Theater. *Canadian Journal of African Studies* 21: 157–74.

Etherton, Michael
1982   *The Development of African Drama*. London: Hutchinson.

Evans-Pritchard, E. P.
1963   Meaning in Zande proverbs. *Africa* 63: 4–7, 109–12.
1964   (Contin.) *Africa* 64: 1–5.

Fabian, Johannes
1971a   *Jamaa: A Charismatic Movement in Katanga*. Evanston: Northwestern University Press.
1971b   Language, History and Anthropology. *Philosophy of the Social Sciences* 1: 19–47.
1974   Genres in an Emerging Tradition: An Approach to Religious Communication. In A. W. Eister, pp. 249–72.
1975   Taxonomy and Ideology: On the Boundaries of Concept Classification. In *Linguistics and Anthropology: In Honor of C. F. Voegelin*, ed. M. Dale Kinkade, Kenneth L. Hale, and Oswald Werner, pp. 183–97. Lisse: Peter de Ridder Press.
1978   Popular Culture in Africa: Findings and Conjectures. *Africa* 48: 315–34.
1979a   Rule and Process: Thoughts on Ethnography as Communication. *Philosophy of the Social Sciences* 9: 1–26.
1979b   Text as Terror: Second Thoughts on Charisma. *Social Research* 46: 166–203.
1979c   The Anthropology of Religious Movements: From Explanation to Interpretation. *Social Research* 46: 4–35.
1979d   Man and Woman in the Teachings of the Jamaa Movement. In *The New Religions of Africa*, ed. Bennetta Jules-Rosette, pp. 169–83. Norwood, N.J.: Ablex.

1982   Scratching the Surface: Observations on the Poetics of Lexical Borrowing in Shaba Swahili. *Anthropological Linguistics* 24: 14–50.

1983   *Time and the Other: How Anthropology Makes Its Object*. New York: Columbia University Press.

1985   Religious Pluralism: An Ethnographic Approach. In *Theoretical and Methodological Explorations in African Religions*, ed. M. Schoffeleers and W. Van Binsbergen, pp. 138–63. London: Kegan Paul International.

1986   *Language and Colonial Power: The Appropriation of Swahili in the Former Belgian Congo, 1880–1938*. Cambridge: Cambridge University Press.

1990   *History from Below: The "Vocabulary of Elisabethville" by André Yav. Texts, Translation, and Interpretive Essay*. Amsterdam-Philadelphia: John Benjamins.

In press   Jamaa: A Charismatic Movement Revisited. In *Religion in Africa: Experience and Expression*, ed. Thomas D. Blakely et al. London: James Currey.

Fabian, Johannes, and Ilona Szombati-Fabian

1980   Folk Art from an Anthropological Perspective. In *Perspectives on American Folk Art*, ed. Ian M. G. Quimby and Scott T. Swank, pp. 247–92. New York: W. W. Norton.

Falasisi (pseud.)

1948   Musique Africaine. A propos des "Petits Chanteurs de la Croix de Cuivre." *La Revue Coloniale Belge* 73: 656–58.

Faik-Nzuji, Cl. Madiya

1976   Art oral traditionnel au Zaire. I. Le proverbe. *Zaire-Afrique* 14: 155–70.

Fenn, Richard K.

1982   The Sociology of Religion: A Critical Survey. In *Sociology: The State of the Art*, ed. Tom Bottomore, Stefan Nowak, and Magdalena Sokolowska, pp. 101–27. Beverly Hills: Sage.

Fernandez, James W.

1986   *Persuasions and Performances: The Play of Tropes in Culture*. Bloomington: University of Indiana Press.

Fetter, Bruce

1976   *The Creation of Elisabethville*. Stanford: Hoover Institution Press.

Fiebach, Joachim

1986   *Die Toten als die Macht der Lebenden. Zur Theorie und Geschichte von Theater in Afrika*. Berlin: Henschelverlag Kunst und Gesellschaft (also in a licensed edition: Wilhelmshaven: Edition Heinrichshofen).

Finnegan, Ruth

1970   *Oral Literature in Africa*. Oxford: Clarendon Press.

Fleishman, Edwin Alan
1984   *Taxonomies of Human Performance: The Description of Human Tasks.* Orlando, Fl.: Academic Press.

Friedrich, Paul
1986   *The Princes of Naranja.* Austin: University of Texas Press.
1988   Multiplicity and Pluralism in Anthropological Construction/ Synthesis. *Anthropological Quarterly* 61: 103–12.

Gansemans, Jos, and Barbara Schmidt-Wrenger
1986   *Zentralafrika. Musikgeschichte in Bildern. Band 1: Musikethnologie. Lieferung 9.* Leipzig: VEB Deutscher Verlag für Musik.

Gascht, A.
1958   *Art au Congo.* Brussels: n.p. (publication for *Exposition Universelle et Internationale de Bruxelles 1958)*

Geertz, Clifford
1973   *The Interpretation of Cultures.* New York: Basic Books.
1980   *Negara: The Theater State in Nineteenth-Century Bali.* Princeton: Princeton University Press.
1988   *Works and Lives: The Anthropologist as Author.* Stanford: Stanford University Press.

Girard, J. A. F.
1981   *Ideology, Local and National: Continuation and Accommodation.* Ph.D. thesis, Michigan State University.

Goody, Jack
1977   *The Domestication of the Savage Mind.* Cambridge: Cambridge University Press.
1986   *The Logic of Writing and the Organization of Society.* Cambridge: Cambridge University Press.

Graham-White, A.
1975   *The Dramas of Black Africa.* New York: Samuel French.

Green, Martin Burgess
1986   *The Triumph of Pierrot: The Commedia dell'arte and the Modern Imagination.* New York: Macmillan.

Harbsmeier, Michael
1989   Writing and the Other: Travellers' Literacy, or Towards an Archeology of Orality. In Schousboe and Larsen, pp. 197–228.

Hare, A. Paul
1985   *Social Interaction as Drama: Applications from Conflict Resolution.* Beverly Hills: Sage.

Harrison, Paul Carter, ed.
1974   *Kuntu Drama.* New York: Grove Press.

Hopkins, Nicholas S.
1972   Persuasion and Satire in the Malian Theatre. *Africa* 42: 217–28.

Hourantier, Marie J.
1984   *Du rituel au théâtre-rituel: contribution à une esthétique théâtrale nègro-africaine.* Paris: Harmattan.

Hulstaert, G.
1958   *Proverbes Mongo.* Tervuren: Musée Royal du Congo Belge.

Hymes, Dell
1974   *Foundations in Sociolinguistics. An Ethnographic Approach.* Philadelphia: University of Pennsylvania Press.
1975   Breakthrough into Performance. In Ben-Amos and Goldstein, pp. 17–74.

Jadot, J. M.
1950   Le Théâtre des marionnettes au Congo Belge. *Institut Royal colonial belge. Bulletin des séances,* 559–70.
1959   *Les écrivains africains du Congo Belge et du Ruanda-Urundi.* Brussels: Académie Royale des Sciences Coloniales.

Jewsiewicki, Bogumil, and David Newbury, eds.
1986   *African Historiographies: What History for Which Africa?* Beverly Hills: Sage.

Kalunga, Mwela-Ubi
1980   Le proverbe taabwa. *Africa* (Rome) 35: 191–216.

Kantshama Badibanga, and Luboya Diambile
1986   La poule chex les Beena Luluwa: analyse linguistique et anthropologique. *Journal des africanistes* 56,1: 113–28.

Kaphagawani, D. N., and H. F. Chidam'modzi
1983   Chewa Cultural Ideals and System of Thought as Determined from Their Proverbs. *Pula* (Botswana Journal of African Studies) 3: 29–37.

Kazadi, Pierre Cary (Kazadi wa Mukuna)
1973   Trends of Nineteenth- and Twentieth-Century Music in the Congo-Zaire. In R. Günther, ed., *Musikkulturen Asiens, Afrikas und Ozeaniens im 19. Jahrhundert.* Regensburg, pp. 267–84.

Keil, Charles
1987   Participatory Discrepancies and the Power of Music. *Cultural Anthropology* 2: 275–83.

Kennedy, S.
1973   *In Search of African Theater.* New York: Scribner's.

Kinkade, M. Dale, Kenneth L. Hale, and Oswald Werner, eds.
1975   *Linguistics and Anthropology: In Honor of C. F. Voegelin.* Lisse: Peter de Ridder Press.

Kiwele, Joseph
1952   *Shura na nyoka—Le crapaud et le serpent.* Elisabethville: CEPSI (*Bulletin du CEPSI* 23).

Korse, P.
1983   Mongo Proverbs of the Basankusu. *Annales Aequatoria* 4: 77–91.

Kramer, Fritz W.
1987   *Der rote Fes. Über Besessenheit und Kunst in Afrika.* Frankfurt:
                Athenäum.

Lakoff, George, and Mark Johnson
1980   *Metaphors We Live By.* Chicago: University of Chicago Press.

Lemaire, Ton
1984   Antropologie en Schrift. In *Antropologie en Ideologie,* ed. Ton
                Lemaire, pp. 103–24. Groningen: Konstaple.

Lenselaer, Alphonse
1983   *Dictionnaire Swahili-Français.* Paris: Karthala.

Lizin, P.
1968   Un scoutisme bien vivant. *Monde et Mission* 5: 26–30.

Low, John
1982   *Shaba Diary: A Trip to Rediscover the "Katanga" Guitar Styles and
                Songs of the 1950's and '60's.* Wien-Föhrenau: E. Stiglmayr.

MacGaffey, Wyatt
1970   *Custom and Government in the Lower Congo.* Berkeley: University
                of California Press.

Mangan, James A.
1986   *The Games Ethic and Imperialism.* New York: Viking.

Marcus, George, and Dick Cushman
1982   Ethnographies as Texts. *Annual Review of Anthropology* 11: 25–69.

Mieder, Wolfgang
1982   *International Proverb Bibliography.* New York: Garland.

Mikanda Kikufi, Tayaya Lubombo, and Kilesa Nona
1980   *Théâtre populaire de Bandundu.* Bandundu: CEEBA.

Mikeno, Simon
1953   Un regard sur le Scoutisme congolais à Léopoldville. *La Voix du
                Congolais* 9: 802–5.

Mitchell, J. Clyde
1968   *The Kalela Dance.* Manchester: Manchester University Press.
                (Originally published in 1956.)

Mpandanjila, M., Bateente, and Ngonga-ke-Mbembe
1986   Devises Luba. *Annales Aequatoria* 7: 303–23.

Mu-Daba Yoka, Lye
1975   La critique coloniale et la naissance du théâtre au Zaire. *Afrique
                Littéraire et Artistique* 37: 83–91.

Mudara, Yoka Lye
1972   Les problèmes du théâtre au Zaire. *Dombi* 3: 3–5.

Mukařowský, Jan
1971   "Prislovi jako soucast kontextu" (The proverb as a part of con-
             text). In *Cestami poetiky a estetiky* (On the trade of poetics and
             aesthetics), 1942–43. Prague: Československý spisovatel, pp.
             277–59.

Ngwenza, Antoine
1946   Le scoutisme et ses bienfaits. *La Voix du Congolais* 2: 408–13.

Nidzgorski, Denis
1980   *Arts du spectacle Africain: Contributions du Gabon.* Bandundu:
             CEEBA.

Nzongola Ntalaja, G., ed.
1986   *The Crisis in Zaire. Myths and Realities.* Trenton, N.J.: Africa
             World Press.

Okpaku, J.
1970   *Contemporary African Drama: A Critical Anthology.* New York:
             Negro Universities Press.

Oyin Ogunba and Abiola Irele
1978   *Theater in Africa.* Ibadan: Ibadan University Press.

Peacock, James L.
1968   *Rites of Modernization: Symbolic and Social Aspects of Indonesian
             Proletarian Drama.* Chicago: University of Chicago Press.

Penfield, Joyce
1983   *Communicating with Quotes: The Igbo Case.* Westport, Conn.:
             Greenwood.

Perrings, Charles
1979   *Black Mineworkers in Central Africa.* London: Heinemann.

Povey, John
1975   The Mufwankolo Theater. *African Arts* 8: 66–67.
1976   The Mwondo Theatre of Zaire. In *African Theatre*, pp. 49–54.

Rabinow, Paul, and William M. Sullivan, eds.
1979   *Interpretive Social Science: A Reader.* Berkeley: University of Cali-
             fornia Press.

Ranger, T. O.
1975   *Dance and Society in Eastern Africa.* Berkeley: University of Cali-
             fornia Press.

Reefe, Thomas Q.
1981   *The Rainbow and the Kings: A History of the Luba Empire to 1891.*
             Berkeley: University of California Press.

Ricoeur, Paul
1979   The Model of the Text: Meaningful Action Considered as Text. In
             Rabinow and Sullivan, pp. 73–101.

Richards, Audrey
1956   *Chisungu: A Girl's Initiation Ceremony Among the Bemba of North-
            ern Rhodesia.* London: Oxford University Press.

Roberts, Allen F.
1986   The Comeuppance of "Mr. Snake," and Other Tales of Survival
            from Contemporary Rural Zaire. In Nzongola, pp. 113–21.

Rodegem, F.
1983   *Paroles de sagesse au Burundi.* Louvain: Peeters.
1985   Proverbes et pseudo-proverbes. *Annales Aequatoria* 6: 67–83.

Rosenthal, Michael
1986   *The Character Factory: Baden-Powell's Boy Scouts and the Impera-
            tives of Empire.* New York: Pantheon.

Ruby, Jay, ed.
1982   *A Crack in the Mirror. Reflexive Perspectives in Anthropology.*
            Philadelphia: University of Pennsylvania Press.

Sacleux, C.
1939   *Dictionnaire Swahili-Français.* Paris: Institut d'Ethnologie.

Schatzberg, Michael G.
1988   *The Dialectics of Oppression in Zaire.* Bloomington: Indiana Uni-
            versity Press.

Schechner, Richard
1982   Collective Reflexivity: Restoration of Behavior. In Ruby, pp 39–
            81.
1985   *Between Theater and Anthropology.* Philadelphia: University of
            Pennsylvania Press.
1986   Magnitudes of Performance. In Turner and Bruner, pp. 344–69.

Scheven, Albert
1981   *Swahili Proverbs.* Washington, D.C.: University Press of America.

Schicho, Walter
1975   Sprachliche Variation als Mittel der Charakterisierung darge-
            stellter Persönlichkeiten in den Stegreiftheaterstücken der
            Gruppe Mufwankolo, Lubumbashi/Zaire. *Grazer Linguistische
            Studien "Sprache und Gesellschaft"* 1: 47–62.

Schicho, Walter, and Mbayabo Ndala
1981   *Le Groupe Mufwankolo.* Vienna: Afro-Pub (Beiträge zur Afrika-
            nistik, vol. 14, Institut für Afrikanistik).

Schipper-de Leeuw, Mineke
1977   *Toneel en maatschapij in Afrika.* Assen: Van Gorcum.
1984   *Théâtre et société en Afrique.* Dakar: Les nouvelles éditions afri-
            caines.

Schousboe, Karen, and Mogens Trolle Larsen, eds.
1989   *Literacy and Society.* Copenhagen: Akademisk Forlag.

Scohy, André
1951   Scenaristes et auteurs dramatiques auront-ils bientôt des con-
             frères congolais? *La Revue Coloniale Belge* 135: 351–52.

Seitel, Peter
1976   Proverbs: A Social Use of Metaphor. In *Folklore Genres*, ed. Dan
             Ben-Amos, pp. 135–43. Austin: University of Texas Press.
1977   Saying Haya Sayings: Two Categories of Proverb Use. In *The
             Social Use of Metaphor: Essays on the Anthropology of Rhetoric*, ed.
             J. David Sapir and J. Christopher Crocker, pp. 75–99. Phila-
             delphia: University of Pennsylvania Press.
1980   *See So That We May See: Performances and Interpretations of Tradi-
             tional Tales from Tanzania.* Bloomington: Indiana University
             Press.

Serres, Michel
1985   *Les cinq sens.* Paris: Bernard Grasset.

Shala Lundula
1985   La notion d'autorité chez les Tetela à travers quelques proverbes.
             Annales Aequatoria 6: 147–63.

Simon, Artur, ed.
1983   *Musik in Afrika.* Berlin: Museum für Völkerkunde.

Singer, Milton
1972   *When a Great Tradition Modernizes: An Anthropological Approach
             to Indian Civilization.* New York: Praeger.

Standard Swahili Dictionary
1939   Under the direction of Frederick Johnson. Oxford: Oxford Uni-
             versity Press.

Street, Brian V.
1984   *Literacy in Theory and Practice.* Cambridge: Cambridge Univer-
             sity Press.

Szombati-Fabian, Ilona, and Johannes Fabian
1976   Art, History and Society: Popular Painting in Shaba, Zaire.
             Studies in the Anthropology of Visual Communication 3: 1–21.

Taabu Sabiti (pseud. Alphonse Lenselaer)
n.d.   [1976] *Proverbes et dictons en Swahili et en Kingwana.* n.p. [Kin-
             shasa]: Editions Saint Paul.

Tannen, Deborah, ed.
1982   *Spoken and Written Language: Exploring Orality and Literacy.* Nor-
             wood, N.J.: Ablex.

Tedlock, Dennis
1972   *Finding the Center: Narrative Poetry of the Zuni Indians.* New
             York: Dial.
1983   *The Spoken Word and the Work of Interpretation.* Philadelphia:
             University of Pennsylvania Press.

Theuws, Jacques A. (Th.)
1954   *Textes Luba (Katanga)*. Elisabethville: CEPSI.
1962   *De Luba-mens*. Tervuren: Musée Royal de l'Afrique Centrale.
1983   *Word and World: Luba Thought and Literature*. St. Augustin: Anthropos.

Theys, G.
1952   Marcel Cornelis et son théâtre de marionnettes au Congo Belge. *Bulletin de l'Union des femmes coloniales* 24,139: 11–13.

Traore, Bakary
1972   *The Black African Theater and Its Social Functions*. Ibadan: Ibadan University Press.

Trussart, J.
1972   Albert Mongita, homme orchestre. *Dombi* 3: 5–7, 15.

Tshibabwa M., and Elia Monongo
1987   Comportement alimentaire en rapport aves le discours Luba-Kasai. *Annales Aequatoria* 8: 59–75.

Turner, Victor
1974   Metaphors of Antistructure in Religious Culture. In Eister, pp. 63–84.
1982   Dramatic Ritual/Ritual Drama: Performative and Reflexive Anthropology. In Ruby, pp. 83–97.
1986   *The Anthropology of Performance*. New York: Performing Arts Journal Publications.

Turner, Victor, and Edward M. Bruner, eds.
1986   *The Anthropology of Experience*. Urbana: University of Illinois Press.

Van Avermaet, E., and B. Mbuya
1954   *Dictionnaire Kiluba-Français*. Tervuren: Musée Royal du Congo Belge.

Van Bulck, Gaston
1936   De invloed van de westersche cultuur op de gesproken woordkunst bij de Bakongo. *Kongo-Overzee* 2/5: 285–93, 3/1: 26–41.

Van Caeneghem, R.
1935   De gierigheid in de spreekworden der Baluba in Baluba-Moyo. *Congo* 2/3: 376–88, 4: 585–97, 5: 727–36.
1937   'Geven aan anderman' in de spreekworden der Baluba-menschen. *Congo* 2/4: 377–411.
1939   De gastvrijheid in de spreekworden der Luba-menschen. *Congo* 1/4: 412–32.

Van der Beeken, Alain
1978   *Proverbes et vie yaka*. St. Augustin: Anthropos.
1982   *Les proverbes yaka au service de l'annonce de l'evangile*. St. Augustin: Anthropos.

Van Spaandonck, Marcel, ed. and transl.
1958   Tumbako ya mu Mpua. Een toneelschets in het Potopot-King-
            wana van Katanga door Christophe Makonga. *Kongo Overzee* 25:
            1–16.

Vansina, Jan
1985   *Oral Tradition as History.* Madison: University of Wisconsin
            Press.

Vaz, Carlos
1978   *Para um conhecimento de teatro africano.* Lisbon: Ulmeiro.

Verhulpen, Edmond
1936   *Baluba et Balubaïsés du Katanga.* Antwerp:

Wannyn, R. L.
1983   *Les proverbes anciens du Bas-Congo. Vol. 1.* Brussels: Editions du
            Vieux Planquesaule.

Warren, L.
1975   *The Theater of Africa: An Introduction.* Englewood Cliffs, N.J.:
            Prentice-Hall.

Washabaugh, William
1979   Linguistic Anti-Structure. *Journal of Anthropological Research* 35:
            30–46.

Weterings, J.
1936–37   Le théâtre et les Nègres. *Beaux Arts* [Brussels] 7: 18–19.

White, Geoffrey M.
1987   Proverbs and Cultural Models: An American Psychology of
            Problem Solving. In *Cultural Models in Language and Thought,* ed.
            Dorothy Holland and Naomi Quinn, pp. 151–72. Cambridge:
            Cambridge University Press.

Wiener, Norbert
1948   *Cybernetics.* New York: John Wiley & Sons.

Wilmsen, Edwin N.
1989   *Land Filled with Flies: The Political Economy of the Kalahari.* Chi-
            cago: University of Chicago Press.

Yanga, Tshimpaka
1977   Inside the Proverbs: A Sociolinguistic Approach. *African Lan-
            guages* 3: 130–57.

Yoka, Lye Mudaba
1982   La conception missionnaire du théâtre naissant en Afrique et
            notamment au Zaire. *Cahiers des Religions Africaines* 16: 267–75.

Young, Crawford, and Thomas Turner
1985   *The Rise and Decline of the Zairian State.* Madison: University of
            Wisconsin Press.

Index

Index 313

New Directions in Anthropological Writing
History, Poetics, Cultural Criticism

GEORGE E. MARCUS
Rice University

JAMES CLIFFORD
University of California, Santa Cruz

GENERAL EDITORS

Power and Performance: Ethnographic Explorations through Proverbial Wisdom and Theater in Shaba, Zaire
Johannes Fabian

Dialogue at the Margins: Whorf, Bakhtin, and Linguistic Relativity
Emily A. Schultz